Cooking with Daniel Boulud

COOKING WITH DANIEL BOULUD

PHOTOGRAPHS BY TODD FRANCE

RANDOM HOUSE NEW YORK

ISBN: 679 40409 0
LC: 93-085747

Designed by Georgiana Goodwin

Manufactured in the United States of America
98765432
First Edition

PREFACE

It was a distinct pleasure for me when Daniel Boulud asked that I write the preface for his book. The first time I met him, in 1982 at the Westbury Hotel, I instantly recognized that he was a very talented chef with great promise. As a classically trained "oldtimer" I was impressed with his background, which began with a three-year apprenticeship at Nandron, an excellent restaurant in Lyons, France. He later spent a year at La Mère Blanc in Vonnas as cook and *chef de parties* (first cook in a station), followed by another year at Roger Vergé's three-star Moulin à Mougins. A stay in Copenhagen as sous chef at the Hotel Plaza les Etoiles continued his outstanding training, after which came a year at Eugénie les Bains, in Michel Guérard's world-renowned three-star restaurant.

His U.S. debut in Washington, D.C., as chef for two years at the European Commission gave him wide experience with international cuisine. He then came to New York to be sous chef at the Westbury Hotel. Next he opened La Régence as executive chef, reigning for two years before coming to Le Cirque in 1986, where he astounded the restaurant world by creating a constant stream of exciting, innovative dishes, to the delight of Sirio Maccioni, Le Cirque's owner and the maestro of fine dining in this country. Daniel's experience at Le Cirque introduced him to the enormous variety of ingredients and the repertoire of ethnic cuisines for which New York restaurants are famous. This, combined with his classic French training, has made him an exceptional chef whose blend of quality and diversity is the hallmark of his inimitable style.

Daniel's great strength is his reliance on the best seasonal products available, which constantly inspire him to new creative heights. He is always searching for new ingredients and produce to stimulate his imagination, and it is a pleasure to experience his intelligence and enthusiasm when he is discussing new dishes. What more can be said except that he is truly an artist.

In addition to our classical training, Daniel and I share a genuine passion for cooking. Even after long hours in a restaurant kitchen, we both enjoy cooking at home for family and friends—the mark of a chef who truly loves his work.

The recipes in this book are based on Daniel's vast and varied cooking experience and include many new ingredients and products that will challenge cooks to create tantalizing dishes at home. The seasonal approach to food is excellent and includes detailed instructions on handling and preparation that will be valuable to home cooks.

Daniel is a friend, artist, and gifted chef. I am proud to know him and look forward to witnessing his continued success in years to come.

PIERRE FRANEY

ACKNOWLEDGMENTS

This book would not have been possible without the help and support of some very talented people:

First I would like to thank my wife, Micky, for her tireless work on the project. She not only helped write the book, but also inspired the concept. It was Micky and her friend Sandra Pralong who in 1988 created with me a twelve-issue newsletter stressing America's seasonal produce, "Easy Cooking with Great Chefs."

And my deep appreciation: To Sirio Maccioni, owner of Le Cirque and one of the world's great restaurateurs. Throughout my six years (1986–1992) as executive chef of Le Cirque, Sirio encouraged me to innovate and develop my personal style. His kindness and support have inspired this book.

To Jason Epstein, America's star editor-publisher, who also happens to be a superb cook. This book would never have been written without his encouragement, enthusiasm, and expertise. He and his wonderful team at Random House and Condé Nast—Rochelle Udell, Janis Donnaud, Georgiana Goodwin, and Beth Pearson, to name only a few—have helped me transform my unwritten knowledge into this cookbook.

To Todd France, a young and gifted photographer. His artistry has perfectly captured my vision and excitement about seasonal American produce. His willingness to accommodate my crazy schedule and his enthusiastic response to my ideas has made our working relationship a most pleasant experience.

To Olivier Guini, the exceptional florist of Les Fleurs de Maxim's, a New York City flower shop owned by Pierre Cardin. The composition of the four seasonal photo spreads would not have been possible without his help and creativity. When arranging the hundreds of ingredients into beautiful still lifes with his magical touch, he truly resembled a master painter creating a chef d'oeuvre.

To Matias Verna, a young chef and carpenter, who built the sets for the spring and summer seasonal still lifes.

To the multitalented Jennifer Newman Brazil, my invaluable assistant. While studying to become a doctor, she found the time to help me every step of the way to organize and style each photo shoot, and to prepare and test the recipes.

To Sottha Khunn, my talented sous-chef for eight years, who supported me throughout this project with his invaluable friendship and boundless assistance.

To my other sous-chefs at Le Cirque—Remi Lauvand, Daniel Baliani, Eric Haillard, and Paul Cunningham—whose devotion and hard work have made this project easier.

Thanks to Alex Lee and Albert Lukas for testing many of the recipes that appear in this book. They also were very helpful with the photographs.

And thanks to Michele Giraldi, Michael Demers, Jonathan Clarke, Robert Hauser,

Adam Cohn, Juan Vargas, Chip Martinson, Frederic Naud, Lee Hanson, Chris Pyun, and Barbara Smilow for help with recipe testing.

To Bob Tabian, my agent at ICM, for his comments, recipe testing, and suggestions on how to make each recipe more understandable for the home cook.

To Jean Tibbetts, a talented author, who helped me write the introduction to each recipe in the book.

Finally, I would like to thank those people who supplied me with the wonderful ingredients and props needed to create the recipes and photographs.

Special thanks to John Weintraub at Dom's Market in New York City, who enthusiastically searched the markets all over the country to bring me the very best produce. He personally carried to my doorstep crates of the freshest and most beautiful vegetables, herbs, and fruit to be found. His passion for quality ingredients makes him a precious ally for us food lovers.

To Rod Mitchell at Browne Trading Co. in Maine for his pristine seafood and invaluable knowledge of the East Coast's underwater bounty; to Marc Sarrazin at De Bragga and Spitler for supplying the best meats in New York City; to Gilles and Muriel Carter at Berry Best Farm, dedicated farmers who sent local fruit and vegetables on the stem for the spring and summer spreads; to Joe Doria, Oscar Bell, and Karla Baumhover at Grace's Marketplace in New York City for their wonderful ingredients used in the fall spread; to Mel Tortorici at Slavin Fish in New York City for his delectably fresh catch of the sea; to Ariane Daguin and George Faison from D'Artagnan in New Jersey, suppliers of the finest game, fowl, poultry, and fresh foie gras; to Jan Greer at Upstate Farm, New York, for her garden-fresh vegetables; to Phil Rozzo at Rozzo and Sons, one of New York City's best fishmongers; to Thierry Farges at Aux Delices des Bois in New York City, a mushroom specialist who provided us with his best specimens; and to Leon Pinto at Gourmand in Washington, D.C., for the gorgeous truffles.

To Michel Bernardaud and Dominique Millet in New York City, who graciously let us use their beautiful china for many of the photographs.

To Jacqueline Coumans and Charles Moriniere at Le Decor Français, who lent us precious fabrics for the fall and winter spreads.

And many thanks to my family, friends, and colleagues whom I have omitted to mention by name, although they have helped me with their love and support at every step of my career.

INTRODUCTION

I would like to share with you my pleasure in finding and cooking the wonderful foods North America produces. Believe it or not, I enjoy preparing a family dinner in our small New York kitchen, even after a harrowing week of supervising the preparation and service of a thousand meals by the staff of fifty professionals at my restaurant, Daniel.

Reflecting on more than twenty-five years of experience in a dozen restaurants, I can derive what all the greatest chefs believe to be the two most important rules of our profession: First, find the best ingredients and, second, respect their flavors when preparing them.

The continual challenge of finding the best ingredients has been part of my life since childhood. The family farm in the Lyons countryside where I grew up produced a wide variety of seasonal crops from the fields, vegetable garden, and orchard. Farm animals included cows for milk, goats for cheese, and pigs for charcuterie, while the farmyard contained geese, ducks, chickens, squabs, rabbits, guinea fowls, and turkeys. The farm's production was sold weekly at the Lyons farmer's market with plenty left over to feed our family. Each new crop was celebrated with lengthy Sunday meals and discussed and compared with previous seasonal bounty. My grandmother Francine, the first person to trust me in a kitchen, would prepare simple but always tasty dishes that were much appreciated by all of us.

Before coming to America, I had assumed that the finest cooking using the best ingredients could be done only in France, where the tremendous variety of excellent ingredients—the meats and fowl, vegetables and herbs, fish and crustaceans, fruits and cheeses—seemed to have no equal in the world. However, I am now convinced that the quality and variety of American bounty is similar to that found in European markets.

In the past decade, an abundance of superior foods, such as high-quality fresh herbs, fruit, vegetables, and free-range poultry has become more generally available throughout the United States due to the growing demand of consumers for better-tasting and more healthful foods. The best example of this is the revival of farmer's markets across the country and the success of specialty food stores. Even supermarkets now recognize the need for developing sections specializing in seasonal, local, and organically grown vegetables and other quality items.

What a wonderful change for the home cook, especially since the enormous variety of ingredients now available at the market is combined with the rich "melting pot" culture of this country. Since I moved to New York City, my cooking has been enriched by the enormous repertoire of ethnic cuisines from Asia, the Middle East, and Latin and South America with their wide variety of produce, as well as by the rejuvenated regional American cooking. Discovering and experimenting with new and unfamiliar ingredients has allowed me to broaden my French repertoire into a more contemporary cooking style adapted for the nineties, keeping in mind quality, taste, health, and simplicity.

But, whether one is preparing a classic French dish or something more exotic, the secret to great cooking remains the quest for excellence in the ingredients you buy. And the key to excellence is respect for nature's seasonal cycle. In France, choosing the best foods for each season is called cuisine du marché, which means first shopping to see what is the best produce available, then planning the meal accordingly. Buying produce at its peak generally means buying it at a favorable price, because supply is usually high. Also, a seasonal variety of foods provides a healthful diet. That is why this book is organized around nature's cycle of seasons.

In the first section of this book, you will find recipes specially created to present the produce from the market lists, which begin on page 327. A short headnote will describe each recipe's characteristics   taste, texture, and visual appeal. Some of the recipes are my signature dishes, such as Crisp Paupiette of Sea Bass in a Barolo Sauce or Maine Sea Scallops in Black Tie; some are tributes to my mentors and colleagues, such as Roasted Guinea Fowl in a Salt Crust Roger Vergé or Lobster and Pompano Sottha Khunn; and some are related to my personal background, such as Gratin of Cardoon Francine, named after my grandmother, and Sweet Apple Alix, my daughter's favorite dessert.

Naturally, I have simplified and adapted each recipe for home use and explained how to prepare it in advance for convenience.

The market lists consist of a seasonal market list of the produce I most often use in my recipes. Each fruit or vegetable listed comes with tips on how to choose the best examples as well as suggestions on how to prepare and combine them in short and easy-to-make recipes. Searching for the best ingredients involves establishing a variety of sources to choose from—local markets, specialty stores, mail-order food companies—and building relationships with growers, suppliers, and vendors who are knowledgeable about quality and freshness. Good restaurants are also excellent sources of information on where to get the best available ingredients.

I hope that the recipes, market lists, and the pictures in this book will help you enjoy the process of searching for and cooking fresh seasonal ingredients.

HAPPY COOKING, DANIEL BOULUD

JULY 1993

CONTENTS

Hors d'Oeuvres page 3

Soups page 31

Salads page 59

Carpaccio and Terrines page 91

Risotto page 105

Pasta page 115

Shellfish page 137

Fish page 163

Poultry page 199

Meat and Game page 219

Side Dishes page 265

Desserts page 293

Seasonal Market Lists page 327

Spring page 327, Summer page 337, Autumn page 347, Winter page 357

Basic Recipes page 369

Basic Chicken or Vegetarian Stock page 370,
Basic Chicken Jus page 371, Basic Puff Pastry page 372

Suppliers page 373

Index page 374

Cooking with Daniel Boulud

Hors d'Oeuvres

Spring   Summer   Autumn   Winter
✽   ⚜   🍃   ❄

Cherry Tomatoes Stuffed with Crab Guacamole ⚜ page 4

Tapenade and Quail Eggs on Toast 🍃 page 5

Red Snapper and Sun-Dried Tomato Roulade with Lime ❄ page 6

Eggplant Dip with Country Bread ⚜ page 8

Basil and Anchovy Dip with Summer Radishes ⚜ page 9

Crispy Rolls of Salsify with Prosciutto and Parmesan 🍃 page 10

Crispy Tomato Toast Michel Guérard ⚜ page 12

Herb, Walnut, and Lemon Dip with Chicken Chunks 🍃 page 13

Beef Sticks with Arugula and a Pickle Dip 🍃 page 14

Smoked Salmon Sticks with a Sherry Dip ❄ page 15

Salmon and Celery "Rillettes" ✽ page 16

Avocado Dip with Sesame Seeds ✽ page 17

Stuffed Baby Artichokes with Almonds and Chives ✽ page 18

Cucumber Cones with Mint and Lime ✽ page 19

Spring Potatoes with Caviar and Chives ✽ page 20

Fresh Sardine Fillets with Arugula ⚜ page 23

Crispy Golden Squid and Celeriac ❄ page 25

Cheese Tartlets with a Sweet Pepper Confit ✽ page 27

Cherry Tomatoes Stuffed with Crab Guacamole

Serves 6 (24 cherry tomatoes)

In summer, when tiny cherry tomatoes are at their plump peak, they are ideal for hollowing, stuffing, and serving with cocktails. Select bright red and yellow ones that are firm and fragrant for this easy-to-prepare appetizer. If crab isn't available, you can use finely diced shrimp, ham, or chicken for the lively guacamole. This recipe can be prepared up to 2 hours in advance; simply refrigerate until ready to serve.

24 large red and yellow cherry tomatoes (1-inch size)

Salt, freshly ground black pepper

1 small ripe avocado, split, pitted, and peeled

Juice of 1/2 lemon

1 tablespoon olive oil

8 drops Tabasco

4 ounces crabmeat

1 tablespoon shallots, finely chopped

1 small clove garlic, peeled and finely chopped

8 sprigs coriander, leaves only, half the leaves chopped

❧ Preparation

Cut a 1/4-inch cap off each tomato. Reserve the caps. Scoop out the seeds and pulp with a tiny spoon or a melon-ball scoop. Season each hollowed tomato with salt and pepper. Set aside.

Mash the avocado with a fork in a bowl, add the lemon juice, olive oil, Tabasco, crabmeat, shallots, garlic, and chopped coriander and mix until smooth. Salt and pepper to taste.

Fill each cherry tomato 1/4-inch above the rim with the crab guacamole. Add a coriander leaf for decoration on top and cover each tomato with its cap.

❧ Presentation

Arrange the remaining coriander leaves on a serving tray and space the stuffed cherry tomatoes evenly in a pattern of your choice. Keep refrigerated until ready to serve.

TAPENADE AND QUAIL EGGS ON TOAST

Serves 4 (24 toasts)

The rustic and pungent Provençal blend of black olives, basil, anchovies, and garlic called tapenade that tops these toasts is garnished with a smooth, colorful, and sweet quail egg. If quail eggs are not available in your specialty food store, use 1 teaspoon chopped hard-boiled egg per toast. Served cold, the tapenade can be prepared up to 1 hour in advance and refrigerated until ready to use.

1 cup small black olives (Niçoise)

4 ounces basil leaves, large leaves separated from small ones

2 cloves garlic, peeled and finely chopped

2 Mediterranean anchovy fillets in oil, drained

1 tablespoon olive oil

Freshly ground black pepper

16 quail eggs (or 4 chicken eggs)

6 slices white bread, toasted

✍ PREPARATION

To pit the olives, place them in a zip-lock bag, seal, and crush with a small mallet or pan. Open the bag and discard the pits. Place the olives, 1/2 of the basil (use the large leaves), 1 clove garlic, the anchovies, olive oil, and pepper in a blender or food processor and process until puréed. Set aside.

Bring 1 quart of water to a boil over medium heat. Add the quail eggs and boil for 3 minutes. Remove from heat and cool under cold running water. Peel the eggs, split them, and set aside. (You have 3 more eggs than necessary to decorate the toasts, so don't worry if you break or have problems peeling one.) If using chicken eggs, boil until hard, 6 to 7 minutes, cool under cold running water, peel, chop, and set aside.

Preheat oven to 350 degrees. Cut each slice of bread into 4 circles with a round 1-1/2-inch cookie cutter. Crisp them in the oven for approximately 5 minutes, let cool, and rub each piece of bread with the remaining clove of garlic. Discard the garlic clove.

Spread the tapenade on each toast. Decorate with half a quail egg (or 1 teaspoon of chopped chicken egg) and a small basil leaf.

✍ PRESENTATION

Arrange the remaining basil leaves on a serving tray and space the toasts evenly. Keep refrigerated until ready to serve.

RED SNAPPER AND SUN-DRIED TOMATO ROULADE WITH LIME

Serves 4 (20 minitoasts)

Inspired by ceviche, the basic combination of fish marinated with lime, this recipe requires very fresh and firm fish fillets, tasty sun-dried tomatoes, lime, and fresh coriander for a sublime flavor. Rolled, chilled, sliced into spirals, then served atop thin rounds of toast, the elements for this hors d'oeuvre can be prepared up to 1 day in advance. The fish roll can be kept in the freezer and defrosted 10 minutes before slicing and assembling.

5 slices white bread

3 tablespoons sweet butter, softened

1 ounce sun-dried tomatoes, 1/2 tablespoon cut into small pieces, the rest whole

Grated zest of 1/2 lime, juice of 1 lime, and 1 lime peeled, segments removed, and cut in small pieces and reserved for decoration

4 drops Tabasco

Salt, freshly ground black pepper

4 ounces skinless red snapper fillet (when using raw fish in recipes, buy only the freshest and finest quality, keep it well chilled, and be sure to use it the same day it is purchased)

2 sprigs coriander, leaves only

✤ PREPARATION

Preheat oven to 350 degrees. Cut each slice of bread into 4 circles with a round 1-1/4-inch cookie cutter. Place them in a baking pan and toast in the oven for 7 to 10 minutes or until lightly colored and dried. Set aside.

Place the butter, whole sun-dried tomatoes, Tabasco, lime zest, and lime juice in a blender or food processor and purée until smooth. Salt and pepper to taste and set aside.

Place a piece of 12-inch-square plastic wrap or parchment paper on a counter. Cut the cold fillets of fish into very thin slices. Arrange the sliced fillet on the plastic wrap to form a rectangle about 7 inches by 4 inches. Cover with a second piece of plastic wrap or paper and flatten the fish evenly with a mallet or small pan. Peel off the top piece of plastic. Season the fish with salt and pepper. Spread the sun-dried tomato butter evenly over the fish rectangle. To roll, lift the bottom sheet of plastic on the long side of the rectangle and roll the fish over the spread butter slowly and tightly, peeling back the plastic as you go. Wrap the roll very tightly in the plastic or paper sheet and freeze until frozen. When ready to serve, remove the plastic or paper and let the roll sit at room temperature for 10 minutes. Slice into 1/4-inch slices and place them over each toast round.

✤ PRESENTATION

Garnish each toast round with a small piece of chopped sun-dried tomato and a coriander leaf. Space the toasts evenly on a tray decorated with coriander leaves and the reserved pieces of lime.

Eggplant Dip with Country Bread

Serves 4 to 6

Eggplant is commonly used in Mediterranean cuisine. Cooked eggplants rarely look great, but when you are familiar with this vegetable, you become addicted to its sharp and delicious taste and the look becomes secondary. For serving ease, you can prepare this Provençal recipe up to 6 hours in advance and refrigerate it—except for the bread, which should be toasted just before serving.

1/4 cup olive oil

3 medium-size eggplants, ends removed, split lengthwise

1/2 cup scallions, white part only, thinly sliced

1 sweet red pepper, split, seeded, in 1/8-inch dice

1/2 small jalapeño pepper, split, seeded, and finely chopped, or a pinch of cayenne pepper (wear plastic gloves when handling jalapeño peppers)

1/4 pound small white mushrooms, sliced

1 large tomato, peeled, seeded, in 1/8-inch dice

2 cloves garlic, peeled and finely chopped

3 sprigs basil: 1 sprig whole, 2 sprigs leaves only, chopped

2-1/2 tablespoons chives, minced

Salt, freshly ground black pepper

1 small loaf country bread, broken into small chunks

❧ Preparation

Preheat oven to 350 degrees. Brush a baking pan with 1 tablespoon of the olive oil. Place the eggplant halves, skin side up, on the baking pan. Bake in the oven for 30 to 45 minutes or until soft and cooked through. Remove from oven and set aside to cool.

Warm 1 tablespoon of the olive oil in a skillet over medium heat. Add the scallions, red pepper, and jalapeño and sweat for 5 minutes without browning. Remove from the pan and set aside. Add the mushrooms to the pan and cook for 5 to 7 minutes or until all moisture has evaporated. Set aside to cool. Scoop out the eggplant pulp onto a large cutting board. Add the mushrooms and finely chop both vegetables. Transfer to a bowl and add the scallion-and-pepper mixture, tomato, 2/3 of the garlic, chopped basil, 3/4 of the chives, the remaining 2 tablespoons oil, and salt and pepper to taste. Mix well with a fork, cover, and refrigerate until needed.

Preheat the broiler. Toss the bread chunks with the remaining garlic and toast them under the broiler, tossing frequently, until golden brown on all sides.

❧ Presentation

Transfer the eggplant dip to a bowl and shape it into a dome using a fork. Decorate the dome with the whole basil leaves and the rest of the chopped chives. Serve the toasted country bread in a basket on the side.

Basil and Anchovy Dip with Summer Radishes

Serves 4

Best described as an *herbs anchoyade*—the lusty anchovy, garlic, and olive oil sauce from the south of France—
this deliciously strong, salty dip provides a great flavor contrast to crisp, peppery pink radishes.
This flavorful dip can be used with many other favorite crudités, such as cherry tomatoes, fresh fennel wedges,
endive leaves, celery sticks, etc. Prepare up to 4 hours beforehand, then chill until serving.

*8 to 10 Mediterranean anchovy fillets in oil,
drained (1 ounce)*

5 sprigs basil, leaves only

1 clove garlic, peeled

1 hard-boiled egg, peeled

1/4 cup extra-virgin olive oil

*Juice of 1 lemon or 1/2 tablespoon
red wine vinegar*

1/2 teaspoon freshly ground black pepper

1 tablespoon water

*2 to 3 bunches small, very firm, pink radishes,
greens trimmed to 1/4 inch, rootlets removed*

❧ Preparation

Place all the ingredients except the radishes in a blender or food processor. Blend until
smooth and pour into a serving bowl.

❧ Presentation

Place the bowl with the anchovy dip in the center of a large plate or tray. Arrange the
radishes around the bowl.

CRISPY ROLLS OF SALSIFY WITH PROSCIUTTO AND PARMESAN

Serves 4 to 6

For those of you who are unfamiliar with this root vegetable, salsify looks like a long, thin, nontapering black carrot. The flesh is white and, once cooked, has a slightly bitter and nutty taste. It is often used for soups, salads, or side dishes. In these satisfyingly crisp, phyllo-wrapped canapés, the vegetable's soft, earthy flavor is wonderfully enriched by salty prosciutto and sharp Parmesan. You can assemble the salsify rolls up to 6 hours in advance, refrigerate, and then bake before serving.

5 to 6 salsify roots (about 1/2 pound), ends cut off and roots peeled

Juice of 1 lemon

Salt, freshly ground black pepper

6 to 8 slices of prosciutto, 8 inches by 3 inches (about 1/4 pound)

4 sheets phyllo dough

2 tablespoons sweet butter, melted

1/2 cup freshly grated Parmesan cheese

4 pinches of freshly ground nutmeg

Fall leaves, for garnish

PREPARATION

Boil the peeled whole roots in a deep pan with 2 quarts water, the lemon juice, and a pinch of salt. When easily pierced with a knife, after approximately 15 to 20 minutes, remove the salsify from the heat, drain, and set aside to cool on a paper towel.

Season each salsify with pepper. Use about 1-1/2 slices prosciutto lengthwise to wrap each root (the width of the slices should fit tightly around the cooked salsify).

Preheat oven to 400 degrees. Place a sheet of phyllo dough on the countertop. Brush the sheet with melted butter and sprinkle it with Parmesan, nutmeg, salt, and pepper. Place a salsify wrapped in prosciutto along the edge of the shorter length of the dough. Tightly wrap the salsify, rolling it 3 times in the dough. Trim off the leftover dough, if any, along the salsify. Repeat with each salsify until they are all wrapped. Brush each roll with butter and sprinkle with or roll them in Parmesan. Place the rolls on a greased baking sheet and bake until golden, approximately 5 to 7 minutes.

PRESENTATION

Cut each roll at an angle in 2-inch-long pieces. Place them on a serving dish over clean and colorful fall leaves.

Note: Salsify can make great chips for snacks. Peel and slice the roots into 2-inch lengths. Thinly slice each piece lengthwise. Heat 1 cup oil to 350 degrees, plunge in the salsify, and fry until golden. Drain the chips on a paper towel and sprinkle with salt.

CRISPY TOMATO TOAST MICHEL GUÉRARD

Serves 4 (20 toasts)

My first encounter with this very refreshing toast the Italians call *crostini* was in 1978 at Michel Guérard's three-star restaurant, Les Prés et Les Sources, in Eugénie-les-Bains. He served it as an *amuse-gueule* ("mouth teaser") and it will always remain my favorite hors d'oeuvre, with the unique sensation of coolness, crispness, and a spicy bite. It's great for summer entertaining and is easy to prepare, and the tomato dip can be made 4 hours in advance and kept very cold until serving. The toast can also be prepared in advance and kept in a dry place.

1 cup ripe tomatoes, peeled, seeded, in 1/4-inch dice, and drained with 1 pinch of salt

3 tablespoons crème fraîche

1 tablespoon chives, finely chopped, plus a few whole chives for garnish

1 tablespoon tarragon, leaves only, finely chopped, a few whole leaves reserved

5 drops Tabasco

Salt, freshly ground black pepper

1 small baguette (approximately 2-1/2 inches in diameter), sliced; or sliced white bread, cut into twenty 2-inch round disks with a cookie cutter

1 clove garlic, peeled

❧ PREPARATION

Preheat oven to 350 degrees. Gently mix the diced tomato, crème fraîche, chopped chives and tarragon, and Tabasco in a serving bowl. Season with salt and pepper to taste. Cover and refrigerate the tomato mixture.

Toast the bread on a baking sheet until crisp, about 5 to 7 minutes, remove, and let cool. Carefully rub the clove of garlic on each toast and discard garlic clove when done.

❧ PRESENTATION

Decorate the tomato mixture with the chives and tarragon leaves. Place the dip in the middle of a tray. Arrange the toast crisps all around.

Herb, Walnut, and Lemon Dip with Chicken Chunks

Serves 4

This astonishingly simple sauce featuring fresh herbs supplies a bright and vibrant accent to sautéed chicken and fresh fennel. Walnuts enrich the dressing, the best of which are the newly harvested, raw, white-meat ones that are available from mid-September to early November. This herb, walnut, and lemon dip can be served with other favorite crudités such as endive and radicchio leaves, or with small chunks of walnut or country sourdough bread. You can prepare this appetizer up to 3 hours before serving.

Four 3-ounce chicken breasts, boneless and skinless

Salt, freshly ground black pepper

2 teaspoons corn oil

2 sprigs tarragon, leaves chopped, stems reserved

5 sprigs Italian parsley, leaves chopped, stems reserved

1 ounce chervil, leaves chopped, stems reserved

2-1/2 tablespoons chives, chopped

1/2 cup walnuts, toasted and chopped

3 tablespoons walnut oil

Juice of 2 lemons

1/2 teaspoon hot pepper oil, or a pinch of hot pepper flakes

1 bulb fennel, halved lengthwise and cut into wedges

Preparation

Salt and pepper the chicken breasts. Warm 1-1/2 teaspoons of the corn oil in a pan over medium heat. Add the chicken breasts and the herb stems. Cook for about 5 minutes. When breasts are colored, turn them over and cover with a lid. Cook for another 5 minutes. Remove the chicken from the pan to a cutting board and let cool. Discard the herb stems and cut the chicken breasts in 1/2-inch chunks.

Blend the herbs, walnuts, walnut oil, lemon juice, hot pepper oil, remaining 1/2 teaspoon corn oil, and salt and pepper to taste in a blender or food processor until smooth. Pour into a serving bowl.

Presentation

Arrange the fennel wedges in a circle on a serving dish. Place the chicken cubes in the middle and stick a toothpick into each one. Serve the dip on the side.

BEEF STICKS WITH ARUGULA AND A PICKLE DIP

Serves 4 to 6 (24 beef sticks)

This casual Italian-style hors d'oeuvre is perfect for summer garden parties. In this version of beef carpaccio, thinly sliced beef is wrapped around *grissini* (bread sticks) and arugula and accompanied by a delightfully piquant pickle dressing. You can also use this dressing over a mixed greens salad covered with thin slices of beef or Swiss dried beef (*bresaola*). The dip can be prepared up to 1 day in advance, but the beef is sliced, assembled, and kept refrigerated an hour before serving.

For the Pickle Dip:

1 hard-boiled egg, peeled

2 cloves garlic, peeled

3 sprigs Italian parsley, leaves only

1 sprig tarragon, leaves only, finely chopped

6 Mediterranean anchovy fillets in oil, drained

6 cornichons

1 tablespoon tiny French capers, drained

2 tablespoons freshly grated Parmesan cheese

1 teaspoon Worcestershire sauce

6 drops Tabasco

1 tablespoon red wine vinegar

1/2 cup olive oil

Juice of 1 lemon

1 tablespoon Dijon mustard

Salt, freshly ground black pepper

For the Beef Sticks:

2 dozen very thin Italian bread sticks (found in Italian specialty shops; the Italian name is grissini)

1/2 pound top round beef, sliced paper thin (ask your butcher to slice it as thin as prosciutto)

1 bunch arugula, leaves only

PREPARATION

For the Pickle Dip:
Finely chop together all the ingredients of the dip in a blender or food processor. Correct the seasoning with salt and pepper.

For the Beef Sticks:
Cut the bread sticks into 4- to 5-inch long pieces. Cut the beef slices in 1-inch wide stripes. Wrap 2 arugula leaves around one end of each bread stick and tightly roll a slice of beef twice around the arugula leaves.

PRESENTATION

Place the pickle dip in a small serving bowl in the middle of a 10-inch round dish. Place the remaining arugula leaves all around and the beef sticks on top, with beef ends pointing toward the bowl.

SMOKED SALMON STICKS WITH A SHERRY DIP

Serves 4 to 6 (about 48 sticks)

This wonderfully tart dressing—studded with sun-dried tomatoes, scallions, and dill—supplies a fine taste complement to these smoked salmon–wrapped cucumber spears. When selecting the best salmon for serving, opt for lox that is not too fatty, has firm translucent slices that are not too thin, and is mild in flavor. The sherry dip can be used as a sauce and served alongside other smoked fish or cold seafood. You can assemble this appetizer and keep it refrigerated up to 3 hours before serving.

1/4 cup sun-dried tomatoes in oil, drained and diced

5 scallions, white part only, thinly sliced

1/2 ounce fresh dill, leaves only, chopped

1/2 cup heavy cream

1 teaspoon ground coriander

1-1/2 tablespoons Spanish sherry vinegar

Salt, freshly ground black pepper

1 long European hothouse cucumber, peeled, split lengthwise, and seeded with a spoon

1/4 pound presliced smoked salmon (lox), each slice cut into strips 1 inch wide and 2 inches long

1 small loaf whole-grain bread, thinly sliced and toasted under the broiler

✤ PREPARATION

Mix the sun-dried tomatoes, scallions, dill, heavy cream, coriander, sherry vinegar, salt, and pepper in a bowl with a fork and refrigerate.

Cut each cucumber half into 4 equal pieces. Split each piece into 6 sticks. Wrap a strip of smoked salmon once around the bottom of each cucumber stick and refrigerate.

✤ PRESENTATION

Serve this hors d'oeuvre on a tray. Pour the dip into a small serving bowl and place it in the center of the tray. Arrange the cucumber and salmon sticks in two little piles on each side of the dip. Place the thin slices of toasted whole-grain bread between the two piles. Dip the cucumber-salmon sticks into the dip and eat with the toast.

SALMON AND CELERY "RILLETTES"

Serves 4 to 6

This chilled lox and cooked salmon spread with celery is a departure from the traditional way of serving that regal cured fish. Equally delicious—yet far more economical—this smooth summer spread can be prepared ahead and kept refrigerated up to 6 hours before serving.

1 very fresh and crisp bunch celery, the large stalks removed from around the heart, the small leaves from the heart reserved for garnish, and the heart finely diced to make 1/2 cup

4 ounces fresh salmon steak, cut 1/2 inch thick

Salt, freshly ground black pepper

Juice of 1 lemon

3 tablespoons crème fraîche or sour cream

3 ounces smoked salmon (lox), in 1/8-inch dice

2 tablespoons chives, finely minced

1 small loaf thinly sliced pumpernickel bread (or toasted white bread)

❀ PREPARATION

Extract the juice from the large celery stalks with a juicer. If you do not have a juicer, chop the stalks, purée in a blender or food processor with 1 cup of water, and strain. Discard the pulp. Bring the celery juice to a boil in a pan over medium heat.

Season the salmon steak with salt and pepper. Plunge the salmon in the boiling celery juice. Simmer for 45 to 60 seconds. Remove the pan from heat and let the salmon cool in the celery juice.

Bring 2 cups of water with a pinch of salt to a boil in a pot over high heat. Plunge in the diced celery heart. Cook until tender, about 5 to 6 minutes, drain, and set aside to cool.

Drain the poached salmon, remove and discard the skin, and pat dry with a paper towel. Discard the celery juice. Break the poached salmon into small chunks and blend gently in a blender or food processor with the lemon juice, crème fraîche or sour cream, and salt and pepper to taste, or mash together in a bowl with a fork. Transfer the salmon mousse into a bowl and mix in the smoked salmon, celery heart dice, and 1/2 of the chives with a spoon. If too dry, add a tablespoon or two more of crème fraîche. Correct the seasoning.

❀ PRESENTATION

Transfer the salmon-and-celery rillettes to a serving bowl, decorate with the small celery leaves, and sprinkle the rest of the chives on top. Serve with the pumpernickel bread.

AVOCADO DIP WITH SESAME SEEDS

Serves 4 to 6

Maybe because I didn't know the taste of avocado when I was growing up, it was love at first bite when I started cooking, first in France and then in America, where I discovered Mexican cuisine. Based on a traditional guacamole, this dish becomes more oriental than Mexican in flavor with its sesame oil and seed additions, for a more-surprising taste. You can prepare this dip up to an hour beforehand to serve with tortilla chips, crispy country bread, or cold grilled chicken wings, or alongside shrimp, steamed lobster, or stone crab claws as a dressing.

1 sweet red pepper, split lengthwise, stem and seeds discarded

1 tablespoon sesame seeds

3 ripe avocados (about one pound), peeled, pitted, and cut into chunks

Juice and grated zest of 1 lime

2 tablespoons sour cream

1 teaspoon dark sesame oil

1 tablespoon shallots, finely chopped

4 sprigs coriander, leaves only, finely chopped

8 drops Tabasco

Salt

❀ PREPARATION

Preheat the broiler. Place the pepper halves under the broiler skin side up. Broil them until the skin turns black, about 10 to 12 minutes. Remove the peppers from the heat, let cool, wash the skin off under cold running water, and pat dry. Finely dice the roasted pepper and set aside.

Toast the sesame seeds in a dry pan over medium heat or under the broiler, tossing often for 1 to 2 minutes or until golden, and set aside.

Mix the avocados, lime juice and zest, sour cream, sesame oil, shallots, coriander, and Tabasco with a fork in a bowl. Add salt to taste.

❀ PRESENTATION

Scoop the dip into a shallow serving dish or bowl. Shape the dip into a rounded dome with a fork and sprinkle the top with the toasted sesame seeds. Arrange the red pepper dice in a ring at the base of the dome.

STUFFED BABY ARTICHOKES WITH ALMONDS AND CHIVES

Serves 4 to 6 (16 baby artichokes)

The artichokes, almonds, and thyme in this appetizer celebrate the Provençal spring harvest. Select young artichokes, firm and compact. You can prepare this dish up to 6 hours in advance and keep refrigerated.

24 baby artichokes, 1-1/2 to 2 ounces each

Juice of 1 lemon

1/2 tablespoon olive oil

1/4 cup onions, peeled and coarsely chopped

2 cloves garlic, peeled and coarsely chopped

1 sprig fresh thyme

1/2 cup white wine

Salt, freshly ground black pepper

2 tablespoons sliced almonds, toasted

1 tablespoon almond or walnut oil (or substitute olive oil)

1 ounce chives: 1/2 cut in 1-inch sticks, 1/2 minced

❁ PREPARATION

With a paring knife, remove the outer leaves of the artichokes, cut off the stems, and shape the bottoms until rounded and smooth. Cut off the top 3/4 inch of the leaves.

Bring 1-1/2 quarts cold water with 1/2 the lemon juice and a pinch of salt to a boil in a large pot over medium heat. Add 16 artichokes and simmer until tender, about 30 minutes. Drain and let cool.

As the artichokes cook, quarter the remaining 8 artichokes. Heat the olive oil in a medium pan over medium heat. Add the onions, garlic, and thyme and sweat until translucent (about 3 to 4 minutes). Add the quartered artichokes and stir well. Add the wine, salt, and pepper. Cover, and cook for 20 minutes or until tender. Remove the lid and let the wine evaporate, then remove from the heat, discard the thyme, and let cool.

Scoop out the center leaves and chokes of each artichoke to form a cavity. Cut 1/4 inch off the bottom of each artichoke and stand them upright on a tray. Add the center leaves, chokes, and trimmings to the quartered artichokes mixture.

Transfer the artichoke mixture to a blender or food processor. Add 1 tablespoon of the almonds, the remaining lemon juice, walnut oil, salt, and pepper and purée. Add the minced chives and mix with a spoon. Transfer the artichoke purée to a zip-lock bag, push the air out, and seal it shut. Cut 1/2 inch off the tip of one of the bottom corners of the bag and pipe the stuffing into the cavity of each baby artichoke to the top.

❁ PRESENTATION

Stud each purée mound with chives and 2 toasted almonds. Arrange the artichokes in rows on a tray and decorate the sides of the tray with additional toasted almonds.

Cucumber Cones with Mint and Lime

Serves 6

Middle Eastern inspired, these bite-size vegetarian treats, which are an adaptation of tabbouleh, are temptingly bright in color and full of flavor. Their couscous filling and fried mint-leaf garnish add refinement to these hors d'oeuvres, which can be assembled up to 3 hours before serving.

2 small European hothouse cucumbers, peeled and cut into 2-inch segments

Grated zest and juice of 4 limes

Salt, freshly ground black pepper

1/4 cup carrots, peeled and finely diced

1/4 cup celery, peeled and finely diced

3 cups instant couscous

3 sprigs fresh mint, leaves only, 1/3 finely chopped

2 sprigs fresh coriander, leaves only, 1/2 finely chopped

4 drops Tabasco

2-1/2 tablespoons olive oil

1/2 cup oil, for frying

❈ Preparation

Slice each cucumber segment diagonally along the length, shaping it into 2 cones. Scoop out and discard the seeds of each piece with a spoon, making a small cavity to be filled with the couscous, and refrigerate. Cover with plastic wrap until needed.

Bring 2 cups water to a boil in a small pot over high heat. Add the lime zest and boil for 5 minutes. Strain out the zest and set it aside. Bring 2 cups water with a pinch of salt to a boil, add the carrots, and cook for 2 minutes. Add the celery and boil for another 5 to 7 minutes. Drain and set aside.

Bring 1 cup water with a pinch of salt to a boil. Put the couscous in a bowl and pour the boiling water over it. Cover with plastic wrap and let the couscous stand for 15 minutes. When cool, add the zest of lime, carrots, and celery, the chopped mint and coriander, lime juice, Tabasco, olive oil, and a few pinches of salt and mix well.

Salt and pepper each piece of cucumber and fill each cavity with the couscous mixture. Refrigerate until needed.

Heat the oil to 325 degrees. Drop the mint leaves into the oil and fry for 30 to 60 seconds or until translucent. Remove the fried leaves with a mesh skimmer to a paper towel.

❈ Presentation

Stud each stuffed cone with 1 or 2 fried mint leaves and fresh coriander. Arrange the cones in rows on a serving tray. Garnish the tray with fresh coriander leaves.

Spring Potatoes with Caviar and Chives

Serves 4 (12 new potatoes)

This stunning hors d'oeuvre combines the ordinary sweet and tender new potatoes with the extraordinary briny caviar, one of nature's greatest delicacies. The tiny potatoes are hollowed out, baked, stuffed with a creamy chive mix, and finally topped with a dollop of caviar. You can cook the potatoes up to 2 hours in advance. When ready to serve, reheat the potato shells before stuffing and topping them with caviar.

12 new potatoes, about 2 ounces each

Salt, freshly ground black pepper

1/2 tablespoon sweet butter

1 cup chicken stock (see page 370)

3 tablespoons crème fraîche or sour cream

1 tablespoon finely chopped chives and 24 chive sticks, 1 inch long, for garnish

12 teaspoons caviar (3 ounces) of your choice

❀ Preparation

Preheat oven to 350 degrees. Peel the potatoes, trimming each down to the size and shape of a small egg, smooth and oval. Scoop out and discard the inside of each potato from one of the tip ends with a small spoon or melon-ball scoop until the potato shell is about 1/4 inch thick. Cut off the tip of the base side of each potato to enable it to stand.

Place the hollowed potato shells in a roasting pan. Season them with salt and pepper inside and out. Put an equal amount of butter into the cavity of each potato along with 1/2 tablespoon of chicken stock. Pour the rest of the stock around the potatoes. Cover with a piece of aluminum foil and bake in the oven for about 20 to 25 minutes. When ready, the potatoes should be tender when pierced but not overcooked or else they will collapse. Test readiness often by piercing them with a small blade while cooking. When done, remove from heat and set aside to cool.

Empty the liquid inside each potato back into the pan and set the potatoes aside. Bring the cooking juices to a boil and cook until reduced to about 2 tablespoons. Brush the outside of the potatoes with the reduced liquid and keep them warm on the side.

Mix the crème fraîche with the chopped chives in a small bowl. Salt and pepper to taste.

❀ Presentation

Arrange the warm potatoes on a small serving dish. Use a small spoon to fill each one halfway with the crème fraîche-and-chive mixture. Mound 1 teaspoon of caviar over the mixture and insert 2 chive sticks into the caviar for decoration.

Fresh Sardine Fillets with Arugula

Serves 4 to 6

This Mediterranean-style hors d'oeuvre, which can also be served as an appetizer, gives center stage to the small but tasty sardine. Its rich flavor is counterbalanced by tangy lemon dressing and peppery arugula garnish. When buying fresh sardines, select those with firm, stiff bodies and bright silvery color. If fresh sardines are not available you can use fresh fillets of mackerel instead, which will require a few more minutes of cooking. All the preparations can be done up to 2 hours in advance and the cooking at the last minute before serving.

3/4 pound very fresh sardines (about 8 to 10 sardines), gutted, washed, and patted dry (if using mackerel instead of sardines, cut the fillets into small strips)

3 tablespoons olive oil

2 sweet red peppers, split lengthwise and seeded

2 lemons: 1 for juice, 1 peeled, seeded, segments removed, and the flesh diced

1 tablespoon small black olives (Niçoise), pitted and finely chopped

2 tablespoons chives, finely chopped

2 sprigs basil, leaves only, chopped

Salt, freshly ground black pepper

1 baguette (or rectangular salted crackers)

1 clove garlic, peeled

1/4 pound arugula, leaves only

❧ Preparation

To fillet the sardines, use plastic disposable gloves to protect your hands from the odor. Cut off the head and tail of each sardine. Hold the sardine in one hand. Place a finger from your free hand on the head side, by the bone. Push your finger into the sardine along the bone, down to the tail, thus removing the top fillet. To remove the bone from the second fillet, just lift the bone up from the head side while holding down the fillet. Once you get the gist of it, it will take you just a few seconds to fillet the sardines. You can also use a small knife and run it along the center bone from head to tail.

Brush 2 sheets of 5-inch-square aluminum foil with a touch of olive oil. Divide the sardine fillets between the 2 sheets. Place them flat, skin side up, and side by side. Refrigerate until needed.

For the Dressing:
Preheat broiler. Broil the peppers skin side up until black. Remove from heat, cool, and peel the blackened skin off under cold running water. Pat dry, cut the peppers in small dice, and set aside.

In a bowl, mix together the diced red pepper, lemon juice, diced lemon, 2-1/2 tablespoons olive oil, black olives, chopped chives, basil, salt, and pepper. Refrigerate until ready to use.

When Ready to Serve:

Preheat broiler. Cut the baguette into 16 to 20 very thin slices at an angle. Toast them under the broiler on both sides, about 3 minutes per side. Let cool and then carefully rub the toasts with the garlic clove. Discard garlic. Place a few arugula leaves on each toast. Set aside.

Preheat a nonstick pan over high heat. Brush the sardine fillets (on their piece of aluminum) with olive oil and season them with salt and pepper. Flip the piece of aluminum into the pan and cook the sardines for 1 minute. If using mackerel, cook for 3 minutes. Remove from heat, place a plate on top of the pan, and flip the pan over, holding the plate in place as you do. Place 1 fillet on each toast. Spoon a little lemon dressing over.

❧ PRESENTATION

Serve the toasts of warm sardines on a large tray decorated with arugula leaves or on small individual plates.

CRISPY GOLDEN SQUID AND CELERIAC

Serves 4 to 6

This combination of crisp fried squid and celeriac slivers with a robust pepper and plum tomato sauce is a superb mingling of tastes and textures. The fiery sauce, which gives a great, flavorful boost to the subtly sweet squid and mild celeriac, can also be served with batter-fried shrimp. You can prepare the dip up to 3 hours in advance as you assemble the ingredients for the squid and celeriac chips. Cook the latter, however, just before serving.

For the Hot Dip:

1 tablespoon olive oil

1/4 cup onions, peeled and coarsely chopped

1 clove garlic, peeled and coarsely chopped

1 sweet red pepper, split, seeded, and coarsely chopped

1 small fresh jalapeño pepper, split, seeded, and coarsely chopped (use disposable gloves when handling); or 5 to 8 drops Tabasco; or 1 teaspoon hot pepper flakes

2 cups ripe plum tomatoes, split, seeded, and coarsely chopped; or canned plum tomatoes, drained, with the seeds squeezed out

Pinch of salt

Pinch of sugar

1/4 cup chicken stock (see page 370) or water

For the Squid:

1/2 pound small squid, cleaned and skinned (see note), flesh washed, patted dry, and cut into 1/3-inch slices

1 cup milk

2 quarts oil, for frying

1/4 pound small celeriac, peeled and sliced paper thin with a vegetable slicer or mandoline

Salt, freshly ground black pepper to taste

1/2 cup all-purpose flour in a large bowl

3 whole eggs, beaten in a large bowl

1 clove garlic, peeled and finely chopped or crushed, mixed with the eggs

1 cup fresh white bread crumbs, finely sifted into a large bowl or deep pan

Pine greens or tree leaves, for garnish

✤ PREPARATION

For the Hot Dip:

Heat the olive oil in a small pan over medium heat. Add the onion, garlic, and red and jalapeño peppers and sweat until the vegetables are soft but not yet colored, approximately 5 to 8 minutes. Stir in the tomatoes and add the salt and sugar, and the chicken stock. Bring to a boil, lower heat, and simmer for 20 to 30 minutes. Remove from heat, transfer to a blender or food processor, and blend coarsely. Taste for seasoning and keep warm until ready to serve.

For the Squid:

Soak the squid slices in the milk for 5 minutes. Heat the oil in a deep skillet to 375 degrees. Fry the celeriac slices in the oil. Cook until golden, approximately 2 to 3 minutes, remove with a skimmer, and drain on paper towels. Sprinkle with salt. Reserve the hot oil. Once all the celeriac is fried, drain the squid thoroughly and discard the milk. (Use disposable gloves to bread the squid to prevent your hands from picking up the odor.) Add the squid one handful at a time to the bowl with the flour and toss them until coated. Shake off excess flour and dip them into the large bowl with the beaten eggs and garlic. Remove and toss them into the bread crumbs. When coated, place them on parchment paper. Fry two handfuls of breaded squid at a time in the 375-degree oil until golden, approximately 2 to 3 minutes. When each batch is done, remove with a fine-mesh or Chinese skimmer to a paper towel and sprinkle with salt.

✤ Presentation

Put the warm tomato dip in the middle of a serving tray. Place the golden squid and celeriac chips all around. Decorate the edges of the tray with clean pine greens or tree leaves. Serve with small cocktail napkins.

Cleaning Squid: To remove the slippery purple-grayish skin from a squid, rub it with kosher or regular salt. The salt will act as an abrasive and the skin will easily come off while rubbing. If using this technique, make sure to rinse the peeled squid completely to wash off any remaining salt.

CHEESE TARTLETS WITH A SWEET PEPPER CONFIT

Serves 4 to 6 (20 to 24 small tartlets)
These tartlets are both creamy and tangy owing to their goat cheese filling and sweet pepper topping.
Fine goat cheese, the pride of many a French farmstead cheese maker, is now produced domestically. This
recipe can be prepared up to 2 hours in advance, then reheated before serving.

For the Dough:

1-3/4 cups all-purpose flour

Pinch of salt

Pinch of sugar

1 egg

1/2 cup sweet butter, softened

1/3 cup cold water

For the Sweet Pepper Confit:

2 tablespoons olive oil

Salt, freshly ground black pepper

Pinch of cayenne pepper

*2 sweet red peppers and 2 sweet yellow peppers,
quartered lengthwise, cored, and seeded*

1 clove garlic, peeled and finely chopped

1 sprig fresh thyme

For the Cheese Mix:

*One 8-ounce log plain white fresh goat cheese,
at room temperature*

3 ounces mascarpone cheese

1 egg yolk

2 whole eggs

2 tablespoons chives, finely chopped

Pinch of freshly grated nutmeg

2 tablespoons freshly grated Parmesan cheese

Salt, freshly ground black pepper

❁ PREPARATION

For the Dough:
Mix the flour, salt, sugar, egg, and butter in a bowl with your hands or in an electric
mixer with the hook attachment at low speed. When the ingredients are half blended
together, add the water, and continue mixing until totally blended (do not overwork the
dough). Shape the dough into a 6-inch square. Wrap the dough in plastic wrap and
refrigerate for 1/2 hour.

For the Sweet Pepper Confit:
Preheat the broiler. While the dough is chilling, brush a baking sheet with 1/2 tablespoon of the olive oil and sprinkle it with salt, pepper, and cayenne pepper. Place the
quartered peppers on the sheet skin side up. Brush the skin with 1/2 tablespoon of the

olive oil and broil until the skin turns black, about 8 to 10 minutes. Remove from heat, cool, and remove the burnt skin under cold running water and pat dry. Set the roasted pepper slices aside.

Heat the remaining tablespoon of olive oil in a pan over low heat. Add the garlic and the sprig of thyme and sweat for 2 minutes (do not color the garlic). Add the sweet pepper, cover with a lid, and gently cook for 15 to 20 minutes. Remove the pan from the heat, let cool, and discard the thyme. Remove the pepper slices with a slotted spoon onto a cutting board. Cut into small diamonds or squares, return them to the cooled cooking oil, and set aside until needed.

Butter 16 to 20 1-1/2-inch tartlet molds and sprinkle them with a pinch of flour (shake off excess flour), or use nonstick molds. Sprinkle the working space needed to roll the dough and a rolling pin with flour. Place the dough in the center of your working space and lightly flour it. Roll the dough on both sides from the center out toward the edges until 1/8 inch thick. Cut out 1 piece of dough for each mold with a 2-1/2 inch round cookie cutter. Place a piece of dough over each of the molds. Press lightly in the corners and along the edges of the mold to line it with the dough. Trim off and discard any dough overlapping the rim. Refrigerate the tartlet shells for 20 to 30 minutes (they can be made a day in advance and kept in the freezer until needed).

Preheat the oven to 325 degrees. Remove the tartlet molds from the refrigerator or freezer. Place a 2-inch square of parchment paper inside each mold and weight it down with dried or baking metal beans (pie weights). Place the tartlet shells on a baking pan and bake for 10 to 15 minutes (do not let the dough color). Remove the molds to cool on a rack.

For the Cheese Mix:
Raise the oven temperature to 350 degrees. While the tartlet shells are baking, mix together the goat cheese, mascarpone, egg yolk, whole eggs, half of the chives, nutmeg, Parmesan, salt, and pepper. Mix well until smooth, transfer the mix into a zip-lock plastic bag, and push the air out of the bag. Cut about 1/3 inch off a corner and pipe filling into each baked tartlet shell to the rim. Bake in the oven for 10 to 12 minutes or until set with the surface lightly colored. Remove to cool on a rack for 3 minutes. Unmold the tartlets and decorate each one with two pieces of red and two pieces of yellow sweet pepper in a checker pattern. Brush the top of the tartlets with a touch of the sweet pepper oil. Reheat the tartlets in the oven for 1 minute before serving.

❀ PRESENTATION

Garnish each tartlet with a pinch of chopped chives, arrange on a serving platter, and serve warm.

Soups

Spring   Summer   Autumn   Winter
✽   ⚜   🍃   ❖

Cold Soups

Cucumber and Coriander Soup with Smoked Trout ✽ page 32

Corn Soup with Nutmeg ⚜ page 33

Asparagus Soup with a Sweet Pepper Coulis ✽ page 34

Green Celery Soup with Pink Radishes ⚜ page 37

Chilled Tomato Soup with a Basil Guacamole ⚜ page 38

Artichoke and Grilled Eggplant Soup with Lemon
        and Thyme ⚜ page 40

Hot Soups

Cabbage and Lobster Soup with Chives 🍃 page 42

Salsify Soup with Bay Scallops and Sorrel ❖ page 45

Cinnamon Squash Soup with Chicken Liver Toasts 🍃 page 46

Eggplant and Crab Garbure with Cumin and
        a Tomato Confit ⚜ page 48

Swiss Chard and Bean Soup with Ricotta Toasts ⚜ page 51

Chicken Bouillon with Lime, Coriander, and Mint ❖ page 52

Curried Cream of Cauliflower and Apple Soup 🍃 page 54

Oyster Mushroom Soup with Walnuts in Red Wine 🍃 page 57

CUCUMBER AND CORIANDER SOUP WITH SMOKED TROUT

Serves 4

Served ice cold, this refreshing and tangy cucumber soup with a rich garnish of diced eggs, tomato, and smoked trout is enhanced by the cool mint and coriander. You can substitute any other firm-fleshed smoked fish in this recipe. This dish can be prepared up to 8 hours in advance. Keep the soup and garnish chilled and add the garnish just before serving.

For the Cucumber Soup:

3 long European hothouse cucumbers peeled, split lengthwise, seeded with a small spoon, in 1/8-inch slices

Juice of 1/2 lemon

1 tablespoon fresh coriander, finely chopped

8 ounces plain yogurt

2 cups chicken stock (see page 370)

4 drops Tabasco

Salt, freshly ground black pepper

For the Garnish:

2 hard-boiled eggs, peeled and coarsely chopped

1/4 cup tomato, peeled, seeded, in 1/8-inch dice

3 ounces smoked fillet of trout, skinless, in 1/8-inch dice (1 whole trout or 2 fillets)

1 tablespoon chives or scallions, finely chopped

1 teaspoon fresh mint leaves, chopped

❊ PREPARATION

For the Cucumber Soup:
In a pot, bring 3 quarts water to a boil with a pinch of salt. Plunge the cucumber slices into the boiling water for 2 minutes. Drain and chill the cucumber slices under cold running water. Squeeze out excess water by pressing the cucumber slices in a colander with the palm of your hand. Put the cucumber slices in a blender or food processor, add the lemon juice, coriander, yogurt, and half of the chicken stock. Blend and add more chicken stock until the soup has a slightly thick consistency. Add the Tabasco and salt and pepper to taste. Strain the soup into a bowl and chill it for 20 minutes in the freezer or refrigerate until needed.

❊ PRESENTATION

Chill the soup bowls in the freezer 5 minutes before serving. Divide the chives and mint evenly among the bowls. Ladle in the ice-cold soup. Or pour the soup into a tureen and sprinkle the garnishes on top.

CORN SOUP WITH NUTMEG

Serves 4

This is a simple and light version of a classic American corn soup, in which the nutmeg enhances
the sweet and mild flavor of the fresh corn without overpowering it. You can garnish this soup with a wide
variety of ingredients, for example small tomato dice, thin slices of celery, and cooked lobster or shrimp
cut into thin slices. You can also serve it warm as a corn chowder adding chopped and cooked vegetables such
as carrots, celery, leeks, potatoes, and garlic. This soup can be prepared up to 8 hours in advance,
cooled, covered , and refrigerated.

3 cups chicken stock (see page 370)

*8 fresh ears of corn, husked, cleaned, kernels
removed (about 2 1/2 cups), cobs reserved*

1 cup milk

1 tablespoon sweet butter

1/2 cup white onions, peeled and chopped

*1/2 teaspoon freshly grated nutmeg plus
1 pinch for garnish*

Pinch of sugar (optional)

4 drops Tabasco

Salt, freshly ground black pepper

1 tablespoon chives, minced

❧ PREPARATION

Bring the chicken stock to a boil in a large stockpot over high heat. Add the reserved
corn cobs and milk and simmer for 5 minutes. Discard the cobs, set the broth aside and
keep it warm. Melt the butter in a medium saucepan over low heat. Add the onions and
sweat until very soft, 4 to 5 minutes, stirring often. Add the corn kernels and the nutmeg. Toss well and sweat for 5 minutes over medium heat (do not color). Add the hot
stock and milk mixture, the pinch of sugar if desired, Tabasco, and salt and pepper to
taste. Bring to a boil and simmer gently for 20 minutes. Let cool and purée in a blender
until very smooth. Taste for seasoning, cover, and chill in the freezer for 45 minutes or
in the refrigerator for 3 to 4 hours. Stir occasionally.

❧ PRESENTATION

Serve in chilled individual soup bowls. Garnish with the minced chives and a pinch of
grated nutmeg.

ASPARAGUS SOUP WITH A SWEET PEPPER COULIS

Serves 4

Served cold or warm, this nonfattening soup is very easy to prepare. The vibrant contrast of colors and flavors—between delicate green asparagus and spicy red pepper—makes this recipe a must for asparagus lovers. This recipe can be prepared up to 8 hours in advance, cooled, then covered and refrigerated until ready to serve.

For the Asparagus Soup:

1 quart chicken stock (see page 370)

1 tablespoon olive oil

1 cup leeks, white part only, split and thickly sliced (about 2 small leeks)

1/4 cup potatoes, peeled, in 1/4-inch dice

24 jumbo asparagus, 2 inches of each hard stem end discarded, the rest in 1/2-inch slices

2 sprigs parsley, leaves only

Salt, freshly ground black pepper

For the Sweet Pepper Coulis:

1/2 tablespoon olive oil

1 tablespoon shallots, peeled and chopped

2 sweet red peppers, split, seeded, and coarsely chopped

1/2 cup chicken stock

6 drops Tabasco

Salt, freshly ground black pepper

❀ PREPARATION

For the Asparagus Soup:
Heat the chicken stock. Warm the olive oil in a pot over medium heat. Sweat the leeks for 5 to 7 minutes until soft (do not let them color). Add the hot chicken stock, potato, and a pinch of salt. Bring to a boil and cook for 6 to 8 minutes. Add the asparagus slices and parsley leaves and boil at high heat until tender, about 5 to 7 minutes. Pour into a blender until half full and carefully blend the soup until smooth. Season to taste with salt and pepper and strain into a bowl. Repeat the same process until all the soup is blended and strained. Place the bowl over ice to cool rapidly (this will allow the soup to keep its vibrant green color). When cooled, cover and refrigerate until ready to serve.

For the Sweet Pepper Coulis:
Heat the olive oil in a small saucepan over medium-low heat. Sweat the chopped shallots and red peppers until soft, approximately 6 to 8 minutes Add the chicken stock, bring to a boil, and cook for 4 to 5 minutes. Pour into a blender and blend until smooth. Add the Tabasco and salt and pepper to taste, strain, let cool, and refrigerate.

❋ PRESENTATION

If serving cold, pour the cold asparagus soup into chilled cups and drizzle the sweet pepper coulis on top in your own design. If serving warm, heat the soup and sweet pepper coulis separately and serve the soup in warm bowls with the coulis drizzled on top.

Green Celery Soup with Pink Radishes

Serves 4

This healthful low-calorie soup combines character with an attractive presentation. The refreshing and pungent taste of green celery and the crunch and peppery taste of radish are enhanced by the flavor of hot curry. This soup can be served with crispy toast rounds. This soup can be prepared up to 8 hours in advance, cooled, covered, and refrigerated until ready to serve.

2 teaspoons olive oil

2 cups leeks, white part only, thinly sliced (about 2 medium leeks)

2 teaspoons Madras curry powder

4 cups celery, green part only, thinly sliced, and 8 celery leaves, chopped for garnish

6 cups chicken stock (see page 370)

1/2 cup potatoes, peeled and coarsely chopped

Salt, freshly ground black pepper

1 bunch small round pink radishes (about 6), cleaned, greens discarded, radishes finely sliced with a vegetable cutter or mandoline, 12 slices reserved for garnish

10 sprigs parsley, leaves only, cleaned

3 drops Tabasco

❧ Preparation

Heat the oil in a pan over medium heat. Add the leeks, curry powder, and celery. Stir with a wooden spoon for 5 to 6 minutes. Add the chicken stock, potatoes, and salt and pepper to taste. Bring to a boil and simmer gently for 15 minutes. Add the sliced radishes and parsley leaves to the soup. Boil for 3 to 4 minutes. Pour the soup into a blender and blend until very smooth. Add the Tabasco and mix well.

Pour the soup into a bowl and chill it in an ice-water bath to cool rapidly. When cold, season to taste and refrigerate until needed.

❧ Presentation

Chill a soup tureen or bowl. Transfer the cold soup to the chilled soup tureen and decorate with the reserved radish slices and sprinkle with the chopped celery leaves.

Chilled Tomato Soup with a Basil Guacamole

Serves 4 to 5

The ultimate thirst quencher full of summer garden flavors, this soup is a must for summer garden parties. It can also be served as a main course by adding diced chilled steamed shrimp, lobster, or crabmeat to the basil guacamole. Prepare the tomato soup 1 day in advance for better taste. The basil guacamole can be prepared 1 to 2 hours in advance.

For the Tomato Soup:

3 cups chicken stock (see page 370)

2 tablespoons olive oil

3/4 cup onions, peeled and thickly sliced

1/2 cup leeks, white part only, thickly sliced (1 small leek)

1/4 cup fresh fennel, thickly sliced

1/4 cup celery, thickly sliced

1 large sweet red pepper, split, seeded, and thickly sliced

2 large cloves garlic, peeled and chopped

Pinch hot pepper flakes or 6 drops Tabasco

Bouquet garni: 2 sprigs of fresh thyme, 1 bay leaf, and 2 sprigs of basil tied together with kitchen string

1 tablespoon Italian tomato paste

1/2 teaspoon salt

3 cups ripe tomatoes, in 1/2-inch dice

1/2 cup tomato juice

Pinch of sugar

For the Basil Guacamole:

2 avocados, split, peeled, pitted, cut in chunks

2 sprigs basil, leaves only, 8 small leaves set aside for garnish, the rest chopped

Juice of 1 lemon

1 tablespoon chives, minced

5 drops Tabasco

Salt

❧ Preparation

For the Tomato Soup:

In a small saucepan, begin heating the chicken stock. Heat the oil in a large pot over medium-high heat. Add the onions, leeks, fennel, celery, red pepper, garlic, pepper flakes, and bouquet garni. Sweat until the vegetables are very soft, approximately 15 to 20 minutes, stirring often. (Do not color; reduce heat if necessary.) Reduce heat to medium, add the tomato paste, and stir for 3 minutes. Add the hot chicken stock, bring to a boil, add the salt, and simmer for 20 minutes. Add the fresh tomatoes, return to a boil, and simmer for 10 minutes. Remove the soup from the heat and set aside to cool. Refrigerate until cold, approximately 2 hours. Discard the bouquet garni. Blend the soup in a blender until smooth. Add the tomato juice, the pinch of sugar, and taste for seasoning. Strain and chill until ready to serve.

For the Basil Guacamole:
Put the avocado, basil, lemon juice, chives, Tabasco, and salt to taste in a bowl. Crush the avocado chunks with a fork and mix the ingredients well, keeping a chunky consistency. Refrigerate until needed.

❧ PRESENTATION

Pour the cold tomato soup into chilled soup bowls. Place a large spoonful of guacamole in the middle and garnish with 2 basil leaves.

Artichoke and Grilled Eggplant Soup with Lemon and Thyme

Serves 4 to 6

Combining many ingredients reminiscent of Provence, this silky smooth soup has
a refreshingly sharp taste of lemon. The soup can be prepared up to 8 hours in advance and kept
refrigerated until needed.

6 large artichokes

*Juice of 2-1/2 lemons and zest of 1 lemon,
finely grated*

5 tablespoons olive oil

Salt, freshly ground black pepper

*2 small eggplants (about 1/3 pound each),
trimmed, peeled, and sliced 1/4 inch thick*

2 quarts chicken stock (see page 370)

1 cup onions, thinly sliced

*2 cups white mushrooms, caps only,
sliced 1/4 inch thick, tossed with the juice of
1/2 lemon*

*2 sprigs thyme: 1 leaves only, finely chopped,
1 whole, for garnish*

1/4 cup heavy cream

2 tablespoons chives, minced

*1/2 cup tomato, peeled, seeded, and cut
into small strips*

*1/4 cup small black olives (Niçoise),
split in half and pitted*

✳ Preparation

Peel off two outer layers of leaves from each artichoke and cut off the stem just below
the bottom. Shape each bottom with a small paring knife until smooth and round. Cut
off the remaining leaves 1/2 inch above the heart. Split the bottoms and scoop out the
chokes with a spoon, discarding chokes and trimmings. Slice into 1/4-inch thick slices
and set aside in 2 cups of water with the juice of 1/2 lemon.

Preheat broiler. Brush a broiler pan with 1 tablespoon of the olive oil, season with salt
and pepper, and cover with the eggplant slices. Brush the top of the slices with 2 tablespoons of the olive oil, season with salt and pepper, and broil for 6 to 8 minutes or until
lightly browned. Turn the slices over and broil for 6 to 8 more minutes. Remove from
pan and set aside to cool.

Bring the chicken stock to a boil in a pot over medium heat. Heat the remaining 2
tablespoons of olive oil in a heavy bottom pot over medium heat. Add the onions and
sweat for 2 to 3 minutes while stirring. Add the mushrooms, the drained artichokes,
and the chopped thyme and sweat for 10 to 15 minutes while stirring often. Add the

juice of 1/2 lemon, the boiling chicken stock, and salt and pepper to taste, and boil for 15 to 20 minutes. When done, remove from heat and let cool for 20 to 30 minutes.

While the soup is cooling, bring 1 cup of water to a boil in a small saucepan, add the grated lemon zest and boil for 2 minutes. Strain out the zest with a fine-mesh strainer and set aside.

When the soup is cool, add half of the broiled eggplant, reserving six of the nicest slices to garnish the top, the heavy cream, blanched lemon zest, and the juice of 1 lemon. Pour the soup into a blender and blend until smooth; taste for seasoning. Strain the soup into a bowl and refrigerate until cold.

Sprinkle the chives, salt, and pepper, and the juice of 1/2 lemon over the tomato strips just before serving the soup.

❧ PRESENTATION

Serve the soup in a large chilled bowl or in individual soup bowls. Garnish with the reserved slices of broiled eggplant, marinated tomato strips, and Niçoise olives. Place a sprig of thyme in the center.

CABBAGE AND LOBSTER SOUP WITH CHIVES

Serves 4

This simple and hearty soup combines the sweetness of cabbage and the slightly briny taste of lobster
with the addition of chives for a refreshing zest. The soup can be prepared 2 to 3 hours in advance and cooled.
When ready to serve, warm the soup in a pot over medium heat.

For the Lobster Stock:

1 leek, split and coarsely chopped

1 carrot, peeled and thickly sliced

1 stalk celery, thickly sliced

1 bay leaf

1 clove garlic, crushed

*2 fresh lobsters, 1 pound each, rinsed
under cold water*

For the Soup:

2 tablespoons sweet butter

1/2 cup onions, peeled and thinly sliced

1/3 cup carrots, peeled, in 1/4-inch dice

1/3 cup celery, in 1/4-inch dice

*1 small head savoy cabbage (1 pound), cored
and thick veins removed with a knife and
discarded, leaves cut in 1/2-inch-square pieces*

Salt, freshly ground black pepper

2 tablespoons chives, minced

PREPARATION

For the Lobster Stock:

Bring 3 quarts water to a boil in a large pot. Add the leek, carrot, celery, bay leaf, and
garlic and boil for 10 minutes. Add the lobsters, cover with a lid, and boil for 4 minutes.
Remove the lobsters and set aside to cool. Keep the lobster stock warm.

To extract the meat from the front claws and tail of the lobster, twist off the front claws
at the first joint near the body. Twist off the whole tail from the body. Break the shell of
the claws and tail with a small mallet or rolling pin. Remove the meat from the pieces
of shell with your fingers or a small fork (reserve all pieces of shell) and slice it in 1/2-
inch pieces. Let cool, then wrap in plastic wrap and refrigerate until needed.

Twist off the 8 hind claws attached to the body and add them to the lobster stock. Clean
the body of guts and fibrous membranes and rinse the pieces of shell under cold running water. Add all pieces of shell to the lobster stock, bring to a boil, and boil for 15
minutes. Strain the stock, discarding the shells and vegetables, and set aside.

For the Soup:

Melt the butter in a large pot over medium-high heat. Add the sliced onions and the
diced carrots and celery and sweat for 3 to 4 minutes, stirring often. Add the cabbage,
mix well, and sweat for 5 minutes more, stirring often. Pour the strained lobster stock
over, add salt and pepper to taste, and cook until the cabbage is soft, approximately 20
to 30 minutes. Keep warm until ready to serve.

☙ PRESENTATION

Divide the pieces of lobster among warm soup bowls and pour the hot soup over. Sprinkle with chives.

SALSIFY SOUP WITH BAY SCALLOPS AND SORREL

Serves 4

One of my favorite winter root vegetables, salsify has a delicate flavor similar to artichokes. In this soup
I have combined salsify with sweet-tasting bay scallops and bitter-tasting sorrel for a sharper edge.
You can prepare this recipe 2 to 3 hours in advance and set it aside to cool, except for the scallops, which should
be cooked just before serving. Reheat the soup over medium heat when ready to serve.

6 cups chicken stock (see page 370)

1 tablespoon sweet butter

*2 cups leeks, white part only, thinly sliced
(2 medium leeks)*

Grated zest and juice of 1 lemon

*3 cups salsify, peeled and sliced into 1/2-inch
pieces (about 1 pound of roots)*

1/2 cup potatoes, peeled, in 1/2-inch dice

1/2 cup heavy cream

5 ounces fresh bay scallops, rinsed and patted dry

Salt, freshly ground black pepper

1/4 pound fresh sorrel leaves, coarsely chopped

✤ PREPARATION

Begin heating the chicken stock. Meanwhile, melt the butter in a stockpot over medium heat. Add the leeks and sweat for 5 to 8 minutes, stirring often (do not color—reduce heat if necessary). Add the grated lemon zest and salsify. Toss well and sweat for 2 to 3 minutes. Add the hot chicken stock, potatoes, and a pinch of salt, bring to a boil, and simmer gently for 20 minutes. Add 1/4 cup of the heavy cream and boil for 8 to 10 minutes more. Pour the soup into a blender and purée in batches until smooth. Keep the soup warm on the side.

Pour 1/4 cup of the salsify soup into a small pan. Add the scallops, salt, and pepper and cook over medium heat for 2 to 3 minutes while stirring. Remove the scallops with a slotted spoon and keep them warm on the side. Reduce the remaining cooking juice in the pan to 2 tablespoons over medium heat. Add the sorrel and cook until wilted and soft, approximately 2 minutes. Remove from heat and cool completely.

Whip the remaining 1/4 cup of cream until firm and add to the sorrel. Adjust seasoning. Refrigerate until ready to serve; just before serving, add the lemon juice to the soup.

✤ PRESENTATION

Divide the scallops among warm soup bowls. Pour the hot soup over and place a spoonful of whipped sorrel cream on top of each portion.

Note: When cooked, sorrel becomes very soft; therefore, you do not need to finely chop it before mixing with the cream for a smooth texture.

Cinnamon Squash Soup with Chicken Liver Toasts

Serves 4

The sweet and woody aroma of cinnamon and fruity orange zest flavor this fall soup. For a spectacular presentation, use a scooped out pumpkin as a soup tureen, with the liver toasts all around. You can prepare the soup 3 to 4 hours in advance and set aside to cool. Reheat the soup in a pot over medium heat and prepare the liver toasts just before serving.

For the Cinnamon Squash Soup:

2 small butternut squash

1 tablespoon sweet butter

1 cup leeks, split, white part only, chopped, 1/4 of the light-green part finely chopped and reserved for garnish

Zest of 1/4 orange, removed in long strips with a vegetable peeler

1/4 teaspoon ground cinnamon or one 2-inch-long cinnamon stick

1-1/4 quart chicken stock (see page 370)

Salt, freshly ground black pepper

For the Liver Toasts:

1/2 tablespoon sweet butter

1 tablespoon shallots, peeled and diced

1 sprig thyme, leaves only, finely chopped

Salt, freshly ground black pepper

3 ounces chicken liver, trimmed

1 tablespoon mascarpone cheese

4 slices country bread

For the Presentation:

1 medium pumpkin to be used as a soup tureen (optional)

4 to 6 cinnamon sticks

4 to 6 long twisted orange peels

Colorful fall leaves, cleaned

Preparation

For the Cinnamon Squash Soup:

Peel the squash by splitting each squash horizontally into 2 or 3 wheels. On a cutting board, run a large knife firmly around the inside of the skin. Discard the seeds and dice the flesh. Melt 1 tablespoon of butter in a cast-iron pot over medium heat. Add the leeks and orange zest and sweat for 5 minutes, stirring often (do not color). Add the diced squash, cinnamon, salt, and pepper, and sweat for 5 minutes, stirring often. Add the chicken stock, bring to a boil, and simmer for 30 minutes. Discard the orange zest and cinnamon stick. Pour the soup into a blender and blend until very smooth. Keep warm until ready to serve. While the soup simmers, blanch the leek greens for 2 minutes in a pot of boiling water. Drain and sprinkle over the soup just before serving.

For the Liver Toasts:

Preheat broiler. Melt the butter in a small pan over medium heat. Add the shallots and the thyme and sweat for 2 minutes. Add the livers and cook for 3 to 4 minutes until done. Salt and pepper to taste, remove from heat, and set aside to cool. Process the livers, shallots and mascarpone in a blender or food processor until puréed. Toast the bread under the broiler. Lct cool and spread the liver mousse on top. Slice each liver toast in half.

 Presentation

If you use a pumpkin as a soup tureen, prewarm the pumpkin for 10 minutes in a 350-degree oven. Garnish the soup with cinnamon sticks and twisted orange peels. Place the pumpkin (or tureen) on a bed of clean leaves and surround with the liver toasts.

Eggplant and Crab Garbure with Cumin and a Tomato Confit

Serves 4

This surprising soup combines Middle Eastern flavor with the feeling of a French country soup. A *garbure* is an earthy soup from the southwest of France often made of cabbage, other vegetables, pork, and a goose confit. To create a leaner soup substitute eggplant and tomato for the cabbage, and crabmeat for the pork and goose. You can also substitute finely sliced cooked lobster or shrimp for the crab in this recipe.
This soup can be prepared 3 to 4 hours in advance. Reheat in a pot over medium heat just before serving.

For the Eggplant and Crab Garbure:

3 small eggplants, peeled and cut into 2-inch-by-1/2-inch sticks

2 quarts chicken stock (see page 370)

1-1/2 tablespoons olive oil

1 cup onions, peeled and sliced 1/4-inch thick

1 cup leeks, white part only, sliced 1/4-inch thick

1 cup carrots, peeled and sliced 1/4-inch thick

1 clove garlic, peeled and finely chopped

1 bay leaf

1 sprig thyme

1 tablespoon ground cumin

1 teaspoon ground coriander

Salt, freshly ground black pepper

1/2 pound jumbo lump or Maine crabmeat

For the Tomato Confit:

3 plum tomatoes, peeled, quartered, and seeded

1 teaspoon ground cumin

1/2 teaspoon ground coriander

1 clove garlic, peeled and sliced

1 tablespoon olive oil

Salt, freshly ground black pepper

1 small bunch chervil or coriander, leaves only, chopped

❧ Preparation

For the Eggplant and Crab Garbure:
In a pot, bring 2 quarts water with 1 tablespoon of salt to a boil. Plunge in the eggplant sticks, boil for 3 minutes, drain, and set aside.

Begin heating the chicken stock. Heat 1 tablespoon of olive oil in a large stockpot over medium heat. Add the onions, leeks, carrots, garlic, bay leaf, thyme, 2-1/2 teaspoons of the cumin, and the coriander. Sweat the vegetables until soft, approximately 6 to 8 minutes, stirring often. Add the warm chicken stock, eggplant, and salt and pepper to taste, bring to a boil, and simmer gently for 30 to 40 minutes. Discard the thyme and bay leaf and set the soup aside until needed.

Season the crabmeat with salt, pepper, and the remaining 1/2 teaspoon cumin. Toss with the remaining 1/2 tablespoon olive oil and set aside.

For the Tomato Confit:
Preheat oven to 350 degrees. Place the pieces of tomato in a roasting pan. Sprinkle with the cumin, coriander, garlic slices, olive oil, and salt and pepper to taste. Bake for 10 to 15 minutes. Discard the garlic slices. Set the confit aside to cool and reheat until warm when ready to serve.

❧ PRESENTATION

Divide the crabmeat evenly among 4 warm soup bowls. Ladle the hot soup over and delicately spoon 3 pieces of tomato confit on top. Garnish with chervil or coriander.

SWEATING: The most important step for cooking a flavorful soup is *sweating*. Sweating means to gradually cook chopped vegetables, greens, or other ingredients in a small amount of oil or butter over low heat until the ingredients' moisture has been released, thus concentrating their flavors. When sweating, stir often, making sure that the ingredients do not color (lower heat if necessary) and wait until the moisture released has evaporated. A soup recipe will tell you in what sequence to sweat its ingredients for best results.

SWISS CHARD AND BEAN SOUP WITH RICOTTA TOASTS

Serves 4

This soup was inspired by a Tuscan regional dish. Swiss chard is a member of the beet family, with a taste similar to that of spinach. The greens combine well with beans and mushrooms in this healthful and tonic soup. The soup can be prepared 2 to 3 hours in advance and set aside to cool. Reheat just before serving over medium heat until hot. The toasts should be made just before serving.

For the Swiss Chard and Bean Soup:

2 quarts chicken stock (see page 370)

1 tablespoon sweet butter

1/2 cup onions, peeled and finely chopped

2 slices bacon, cut into 1/4-inch pieces

2 cups firm white mushrooms, caps only, in 1/4-inch dice

1 clove garlic, peeled and finely chopped

Pinch of freshly grated nutmeg

1 cup fresh cranberry beans, shelled (about 3 pounds fresh cranberry beans in the shell); or 1/2 cup dried cranberry beans, presoaked overnight in cold water, then drained

1 pound Swiss chard, leaves only (stalks and hard veins removed), coarsely chopped

1/2 teaspoon salt

Pinch of freshly ground black pepper

For the Ricotta Toasts:

1/4 pound ricotta cheese (made from Buffalo milk, if possible, for a richer taste)

4 thin slices country bread

1 tablespoon freshly grated Parmesan cheese

1 teaspoon freshly grated nutmeg

PREPARATION

For the Swiss Chard and Bean Soup:

Heat the chicken stock in a pot over medium heat until warm. Melt the butter in a large stockpot over medium-high heat. Add the onions, bacon, mushrooms, garlic, and nutmeg and sweat for 5 to 8 minutes, stirring often. Add the warm chicken stock and the beans, bring to a boil, and simmer gently for 20 minutes (simmer for 35 to 40 minutes if using dried beans). Add the Swiss chard, salt, and pepper and boil gently for another 15 minutes. Correct the seasonings and keep warm on the side.

For the Ricotta Toasts:

Preheat broiler. Spread the ricotta on each slice of bread. Sprinkle with Parmesan cheese and nutmeg. Toast under the broiler for 3 minutes or until golden.

PRESENTATION

Serve in large soup bowls with the warm toasts on the side or floating atop the soup.

Chicken Bouillon with Lime, Coriander, and Mint

Serves 6

My right-hand man for the past eight years, Sottha Khunn, always made this healthful and invigorating winter soup, inspired by his native country of Cambodia, for the kitchen staff on chilly days when we needed a boost of energy. The pungent coriander, the cool mint, and the zesty lime that flavor this chicken broth give a strong Oriental touch. You can prepare this soup 3 to 4 hours in advance and set aside to cool. Just before serving, heat the soup over medium heat.

For the Chicken Bouillon:

1 chicken, about 2-1/2 pounds, cleaned and trussed

1 leek, split, white part only

1 large carrot, peeled and split lengthwise

1 stalk celery, cut into 3 equal pieces

1 large whole onion, peeled

Peel of 1 lime

1 clove garlic, peeled

1 teaspoon coriander seed

1 stalk lemongrass, crushed with a mallet, or 1 slice fresh gingerroot, 1/3 inch thick

1 small bay leaf

4 white peppercorns

1-1/2 teaspoons salt

For the Garnish:

1 small leek, white part only, in 1/8 inch slices

1/2 cup carrots, peeled, in 1/4- inch dice

1/2 cup celery, in 1/4-inch dice

5 sprigs coriander, leaves only, chopped

2 sprigs fresh mint, leaves only, chopped

3 limes: 2 limes peeled, sectioned and diced, 1 lime cut into 6 wedges

✣ Preparation

For the Chicken Bouillon:
Place the chicken, vegetables, lime peel, garlic, spices, and salt in a large stockpot. Cover with cold water 2 inches above the chicken and bring to a boil over high heat. When the water is boiling, reduce the heat and simmer for 35 to 45 minutes. Skim the surface from time to time. Remove the chicken carefully from the pot and set aside to cool. Strain the bouillon into a bowl and discard the vegetables and spices. (You should have approximately 3 quarts left.) Remove the legs, thighs, and breasts and peel off the skin. Shred the meat and set aside. Discard the skin, bones, and carcass.

Pour the bouillon back into the stockpot over medium heat, bring to a boil, and cook until reduced by half. Skim off impurities from time to time.

For the Garnish:
Add the leek, carrot, and celery garnish to the broth and boil until tender, approximately 10 minutes. Remove the vegetables with a mesh skimmer and set them aside. Taste the bouillon for seasoning and, when ready to serve, strain into a soup tureen.

Divide the shredded meat, vegetables, chopped coriander and mint leaves, and the diced lime evenly among 6 soup bowls.

✤ Presentation

Ladle the hot bouillon evenly into each bowl at the table. Serve a lime wedge on a small plate on the side for an extra zesty lime taste.

CURRIED CREAM OF CAULIFLOWER AND APPLE SOUP

Serves 4 to 6

Smooth and creamy, with a sweet and spicy taste, this soup can be made a more complete meal by adding slices of cooked lobster or shrimp. You can prepare this recipe in advance and reheat it just before serving. You can also serve this soup with dried apple chips. Slice 1 whole apple very thin. Place the slices in a nonstick pan, and let dry in a 250-degree oven for 15 to 20 minutes or until done.

For the Curried Cream of Cauliflower:

4 cups chicken stock (see page 370)

1-1/2 tablespoons sweet butter

1 cup onions, chopped

2 teaspoons Madras curry powder

1/2 teaspoon saffron threads or 2 pinches of saffron powder

1 cup Golden Delicious (or other apple), peeled, split, cored, and sliced

4 cups cauliflower (about 1 medium head), greens and stem discarded, head broken up into small florets

1 cup heavy cream

Salt, freshly ground black pepper

1 tablespoon chives, minced

For the Curried Apple Dice:

1 cup Golden Delicious apple, peeled, split, cored, in 1/4-inch dice

1 teaspoon Madras curry powder

1/4 teaspoon saffron threads or 1 pinch of saffron powder

Salt, freshly ground black pepper

PREPARATION

For the Curried Cream of Cauliflower:

Warm the chicken stock over medium heat. Melt the butter in a cast-iron pot over medium-low heat. Add the onions, curry powder, and saffron and sweat for 2 minutes, stirring often. Add the sliced apple and sweat for another 5 minutes, stirring often. Add the cauliflower and warm chicken stock and bring to a boil. Boil until the cauliflower is tender when pierced with a knife, approximately 20 minutes. Add the cream and cook for 3 more minutes. Salt and pepper to taste. Transfer the soup in batches to a blender or food processor and purée at high speed until very smooth. Keep warm until ready to serve or refrigerate when cool and reheat just before serving.

For the Curried Apple Dice:

Place the apple dice with 1 tablespoon of water in a pan over medium heat. Add the curry powder, saffron, and salt and pepper to taste. Mix well, cover with a lid, and cook for 3 minutes over medium heat. Strain and keep warm on the side.

◢ PRESENTATION

Ladle soup into 4 heated soup bowls. Evenly divide the diced curried apple over the top, and then garnish with the chives.

OYSTER MUSHROOM SOUP WITH WALNUTS IN RED WINE

Serves 4

This recipe makes perfect use of oyster mushrooms, the slightly bitter and tasty variety that imparts a wonderful earthy taste when boiled in the soup. This soup can be prepared 2 to 3 hours in advance and set aside to cool. Reheat just before serving in a pot over medium heat.

For the Oyster Mushroom Soup:

1 1/2 quarts chicken stock (see page 370)

1 tablespoon sweet butter

1 cup leeks, white part only, thinly sliced (about 2 small leeks)

1 sprig thyme

1 bay leaf

4 cups oyster mushrooms, cleaned, stems discarded, sliced (about 2 pounds whole)

1 cup potatoes, peeled, in 1/4-inch dice

Salt, freshly ground black pepper

1 cup heavy cream

1/4 cup of chives, minced

For the Walnuts in Red Wine:

2 cups red wine

1/2 cup walnut halves

1 bay leaf

5 peppercorns

1 clove

1 teaspoon sugar

PREPARATION

For the Oyster Mushroom Soup:

Begin heating the chicken stock. Melt the butter in a large pot over medium heat. Add the leeks, thyme, and bay leaf and sweat until soft, approximately 4 to 5 minutes, stirring often. Add the mushrooms and stir for 10 minutes or until all moisture has evaporated. Add the warm chicken stock, potatoes, and salt and pepper to taste. Bring to a boil and simmer for 15 minutes. Add the cream and boil for 5 minutes more. Discard the thyme and bay leaf and purée the soup in batches until smooth in a blender or food processor. Pour the blended soup back into the pot and keep warm until needed.

For the Walnuts in Red Wine:

In a small saucepan over high heat, combine the red wine, walnuts, bay leaf, peppercorns, clove, and sugar and bring to a boil. Simmer until reduced to 1 tablespoon, approximately 12 to 15 minutes. Remove the walnuts with a slotted spoon and set aside to cool. Strain the reduced red wine and add it to the soup. Slice the walnuts when cool and set aside.

PRESENTATION

Pour the hot soup into a warm tureen. Garnish with the sliced walnuts and minced chives.

Salads

SPRING   SUMMER   AUTUMN   WINTER
❁   ⚜   🍃   ❅

WARM SALADS

SALMON SALAD WITH FENNEL, WALNUTS, AND CHIVES ❅ PAGE 61

SALAD OF CRISPY SWEETBREADS WITH CURLY CHICORY
    AND CONDIMENTS ❅ PAGE 62

QUAIL SALAD WITH SWEET POTATOES, RED CABBAGE,
    AND CELERIAC CHIPS ❅ PAGE 64

TUNA SALAD WITH CRANBERRY BEANS AND BLACK OLIVES ⚜ PAGE 67

SPINACH AND WHITE ASPARAGUS SALAD WITH PRAWNS
    IN A PESTO SAUCE ❅ PAGE 68

CHICKEN SALAD TEPEE WITH WALNUTS AND CHIVES ❁ PAGE 69

COLD SALADS

THE BEST CHILLED TOMATO SALAD ⚜ PAGE 73

CRAB SALAD WITH BABY ARTICHOKES AND A LEMON CONFIT ❁ PAGE 74

SMOKED FISH WITH POTATOES AND QUAIL EGGS ❅ PAGE 76

SQUID AND ARUGULA SALAD WITH SESAME SEEDS ⚜ PAGE 78

CHICKEN CURRY SALAD LE CIRQUE ⚜ PAGE 80

CHICKEN SALAD IN A SPRING VEGETABLE BROTH ❁ PAGE 82

LOBSTER SALAD LE RÉGENCE ⚜ PAGE 84

CELERIAC AND ESCAROLE SALAD WITH APPLE CHIPS ❅ PAGE 86

SMOKED TROUT AND RADICCHIO SALAD WITH POMELO 🍃 PAGE 89

opposite page: Chicken Curry Salad Le Cirque

SALMON SALAD WITH FENNEL, WALNUTS, AND CHIVES

Serves 4

One of the most savory food pairings in Provençal cuisine is that of grilled fish and dried fennel.
The salmon's fatty, full flavor is offset perfectly by the fennel's crisp, fresh texture and forward, aniselike taste.
To ensure that the salmon remains moist for this salad, cook it only until it is rare to medium-rare.
Except for searing the salmon and any final seasoning, this salad can be prepared up to 2 hours before serving.

8 baby artichokes

Juice of 1 lemon

2 large bulbs fennel (about 3/4 pound each)

1 tablespoon corn oil

4 fresh salmon fillets, 6 ounces each, 1-inch thick, skinless

Salt, freshly ground black pepper

2 medium plum tomatoes, cored and cut in thin slices horizontally

1/4 cup walnut halves, coarsely chopped

2 tablespoons chives, minced

3 tablespoons walnut oil

1 tablespoon Spanish sherry vinegar or the juice of 1 lemon

✤ PREPARATION

Cut and remove the stem and the outer leaves of the baby artichokes. With a paring knife, trim the bottom and cut off the leaves 1/2 inch above the heart. Place the artichokes in a pot with 1 quart cold water, half of the lemon juice, and a pinch of salt. Bring to a boil and cook for 15 to 20 minutes, or until tender when pierced with a knife. Remove from heat, drain, and set aside to cool. Quarter the artichoke hearts and set aside.

Trim off the top greens and the outer stalks of the fennel bulbs. Chop the fennel scraps roughly and set them aside (they will be cooked along with the salmon). Slice the fennel bulbs very thin with a vegetable slicer, mandoline, or food processor. Place the sliced fennel in a bowl, drizzle the remaining lemon juice over, cover, and refrigerate until needed.

Heat the corn oil in a pan over high heat. Season the salmon fillets with salt and pepper. Place the salmon in the hot pan, scatter the fennel scraps over the salmon, and cook for 5 minutes. Turn the salmon over, place the fennel scraps back on the salmon and cook for another 3 to 5 minutes. Transfer the salmon to a serving plate and discard the fennel scraps.

Combine the sliced fennel with the baby artichokes, sliced tomatoes, walnuts, 1/2 of the chives, walnut oil, sherry vinegar, and salt and pepper to taste. Toss lightly.

✤ PRESENTATION

Place the vegetable salad over the warm salmon and sprinkle with the remaining chives.

Salad of Crispy Sweetbreads with Curly Chicory and Condiments

Serves 4

Calf sweetbreads can be roasted, grilled, sautéed, braised, poached, or deep-fried. For this salad they are brushed with mustard then quickly seared to create a crisp crust yet a buttery-smooth texture. Their mild flavor demands a strong dressing, like the cornichon, caper, and horseradish one here. The ingredients can be prepared up to 3 hours in advance and kept refrigerated, the sweetbreads sautéed and the salad seasoned just before serving.

For the Sweetbreads:

3/4 pound sweetbreads, soaked in ice water overnight

Salt, freshly ground black pepper

3 tablespoons all-purpose flour

3 tablespoons Dijon mustard

1 teaspoon Colman's dry mustard

2 sprigs tarragon, leaves only, chopped

1 cup white bread crumbs (about 8 slices white bread, crust removed, finely ground)

2 tablespoons corn oil

For the Dressing:

1 small sweet red pepper, split lengthwise and seeded

1 tablespoon tiny French capers

1 tablespoon cornichons, thinly sliced

1 teaspoon grated fresh horseradish

1 hard-boiled egg, peeled and chopped

1 tablespoon shallots, chopped

2 sprigs tarragon, leaves only, 1 sprig chopped, 1 sprig whole leaves reserved for decoration

3 tablespoons tarragon vinegar

1/2 cup olive oil

Salt, freshly ground black pepper

For the Salad:

1/2 pound or 2 heads curly chicory

1/2 pound mâche

✤ Preparation

For the Sweetbreads:

Rinse the sweetbreads thoroughly. Place them in a pot with 2 quarts cold water. Bring gently to a boil over medium heat and boil for 1 minute. Remove from heat, drain, and cool under cold running water. Drain and pat the sweetbreads dry with a paper towel. Trim off any fat and membranes and cut into eight 1/2-inch slices. Salt and pepper each slice and roll them in flour, shaking to remove any excess flour. Set aside.

Combine the Dijon and dry mustards with the chopped tarragon. Brush one side of each sweetbread slice with the mustard mixture.

Spread half of the bread crumbs on the bottom of a shallow baking pan. Place the sweetbreads mustard side down on the bread crumbs. Brush the other side with the rest of the mustard mixture and sprinkle with the remaining bread crumbs. Press the crumbs on the sweetbreads with the palm of your hand to make them adhere, and refrigerate until ready to fry.

Warm the corn oil in a nonstick pan over medium heat. Add the pieces of sweetbreads and cook until golden and crispy, about 5 minutes on each side. Keep warm.

For the Dressing:
Preheat broiler. Place the red pepper halves skin side up on a greased baking sheet. Broil until the skin turns black, approximately 5 to 7 minutes. Remove from heat, let cool, and wash the skin off under cold running water; pat dry, and dice.

Combine the sweet pepper dice with the rest of the dressing ingredients in a bowl. Salt and pepper to taste.

✤ PRESENTATION

Evenly divide and arrange the chicory and mâche among the plates. Place the warm and crispy sweetbreads on top. Spoon the dressing onto the sweetbreads and the salad. Sprinkle with tarragon leaves.

Quail Salad with Sweet Potatoes, Red Cabbage, and Celeriac Chips

Serves 4

With its sweet potatoes and peanuts, this broiled quail salad has a light Southern accent.
The sweet potatoes brighten this bird's mild gamy flavor and balance the tart pickled red cabbage; the peanuts
and fried celeriac add crunch. The salad can be prepared up to 3 hours in advance, but cook the quails and the
celeriac just before serving. You can substitute chicken breasts or squabs if quail are not available.

2 slices bacon

2 medium sweet potatoes, peeled

4 cloves

*1 small head red cabbage (about 12 ounces),
outer leaves discarded, cabbage split lengthwise,
core removed, leaves shredded
or cut into a matchstick julienne*

1/2 cup red wine vinegar

4 jumbo quails, boneless

Salt, freshly ground black pepper

1-1/2 cups peanut oil

*1 small celeriac (about 1/4 pound), peeled
and thinly sliced*

1 tablespoon shallots, peeled and chopped

2 tablespoons peanuts, coarsely chopped

1 sprig parsley, leaves only, finely chopped

1/2 teaspoon garlic, finely chopped

❖ Preparation

Preheat oven to 350 degrees. Wrap a slice of bacon around each sweet potato and stud each with 2 cloves. Wrap each sweet potato in foil and bake for 45 to 50 minutes, until tender. Discard the foil and the cloves. Dice the sweet potatoes into 1/2-inch cubes and slice the bacon into small pieces. Place together in a bowl and keep warm.

Put the cabbage in a bowl. Bring 6 tablespoons of the vinegar to a boil and pour over the cabbage. Toss, put in a colander, and drain for 30 minutes. (This pickles the cabbage.)

Preheat broiler. Brush the quails with some of the peanut oil, season with salt and pepper, and broil for 5 to 7 minutes on each side. Split the quails and keep warm on the side.

Set 3 tablespoons of the peanut oil aside and heat the rest to 350 degrees in a fryer or deep skillet. Add the celeriac and fry until golden, about 2 minutes. Remove the celeriac chips with a slotted spoon, drain on paper towels, and sprinkle with salt. Set aside.

To serve, toss the cabbage, shallots, peanuts, parsley, garlic, the 2 tablespoons red wine vinegar, and the 3 tablespoons peanut oil with the warm sweet potato and bacon.

❖ Presentation

In the center of a plate or platter, shape the sweet potato and cabbage salad into a dome. Place the warm quail on top. Decorate with the celeriac chips and serve warm.

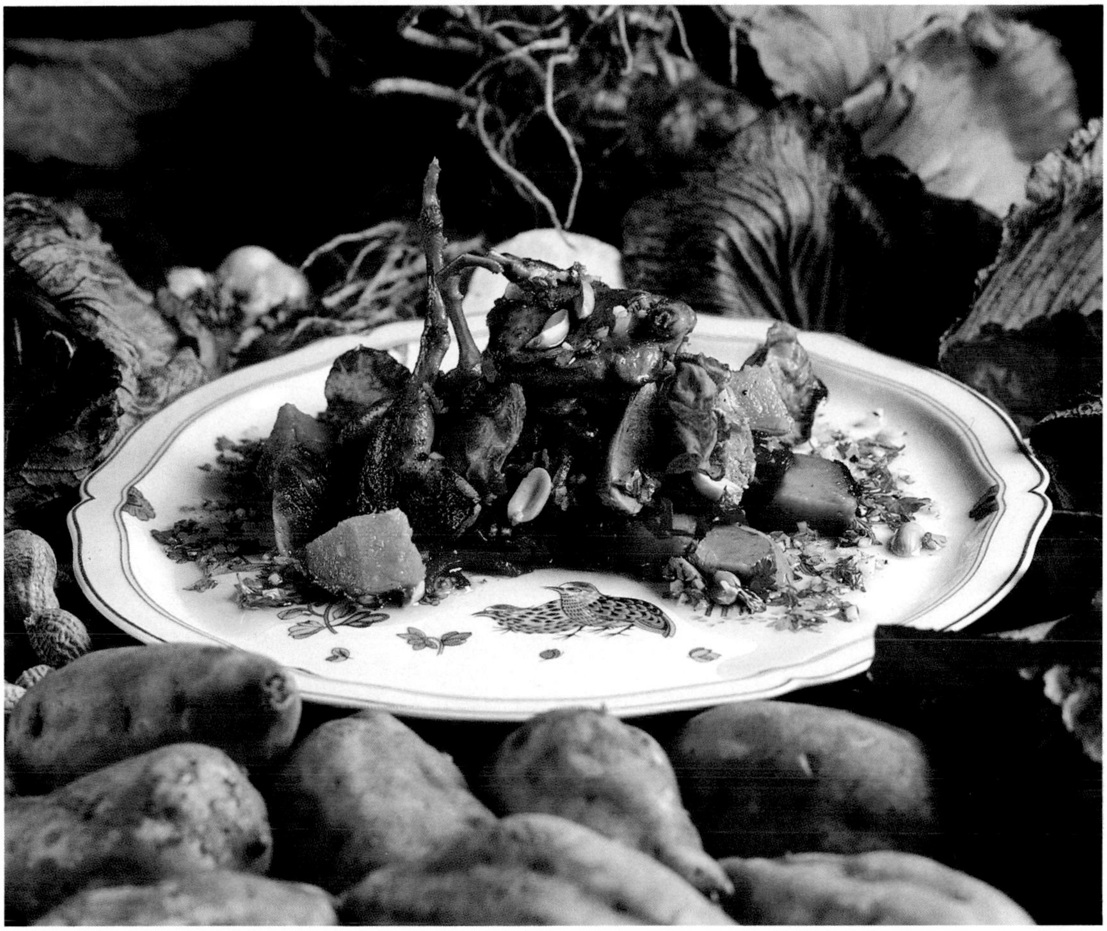

TUNA SALAD WITH CRANBERRY BEANS AND BLACK OLIVES

Serves 4

Widely available during the summer, fresh and flavorful cranberry beans are paired with some of the best tuna in the world—which is found off the Atlantic coast from Montauk to Maine. I also enjoy making this dish on the weekend with tuna cooked on the barbecue. For serving ease, prepare the ingredients up to 2 hours beforehand, but save the tuna's searing and final assembly until just before serving.

1 small onion, peeled and split

1 clove garlic, peeled

1 bay leaf

1 sprig thyme

1 teaspoon salt

1 pound fresh cranberry beans, shelled

1/2 cup tomato, peeled, seeded, in 1/4-inch dice

1/4 cup small black olives (Niçoise), pitted

2 tablespoons chives, finely chopped

2 sprigs tarragon, leaves only, finely chopped

6 tablespoons olive oil

2 tablespoons Spanish sherry vinegar

Salt, freshly ground black pepper

One 14-ounce fresh tuna steak, sushi quality, cut 1 inch thick

1 teaspoon crushed black peppercorns

1 bunch arugula, leaves only

❧ PREPARATION

In a pot over medium heat, add 2 quarts water, the onion, garlic, bay leaf, thyme, 1 teaspoon salt, and cranberry beans. Bring to a boil and simmer for about 20 to 30 minutes or until the beans are soft but not bursting. Drain and discard the onion, garlic, bay leaf, and thyme.

Combine the beans, tomato, Niçoise olives, chives, tarragon, 5 tablespoons of the olive oil, sherry vinegar, and salt and pepper in a bowl. Toss well and keep warm on the side.

Heat the remaining tablespoon olive oil in a nonstick pan over high heat. Season the tuna with salt and the crushed pepper. Cook the tuna in the hot pan for 5 minutes, turn over, and cook for another 4 to 5 minutes. If you like tuna rare, remove it from the pan. For medium rare, cook for another 2 minutes on each side. For medium, another 3 minutes. Cut the tuna steak into four pieces.

❧ PRESENTATION

Arrange a dome of arugula on the center of a platter. Place the thick slices of tuna on top. Spoon the bean salad over the tuna. Serve warm.

Spinach and White Asparagus Salad with Prawns in a Pesto Sauce

Serves 4

Roger Vergé, the master chef of the restaurant Le Moulin de Mougins, in France, enjoys casual and light dishes. His cuisine has long been an inspiration to my cooking. I once made for him this delicious salad from ingredients that were on hand. Except for the shrimp, everything can be prepared up to 3 hours before serving.

1/4 pound white or green asparagus, hard ends discarded, peeled and cut diagonally in 1/2- inch pieces

1 bunch basil leaves (approximately 2 ounces)

5 tablespoons olive oil

Salt, freshly ground black pepper

1 cup plus 1 tablespoon oil, for frying

Pinch of sugar

16 fresh blue prawn or large fresh shrimp,

shelled and deveined, heads removed

minced zest of 1 lemon and juice of 2 lemons

1 pound young spinach leaves, stems discarded

1/4 pound cherry tomatoes, thinly sliced

2 tablespoons chives, minced

1/4 pound small white mushrooms, very white and firm, caps only, thinly sliced

1/4 cup black Niçoise olives, pitted and chopped

✤ Preparation

Bring 2 quarts water with 2 tablespoons salt to a boil in a pot over high heat. Plunge in the asparagus slices and boil until tender but still firm, about 4 to 6 minutes. Drain, chill under cold running water, and drain again. Set aside on paper towels to dry.

In a food processor, purée 2/3 of the basil with the olive oil, salt, and pepper. Set aside.

Heat 1 cup of the frying oil in a deep skillet to 325 degrees. Fry the remaining basil leaves, two at a time for 1 minute. Remove them, drain, and sprinkle with salt.

Heat the tablespoon frying oil in a skillet over high heat. Season with a pinch of sugar. Salt and pepper the shrimp, and cook them in the oil for 2 to 3 minutes on each side. Remove them and toss with half each of the basil oil and lemon juice and zest.

Combine the spinach leaves with the asparagus, tomatoes, chives, remaining lemon juice and zest, and 2 tablespoons of basil oil. Salt and pepper to taste and toss gently.

✤ Presentation

Shape the salad into a dome on a platter. Arrange the shrimp around it and sprinkle with the mushrooms, olives, and basil oil. Garnish with the fried basil leaves.

CHICKEN SALAD TEPEE WITH WALNUTS AND CHIVES

Serves 4

This low-calorie salad—with its great balance of tastes, textures, and presentation—has always been
a popular dish on my menu and a perfect meal for a light and healthful lunch. The salad's title suggests its
whimsical appearance, and while the ingredients can be prepared 1 to 2 hours in advance,
the dish is best assembled and seasoned just before serving.

*4 chicken breasts, 6 ounces each,
boneless and skinless*

Salt, freshly ground black pepper

3 tablespoons peanut oil or olive oil

*1/2 pound haricots verts (very thin green
beans), ends trimmed*

*1/2 pound regular-size or 8 jumbo green
asparagus, stems peeled*

*1 pint red and yellow cherry tomatoes,
quartered*

*4 very firm medium white mushrooms,
caps only, sliced*

*1 ripe avocado, peeled, pit removed,
in 1/2-inch dice*

2 tablespoons walnuts, coarsely chopped

2 tablespoons chives, minced

2 tablespoons walnut oil or olive oil

*2 tablespoons Spanish sherry vinegar or
lemon juice*

2 Belgian endives, leaves separated

1 bunch arugula, leaves only

1 head radicchio, leaves separated

1 ounce chervil, leaves only

❊ PREPARATION

Preheat oven to 425 degrees. Salt and pepper the chicken breasts. Heat 1/2 tablespoon
of the peanut oil in a roasting pan on top of the stove over high heat. Add the chicken
breasts and sauté them for 3 to 4 minutes on one side. Turn the breasts over and finish
roasting in the oven for another 8 to 10 minutes. Remove from the oven and set aside to
cool for 15 minutes.

Bring 3 quarts water with 1 tablespoon salt to a boil over high heat. Add the haricots
verts and boil for 5 to 6 minutes. Transfer the beans with a mesh strainer to a colander
and cool with cold running water. Drain and set aside. Plunge the asparagus into the
same boiling water. Boil for 6 to 7 minutes for jumbo asparagus and 4 to 5 minutes for
regular-size asparagus. Drain the asparagus in a colander and chill under cold running
water. Cut the tips 2 inches long, slice 3/4 of the stem into 1/2-inch pieces, and set aside.
Discard the tough ends of the stems.

In a bowl combine 1/2 of the cherry tomatoes, the mushrooms, the avocado, 3/4 of the
haricots verts, the sliced asparagus, 1 tablespoon of the walnuts, 1 tablespoon of the
chives, 1-1/2 tablespoons of the peanut oil, 1 tablespoon of the walnut oil, 1 tablespoon

of the sherry vinegar, and salt and pepper to taste. Gently toss until well mixed.

Slice the chicken breasts widthwise into 5 to 6 slices per breast. Stack the slices on a plate and warm in the oven for 2 minutes.

In a small bowl, combine the remaining tablespoon peanut oil, walnut oil, sherry vinegar, chives, walnuts, and salt and pepper to taste.

❀ Presentation

Arrange 5 endive leaves, tips outward like the petals of a daisy, on each of 4 large serving plates. Place 1 arugula leaf between each endive leaf. Construct a small basket with about 4 leaves of radicchio in the center of each endive flower. Fill the baskets with the vegetable salad. Lean 5 to 6 slices of warm chicken breast all around the baskets, forming a tepee. Garnish the tepee, endive, and arugula with the asparagus tips, remaining cherry tomatoes, and haricots verts. Drizzle the remaining dressing evenly over each salad and sprinkle with the chervil leaves and a pinch each of salt and pepper.

Keeping Knives Sharp: Always keep your knives sharp for easier and safer use. Store them in a wooden knife block instead of a kitchen drawer where blades can be bumped or chipped (and can cause accidental cuts).

THE BEST CHILLED TOMATO SALAD

Serves 4

This salad of sliced, seasoned, then reassembled tomatoes is peerless in taste and presentation.
It's also a snap to prepare and requires only one simple key to success: executing the very thinnest, most
uniform, horizontal slices. This exposes the greatest amount of flesh for seasoning and allows
for neat stacking. This salad should be seasoned and chilled at least 2 hours in advance, then stacked just
before serving. (Tomato salad is also delicious at room temperature but chilling it, as in this recipe,
is more refreshing on a hot summer day.)

*4 large vine-ripened tomatoes (about 6 ounces
each), peeled and cut in very thin slices
horizontally (about 10 to 12 slices each)*

Salt, freshly ground black pepper

2-1/2 tablespoons Spanish sherry vinegar

1/4 cup olive oil

1 tablespoon shallots, peeled and minced

2 tablespoons chives, minced

8 quail eggs (or 2 chicken eggs)

1 bunch arugula or lettuce, leaves only

1 bunch chervil, leaves only

❧ PREPARATION

Lay the tomato slices in a large pan in the order in which they were cut (each tomato
will be reconstructed later). Season each slice with a pinch of salt, pepper, a splash of
vinegar, and a little olive oil. Sprinkle with the shallots and 3/4 of the chives. Place the
pan of tomatoes as well as the serving plates in the coldest spot of the refrigerator for at
least 1 hour (or 10 to 15 minutes in the freezer).

Boil the quail eggs for 3 minutes. Cool them under cold running water. Shell and split
them in half. If using chicken eggs, boil for 6 to 7 minutes, shell, and split in quarters.

❧ PRESENTATION

Arrange the arugula or lettuce leaves in a circle in the middle of each cold serving plate.
Reassemble each tomato by piling up the slices in the center of the plate. Sprinkle with
the remaining chives. Decorate each tomato with the quail eggs, sprinkle with chervil
leaves, and spoon over the leftover dressing from the pan.

Crab Salad with Baby Artichokes and a Lemon Confit

Serves 4

This elegant salad combines the delicate and briny flavors of crabmeat, the tender delicacy of baby artichokes, and the nutty taste of mâche with a slightly sharp lemon confit. You can prepare the ingredients for the salad up to 3 hours before serving. Keep refrigerated and assemble just before serving.

12 baby artichokes

2 lemons, plus juice of two more

1 cup oil, for frying

12 ounces fresh jumbo lump crabmeat

3 basil sprigs, leaves only, 12 small leaves reserved for garnish, the rest coarsely chopped

3 tablespoons chives, finely chopped

1 cup plum tomatoes, peeled, seeded, in 1/4-inch dice

1/4 cup olive oil

Salt, freshly ground black pepper

4 ounces mâche or arugula

✿ Preparation

Pull off the outer leaves of the artichokes. With a paring knife, cut off the stem at the base of the artichoke and shape the bottom until round and smooth. Trim about 3/4 inch off the tip of the leaves. Discard any trimmings.

Rub each baby artichoke with 1/2 lemon to prevent discoloration. Squeeze this same 1/2 lemon and strain the juice into 1 quart water in a pot. Add a pinch of salt, 10 of the trimmed baby artichokes, and boil until fork tender, approximately 20 minutes over high heat. When done, drain the artichokes and set aside to cool.

Heat the frying oil to 350 degrees. Slice the 2 remaining raw artichokes horizontally in very thin slices with a mandoline or knife. Plunge them into the hot oil and fry them until golden. Remove the artichoke chips with a slotted spoon and set them on a paper towel to drain. Sprinkle with salt and set aside to cool.

Remove the zest of 1 lemon with a vegetable peeler and cut into a julienne (matchstick size). Bring 1 quart water to a boil in a small pot over high heat and boil the lemon julienne for 15 minutes. Drain and set aside to cool. With a paring knife, cut off the lemon rind from top to bottom, and remove each wedge, freeing the flesh from the membrane. Remove any seeds. Set the fillets of lemon aside.

Combine the crabmeat in a bowl with the lemon julienne, chopped basil and chives, diced plum tomatoes, juice of 2 lemons, 3 tablespoons of the olive oil, and salt and pepper to taste. Toss well.

Split the cooled baby artichokes lengthwise and toss them in a bowl with the mâche lettuce, the juice of the remaining 1/2 lemon, the remaining 1 tablespoon olive oil, and salt and pepper to taste.

❀ PRESENTATION

Serve this salad on individual serving plates. Fill a small cup or mold with the crab mixture and invert it onto a salad plate for a dome shape. Arrange 5 baby artichoke halves around the base of the dome with a few mâche leaves. Place 2 fillets of lemon and 3 small basil leaves on top of the crab. Sprinkle with a few artichoke chips.

SMOKED FISH WITH POTATOES AND QUAIL EGGS

Serves 4

This salad of smoked sturgeon, salmon, and eel—which brings back fond memories of my two years as
a chef in Denmark, a country famous for its smoked seafood—is perfect for Sunday brunch. It can
be prepared and refrigerated up to 3 hours in advance, seasoned and assembled before serving, and lends itself
well to substitutions—such as smoked trout and whitefish—should sturgeon or eel be unobtainable.

1/4 pound small red-skinned potatoes, peeled

*2 sprigs parsley, leaves finely chopped,
stems set aside*

*1 sprig tarragon, leaves finely chopped,
stem set aside*

*2 large leeks, white part only, peeled and
split 3/4 lengthwise*

*1/2 tablespoon shallots, peeled and
finely chopped*

2 ounces smoked sturgeon, in 1/4-inch dice

2 ounces smoked eel, meat only, in 1/4-inch dice

*1-1/2 tablespoons Spanish sherry vinegar or
the juice of 1-1/2 lemons*

2 tablespoons plus 1 teaspoon olive oil

Salt, freshly ground black pepper

3 tablespoons heavy cream

*1 tablespoon chives, finely chopped,
or a dollop of caviar*

*8 quail eggs, carefully cracked into 4 small cups
(2 eggs per cup)*

2 ounces smoked salmon, thinly sliced

✤ PREPARATION

Bring 2 quarts water and the potatoes to a boil with a pinch of salt in a large pot over
high heat. Tie the parsley and tarragon stems together with a string and add to the
potatoes along with the leeks. Boil until tender when pierced with a knife, approximately 20 to 30 minutes. Drain and set aside to cool. Dice the potatoes into 1/4-inch
cubes and place them in a bowl. Dice 1 of the leeks into 1/4-inch pieces, combine with
the diced potatoes, and set aside. Discard the herb stems.

Split the second leek lengthwise and separate the layers. Trim the leek strips to a
1-inch width. Construct four rings, 3 to 4 inches in diameter and 1 inch high, to contain
each serving of salad in the following way: Place two leek strips end to end, overlapping by 1 inch, to obtain a 10- to 12-inch long band. Overlap a third layer over the second layer to complete the band. Take a glass or any other round object with a 3- to
4-inch diameter and lay it at the end of the three-part strip. Roll the leek strip around
the glass to form a ring, place the ring on one of the serving plates, and
delicately push the leek ring off the glass onto the center of the plate. Repeat the same
procedure for the other 3 bands.

In a bowl, combine the shallots, parsley, tarragon, smoked sturgeon, smoked eel, 1/2 tablespoon of the sherry vinegar, 2 tablespoons of the olive oil, and salt and pepper to taste with the diced potatoes and leek and toss well. Set aside.

Combine the heavy cream with the remaining tablespoon of sherry vinegar, chives, salt, and pepper and set aside.

Warm the remaining teaspoon of oil in a large nonstick pan. Sprinkle salt and pepper evenly over the pan. Gently add the pairs of quail eggs, making sure each pair stays separate from the other pairs in the pan. When the whites are cooked, remove eggs from heat.

✤ PRESENTATION

Divide the salad among the leek rings. Place the smoked salmon on top of each serving. Place each pair of quail eggs on top of each smoked fish ring. Spoon the vinegar cream around the smoked fish ring and serve while the quail eggs are still warm.

SQUID AND ARUGULA SALAD WITH SESAME SEEDS

Serves 4

Tender and exquisitely chewy, snow-white squid is one of the most delectable seafoods and a particular favorite in Mediterranean cuisines. Since its flavor is mild, it is best served with a powerful, zesty sauce—such as this recipe's sharp, sesame-shallot vinaigrette. If fresh squid is not available, you can substitute poached scallops, shrimp, or swordfish, but adjust cooking time accordingly. The squid can be prepared up to 3 hours in advance and kept refrigerated until ready to serve. The remaining ingredients should be assembled just before serving.

1 sprig thyme

1 bay leaf

10 coriander seeds

Juice of 2 lemons

1/2 pound squid, cleaned, washed, and drained (see page 26)

2 sweet red peppers, split and seeded

3 tablespoons olive oil

1 small clove garlic, peeled and chopped

2 sprigs fresh coriander, leaves only, chopped

1/2 tablespoon light sesame oil or 1 teaspoon dark sesame oil

1 tablespoon shallots, peeled and finely chopped

1 sprig fresh mint, leaves only, half of them chopped

2 bunches arugula, leaves only

1 tablespoon chives, minced

1/2 tablespoon sesame seeds

Salt, freshly ground black pepper

❧ PREPARATION

In a large pot over high heat, combine 1 quart water with 1 teaspoon salt, thyme, bay leaf, coriander seeds, the juice of 1/2 lemon, and freshly ground black pepper. Bring to a boil and cook for 3 minutes. Add the squid and boil again for another 2 to 3 minutes. Drain the squid and set aside to cool. Discard the cooking liquid with the herbs and condiments. Slice the squid into 1/4-inch pieces and set aside.

Preheat the broiler. Brush the skin of the red pepper with 1/2 tablespoon of the oil and place on a baking sheet. Cook under the broiler until the skin turns black, approximately 5 to 7 minutes. Remove from heat, let cool, and wash the burnt skin off under cold running water. Pat dry and cut the roasted pepper into thin strips. Set aside.

In a bowl, mix the squid, the red pepper strips, the juice of 1 lemon, 1-1/2 tablespoons of the olive oil, the garlic, 1/2 of the chopped coriander leaves, the sesame oil, the shallots, the chopped mint leaves, and salt and pepper to taste.

In a separate bowl, mix the arugula with 1/2 of the chives, 1/2 of the sesame seeds, juice from 1/2 lemon, the remaining tablespoon olive oil, and salt and pepper to taste.

Toast the sesame seeds in a dry pan over medium heat or under the broiler, tossing often for 1 to 2 minutes or until golden, and set aside.

❧ PRESENTATION

Divide the arugula among the plates and spoon even amounts of the squid on top of each bed of leaves. Sprinkle with the remaining minced chives, toasted sesame seeds, coriander leaves, and mint leaves. Serve very cold.

CHICKEN CURRY SALAD LE CIRQUE

Serves 4 to 6

This cool chicken curry salad is perfect for a summer buffet. It's fragrant, beautiful with its
13 colorful garnishes, and balanced in flavor, since its seasonal fruits and vegetables supply enough acidity to
contend with the curried chutney-laced dressing. This refreshing dish can be prepared in large
quantities a full day in advance.

For the Chicken:

2 pounds chicken breast, skinless and boneless

Salt, freshly ground black pepper

1/2 tablespoon Madras curry powder

1/2 tablespoon oil, for cooking

For the Sauce:

1 cup onions, peeled and chopped

1 clove garlic, peeled and chopped

1/2 tablespoon corn oil

2 tablespoons Madras curry powder

Pinch of saffron

1/2 cup chicken stock (see page 370)

3 tablespoons mayonnaise

2 tablespoons crème fraîche

1/2 tablespoon Dijon mustard

1/2 tablespoon mango chutney

Juice of 1 lime

5 drops Tabasco

For the Condiments:

2 tablespoons unsweetened grated coconut

1 banana, peeled and sliced

1 small mango, peeled, in 1/2-inch dice

1 apple, peeled, cored, in 1/2-inch dice

1/4 cup raisins

1/4 cup shelled toasted peanuts

*1 large tomato, peeled, cored, seeded,
in 1/2-inch dice*

*1/2 cup freshly shelled green peas,
boiled for 3 minutes in salted water
(1/2 pound in the pod)*

1/4 cup red onions, peeled, in 1/4-inch dice

1 small red pepper, seeded and thinly sliced

1 small bulb fennel, thinly sliced

1/2 cup mango chutney

1/2 cup crème fraîche

For the Garnishes:

1 head radicchio, leaves separated

1 bunch arugula, leaves only

2 sprigs fresh coriander, leaves only

2 tablespoons chives, cut in 1/2-inch sticks

Unsweetened shredded coconut

1 tablespoon raisins

1 tablespoon chopped peanuts

✤ PREPARATION

For the Chicken:
Season the chicken breasts with salt and pepper to taste, and the curry powder. Warm the oil in a pan over high heat. Sauté the breasts of chicken on both sides until done, about 7 minutes on each side. Reduce heat and cover the pan for the last 3 minutes of cooking. Remove from the pan and set aside to cool. Cut the breasts in small, finger-size strips, about 2 inches long, and keep refrigerated until needed.

For the Sauce:
Sweat the onion and garlic in corn oil until soft in a pan over medium heat. Add the curry and saffron and cook for 3 minutes. Add the chicken stock and reduce to 2 table-spoons. Remove from heat and set aside to cool. Combine the curried onions with the remaining sauce ingredients in a food processor or blender and purée until smooth.

Thoroughly mix the sauce with the finger-size chicken, cover, and refrigerate until ready to serve.

For the Condiments:
Place the condiments in small individual cups and refrigerate until needed.

✤ PRESENTATION

Arrange the radicchio and arugula leaves on a large serving platter or bowl. Fill with the chicken curry salad molded into a dome shape. Garnish the chicken salad with coriander leaves, chives, a touch of coconut, raisins, and peanuts. Place the bowl in the center of a large tray or on a buffet with the condiments in small cups all around.

Chicken Salad in a Spring Vegetable Broth

Serves 4

This is my version of a sublime chicken salad: an unusual combination of creamy, dressed chicken and vegetables surrounded by lightly jelled consommé. Served well chilled, this superb summer entrée can be prepared well in advance—up to a day. You can also minimize its calories—if you wish—by substituting low-fat plain yogurt for the crème fraîche.

1 chicken (about 2-1/2 pounds), trussed

1 sprig fresh thyme

1 cup carrots, peeled, in 1/4-inch dice

1/3 cup celery, in 1/4-inch dice

1/2 cup leeks, white part only, in 1/4-inch dice

1 small white onion, peeled and studded with 2 cloves

2 cloves garlic, peeled and sliced

Salt, freshly ground black pepper

3 gelatin sheets or 1 small packet plain Knox gelatin powder

Juice of 2 lemons

1/3 cup plain low-fat yogurt

1/4 cup crème fraîche

4 sprigs coriander, leaves only, a few reserved for garnish, the rest chopped

4 sprigs dill, leaves only, a few reserved for garnish, the rest chopped

✻ Preparation

Place the chicken in a pot that holds it snugly. Cover with cold water to 1 inch above the chicken. Bring to a boil and simmer over medium-high heat for about 10 to 15 minutes. Skim the surface with a spoon. Add the thyme, carrots, celery, leeks, studded onion, garlic, and 1 teaspoon salt and simmer for another 25 minutes. Discard the onion and thyme. Remove the chicken and set aside to cool. Remove the vegetables with a slotted spoon and set aside. Reduce the bouillon to about 2 cups of liquid over medium heat, while degreasing the broth with a small ladle, about 15 to 20 minutes. Add the gelatin, stir well, strain through a fine-mesh strainer, and let cool. Gently fold in the vegetables, cover with plastic wrap, and refrigerate for 2 hours.

Remove and discard the skin of the chicken. Remove the meat from the bones, discard the bones and carcass, dice the meat in 1/2-inch pieces, and refrigerate. When the diced chicken is cold, toss it with the lemon juice, yogurt, crème fraîche, chopped coriander, chopped dill, and salt and pepper to taste.

✿ PRESENTATION

Chill 4 deep serving plates in the freezer. Fill a small cup or mold with the chicken salad and invert it onto the middle of each cold plate for a dome shape. Spoon the lightly jelled chicken broth all around. Sprinkle with coriander and dill leaves.

LOBSTER SALAD LE RÉGENCE

Serves 4

I made this luxurious salad combining lobster, black truffles, and delicious vegetables for the 1984 opening of Le Régence, the restaurant in New York's Plaza Athénée Hotel, when I was its executive chef. This salad has since become a signature dish. It can be prepared up to 3 hours in advance and seasoned just before serving.

For the Salad:

2 large artichokes

Juice of 1 lemon

1 tomato, cored

2 ounces haricots verts (very thin green beans), ends removed

8 asparagus, peeled, hard ends removed

4 live lobsters, 1-1/2 pounds each

2 tablespoons Spanish sherry vinegar

1 teaspoon crushed black peppercorns

1 ounce black truffles (fresh or canned), chopped, juice reserved

12 leaves Boston lettuce heart

1 avocado, peeled, pitted, quartered, and sliced

2 tablespoons fresh chervil, leaves only

For the Dressing:

6 tablespoons olive oil

4 teaspoons Spanish sherry vinegar

2 teaspoons aged red wine vinegar

1 tablespoon chervil leaves

Salt, freshly ground black pepper

❊ PREPARATION

For the Salad:

Remove and discard the leaves of the artichokes. Shape the artichoke hearts with a paring knife until round and smooth. Bring 2 quarts water with the lemon juice and a pinch of salt to a boil in a large pot over high heat. Add the artichoke hearts and boil for 20 minutes until tender. Drain and set aside to cool. Scoop out and discard the chokes, split and slice the hearts. Set aside.

Boil 2 quarts water, add the tomato for 30 seconds, remove, and cool under cold water. Peel the skin, split, seed, and finely dice the tomato pulp. In the same water add a tablespoon salt and plunge in the haricots verts for 6 minutes. Drain and chill them in cold water, then drain again. Set aside.

Bring 2 quarts salted water to a boil in a stockpot. Add the asparagus, tips up. Boil until tender, approximately 5 to 7 minutes. Drain and chill them in cold water, then drain again. Cut each asparagus in 4 1-inch segments and discard the rest of the stems. Set aside.

Bring 1 gallon salted water with the vinegar and crushed peppercorns to a boil. Plunge in the lobsters, cover, and poach for 7 minutes. Remove the lobsters and set aside to cool. To remove the lobster meat, break off the tails and claws. Crush the shells with a small mallet, extract the meat, and discard the shells. Cut the lobster tails lengthwise in a fan shape by making 4 slits lengthwise 3/4 up the tail. Split the claws.

For the Dressing:
Mix together the ingredients and any reserved truffle juice in a bowl.

❀ PRESENTATION

Arrange the Boston lettuce leaves on the center of each plate. Build a mound with even amounts of haricots verts, asparagus, and sliced artichoke hearts and avocado on top of the lettuce. Place a lobster tail over each dome of vegetables with the claws on top. Sprinkle with diced tomato, chervil leaves, and the chopped black truffles. Serve the dressing on the side.

Note: Fresh black truffle season is mid-December until mid-March, but during the off-season you can buy canned black truffles and use the juice to make the dressing.

CELERIAC AND ESCAROLE SALAD WITH APPLE CHIPS

Serves 4

This is a variation of one of the most popular and traditional bistro dishes: celery *rémoulade*—blanched, julienned celeriac dressed in a mustard mayonnaise. This version, however, is far more flavorful with added bacon to impart a warm, smoky edge, crisp apple slivers to provide sweetness and texture, and escarole to underscore celeriac's wonderful tang. You can prepare this celeriac salad up to 4 hours in advance and keep refrigerated until ready to serve. Assemble the remaining ingredients and season just before serving.

3/4 pound celeriac, peeled and washed under cold running water

2 lemons

2 Granny Smith apples, peeled and cored, one apple in 1/4-inch dice and sprinkled with lemon juice, the other horizontally sliced paper thin with a mandoline or vegetable slicer (about 20 doughnut-shaped slices)

2 slices bacon, 1/4 inch thick

1-1/2 tablespoons Dijon mustard

2 tablespoons crème fraîche

2 tablespoons mayonnaise

2 tablespoons chives, minced

Salt, freshly ground black pepper

2 heads escarole or endive, leaves separated

2 tablespoons olive oil

✤ PREPARATION

Bring 1 quart water with a pinch of salt to a boil in a pot over high heat. Rub the celeriac with 1/2 lemon to keep it white. Cut the celeriac into a julienne (matchstick size), place it in a bowl, and squeeze the same lemon half over it. Plunge the celeriac into the boiling water for 3 to 4 minutes. It should still be slightly firm when cooked. Drain, cool under cold running water, and dry well on paper towels. Combine in a bowl with the diced apple and set aside.

Preheat oven to 350 degrees. Place the apple slices on a baking sheet and dry them in the oven for 10 to 15 minutes. The apple chips should be slightly colored. Remove from heat and set aside in a dry spot.

Cook the bacon in a nonstick pan over medium heat until golden and crisp. Remove from heat, cut into small pieces, and add to the bowl with the celeriac julienne and diced apple.

Combine the celeriac-apple-bacon mixture with the juice of 1 lemon, mustard, crème fraîche, mayonnaise, and 1/2 of the chives. Toss well and salt and pepper to taste.

Toss the escarole with the juice of 1/2 lemon and the olive oil. Salt and pepper to taste.

❖ PRESENTATION

Arrange the escarole on the bottom of a platter. Spoon the celeriac mixture into the middle. Decorate with the apple chips and sprinkle with the remaining chives.

SMOKED TROUT AND RADICCHIO SALAD WITH POMELO

Serves 4

This autumn salad is a delightful contrast of tastes and textures. Its rich, smoky trout is pleasantly offset by slightly bitter radicchio and lightly acidic pomelo—a citrus that some call Chinese grapefruit. Moist and tender fish, meanwhile, is nicely counterpointed by a topping of toasted croutons, walnuts, and coconut. You can prepare this salad up to 3 hours beforehand; just add the dressing prior to serving.

1/2 tablespoon shredded unsweetened coconut

2 slices white bread, trimmed, in 1/2-inch dice

1 clove garlic, peeled and finely chopped

1 tablespoon walnut oil

3 tablespoons heavy cream

1 tablespoon Spanish sherry vinegar

Salt, freshly ground black pepper

8 ounces radicchio (3 to 4 medium heads), 8 large leaves reserved, the remaining leaves cut into 1/4-inch strips

8 walnut halves, coarsely chopped

2 sprigs fresh coriander, leaves only, 1/4 of the leaves reserved and the rest finely chopped

3 fillets smoked trout, 8 ounces each, skinned, in 1/2-inch dice

3 scallions, white part only, thinly sliced

1/4 pomelo, peeled, segments separated, split open, and shredded by hand; or 1 pink grapefruit, peeled and segments cut in small pieces

PREPARATION

Preheat oven to 325 degrees. Toast the coconut until lightly brown, approximately 5 minutes. Remove and set aside.

Mix the diced bread, garlic, and walnut oil on a baking pan. Toast in the oven for 5 to 7 minutes. Remove and set aside.

Combine the heavy cream and the sherry vinegar, adding salt and pepper to taste. Pour 3/4 of the dressing onto the radicchio strips. Add the chopped walnuts, chopped coriander, smoked trout, scallions, and 1/2 of the pomelo or grapefruit. Toss well. Salt and pepper to taste.

PRESENTATION

On a platter, construct a bowl with the whole radicchio leaves. Fill the center with the trout salad. Sprinkle with the toasted coconut, croutons, the rest of the pomelo or grapefruit, and the coriander leaves. Drizzle the remaining dressing over the top.

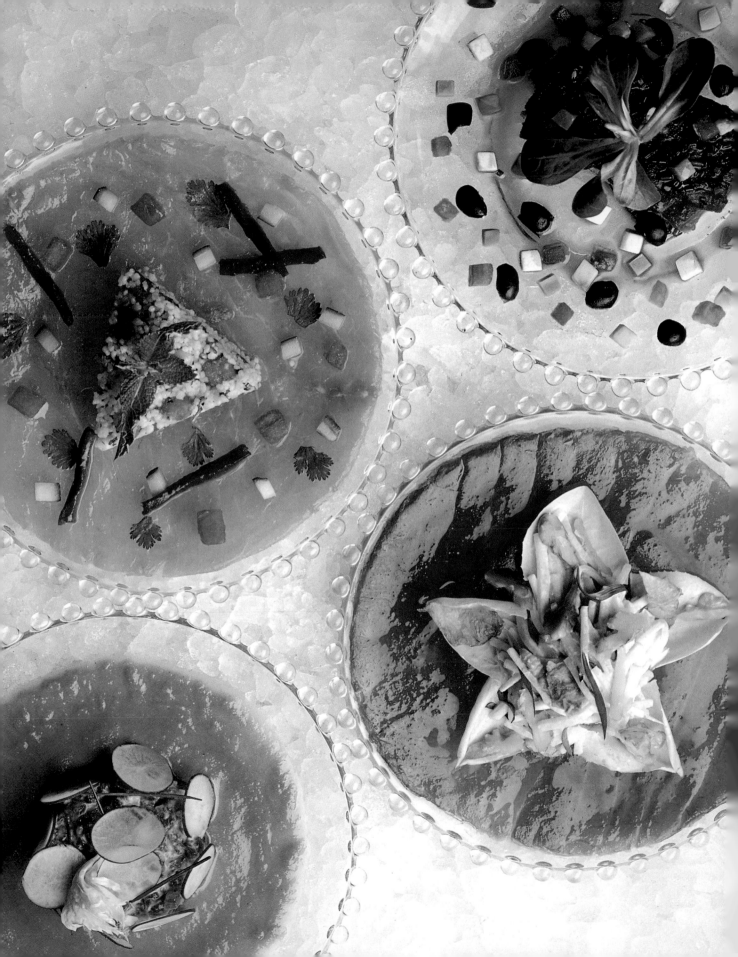

Carpaccio and Terrines

Spring   Summer   Autumn   Winter
❀   🌿   🍃   ❄

Curried Tuna Tartare with Pink Radishes and
    a Green Celery Sauce 🌿 page 92

Napoleon of Tuna with a Mosaic Salad 🌿 page 94

Carpaccio of Salmon with Minted Couscous ❀ page 96

Carpaccio of Tuna with Celeriac and Tarragon ❄ page 98

Carrot, Artichoke, and Broccoli Terrine ❀ page 100

Beef Shank and Leek Terrine 🍃 page 102

CURRIED TUNA TARTARE WITH PINK RADISHES AND A GREEN CELERY SAUCE

Serves 4

This handsome warm-weather first course may well be the quintessential tuna tartare. Its fiery curry flavor and peppery radish accompaniment balance well with the cool celery coulis while wisps of deep-fried celery leaves add a smooth crunch. The ingredients for this dish can be prepared up to 3 hours in advance, refrigerated, and arranged just before serving. Salmon can be substituted for the tuna if the latter is unavailable.

For the Curry Sauce:

1 teaspoon oil, for frying

1 tablespoon onion, peeled and finely chopped

1 tablespoon apple, peeled, cored, and finely chopped

2 teaspoon Madras curry powder

1 tablespoon mayonnaise

2 teaspoons Dijon mustard

1 tablespoon mango chutney

1 tablespoon créme fraîche

2 drops Tabasco

Salt

For the Tuna Tartare:

12 ounces very fresh tuna, sushi quality, cut into 1/4-inch-thick slices. Cut each slice into thin strips, about 1/4 inch wide. Cut each strip into 1/4-inch small dice. Refrigerate until needed. (When serving raw fish, you must buy extra-fresh fish of the highest quality and serve it the same day.)

1 bunch round red radishes, stems and rootlets discarded, 4 cut into paper-thin slices with a vegetable cutter or mandoline and reserved in ice water, the remainder in 1/8-inch dice.

1 small rib of celery in 1/8-inch dice

1 tablespoon chives, chopped fine, plus 4 blades in 2-inch pieces for decoration

Salt, freshly ground black pepper

For the Celery Sauce:

1/4 cup oil, for frying

1/2 cup leek, white part only, (about 1 medium leek), sliced fine, or 1/2 cup onion, peeled and sliced fine

2 teaspoons Madras curry powder

2 cups chicken stock (page 370)

1/4 cup potato, peeled, in 1/4-inch dice

2 cups celery, sliced into 1/4-inch-thick segments, heart leaves reserved for frying

3 sprigs of Italian flat-leaf parsley, leaves only, cleaned

Pinch of salt

❧ PREPARATION

For the Curry Sauce:
Heat the oil in a small pot over medium heat. Add the onion, the apple, and the curry and sweat for 4 to 5 minutes, stirring often. Add 2 tablespoons of warm water and cook for 3 minutes more while stirring to make a paste. Remove from heat, let cool, and mix in the mayonnaise, mustard, mango chutney, créme fraîche, Tabasco, and salt. Pour the curry sauce into the container of a blender or food processor and blend until smooth. Set aside.

For the Tuna Tartare:
Combine the diced tuna, radishes, celery, and the chopped chives in a bowl. Add the curry sauce, mix well, and season with salt and pepper to taste. Cover with plastic wrap and refrigerate until ready to serve.

For the Celery Sauce:
Heat 1/2 tablespoon of the oil in a small pot over medium heat. Sweat the leek or onion with the curry powder until soft. Add the chicken stock and the potato, bring to the boil, and cook for 4 to 5 minutes. Add the celery, parsley, and salt, and boil for another 4 to 5 minutes. Pour into a blender and blend until smooth (if the sauce is too thick, add 1/2 tablespoon of water). Strain the celery sauce into a small bowl and cool on ice before refrigerating until needed. Heat the rest of the oil to 350 degrees and plunge in the celery leaves until fried (about 2 minutes). Remove with a mesh strainer and drain over a paper towel. Discard the oil when cool. Drain the radish slices and dry on paper towels.

❧ PRESENTATION

Place a round cookie cutter, 2-1/2 inches wide and 1 inch high, in the middle of a serving plate. fill the ring with 1/4 of the tuna tartare and gently press on the tartare to compact it in the ring. Remove the ring and repeat the process with the 3 other chilled serving plates. Place 1/4 of the thin slices of radishes around and over each tartare. Sprinkle 1/4 of the fried celery leaves on top and stick 2 chive sticks into the top of each one. Pour 1/4 of the celery sauce around the tartare. Serve the remaining celery sauce and slices of toasted country bread on the side.

NAPOLEON OF TUNA WITH A MOSAIC SALAD

Serves 4

This great example of a savory napoleon is a refreshing appetizer of layered tuna and crispy garlic toast with a colorful diced vegetable salad. All the ingredients can be prepared 1 hour in advance, kept refrigerated, then assembled and seasoned just before serving. You can substitute fresh salmon for the tuna.

For the Mosaic Salad:

2 large artichokes, rinsed

Juice of 2 lemons

1 large tomato, peeled, cored, split horizontally, seeded with a teaspoon, in 1/8-inch dice

4 large white mushrooms, very fresh and firm, caps only, in 1/8-inch dice

1 small avocado, firm but ripe, split, pitted, peeled, in 1/8-inch dice

1/4 cup small black olives (Niçoise), pitted and coarsely chopped

3 tablespoons olive oil

Salt, freshly ground black pepper

2 tablespoons chives, chopped

1 bunch watercress or mâche, leaves only, cleaned

For the Napoleon of Tuna:

6 thin slices white bread

1 clove garlic, peeled

8-ounce slice tuna fillet, sushi quality, center cut, about 1 inch thick, well chilled (when serving raw fish, you must buy extra-fresh fish of the highest quality and serve it the same day)

1/2 tablespoon lemon juice

1 tablespoon olive oil

1/2 tablespoon chives, finely minced

Salt, freshly ground black pepper

❋ PREPARATION

For the Mosaic Salad:

Peel off the outer leaves of each artichoke, cut off the stem below the heart, and shape the heart with a paring knife until round and smooth. Cut off and discard the top leaves 1/2 inch above the heart. Bring 1 quart of water with 1 teaspoon of salt and the juice of 1 lemon to a boil. Boil the artichoke hearts until fork-tender, approximately 30 minutes. Drain, cool, and scoop out the chokes with a spoon. Dice the hearts into 1/8-inch cubes and set aside in a bowl. Add the diced tomato, mushrooms, avocado, and Niçoise olives to the bowl with the diced artichokes, cover, and refrigerate until ready to serve. Just before serving, mix the vegetables with 1 tablespoon of the lemon juice, 2 tablespoons of the olive oil, the chives, and salt and pepper to taste.

For the Napoleon of Tuna:

Preheat oven to 325 degrees. Stack the slices of bread and trim off the crusts. Cut the square bread stack into 2 even rectangular ones. Place the 12 pieces of bread in a single layer on a baking sheet with a rack or another pan on top to prevent them from curling when drying. Bake them in the oven for 6 to 8 minutes or until golden. Remove from heat and set aside to cool. Carefully rub each dried toast with the garlic clove and discard the garlic or chop the clove and add it to the vegetable salad.

With a sharp knife, cut the cold tuna at an angle into 12 thin slices 1/4 inch thick, about the size of the toast. Place the tuna slices on a plate and season them with the lemon juice, olive oil, chives, and salt and pepper. Place a slice of tuna on each slice of toast and then assemble these to make 4 napoleons of 6 layers each (three toast, three tuna).

❖ PRESENTATION

Place each napoleon in the middle of a chilled individual serving plate. Evenly spread a thick layer of vegetable salad on top of and around each napoleon. Place a small, tight bunch of watercress or mâche leaves on each vegetable-salad-topped napoleon. Drizzle the sandwich and plate with the remaining tablespoon of olive oil and remaining lemon juice. Serve immediately so that the toast remains very crisp.

Carpaccio of Salmon with Minted Couscous

Serves 4

This dish combines the sweet taste of raw salmon marinated in a tangy lemon-and-olive-oil dressing with refreshing minted couscous, cucumbers, and tomatoes for a Middle Eastern sensation. You can prepare and refrigerate the wrapped salmon carpaccio disks and the ingredients for the couscous salad up to 2 hours in advance. Season only when ready to serve.

For the Salmon Carpaccio:

8 ounces salmon steak, 1 inch thick, bones and skin discarded, cut into 4 equal 1/4-inch-thick slices (when serving raw fish, you must buy extra-fresh fish of the highest quality and serve it the same day)

1 medium sweet red pepper, split and seeded

1 tablespoon lemon juice

Salt, freshly ground black pepper

3 tablespoons olive oil

For the Minted Couscous:

1 European hothouse cucumber (about 12 ounces) peeled, split, seeded with a small spoon, in 1/8-inch dice

1 large tomato, peeled, split, seeded, in 1/8-inch dice

1/2 cup instant couscous

Zest of 1 lemon, grated

2 sprigs fresh mint, leaves only, 4 leaves reserved for garnish, the rest chopped

3 tablespoons lemon juice

3 tablespoons olive oil

Salt, freshly ground black pepper

3 sprigs fresh coriander, leaves only

✿ Preparation

For the Salmon Carpaccio:

Lay an 11-inch-square sheet of plastic wrap flat on the counter. Place 1 slice of salmon in the middle and cover with a second 11-inch square of plastic. Gently flatten the salmon with a meat pounder, mallet, or heavy skillet into a disk about 6 inches in diameter, shaping it as round and thin as possible. Repeat the same process with the other 3 pieces of salmon. Stack the 4 wrapped salmon disks on a plate and refrigerate until needed.

Preheat broiler. Place the red pepper halves skin side up on an oiled baking sheet and broil until the skin becomes black, approximately 8 to 10 minutes. Remove from heat, let cool, and peel the blackened skin off under cold running water. Pat dry with paper towel, cut the pepper into matchsticks, and set aside.

In a cup, mix the lemon juice with a pinch of salt and pepper. Add the olive oil and stir well. Set the carpaccio dressing aside until needed.

Refrigerate 4 large serving plates for 15 minutes or freeze for 3 to 5 minutes before serving.

For the Minted Couscous:
Place the cucumber and tomato in a strainer. Sprinkle with a pinch of salt and let drain for 10 minutes.

Bring 3/4 cup water with a pinch of salt to a boil in a small pot. Add the couscous, stir once, remove from heat, cover with a lid, and let the grains absorb the moisture for 10 minutes while cooling. When cool, transfer to a shallow bowl and refrigerate.

In a small saucepan, bring 1 cup of water with the lemon zest to a boil. Boil for 5 minutes, strain out the zest, and set aside.

In a bowl, gently mix the cucumber, tomato, 1/2 of the chopped mint, 1/2 tablespoon of the lemon juice, 1-1/2 tablespoons of the olive oil, and salt and pepper with a spoon.

In a second bowl, mix the couscous with the remaining 1/2 tablespoon lemon juice, the remaining 1-1/2 tablespoons olive oil, the remaining chopped mint, the blanched lemon zest, and pepper to taste.

Remove the wrapped salmon slices and cold plates from the refrigerator. Discard the top layer of plastic from each salmon disk and place one disk per plate, salmon side down. Discard the top sheets of plastic and drizzle the carpaccio dressing equally over each salmon disk.

Fill a small round cup halfway with the cucumber and tomato salad, then fill it up with the couscous. Press lightly on the surface to pack the salad inside. Invert the cup of salad onto the center of one of the seasoned salmon disks and tap on all sides of the cup to loosen the couscous salad. Repeat the process for the other 3 salmon carpaccios.

❀ PRESENTATION

Garnish each salmon carpaccio with the red pepper strips and coriander leaves. Place a mint leaf on top of each minted couscous salad.

Note: If you prefer to serve the salmon cooked and warm, just put each plate (do not refrigerate them beforehand) with the marinated salmon disk under the broiler for 2 minutes before topping it with the cool minted couscous salad.

CARPACCIO OF TUNA WITH CELERIAC AND TARRAGON

Serves 4

This tasty appetizer combines cool tuna with an earthy celeriac salad seasoned with a spicy mustard dressing. You can prepare this dish up to 2 hours in advance, cover, and keep refrigerated until needed. Season the tuna and celeriac salad just before serving.

8 ounces tuna steak, sushi quality, 1 inch thick, cut in 4 equal round slices, about 3 inches in diameter and 1/4 inch thick (when serving raw fish, you must buy extra-fresh fish of the highest quality and serve it the same day)

1 cup oil, for frying

1 pound celeriac, peeled, 1/4 sliced into very thin disks with a vegetable slicer, mandoline, or food processor and the remaining cut in a julienne (matchstick size)

1 teaspoon salt

Juice of 1 lemon

1 tablespoon Dijon mustard

1 tablespoon Spanish sherry vinegar

3 tablespoons crème fraîche or low-fat yogurt

1 tablespoon mayonnaise

Salt, freshly ground black pepper

3 Belgian endives, 2 inches of the tips cut off and reserved for decoration, the rest of the leaves finely sliced (discard the hard core)

3 sprigs tarragon, leaves only: 2 sprigs chopped, 1 sprig whole for garnish

1 tablespoon shallots, finely chopped

1/4 cup sliced walnuts

1 small loaf country bread, thinly sliced, and toasted just before serving

✤ PREPARATION

Lay 1 sheet of 11-inch-square plastic wrap flat on the counter. Place 1 piece of tuna in the middle and cover with a second 11-inch-square piece of plastic wrap. Gently flatten the tuna with a meat pounder, mallet, or heavy skillet into a disk about 6 inches in diameter, making it as round and thin as possible. Repeat with the 3 other tuna slices. Stack the 4 wrapped tuna disks on a plate and refrigerate until needed.

Heat the oil to 325 degrees. Fry the thin celeriac slices for 2 to 3 minutes or until light golden brown. Remove with a slotted spoon and drain on a paper towel. Sprinkle the chips with salt and set aside.

Bring 1 quart water with 1 teaspoon salt and the lemon juice to a boil. Boil the julienned celeriac for 4 to 5 minutes (although cooked, it should still be slightly crunchy). Drain and set aside to cool.

Mix the mustard, sherry vinegar, crème fraîche, mayonnaise, and salt and pepper to taste in a small bowl until smooth.

Refrigerate 4 large serving plates for 15 minutes or freeze them for 3 to 5 minutes before serving.

When ready to serve, mix the sliced endive with the blanched celeriac, chopped tarragon leaves, shallots, and walnuts in a bowl. Add 2/3 of the dressing, toss well, and taste for seasoning.

Remove the wrapped tuna disks and cold plates from the refrigerator. Discard the top layer of plastic wrap from each tuna disk and place one disk on each plate, tuna side down. Discard the top sheets of plastic and season each disk with salt and pepper.

✤ PRESENTATION

Arrange a circle of endive tips, tips facing out, on the center of each tuna carpaccio. fill the center of each endive circle with the celeriac salad. Cover with the celeriac chips and drizzle the remaining dressing over each tuna carpaccio in a zigzag design. Decorate each salad with a few tarragon leaves. Serve warm toasted country bread on the side.

Note: If you prefer to serve the tuna cooked, just put each plate (do not refrigerate them beforehand) with the tuna disk under the broiler for 2 minutes. Arrange the salad over the warm tuna.

CARROT, ARTICHOKE, AND BROCCOLI TERRINE

Serves 6 to 8

Even children will enjoy this healthful, delicious, and colorful vegetarian terrine. For a main course,
serve a generous slice on a bed of seasonal mixed greens. You can prepare the terrine 2 days beforehand, and its
tomato dressing, a few hours prior to serving.

For the Terrine:

4 large or 5 medium artichokes

Juice of 1 lemon

1-1/2 pounds carrots, peeled

3 eggs

1 tablespoon all-purpose flour

1/2 cup heavy cream

Salt, freshly ground black pepper

5 sprigs tarragon, leaves only, chopped

*3/4-pound head broccoli, cut into florets,
thick stems discarded*

1 tablespoon olive oil

Chervil and tarragon leaves, for garnish

For the Tomato Dressing:

*2 cups tomatoes, peeled, seeded,
and chopped*

1 tablespoon Spanish sherry vinegar

3 tablespoons olive oil

3 drops Tabasco

Salt, freshly ground black pepper

3 sprigs tarragon, leaves only, chopped

❋ PREPARATION

For the Terrine:

Remove all the leaves around the bottom of the artichokes. With a paring knife, shape
the bottoms until round and smooth. Cut off and discard the leaves 1 inch above the
heart. Bring 2 quarts salted water with the lemon juice to a boil, add the artichoke bottoms, and boil until easily pierced with a knife, about 20 to 30 minutes. Drain, let cool,
and scrape out the chokes with a spoon. Discard the chokes and set the bottoms aside.

Preheat oven to 300 degrees. Boil the carrots in salted water for about 30 minutes or
until tender, and drain. Dice 1/3 of the carrots and set aside. Place the rest of the carrots
side by side on a greased baking sheet and dry for 20 minutes or until part of their
moisture has evaporated. Remove from heat and transfer to a blender or food processor.
Purée the dried carrots until very smooth. Add the eggs, flour, cream, and salt and
pepper to taste, and process until well blended. Pour the mixture into a bowl, add the
carrot dice and chopped tarragon, and set aside.

Boil the broccoli florets in salted water for 3 minutes. Cool under cold running water,
drain, and set aside.

Raise the oven temperature to 325 degrees. Brush a 10-by-3-1/2-by-3-inch terrine with the olive oil. Line the terrine with parchment paper, overlapping the edges by 2 inches. Brush the inside of the parchment with oil. Spoon a 1/2-inch-thick layer of carrot mixture into the terrine and cover with the broccoli florets in a tight and flat bed. Spoon a second layer of the carrot mixture onto the broccoli, then place the artichoke bottoms along the length of the terrine. Cover with the remaining carrot mixture. Use the overlapping parchment paper to seal the terrine and place it in a deep ovenproof pan filled with 1-1/2 inches of boiling water. Bake for 75 to 90 minutes, removing the paper after 30 minutes of cooking. The terrine is done when the mixture is set. Remove from heat, set on a rack to cool, and refrigerate for 1 day before serving or freeze for 2 hours.

For the Tomato Dressing:
Purée the tomato in a blender or food processor and drain in a colander lined with cheesecloth for a few hours to extract the water. Mix the drained tomatoes in a bowl with the vinegar, olive oil, Tabasco, salt and pepper to taste, and chopped tarragon until well blended.

❀ PRESENTATION

To remove the terrine from the mold: Place a cutting board on the terrine, flip the terrine onto the board, and remove the parchment paper. Cut the terrine into 1/2-inch-thick slices. Place a slice in the center of a cold plate and pour the tomato dressing around. Garnish with the chervil and tarragon leaves.

BEEF SHANK AND LEEK TERRINE

Serves 10

This tasty terrine has the simplicity of a peasant dish, for it utilizes an economical cut of meat and ever-abundant garden vegetables. Beef shank is gelatin rich, with a full flavor that provides a delicious stock to bind the ingredients together. This recipe should be prepared 1 to 2 days before serving.

1 whole beef shank, about 6 pounds, trimmed of fat, the bone trimmed short enough to fit in a large pot

2 large onions, peeled and each studded with 1 clove

2 stalks celery, cut in half

2 large carrots, peeled and split lengthwise

1 bay leaf

2 sprigs fresh thyme

6 sprigs tarragon, leaves chopped and reserved

2 teaspoons salt

10 black peppercorns

10 medium leeks (cut lengthwise halfway), white part only

2 packets unflavored Knox gelatin, softened in a cup of cold water, excess water drained when soft

1 cup heavy cream

2 tablespoons Dijon mustard

2 tablespoons freshly grated horseradish

2 teaspoons hot English mustard or Colman's dry mustard

1 tablespoon tiny French capers, chopped

1 tablespoon chopped cornichons

1 tablespoon chopped parsley

1 tablespoon chopped chives

2 tablespoons Spanish sherry vinegar

Salt, freshly ground black pepper

Chives and tarragon leaves, for garnish

PREPARATION

Place the shank in a stockpot. Cover with cold water 4 inches above the meat and bring to a boil. Skim the surface and lower heat to simmer. Add the onions, celery, carrots, bay leaf, thyme, tarragon stems, salt, and peppercorns and gently simmer for 2 hours and 15 minutes. Add the leeks and simmer for another 30 to 45 minutes or until fork tender. Remove the leeks to a plate and let cool. Remove the beef to a cutting board and let cool. Strain the broth into a large bowl, discard the vegetables, herbs, and spices, and return the broth to the stockpot. Over high heat, reduce to 1 quart liquid. Add the softened gelatin to the reduced broth while stirring, strain again, and set aside to cool.

Shred the beef into small pieces with your fingers, discarding any fat and nerves. Mix the chopped tarragon leaves with the beef. Spoon a layer of beef, 1 inch thick, onto the bottom of a 10-by-4-by-4-inch terrine. Place 3 white leeks, end to end, over the center of

the meat, forming 1 long white leek the length of the terrine. Cover with another 1-inch layer of beef and another row of leeks. Cover with beef almost to the top of the mold. Pour the reduced broth with gelatin into the mold, up to the level of the beef. Press lightly to compact the terrine, cover with plastic wrap, and refrigerate until set (4 hours minimum).

To unmold the terrine, warm its bottom and sides in a bath of hot water for 30 seconds. Then slip the blade of a knife between the terrine and the sides of the mold to separate the terrine from the sides. Place a platter on top of the terrine and, holding it firmly, flip platter and terrine over. Tap the bottom until the terrine comes loose. Cut 3/4-inch slices with an electric knife or a very sharp slicing knife.

For the sauce, mix together the remaining ingredients (except the chives and tarragon leaves) in a small bowl.

PRESENTATION

Place 1 slice of terrine in the center of each chilled plate. Pour the sauce around. Garnish with chives and tarragon leaves.

Risotto

Spring Summer Autumn Winter
❋   ✲   🍃   ✦

Beet and Watercress Risotto with Pancetta ✦ page 106

Acorn Squash Risotto with Spices ✦ page 107

Corn Risotto with Bacon and Chanterelles ✲ page 109

Green Risotto with Roasted Squab and Garlic Cloves ❋ page 110

Gulf Shrimp and Sugar Pea Risotto with Rosemary ❋ page 112

Crab and Radicchio Risotto with Basil 🍃 page 113

BEET AND WATERCRESS RISOTTO WITH PANCETTA

Serves 4

Ruby red beets and emerald green watercress make this risotto as vibrant in color and spectacular in appearance as it is deep in taste. For serving ease, prepare the ingredients up to 2 hours in advance, then cook and combine 20 minutes before serving.

1/4 pound small beets, greens discarded, beets washed

1/4 pound pancetta, in 1/4-inch dice

2 quarts chicken stock (see page 370)

3 tablespoons sweet butter

2 tablespoons shallots, peeled and finely chopped

1 sprig thyme

1 cup Italian arborio rice superfino

1/4 cup red wine

3 bunches watercress, leaves only

3 tablespoons freshly grated Parmesan cheese

Salt, freshly ground black pepper

✢ PREPARATION

Boil the beets until fork-tender, approximately 40 to 60 minutes, in salted water. Cover your cutting board with parchment paper to protect it from beet stains and wear plastic gloves to protect your hands. Peel and chop the beets into 1/4-inch dice and set aside.

Warm a nonstick pan over high heat and add the pancetta. Cook it until lightly crisp on all sides, approximately 8 to 10 minutes, and set aside.

Bring the chicken stock to a boil in a pot and lower heat to keep it at a low simmer.

Melt 1 tablespoon of the butter in a medium enameled cast-iron pot over medium heat. Sweat the chopped shallots for 3 minutes. Add the fresh thyme and rice and stir well for 3 minutes, until the rice is well coated (do not let the rice color). Add the red wine, mix well, and let the rice absorb it. Slowly stir in chicken stock to the level of the rice (about 1 cup) and simmer. Stir constantly and add more chicken stock, 1/2 cup at a time, as it is absorbed by the rice. After 15 to 18 minutes of cooking (or until the rice is al dente), mix in the diced beets, 1/2 of the cooked pancetta, 3/4 of the watercress leaves, the grated Parmesan cheese, and the remaining 2 tablespoons butter. Salt and pepper to taste. Discard the sprig of thyme.

✢ PRESENTATION

Transfer the risotto to a warm bowl and sprinkle with the remaining watercress leaves and pancetta.

Note: If you find the risotto too sweet, add a splash of vinegar.

ACORN SQUASH RISOTTO WITH SPICES

Serves 4

With the combination of Virginia ham, acorn squash, and spices, this risotto has a true American feeling. It is assuredly dramatic when presented in the suggested green squash shells. You can prepare the ingredients up to 2 hours beforehand, then cook and combine 20 minutes before serving.

4 green acorn squash (about 1 pound each), lids cut off 1 inch below the stem and reserved, seeds scooped out and discarded

1 cinnamon stick, broken into four 1-inch-long pieces

4 cloves

4 pinches of ground allspice

4 pinches of freshly grated nutmeg

1 bay leaf, broken into 4 pieces

3 quarts chicken stock (see page 370)

3 tablespoons sweet butter

Salt, freshly ground black pepper

2 tablespoons shallots, peeled and finely chopped

1 cup Italian arborio rice superfino

1/2 pound seasonal mushrooms, cleaned and sliced 1/4 inch thick

1/4 pound smoked Virginia ham, in 1/4-inch dice

2 tablespoon freshly grated Parmesan cheese

✤ PREPARATION

Preheat oven to 400 degrees. Place the acorn squash upright close together in an oven-proof pan just big enough to fit them all in or steady the squash by resting them on aluminum foil rings. In each one place a stick of cinnamon, 1 clove, 1 pinch each of allspice and nutmeg, and 1/4 of a bay leaf. Fill each squash with chicken stock to 3/4 full and add 1/4 tablespoon of butter and a pinch of salt and pepper. Cover with the lids and bake in the oven for 1 hour or until the flesh is fork tender. Remove the squash from the oven to cool for a few minutes and lower heat to 200 degrees.

Set the lids aside and pour the liquid inside each squash through a strainer set over a pot. Reserve the spiced chicken stock for cooking the risotto. Delicately scoop out 4 to 6 tablespoons of flesh from each squash, cut the flesh into small pieces, and set aside.

Keep the squash shells with their lids in the warm oven until needed.

Bring the reserved spiced chicken stock to a simmer. Melt 1 tablespoon of the butter in a medium enameled cast-iron pot over medium heat. Add the shallots and cook for 2 to 3 minutes. Add the risotto and stir with a wooden spoon for 2 minutes until well coated (do not let the rice color). Add the mushrooms, sweat 2 minutes, and slowly stir in spiced chicken stock to the level of the rice (about 1 cup) and simmer. Stir constantly. Add more chicken stock, 1/2 cup at a time, as it is absorbed by the rice. (Add some regular chicken stock if you run out of the spiced stock.) After 16 to 18 minutes, when the rice has absorbed about 4-1/2 to 5 cups of liquid, add the diced acorn squash flesh, the ham, the Parmesan, the remaining tablespoon butter, salt, and pepper. Stir well and add a splash of chicken stock if the risotto is getting too thick. (Risotto should be moist but not runny.) Remove from heat, divide evenly among the warmed acorn squash shells, and cover each squash with its lid.

✣ PRESENTATION

Arrange the acorn squash on a large platter over a bed of clean winter greens, such as pine needles.

Corn Risotto with Bacon and Chanterelles

Serves 4 to 6

This summer risotto is sweet and smoky and the fine chanterelles elevate the dish to an earthy yet delicate preparation. You can prepare the ingredients for this risotto up to 2 hours in advance, then cook and combine them 20 minutes before serving.

7 slices of 1/4-inch-thick bacon (6 ounces)

4 cups chicken stock (see page 370)

4 ears corn, husks and silk removed

3 tablespoons sweet butter

2 cups chanterelle mushrooms (about 1/2 pound)

Salt, freshly ground black pepper

1 tablespoon chives, minced

1/4 cup scallions, minced (about 4 scallions)

1-1/2 cups Italian arborio rice superfino

1/4 cup dry white wine

2 tablespoons freshly grated Parmesan cheese plus more for serving

4 fresh sage leaves, chopped

❧ Preparation

Preheat oven to 400 degrees. Place the bacon on a baking sheet and cook in the oven until brown, about 10 minutes. Remove to a paper towel. When cool, chop in small pieces and set aside.

Bring the chicken stock to a boil in a pot and lower heat to a low simmer.

Boil the corn in salted water for 3 minutes, drain, and set aside to cool. Remove the kernels from the cobs with a knife. Set 1/4 cup of whole kernels aside. Purée the rest with 1/4 cup warm chicken stock in a food processor until smooth and set aside.

Melt 1 tablespoon of butter over high heat. Add the chanterelles, salt and pepper to taste, and toss well until lightly colored, 5 to 8 minutes. Add 1/2 of the chives and keep warm.

Melt 1 tablespoon of the butter in a medium pot over medium heat. Add the scallions and sweat for 2 minutes. Add the rice and stir for 3 minutes until well coated (do not brown). Add the wine, mix, and let evaporate, about 2 minutes. Slowly stir in warm chicken stock to the level of the rice (about 1 cup) and simmer. Stir continually and add the rest of chicken stock, 1/2 cup at a time, as it is absorbed by the rice. In 16 to 18 minutes, when done, mix in the remaining tablespoon butter, the Parmesan cheese, the corn purée, whole corn kernels, sage, 1/2 of the bacon, 1/2 of the chanterelles, salt and pepper. Add more chicken stock if needed to moisten the risotto. Remove from heat.

❧ Presentation

Serve the risotto on warm plates. Top with the bacon, chanterelles, and chives.

GREEN RISOTTO WITH ROASTED SQUAB AND GARLIC CLOVES

Serves 4 to 6

This risotto's beautiful green color results from an intense parsley purée and that, coupled with
its roasted garlic garnish, becomes a delectable combination. The emphatic flavors are
great complements to roasted squab. You can prepare the ingredients for the risotto 2 hours in advance,
then cook and combine them 20 minutes before serving.

*4 squabs, ready to roast, 16 ounces each
(use Cornish hens if squabs are not available)*

Salt, freshly ground black pepper

1 tablespoon oil, for cooking

12 cloves garlic, skin left on

7-1/4 cups chicken stock (see page 370)

3 ounces parsley, leaves only

3 tablespoons sweet butter

2 tablespoons shallots, peeled and finely chopped

1-1/4 cups Italian arborio rice superfino

1/2 cup freshly grated Parmesan cheese

❃ PREPARATION

Preheat oven to 450 degrees. Season the squabs with salt and pepper. Heat the oil in a
deep ovenproof pan on the stove over high heat. Cook each squab with one side of its
breast down in the pan for 2 minutes, then shift each squab onto the other side of its
breast and cook for 2 more minutes. Add the garlic cloves. Turn the squabs over and
roast them in the oven for 20 to 25 minutes. Remove from heat, place the squabs on a
cutting board to cool, and reserve the garlic to garnish the risotto. When cool enough to
handle, cut off the breast and leg meat with a sharp knife, mince, and set aside.

Combine the squab carcasses, the defatted pan juices, and 7 cups of the chicken stock in
a large pot over medium heat. Bring to a boil and cook for 20 minutes or until the liquid is reduced to 5 cups of stock. Strain the stock into a pot and discard the carcasses.
Reduce heat to low and keep at a simmer until needed to cook the risotto.

While the squabs are roasting in the oven, cook the parsley in a quart of boiling salted
water for 5 minutes. Drain, transfer to a blender with the remaining 1/4 cup of chicken
stock, blend until very smooth, and set aside.

Heat 1 tablespoon of the butter in a large pot over medium heat. Add the shallots and
sweat for 2 minutes. Add the risotto and stir with a wooden spoon for 4 minutes or
until the rice is well coated (do not let the rice brown). Slowly stir in squab stock to the
level of the rice (about 1 cup) and simmer. Stir continually and add more stock, 1/2 cup
at a time, as the rice absorbs the liquid. After 16 to 18 minutes, you will have used about
5 cups of stock. Make sure the rice always remains moist. When the rice is done, add
the parsley purée, the Parmesan cheese, the remaining 2 tablespoons butter, and the

minced squab. Mix well, salt and pepper to taste, and remove from heat. If too thick, add a little more stock. (The risotto should be moist but not runny.)

❋ PRESENTATION

Transfer the risotto to a large warm serving bowl. Arrange the roasted garlic in a circle on top of the risotto. To eat the garlic, hold one end with your fingers, squeeze, pop the roasted garlic into your mouth with your teeth, and discard the skin.

GULF SHRIMP AND SUGAR PEA RISOTTO WITH ROSEMARY

Serves 4

This colorful risotto combines delicate and briny shrimp with sweet and tender sugar peas. Gulf shrimp are harvested in the Gulf of Mexico, and are the variety usually found fresh at market (frozen shrimp are often from South America or other continents). Rosemary, one of the best accompaniments to peas, adds character to the elegant flavors of this dish. Its simplicity will conquer any seafood lover. The ingredients can be prepared up to 2 hours in advance, the shrimp and rice cooked 20 minutes before serving.

1-1/2 quarts chicken stock (see page 370)

2 tablespoons sweet butter

1/4 cup onions, peeled and finely chopped

3 sprigs rosemary: 1/2 sprig leaves only, chopped, 2-1/2 sprigs for garnish

1 cup Italian arborio rice superfino

1/4 cup dry white vermouth (Noilly Prat) or white wine

1/4 pound sugar snap peas or snow peas, trimmed at both ends, cut in 1/2-inch diagonal slices, and refrigerated until ready to use

16 small (under 15 per pound) shrimp, peeled, deveined, each shrimp cut into 3 pieces (refrigerate until ready to use)

1 tablespoon freshly grated Parmesan cheese

Salt, freshly ground black pepper

❋ PREPARATION

Bring the chicken stock to a boil in a pot and lower heat to a low simmer.

Melt 1/2 tablespoon of the butter in a medium cast-iron pot over medium-low heat. Add the chopped onions and chopped rosemary and sweat for 2 minutes. Add the risotto and stir with a wooden spoon for 4 minutes until well coated (do not color the rice). Pour the vermouth or white wine over the rice, stir, and let the liquid evaporate. Slowly stir in chicken stock to the level of the rice (about 1 cup) and simmer. Stir continuously and add more chicken stock, 1/2 cup at a time, as it is being absorbed by the rice. Add the sugar snap peas after 10 minutes. Add the shrimp, remaining 1-1/2 tablespoons butter, and Parmesan cheese once the risotto has cooked for 15 minutes. The risotto should cook in 16 to 18 minutes and you should have about 1/4 cup chicken stock left over. Add more stock if needed (the risotto should remain moist). Salt and pepper to taste.

❋ PRESENTATION

Transfer the risotto to a warm bowl or individual soup bowls and decorate with a few short sprigs of rosemary.

CRAB AND RADICCHIO RISOTTO WITH BASIL

Serves 4

The temptingly tart elongated radicchio that is native to the northeastern Italian region known as the Veneto is sautéed along with crabmeat to create a contrast of sweetness with a slight bitterness boosted by garlic and basil butter. The ingredients can be prepared 2 hours in advance, then cooked and combined 20 minutes before serving.

6 basil sprigs, leaves only, 8 nice leaves reserved for decoration

3 tablespoons sweet butter, softened

1 tablespoon olive oil

1/2 pound fresh jumbo lump crabmeat

8 ounces radicchio di Treviso, sliced into 1/2-inch segments (American radicchio can be substituted)

1 teaspoon garlic, finely chopped

Salt, freshly ground black pepper

2 quarts chicken stock (see page 370)

2 tablespoons onions, peeled and finely chopped

1-1/4 cups Italian arborio rice superfino

3 tablespoons dry white vermouth (Noilly Prat)

Freshly grated Parmesan cheese

Olive oil

PREPARATION

Blend the basil with 2 tablespoons of the butter in a spice grinder or mini food processor until it becomes a paste. Remove to a small cup and refrigerate until ready to use. Heat the olive oil in a large pan over high heat. Add the crabmeat and toss for 1 minute. Add the radicchio, toss well, and cook for another 3 to 4 minutes. Add the garlic, salt and pepper to taste, and toss well. Set aside until needed.

Bring the chicken stock to a boil in a pot and lower heat to a low simmer.

Melt the remaining tablespoon butter in a medium cast-iron pot over medium heat. Add the onions and sweat for 2 minutes. Add the risotto and stir for 2 minutes until well coated (do not color the rice). Add the vermouth, mix well, and let it evaporate. Slowly stir in chicken stock to the level of the rice (about 1 cup) and simmer. Stir continually and add more stock, 1/4 cup at a time, as it is absorbed by the rice. The risotto should cook in 16 to 18 minutes and be moist but not runny. When the risotto is cooked, stir in the basil butter and 1/2 of the crab mixture. Salt and pepper to taste.

PRESENTATION

Transfer the risotto to a warm bowl. Spoon the remaining crab mixture over the top and decorate with the reserved basil leaves. Serve with the Parmesan cheese and olive oil on the side.

Pasta

Spring   Summer   Autumn   Winter

❁   ⚜   🍃   ❈

Lobster Ravioli on Spinach Leaves in a Ginger Broth ⚜ page 117

Gulf Shrimp and Butterfly Dynamite ❈ page 119

Fettuccine with Mushrooms, Sweet Garlic, and Thyme 🍃 page 121

Vegetarian Penne 🍃 page 123

Trenette with Crabmeat and Lemongrass ❈ page 125

Spaghetti Sirio Maccioni (Spaghetti Primavera) ❁ page 126

Pappardelle Meridionale ⚜ page 128

Herb Ravioli with Basil Oil and a Tomato Coulis ⚜ page 130

Ruote with Scallops, Peas, and Black Truffles ❁ page 134

LOBSTER RAVIOLI ON SPINACH LEAVES IN A GINGER BROTH

Serves 4

In 1984, I made this lobster ravioli for the opening menu of the Hotel Plaza-Athénée restaurant Le Régence, and since then it has become a trademark dish that remains on the menu today. The ravioli can be assembled up to 4 hours in advance, then steamed just before serving—as you prepare the ginger broth.

For the Lobster Ravioli:

1 tablespoon white vinegar

2 live lobsters (about 1 pound each)

1 tablespoon sweet butter

1/4 cup fennel bulb, trimmed and finely chopped in a blender or food processor

1/4 cup carrots, peeled and finely chopped in a food processor

1/4 cup celery, finely chopped in a food processor

1/4 cup leeks, white part only, finely chopped in a food processor

1 sprig thyme

1 teaspoon gingerroot, peeled and finely chopped or grated

3 tablespoons water

32 wonton skin wrappers (3 by 3 inches)

1 egg, beaten

Salt, freshly ground black pepper

For the Spinach Leaves:

1/2 pound spinach, leaves only, thoroughly washed

For the Ginger Broth:

1/4 cup dry white vermouth (Noilly Prat)

1 teaspoon gingerroot, peeled and finely chopped or grated

2 tablespoons sweet butter

Salt, freshly ground black pepper

1/4 cup tomato, cored, peeled, seeded, in 1/4-inch dice

❦ PREPARATION

For the Lobster Ravioli:
Bring 5 quarts water with the white vinegar and 1 tablespoon salt to a boil. Plunge in the lobsters, cover tightly, and boil for 6 to 7 minutes. Remove the lobsters, set aside to cool, and discard the cooking water. Break the shell of the tails and claws with scissors or a small mallet. Remove the meat and discard the shells and the rest of the lobsters. Reserve 8 slices of lobster tail for decoration on a small plate, cover, and refrigerate until needed. Dice the rest of the lobster meat into 1/8-inch cubes and set aside in a bowl.

Warm the butter in a small pan over medium heat. Sweat the fennel, carrots, celery, leeks, and thyme. Add the gingerroot and cook for 2 minutes. Add the water, cover, and cook for 8 to 10 minutes or until the moisture has evaporated. Set aside to cool. Discard the thyme, and season with salt and pepper. Add the mixture to the diced lobster.

Place a wonton sheet on the counter. Brush lightly with the beaten egg and place 1 compact tablespoon of the lobster and vegetable mixture in the center. Cover with a second wonton skin, press with your fingers all around the lobster mixture to seal the ravioli, and cut with a 2-1/2-inch-round cookie cutter to make a circular ravioli. Make sure all the ravioli are well sealed. Repeat the same procedure until you have used all of the lobster mixture to make 16 ravioli. Set the ravioli aside on a plate, cover with plastic wrap, and refrigerate until needed.

For the Spinach Leaves:
Bring 1 quart water with 1 teaspoon salt to a boil, plunge the spinach in for 1 minute, drain, and keep warm on the side.

For the Ginger Broth:
Just before serving make the ginger broth. In a small pot, boil the vermouth with the gingerroot until reduced by half. Over low heat, whip in the butter until blended. Salt and pepper to taste. Strain into a small bowl, add the tomato dice, mix and keep warm on the side.

In a large pan that easily holds all the ravioli, simmer 1 cup water with a pinch of salt over low heat. Add the ravioli, cover, and simmer for 3 minutes. Remove and drain.

❧ PRESENTATION

Equally divide the spinach among 4 warm, deep plates. Place 4 ravioli on each bed of spinach and spoon the ginger broth evenly over the top of each serving. Garnish with 2 reserved slices of lobster tail per plate.

MAKING GINGER-FLAVORED OIL: When peeling fresh gingerroot, save the peel and place it in a small pot, cover with vegetable oil, and cook over very low heat for 10 to 15 minutes. Cool, strain the flavored oil, and discard the peel. Store the oil in a sealed glass jar and use for sautéing vegetables or seafood, with salad greens, sauces, etc.

GULF SHRIMP AND BUTTERFLY DYNAMITE

Serves 4

This dish lives up to its name, for it is a virtual explosion of tastes—sweet but briny shrimp, barely bitter broccoli rabe, fiery-hot jalapeño pepper, smoky bacon, and tangy olives and tomatoes. You can prepare the ingredients 2 to 3 hours before serving and refrigerate, then sauté the shrimp and vegetables while the pasta is cooking, 10 minutes before serving.

1 pound broccoli rabe, bottom leaves removed, florets with stems cut 2-1/2 to 3 inches long; or 1 pound broccoli, florets only, split into small pieces

4 slices bacon, in 1/4-inch dice

3-1/2 tablespoons olive oil

12 ounces dried butterfly (or bow tie) pasta

Salt, freshly ground black pepper

1 pound fresh gulf shrimp (about 16 to 20 shrimp), peeled and deveined

3 cloves garlic, peeled and chopped

1 small jalapeño pepper, finely chopped

1/3 cup onions, peeled and finely chopped

1 small sprig fresh rosemary, leaves only, chopped

2 tablespoons tiny French capers

1-1/2 tablespoons sun-dried tomatoes, diced

1/2 cup small black olives (Niçoise), pitted

1/4 cup green olives, pitted and diced

2 cups fresh plum tomatoes, split, cored, seeded, in 1/4-inch dice

❖ PREPARATION

Bring 2 quarts water with 1 tablespoon salt to a boil. Add the broccoli rabe and boil for 2 to 3 minutes. Drain, cool under cold running water, drain again, and set aside.

Cook the diced bacon in a pan over medium heat until slightly brown and crisp. Remove with a slotted spoon, dry on paper towels, and reserve for garnish.

Bring 4 quarts water with 1 tablespoon salt and 1/2 tablespoon of the olive oil to a boil in a large pot over high heat. Add the pasta and boil for 5 to 8 minutes.

While the pasta is cooking, heat 2 tablespoons of the olive oil in a large sauté pan over high heat. Salt and pepper the shrimp and sauté them for 30 seconds while tossing constantly. Add the chopped garlic, jalapeño pepper, onions, and rosemary and continue tossing for 1 minute. Add the capers, sun-dried tomatoes, black and green olives, fresh tomatoes, and the broccoli rabe or broccoli while tossing for 2 to 3 minutes more. Salt to taste and set aside. Drain the pasta and toss in a warmed serving bowl for 2 minutes with the shrimp mixture.

✤ PRESENTATION

Drizzle the remaining tablespoon olive oil over the warm pasta and shrimp and sprinkle the bacon on top. Serve on warm plates.

FETTUCCINE WITH MUSHROOMS, SWEET GARLIC, AND THYME

Serves 4 to 6

Fettuccine is one of the finest vehicles for cream sauces; long and moderately thick, it provides ample surface for carrying the pungent and rich taste of this creamy mushroom and garlic sauce. The ultimate complement to this dish would be fresh Italian Alba white truffles shaved over the pasta at the table, an expensive but unforgettable treat! The sauce and ingredients may be prepared up to 2 hours in advance and cooled on the side, while the mushrooms and pasta should be cooked 6 to 8 minutes before serving.

For the Sauce:

8 cloves garlic, peeled

1 tablespoon sweet butter

2 tablespoons shallots, peeled and coarsely chopped

1 sprig fresh thyme, leaves only, coarsely chopped

2 cups heavy cream

1/2 cup freshly grated Parmesan cheese

Salt, freshly ground black pepper

1 pound assorted seasonal mushrooms, caps only, cleaned and sliced 1/4 inch thick

1/4 cup chicken stock (see page 370)

For the Pasta:

1 tablespoon coarse sea salt

1 tablespoon oil, for cooking

1-1/2 pounds fresh fettuccine or 1 pound dried

PREPARATION

For the Sauce:

Boil the garlic cloves in a quart of water over medium heat for 5 minutes. Change the water and repeat the process twice so the garlic will lose its strong flavor.

Melt 1/2 tablespoon of the butter in a pot over medium heat. Add the chopped shallots and thyme and the cooked garlic and sweat for 2 minutes. Add the cream, 1/4 cup of the grated Parmesan cheese, and salt and pepper to taste. Boil for 2 minutes then pour into a blender. Purée until smooth, test for seasoning, and keep warm on the side.

Melt the remaining 1/2 tablespoon butter in a large pan over high heat. Add the mushrooms, salt, and pepper and sauté for 5 to 8 minutes or until all liquid released by the mushrooms has evaporated. Set aside.

Bring the chicken stock to a boil in a pot and lower the heat to a slow simmer. Use it just before serving to dilute the cream sauce to the desired consistency. The sauce should be neither too thick nor too runny.

For the Pasta:

Bring a large pot of water with the coarse salt and oil to a boil. (The oil will prevent the pasta from sticking together.) Add the fettuccine and boil over high heat for 3 minutes if using fresh pasta, 8 minutes if using dried. The pasta should be al dente. Drain and set aside.

PRESENTATION

Pour the sauce into a large, warm serving bowl, then add the steaming pasta. Place the mushrooms in a separate bowl. If you toss the pasta while at the table, it will stay hot longer. Serve in warm deep plates and garnish generously with the mushrooms. Sprinkle with the remaining Parmesan cheese.

VEGETARIAN PENNE

Serves 4 to 6

For one mid-fall dinner, Bill Cosby requested a strictly vegetarian pasta to conform with his diet and I complied by creating this dish: a spontaneous array of the seasonal produce we had on hand. Except for the pasta and the tossing of the vegetables, which require last-minute cooking, you can prepare this recipe up to 3 hours in advance and keep refrigerated. All the ingredients can be cooked 15 minutes before serving.

2 large artichokes

Juice of 1 lemon

1/4 cup olive oil, plus more for serving

2 cups eggplant, in 1/4-inch dice

3 ounces chanterelle mushrooms, cleaned and sliced, and 3 ounces fresh porcini, sliced; or 6 ounces of any other kind of seasonal mushrooms, sliced

1/4 cup scallions, white part only, minced

2 cloves garlic, peeled and chopped

1/4 cup sun-dried tomatoes, diced

1/4 cup small black olives (Niçoise), pitted

2 tablespoons tiny French capers

Salt, freshly ground black pepper

6 drops Tabasco

10 to 12 ounces penne pasta (small tubular pasta cut on the diagonal)

2 tablespoons sweet butter

2 sprigs basil, leaves only, chopped

1/4 cup freshly grated Parmesan cheese

PREPARATION

Bring a large pot of salted water to a boil to cook the penne. Reduce heat to a simmer until ready to use.

Peel off the leaves around the bottom of the artichokes. Cut off the stem and shape the bottom with a paring knife until smooth and round. Cut off the remaining leaves 1/2 inch above the heart. Boil the artichokes in 1 quart water with the lemon juice and 1 teaspoon salt until tender when pierced with a knife, about 25 minutes. Drain, let cool, and scoop out the chokes with a spoon. Slice the bottoms into thin wedges and set aside.

Heat 2 tablespoons of the olive oil in a nonstick pan over high heat. Add the eggplant and toss until golden brown, about 5 to 7 minutes. Remove the cooked eggplant with a slotted spoon and drain on paper towels.

In the same hot pan, add the remaining 2 tablespoons olive oil, the chanterelles, and the porcini. Toss while cooking until all moisture is released and evaporated. Add the scallions and toss for a few minutes. Add the artichoke wedges, eggplant, garlic, sun-dried tomatoes, Niçoise olives, capers, salt, pepper, and Tabasco and toss well for another 5 to 7 minutes.

Return the simmering water for the pasta to a high boil. Add the penne and cook al dente, approximately 10 to 12 minutes. Drain and toss the penne in the pot with the butter and basil.

PRESENTATION

Transfer the penne to a large hot bowl or plate. Spread the vegetables over the top and serve with Parmesan cheese as well as olive oil on the side.

TRENETTE WITH CRABMEAT AND LEMONGRASS

Serves 4

Of all the exotic herbs prevalent in Thai, Cambodian, and Vietnamese cooking, lemongrass is a personal favorite for its delicate and refreshing, lemony, gingery taste. It complements fish, shellfish, and chicken and its flavor is best extracted, as in this recipe, through infusion. Here that infusion is used to cook and flavor the trenette, a pasta in the shape of a long flat ribbon. The basic ingredients can be prepared up to 1 hour in advance; the crab and pasta are cooked 10 minutes before serving.

10 stems lemongrass, top branches removed, 8 stems whole, 2 stems tender white part only, minced

1 tablespoon sesame oil

1/4 cup onions, peeled, in 1/8-inch dice

1/2 cup green pepper, seeded, in 1/8-inch dice

1/2 tablespoon garlic, peeled and finely chopped

Finely grated zest and juice of 1/2 lemon

2 pinches of cayenne pepper

1 cup plum tomatoes, peeled, seeded, and coarsely chopped

3/4 pound fresh jumbo lump crabmeat

2 tablespoons sweet butter

Salt

1/2 pound trenette pasta

Freshly ground black pepper

1 tablespoon toasted peanuts, finely crushed

3 sprigs coriander, leaves only

✤ PREPARATION

Crush 8 stems (solid part only) of lemongrass with a mallet. Bring 3 quarts water with 1 tablespoon salt and the crushed lemongrass to a boil in a large pot. When the water starts to boil, remove from heat, cover tightly, and infuse for 20 minutes. Strain into a large bowl, return the infusion to the pot, and discard the crushed lemongrass.

Heat the sesame oil in a large pan over medium heat. Add the diced onions and green pepper, garlic, and the grated lemon zest and sweat for 5 to 7 minutes. Toss often. Add the cayenne pepper, tomatoes, crabmeat, 1 tablespoon of the butter, and salt and cook for 2 to 3 minutes while tossing. Add the lemon juice, mix, and set aside.

Bring the lemongrass infusion to a boil. Add the pasta and cook for 6 to 7 minutes, until al dente. Drain, put the pasta back in the pot, and toss with the remaining tablespoon butter, the minced lemongrass, and pepper.

✤ PRESENTATION

Transfer the pasta to a large warm bowl. Spread the crabmeat garnish over the top. Sprinkle with the peanuts and coriander leaves.

Spaghetti Sirio Maccioni (Spaghetti Primavera)

Serves 4

This inspired combination of crisp spring vegetables, cream, and toasted pine nuts dressed with tomato sauce has been one of the most popular pasta dishes served at Le Cirque for nearly two decades. It was originally the creation of Sirio Maccioni, the restaurant's owner, at a weekend gathering for friends and family where he used fresh spring vegetables in a spontaneous and delicious way. The sauce and vegetables may be prepared up to 3 hours in advance, the pasta cooked and the vegetables tossed 10 minutes before serving.

1/2 cup olive oil

1/2 cup freshly shelled peas
(about 1 pound in the pod)

3/4 cup heavy cream

3 tablespoons mascarpone cheese

3 tablespoons sweet butter

1/4 cup freshly grated Parmesan cheese

2 pinches of salt

Freshly ground black pepper

2 tablespoons pine nuts

1 cup white mushrooms, caps only,
sliced 1/8 inch thick

1 cup zucchini, split and
sliced 1/8 inch thick

1 cup broccoli florets

12 pencil-thin asparagus, green part only,
cut in 1-inch segments

1 tablespoon garlic, peeled and finely chopped

3 sprigs basil, leaves only, finely chopped

1 cup plum tomatoes, seeded, in 1/2-inch dice

1/2 pound No. 3 spaghetti

2 tablespoons chives, chopped

❀ Preparation

Bring 1 gallon water with 2 tablespoons salt and 1 tablespoon of the olive oil to a boil in a pasta pot or stockpot. Reduce heat to a low simmer until ready to cook the pasta.

While the water for the pasta is warming, bring 2 quarts of water with 1 tablespoon salt to a boil in a small pot over high heat. Add the fresh peas and boil for 3 minutes. Drain, cool the peas under cold running water, and drain again. Keep warm on the side.

In a small pot over low heat, combine the heavy cream, mascarpone, butter, Parmesan, salt, and pepper. Cook slowly for 5 minutes or until the sauce lightly thickens. Set aside and keep warm. Heat 2 tablespoons of the olive oil in a pan over high heat. Add the pine nuts, toss, and toast until very light brown. Add the sliced mushrooms, zucchini, broccoli, and asparagus and toss well for 5 to 7 minutes. Salt and pepper to taste, set aside, and keep warm.

Heat the remaining tablespoon olive oil in a small pan over medium heat. Add the garlic and basil and cook for 2 minutes (do not brown the garlic). Add the diced tomatoes, salt, and pepper and cook for another 3 to 4 minutes.

Return the water in the pasta pot to a boil. Plunge the spaghetti into the boiling water. Stir and cook for 5 to 7 minutes. Drain and return the spaghetti to the pot. Add the Parmesan cream sauce, chives, and half of the peas, sautéed vegetables, and tomato mixture. Toss well for 2 minutes and add a little Parmesan if the sauce needs thickening, or a few tablespoons of hot water if too thick.

❊ PRESENTATION

Pour the creamy spaghetti into a warm serving bowl. Sprinkle the remaining peas, sautéed vegetables, and tomato mixture on top. Garnish with basil leaves and serve grated Parmesan on the side.

Pappardelle Meridionale

Serves 4

Pappardelle, the broadest of the long noodles and a traditional Tuscan pasta shape, is essential to carrying rich, succulent sauces such as this southern-style (*meridionale*) one with its eggplant, garlic, tomatoes, olives, and fresh sardines. The sauce can be prepared up to 3 hours in advance, then reheated as you cook the pasta and sardines 8 to 10 minutes before serving.

1/2 pound eggplant, peeled and cut into sticks 2 inches long and 1/4 inch wide

Zest of 1 lemon, finely chopped

1/4 cup olive oil

1/2 cup sweet white onions, peeled and finely chopped

1 tablespoon garlic, peeled and finely chopped

1/4 teaspoon hot pepper flakes

1 yellow sweet pepper, split, cored, and finely chopped

1 large bay leaf

One 16-ounce can imported plum tomatoes, drained (1/2 cup juice reserved), split, seeded, and chopped

1 pound fresh tomatoes, peeled, cored, split, seeded, and finely chopped

Pinch of sugar

1/4 cup small black olives (Niçoise), pitted

12 fresh sardine or anchovy fillets (if using fresh sardines, see page 23 for instructions on how to remove the fillets)

1 pound pappardelle pasta (wide ribbon pasta)

2 sprigs basil, leaves only

Salt, freshly ground black pepper

❧ Preparation

In a pot, bring 1 quart water with 1 teaspoon salt to a boil. Add the eggplant and boil for 2 minutes. In a colander, drain and press the eggplant well to remove all cooking water. Set aside.

In a small pot, bring 2 cups water to a boil. Add the chopped lemon zest and boil for 5 minutes. Strain and reboil the zest in clean water for another 5 minutes. Strain out the zest and set it aside.

Heat 2 tablespoons of the olive oil in a large pan over medium heat. Add the onions, garlic, hot pepper flakes, sweet pepper, and bay leaf. When the onions are soft and translucent, approximately 5 minutes, add the canned and fresh tomatoes, the 1/2 cup reserved tomato juice, and a pinch each of salt and sugar, and simmer for 20 minutes. Add the eggplant and Niçoise olives and cook for another 10 minutes. Discard the bay leaf, add the lemon zest, toss, and taste for seasoning. Keep warm on the side.

Bring 1 gallon water with 2 tablespoons salt to a boil in a large pot over high heat to cook the pasta.

If using fresh sardines, heat 1/2 tablespoon of the olive oil in a nonstick pan over high heat. Salt and pepper the sardine fillets and sear them on the skin side for 1 to 2 minutes. Turn them over and keep warm on the side. If using canned sardines, don't cook them, just remove the bones and toss them quickly in olive oil.

Plunge the pappardelle in the boiling water for 4 minutes if fresh, 7 to 8 minutes if dried, until al dente, stirring from time to time. Drain, return the pasta to the pot, toss with 1 tablespoon of the olive oil, and salt and pepper to taste.

❋ Presentation

Transfer the pappardelle to a warm serving bowl. Spoon the vegetable mix evenly over the pasta. Arrange the sardine fillets over the vegetable mix, decorate with basil leaves, and drizzle the remaining 1/2 tablespoon olive oil over the top. Serve on warm plates.

HERB RAVIOLI WITH BASIL OIL AND A TOMATO COULIS

Serves 4 to 6

The verdant, full-flavored profusion of herbs and greens in this ravioli creates a burst of taste tempered by a lightly sweet and silky tomato sauce. This three-part recipe can be prepared up to 24 hours in advance; you can freeze the ravioli and refrigerate the basil oil and tomato coulis until ready to cook, combine, and serve.

For the Ravioli Dough:

1 pound all-purpose flour

1/4 pound semolina flour

5 medium eggs

1/2 teaspoon salt

1 egg beaten with 1 tablespoon water

For the Herb Mix:

1/2 tablespoon olive oil

1/2 cup onions, peeled and finely chopped

1 sprig rosemary, leaves only, finely chopped

1 sprig thyme, leaves only, finely chopped

Pinch of freshly grated nutmeg

1 clove garlic, peeled and finely chopped

1-1/2 teaspoons salt

1/2 pound Swiss chard, leaves only

1/3 pound arugula, leaves only

1/2 pound spinach, leaves only

2 ounces watercress, leaves only

3 tablespoons chives, coarsely chopped

2 ounces chervil, leaves only

3 sprigs dill, leaves only, chopped

3 sprigs tarragon, leaves only, chopped

5 sprigs coriander, leaves only, chopped

3 tablespoons mascarpone cheese

2 tablespoons ricotta cheese, more if needed

1 tablespoon grated Parmesan cheese

Salt, freshly ground black pepper

For the Tomato Coulis:

1 tablespoon olive oil

1/4 cup onions, peeled and finely chopped

3 cloves garlic, peeled and finely chopped

1 bay leaf

1 sprig fresh thyme

One 16-ounce can imported plum tomatoes, drained and squeezed to remove any excess water

3 pounds ripe tomatoes, split, seeded, and finely chopped

1 stalk celery, cut into 4-inch-long pieces and tied together with a piece of kitchen string

Pinch of sugar

Salt, freshly ground black pepper

For the Basil Oil:

1/4 cup olive oil

6 sprigs basil, leaves only

Salt, freshly ground black pepper

❧ PREPARATION

For the Ravioli Dough:
Combine both flours, the eggs, and the salt in a bowl by hand or in a food processor (use the plastic blade) and process for 2 minutes. Transfer to a floured work surface and knead the dough by hand until well combined, about 5 to 8 minutes. Wrap in plastic wrap and refrigerate until needed.

For the Herb Mix:
Heat the olive oil in a small pan over medium heat. Add the onions, rosemary, thyme, nutmeg, and garlic and sweat for 8 to 10 minutes without coloring the onions (add a few tablespoons water if needed to keep moist while cooking). Remove from heat and set aside to cool.

Bring 3 quarts water with 1-1/2 teaspoons salt to a boil in a large pot over medium heat. Add the Swiss chard and boil for 2 minutes. Add the arugula and boil for 2 minutes more. Add the spinach and watercress and boil for another 3 to 4 minutes. Drain and chill the greens under cold running water, drain again, and press inside a colander very firmly with your hands to remove any excess water.

Transfer the cooked greens to a blender or food processor, add the cooked onions, 3/4 each of the chives, chervil, dill, tarragon, and coriander, along with all of the mascarpone, ricotta, Parmesan cheese, and salt and pepper to taste, and purée until smooth, about 3 to 4 minutes. From time to time, scrape down the sides of the blender or food processor to avoid lumps. If the herb mixture is too dry, add 1 more tablespoon of ricotta cheese (the mixture should be very green and smooth). Taste for seasoning before putting in a zip-lock bag. Press any air out of the bag, seal, and refrigerate until needed.

To make the ravioli:
Remove the ravioli dough from the refrigerator and unwrap. Sprinkle the counter and rolling pin with flour. Divide the dough into 4 equal pieces. Flatten each piece into a 3-inch square with the rolling pin. Roll the pieces of dough through a pasta machine until about 12 inches by 5 inches and thin enough to see your hand through. If using a ravioli tray, make sure the 4 sheets of dough are slightly larger and longer than your ravioli tray. Cut a 1/2-inch tip off one of the bottom corners of the plastic bag containing the herb mixture and use it as a piping bag.

Here are two ways to make the ravioli:
1. Place a layer of dough over a ravioli tray (2-inch-square size with 12 shallow bowls). Push lightly with your finger into each hole to line the hole with the dough. Brush the dough with a little egg and water wash along the ridges of each hole. Pipe 1 teaspoon of the herb mixture into each hole. Cover the top of the filled ravioli tray with a second sheet of pasta. Apply even pressure with your fingers over the top layer of pasta to seal each ravioli and roll a rolling pin over the ridging to sever each ravioli. Line a flat baking

sheet the size of the ravioli tray with a piece of parchment paper sprinkled with flour. Flip the ravioli tray onto the baking sheet and gently shake the tray to release the ravioli onto the parchment paper. Repeat the same process with the rest of the dough and filling. Cover with a dry towel and refrigerate until ready to cook.

2. Place a layer of dough on a flat surface. Brush it with the egg and water wash. Pipe 1 teaspoon of the herb mixture evenly every 2 inches along the length in 2 to 3 rows to make at least 12 ravioli. Cover with the second sheet of dough. Press well with your fingers all around each ravioli. Cut them out with a fluted rolling cutter or knife for square shaped ones, or use a small round cookie cutter for round ravioli. Repeat the same process with the rest of the dough and filling. Place the ravioli on a baking sheet lined with parchment paper sprinkled with flour, cover with a dry towel, and refrigerate until ready to serve.

For the Tomato Coulis:
Warm the olive oil in an enameled cast-iron pot over medium heat. Add the onions, garlic, bay leaf, and thyme and sweat for 5 to 7 minutes until soft and translucent. Add both the canned and fresh tomatoes, celery, sugar, and salt and pepper to taste. Mix well, reduce heat to low, and cook for 30 to 40 minutes or until soft. Remove from heat, discard the thyme, bay leaf, and celery. Transfer the tomato mixture to a blender or food processor and purée until smooth. Keep warm until needed.

For the Basil Oil:
Blend the olive oil with the basil leaves in a blender or food processor until smooth. Salt and pepper to taste and strain through a cheesecloth or cotton towel into a small bowl. Refrigerate until needed.

To cook the ravioli:
Bring 1 gallon of water with 1 tablespoon salt to a boil. Plunge in the ravioli and boil for 3 minutes. Delicately remove the ravioli with a mesh strainer and toss them gently in a pan with the basil oil over medium heat for a few minutes. Taste for seasoning.

❧ PRESENTATION

Spoon the warm tomato coulis onto the bottom of warm individual plates or a platter. Divide the ravioli evenly among the serving plates over the tomato coulis. Sprinkle the remaining chives, chervil, dill, tarragon, and coriander leaves on top of the ravioli. Serve with grated Parmesan cheese on the side.

RUOTE WITH SCALLOPS, PEAS, AND BLACK TRUFFLES

Serves 4 to 6
Ruote, also called trulli, is a pasta shaped like small wheels
and goes perfectly with this spring preparation rich in vegetables and caramelized scallops. The preserved
winter black truffles give an elegant and earthy taste. The vegetables can be prepared an hour before serving,
but the assembling and cooking should be done 12 to 15 minutes before serving.

3 tablespoons olive oil

3 tablespoons sweet butter

*1/4 cup carrots, peeled and cut into julienne
(matchstick size)*

*1/4 cup leeks, white part only, sliced 1/4 inch
thick (1 medium leek)*

1/4 cup celery, peeled and sliced 1/4 inch thick

Salt, freshly ground black pepper

*1/4 cup zucchini, trimmed and cut
into julienne*

*1/4 cup freshly shelled peas
(about 1/2 pound in the pod)*

*1/4 cup fresh fava beans, shelled and
peeled (plunge for 1 minute in boiling
water, drain, cool under cold running water,
pierce a slit on one side, and squeeze
the fava out of the skin)*

10 to 12 ounces ruote pasta

*8 ounces Maine sea scallops, cut into
2 or 3 slices 1/4 inch thick;
or bay scallops, washed and patted dry*

1 tablespoon all-purpose flour

*2-ounce jar black truffles, juice reserved,
cut into julienne*

❀ PREPARATION

Heat 1/2 tablespoon of the olive oil with 1/2 tablespoon of the butter in a large pan over medium heat. Add the carrots, leeks, celery, salt, and pepper and toss well for 3 to 4 minutes. Add 2 tablespoons water, cover with a lid, and cook for 3 to 4 minutes. Remove the lid, add the zucchini, fresh peas, 2 tablespoons water, mix well, cover with a lid, and cook for another 3 minutes. Remove the lid, add the fava beans, toss for 1 minute, and set aside.

Bring 4 quarts water with 1 tablespoon salt and 1/2 tablespoon of the olive oil to a boil in a large pot over high heat. Add the pasta and boil for 7 to 9 minutes.

While the pasta is cooking, prepare the scallops. Season the scallops with salt and pepper and dust them with flour. Heat a large pan over high heat, and when hot add the remaining 2 tablespoons olive oil. Carefully add the scallops and, once slightly colored, about 1-1/2 to 2 minutes, turn them over and cook for 1 more minute. Pour the reserved truffle juice over the scallops, add the cooked vegetables and the black truffles. Toss well for 2 to 3 minutes, adding 3 to 4 tablespoons water if too dry.

When the pasta is done, drain, return to the pot, and add the remaining 2-1/2 tablespoons butter and salt and pepper to taste, and toss quickly for 1 minute. Add the scallops, truffles, and vegetables mixture and toss well for 1 minute. Taste for seasoning.

❉ PRESENTATION

Transfer to a large, warm serving bowl and serve immediately. Serve extra olive oil on the side.

Drizzle the remaining tablespoon olive oil over the warm pasta and shrimp and sprinkle the bacon on top. Serve on warm plates.

SHELLFISH

SPRING   SUMMER   AUTUMN   WINTER
❋   ⚜   🍃   ❆

BROILED BLUE PRAWNS WITH GINGER ❋ PAGE 138

SOFT-SHELL CRAB AND CAULIFLOWER GRENOBLOISE ❋ PAGE 140

MUSSELS AND BABY VEGETABLE STEW WITH BASIL ❋ PAGE 142

CORN CRÊPES WITH LOBSTER AND BACON ⚜ PAGE 144

GULF SHRIMP WITH SWEET RED PEPPER AND
      ZUCCHINI CUSTARD ⚜ PAGE 147

LOBSTER WITH A FAVA PURÉE AND BLACK TRUMPETS ⚜ PAGE 149

MAINE SEA SCALLOPS IN BLACK TIE ❆ PAGE 151

SWEET-WATER PRAWN AND CHANTERELLE CASSEROLE
      WITH GARLIC 🍃 PAGE 154

SEA SCALLOPS WITH MASHED POTATOES AND
      A RED ONION CONFIT 🍃 PAGE 155

MARINIÈRE OF LITTLENECK CLAMS AND SALMON WITH
      CHAMPAGNE AND CAVIAR ❆ PAGE 156

STUFFED TOMATOES WITH CRAB AND FENNEL COULIS ⚜ PAGE 157

SEA SCALLOPS WITH FRESH FENNEL AND CUMIN ❆ PAGE 159

MARYLAND CRAB AND CARROT GRATIN WITH CORIANDER ❋ PAGE 161

opposite page: Sea Scallops with Mashed Potatoes and a Red Onion Confit

Broiled Blue Prawns with Ginger

Serves 4

To ensure that the blue prawns featured in this dish cook to a uniform, succulent state, they are sautéed briefly on both sides, coated with zesty ginger butter, and briefly broiled to develop their fragrant crust. A simple garnish of tender snow peas and sweet peppers provides the complement. The butter can be prepared up to 4 hours in advance and the prawns and vegetables cooked 8 to 10 minutes before serving. You can prepare this recipe with large shrimp or scallops if blue prawns are not available.

For the Ginger Butter:

3 ounces gingerroot, peeled and thinly sliced

3 slices white bread, crusts discarded

6 tablespoons sweet butter, at room temperature

Salt, freshly ground black pepper

For the Blue Prawns:

16 blue prawns with heads on (2 ounces each or 2 pounds total), tail shells removed (do not break the tail from the body), legs, claws, and antennae cut off with scissors

Salt, freshly ground black pepper

1 tablespoon sweet butter

1 cup spring onions or scallions, white part only, peeled and sliced 1/4 inch thick

3/4 cup sweet red pepper, split, cored, and sliced 1/8 inch thick

3/4 cup snow peas, ends trimmed

2 tablespoons gingerroot, finely grated

❋ Preparation

For the Ginger Butter:

Bring 1 quart water to a boil in a saucepan over medium heat. Add the gingerroot and boil for 20 minutes or until tender. Drain, let cool, and finely chop.

Put the bread in a blender or food processor and grind well. Add the gingerroot, butter, and salt and pepper to taste and mix until smooth. Transfer the ginger butter to a zip-lock bag, press the air out of the bag, and seal. Keep cool until needed, or leave at room temperature if using right away.

For the Blue Prawns:

Preheat the broiler. Salt and pepper the prawns. Melt the butter in a large pan over high heat. Add the prawns and sauté for 1 minute on each side. Transfer the prawns to an ovenproof pan and set aside to cool.

Add the spring onions and red pepper to the hot pan used to cook the prawns and sweat for 3 minutes over medium heat. Add the snow peas and cook for another 5 to 8 minutes. Wrap the grated gingerroot in a piece of cheesecloth or a cotton kitchen towel and squeeze the juice over the vegetables. Discard the leftover gingerroot. Salt and pepper the vegetables to taste and set aside.

Bring the ginger butter to room temperature 30 minutes before cooking the shrimp. Cut off a bottom corner of the zip-lock bag and pipe the ginger butter evenly onto the prawns from head to tail (top side only). Broil the prawns for 3 to 4 minutes or until golden brown.

❋ PRESENTATION

Arrange the warm vegetables in the middle of a large oval or round dish. Arrange the prawns in a crown on top and pour the melted ginger/prawn butter from the broiling pan over the prawns and vegetables.

STORING FRESH BLUE PRAWNS: The color of the blue prawn is bluish-green when raw and pink when cooked. When fresh, the shell of the blue prawn is very shiny and easy to remove, and the flesh is firm. To store, cover the prawns with a damp cloth. Place a zip-lock bag filled with ice over the cloth, and keep in the coldest spot of your refrigerator.

SOFT-SHELL CRAB AND CAULIFLOWER GRENOBLOISE

Serves 4

When selecting soft-shell crabs, make sure they are firm, plump, and alive. Sauté them quickly, then top
with the capers, herbs, lemon, and brown butter garnish; a bed of cauliflower florets creates a delicious contrast.
You can clean the crabs and poach the cauliflower up to 1/2 hour in advance, then sauté both
6 to 8 minutes before serving.

8 live soft-shell crabs (about 2 ounces each)

*1 head of cauliflower, cut in small florets,
stems and leaves discarded*

1 cup milk in a shallow dish

1 cup flour in a bowl

1/4 cup sweet butter

Salt, freshly ground black pepper

*2 slices white bread, crusts discarded,
cut in half*

1/4 cup tiny French capers

1 tablespoon chives, finely chopped

1 tablespoon parsley, leaves only, finely chopped

1 tablespoon fresh tarragon leaves, finely chopped

2 lemons: 1 for juice, 1 peeled, seeded, and diced

❊ PREPARATION

To clean the soft-shell crabs, cut off the gills (a cottonlike membrane under each side of
the head) by lifting the sides of the upper shell and snipping with scissors, and cut off
the turned-under tail as well as the head directly behind the eyes. Scrape out the innards
through the opening at the head with a knife and rinse the opening under cold water.
Pat the crabs dry with paper towels and refrigerate them until needed.

Bring 3 quarts water with 1 tablespoon salt to a boil in a pot over high heat. Add the
cauliflower and boil for 7 to 8 minutes or until fork tender. Drain and set aside.

Dip the crabs in the milk. Dredge them one by one in the flour, shaking off any excess.
Melt 1/2 tablespoon of the butter in a large nonstick pan over high heat. Add the crabs,
bottom side up, and season them with salt and pepper. Cook for 3 to 4 minutes or until
crisp and colored. Turn the crabs over, add another 1/2 tablespoon butter, and cook for 3
more minutes. Transfer the crabs to a plate and keep them warm. Add 1 tablespoon of
the butter and the cauliflower to the same pan in which the crabs were cooked. Salt and
pepper to taste and toss well for 3 to 4 minutes. Keep warm.

Toast the bread under the broiler until golden on both sides. Heat the remaining 2
tablespoons butter until light brown in a clean pan over medium heat.

 PRESENTATION

Place 2 soft-shell crabs on each piece of toast in the center of a serving dish. Arrange the cauliflower all around. Sprinkle with the capers, fresh herbs, diced lemon, and lemon juice. Pour the brown butter over the crabs and serve immediately.

BUYING SOFT-SHELL CRABS: From Maryland to Louisiana, the East Coast blue crab, caught immediately after shedding its shell, is the delicacy known as soft-shell crab. Available primarily in the spring, live crabs of small size—2-1/2 to 3-1/2 inches—are best.

MUSSELS AND BABY VEGETABLE STEW WITH BASIL

Serves 4

This light recipe integrates the flavors of its ingredients by using the mussel juices to cook the spring vegetables, and is accented with fragrant fresh basil. If some of the baby vegetables called for are not available at your market, you can substitute regular-size vegetables of the same variety cut into small pieces. You can prepare this dish up to 2 hours in advance then reheat it 5 minutes prior to serving.

For the Mussels:

2 pounds mussels (discard any open mussels, clean the closed mussels with a scrub brush under cold running water, and pull off the beards with your fingers)

1 cup dry white wine

2 tablespoons shallots, peeled and coarsely chopped

1/4 teaspoon ground black peppercorns

2 sprigs parsley

1 bay leaf

1/2 teaspoon Madras curry powder

For the Stew:

1/2 cup shelled fresh fava beans (about 3/4 pound unshelled) or 1/2 cup shelled fresh peas (about 1/2 pound unshelled)

1/4 cup olive oil

4 baby leeks or scallions, white part only, cut into 1/2-inch slices

8 pearl onions, peeled (see page 213)

8 baby carrots, peeled, top greens trimmed to 1/2 inch

8 baby turnips, peeled, top greens trimmed to 1/2 inch

1 cup chicken stock (see page 370) or water

Salt, freshly ground black pepper

6 baby zucchini, sliced 1/4 inch thick

6 baby eggplants, peeled and sliced 1/4 inch thick

3 sprigs basil, leaves only

8 or 12 cherry tomatoes, blanched for 30 seconds in boiling water and peeled

❋ PREPARATION

For the Mussels:

Place the mussels with all the other ingredients in a pot over high heat. Cover and cook, tossing often until the mussels start to open, approximately 4 minutes. Remove the mussels with a slotted spoon as they open and let them drain in a colander. When all the mussels have opened, strain the cooking liquid and set aside in a cup.

Reserve 4 unshelled mussels for decoration and remove the rest of the mussels from their shells. Discard the shells and set the mussels aside.

For the Stew:

To peel the fava beans, bring 1 quart water to a boil in a pot over high heat. Plunge in the fava beans and boil for 1 minute. Drain and cool the beans under cold running water. Make a small incision with your finger at one end of each bean and pop the bean out of its shell. Discard the shells and set the beans aside.

Heat 1 tablespoon of the olive oil in a pot over medium heat. Add the leeks, onions, carrots, and turnips and sweat for 6 to 8 minutes, stirring often. Add the strained mussel liquid, the chicken stock, and a pinch of salt and pepper, bring to a boil, and gently boil for 10 minutes.

Add the zucchini and eggplant and boil for 5 to 7 more minutes. Remove the vegetables with a mesh skimmer to a colander, drain, and set aside.

Strain the vegetable cooking broth through a Chinese strainer (a cone-shaped, fine-meshed strainer) into a bowl, transfer the strained broth back into the pot, and bring to a boil. Add the fava beans and boil for 3 to 4 minutes. Transfer the broth with the fava beans into a blender or food processor, add 1/2 of the basil leaves, and blend until smooth. While blending, slowly add the remaining 3 tablespoons olive oil. Add salt and pepper to taste. Strain the broth into a large pot. Carefully add the mussels and vegetables to the pot and mix. Add the cherry tomatoes and reheat over medium heat.

❁ PRESENTATION

Transfer the mussel and baby vegetable stew to a warm soup tureen or shallow plate. Decorate with the unshelled mussels and the remaining basil leaves.

CORN CRÊPES WITH LOBSTER AND BACON

Serves 4

This colorful warm-weather entrée of bacon-wrapped lobster pieces on top of corn crêpes combines traditional American ingredients that are readily available in the summer. You can cook the crêpes and diced vegetable garnish up to 3 hours beforehand and reheat them as you cook the lobster 10 minutes before serving.

4 large ears corn, husked and silked

3 live lobsters, 1 pound each

5 slices bacon, at room temperature, each slice cut into 4 equal segments

2-1/2 tablespoons sweet butter, more if needed

1 tablespoon shallots, peeled and chopped

1/2 cup carrots, peeled, in 1/4-inch dice

1/2 cup celery, trimmed, in 1/4-inch dice

1/2 cup white mushrooms, caps only, in 1/4-inch dice

1/2 cup chicken stock (see page 370)

Salt, freshly ground black pepper

1 tablespoon Spanish sherry vinegar

1/2 cup milk

3 eggs

Pinch of freshly grated nutmeg

1/2 teaspoon baking powder

1/2 cup all-purpose flour

4 sprigs fresh Italian parsley, leaves only, coarsely chopped

❧ PREPARATION

Bring 3 quarts water with 1 tablespoon salt to a boil in a large pot over high heat. Add the corn and boil for 3 minutes. Remove the corn with a mesh skimmer and set aside to cool. Slice the kernels off the cob by running a knife along the cob under the kernels. Set the corn kernels aside and discard the cobs. (You should have about 1 cup kernels.)

Return the water in the large pot to a boil, add the lobsters, and boil for 1 minute. Remove the partially cooked lobsters and set aside to cool. Discard the boiling water.

To remove the lobster meat from the shell, detach the tail from the body with a knife. Twist the claws off the body or use heavy scissors to cut them off. Crack the shell with a mallet and remove the meat from the tail and claws. Discard the body and the pieces of shell or freeze for lobster stock.

Cut the meat of each tail into 4 equal slices. Wrap each piece of tail and claw meat with a piece of bacon (18 pieces total). Set aside and refrigerate until needed.

Melt 1/2 tablespoon of the butter in a pan over medium heat. Add the shallots, carrots, celery, and diced mushrooms and sweat for 3 minutes. Add the chicken stock, salt, and pepper, bring to a boil, and gently boil for 6 to 8 minutes.

Strain the vegetables in a colander set over a bowl, reserving the broth to make the sauce. Set the vegetables aside.

Combine the broth and vinegar in a small pot over high heat. Reduce to about 1/4 cup. Whip in 1-1/2 tablespoons of the butter and salt and pepper to taste. Keep the sauce lukewarm on the side.

Combine 3/4 of the corn kernels with the milk, eggs, nutmeg, salt, and pepper in a blender or food processor and blend until smooth. Pour the corn mixture into a bowl, add the baking powder and flour, and mix well.

Melt the remaining 1/2 tablespoon butter in a large nonstick pan, about 10 inches in diameter, over medium heat. Pour 1 tablespoon of the corn crêpe mixture near the edge of the pan, then continue pouring 1 tablespoon of the mix every 2 inches all around the pan and in the center until you have 8 mini-crêpes evenly spaced. Cook for about 2 minutes or until golden (lift the edge of the first crêpe with a spatula to check the color). Flip the crêpes over with a spatula and cook the other side for the same amount of time. Repeat the same process until you have a total of 18 mini-crêpes. (Use more butter as needed.) Set the warm crêpes on the side.

Wipe the pan in which you made the crêpes with a paper towel and place it over high heat. Add the pieces of lobster wrapped in bacon and cook for 3 to 4 minutes on each side until brown and crispy and most of the fat has been rendered. Remove from pan and keep warm. Discard the melted fat from the pan and add the diced vegetables and remaining corn kernels and toss for 3 to 5 minutes over medium heat or until warm.

❧ PRESENTATION

Place the corn crêpes on a large, warm platter. Place a wrapped lobster piece on each crêpe with the diced vegetables spread over the top. Sprinkle with chopped parsley and serve the vinegar sauce on the side.

Gulf Shrimp with Sweet Red Pepper and Zucchini Custard

Serves 4

Orange zest, garlic, and thyme impart fine Mediterranean flair to this roasted shrimp entrée
with its zucchini flan accompaniment. The individual flan and finishing sauce can be prepared up to 2 hours
beforehand; the shrimp require last-minute cooking.

For the Zucchini Custard:

Two 1-inch pieces orange zest, cut into a
julienne (matchstick size)

One 2-inch piece gingerroot, peeled with a
knife and cut into a julienne (matchstick size)

1 tablespoon olive oil

1 tablespoon shallots, peeled and chopped

2 cups very fresh and green zucchini,
sliced 1/4 inch thick

Salt, freshly ground black pepper

1 whole egg and 1 egg yolk

1/2 cup heavy cream

1 tablespoon sweet butter, melted

For the Shrimp and Red Pepper Sauce:

2 pounds fresh shrimp with the heads on
or 1-1/4 pounds tails only (Peel off the shell
around the tail of the shrimp, reserve
the shells. Remove the heads and reserve.
Devein the shrimp with a small knife.
Refrigerate until needed.)

Coarsely chop the following: 2 medium shallots,
peeled; 2 small carrots, peeled; 1 clove garlic,
peeled; 1 sprig thyme, leaves only; 1/2-inch slice
gingerroot, peeled; 1-inch piece orange zest

1/4 cup olive oil

1/2 cup dry white wine

2 cups chicken stock (see page 370)

1 red pepper, quartered, cored, and seeded

3 drops Tabasco

Salt, freshly ground black pepper

❧ Preparation

For the Zucchini Custard:

Bring 1 quart water to a boil in a small pot over medium heat. Add the orange zest and
gingerroot and boil for 10 minutes or until tender. Drain and set aside.

Preheat oven to 300 degrees. Heat the olive oil in a pan over medium heat. Add the
shallots, zucchini slices, 1/2 of the orange zest and gingerroot, and salt and pepper to
taste. Toss often and cook for 10 minutes until the zucchini are tender but firm (do not
let them color). Add a drop of water if more moisture is needed while cooking. Drain
the zucchini, reserve 16 slices for decoration, and transfer the rest to a food processor or
blender. Once the zucchini are room temperature, add the whole egg, egg yolk, and
heavy cream and blend until smooth. Salt and pepper to taste.

Brush four small pie pans (5 inches in diameter by 1 inch deep) or disposable tart tins with the melted butter and fill with the zucchini mixture. Place in a shallow pan with 1/2 inch of hot water, cover with aluminum foil, and cook in the oven until the custard is set, about 45 minutes. Remove and set aside.

For the Shrimp and Red Pepper Sauce:
Combine the shrimp heads and shells with the chopped ingredients in a bowl. Heat 1 tablespoon of the olive oil in a pan over medium heat. Add the shrimp shell and vegetable mixture and sweat for 5 to 7 minutes, stirring often. Add the white wine, bring to a boil, and gently boil for 5 minutes. Add the chicken stock and reduce to 1/4 cup over medium heat. Strain the stock over a bowl and set the strained stock aside. Discard the shells and vegetables.

Bring 1 quart water to a boil in a small pot over medium heat. Add the red pepper and boil until soft, about 10 minutes. Drain and transfer to a blender or food processor. Add the shrimp stock and Tabasco and blend until smooth. Gently pour in 2 tablespoons of the olive oil while blending. Salt and pepper to taste. Keep warm on the side.

Heat the remaining tablespoon olive oil in a large pot over high heat. Add the shrimp tails and sprinkle with salt and pepper. Toss well for 3 minutes. Add the remaining zucchini slices and orange zest and gingerroot and toss well for another minute. Remove from heat.

❧ PRESENTATION

Unmold the zucchini cups in the middle of a warm platter. Place the shrimp with the zucchini slices, orange zest, and gingerroot all around them. Spoon a few drops of red pepper sauce around the shrimp and serve the rest of the sauce in a small bowl on the side.

USING SHRIMP: When buying raw shrimp, look for firm flesh and a shiny shell with a sweet smell (stale shrimp smell of ammonia). To prepare shrimp, remove the heads (if any) and the shell with your hands. To devein, make a small incision along the tail and remove with the tip of a sharp paring knife. Don't overcook shrimp or they will be tough and chewy. Don't refrigerate cooked shrimp, serve them immediately.

LOBSTER WITH A FAVA PURÉE AND BLACK TRUMPETS

Serves 4

Dramatic is the best way to describe this summer entrée of sweet ruby-red lobster, creamy pastel green fava purée and inky sautéed black mushrooms—which tastes as winning as it looks. You can prepare the fava purée as well as the rest of this recipe up to 2 hours in advance, then reheat and assemble it 5 minutes before serving.

For the Lobster:

2 tablespoons white vinegar

4 live lobsters, 1 pound each

1 tablespoon olive oil

1 pound chicken bones or wings, cut into pieces

1 sprig fresh rosemary

3 garlic cloves, peeled and crushed

1 shallot, peeled and sliced

1/4 cup dry white vermouth (Noilly Prat)

2 plum tomatoes, cut into cubes

3 cups chicken stock (see page 370)

1 tablespoon sweet butter

Salt, freshly ground black pepper

For the Fava Purée:

2 cups shelled fresh fava beans (about 3 pounds in the shell)

2-1/2 tablespoons sweet butter

1/2 cup onions, peeled and chopped

1 sprig fresh rosemary

Salt, freshly ground black pepper

For the Black Trumpet Mushrooms:

1/2 tablespoon sweet butter

1/4 pound fresh black trumpets, caps only, rinsed and drained

Salt, freshly ground black pepper

❧ PREPARATION

For the Lobster:

Bring 1 gallon water with the white vinegar to a boil. Plunge in the lobsters, cover tightly, and return to a simmer. Simmer for 4 minutes, drain, and set the lobsters aside to cool.

To remove the lobster meat from the shell, detach the tail from the body with a knife. Twist the claws off the body or use heavy scissors to cut them off. Carefully crush the shell with a mallet and remove the meat from the tail and claws. Set the pieces of shell and meat aside separately. Split the body lengthwise with a long kitchen knife and discard the gills and stomach. Rinse out the body shells and set them aside with the rest of the shells.

Preheat oven to 425 degrees. Heat the olive oil in a shallow roasting pan. Add the chicken bones or wings and brown them for 10 minutes on top of the stove. Add the lobster shells, rosemary, garlic and shallot, stir well, and roast for another 20 minutes. Add the vermouth and tomatoes and cook for another 10 minutes. Add the chicken stock and boil for 30 minutes. Strain over a bowl and discard the solids. Return the strained sauce to the pot and reduce on top of the stove to 1/4 cup over medium heat. Add the butter and season to taste with salt and pepper. Skim the surface and set aside.

For the Fava Purée:
Bring 1 quart water to a boil in a pot over high heat. Plunge in the fava beans and boil for 1 minute. Drain and cool the beans under cold running water. Make a small incision with your finger at one end of each bean and pop the bean out of its shell. Discard the shells and set the beans aside.

Melt 1/2 tablespoon of the butter in a pan over medium heat. Add the onions and rosemary and sweat until soft, about 5 minutes. Add the fava beans and 2 to 3 tablespoons water and and cook for 5 minutes while tossing often. Discard the rosemary sprig and transfer the fava and onion mixture to a blender or food processor. Add the remaining 2 tablespoons butter, salt, and pepper and purée until smooth. Keep the purée warm on the side.

For the Black Trumpet Mushrooms:
Melt the butter in a pan over high heat. Add the black trumpets and toss well for 2 minutes. Salt and pepper to taste and keep warm on the side.

When ready to serve, warm up the lobster jus and stir in the butter, salt, and pepper. Split the lobster tail and add to the jus along with the claws. Warm the lobster meat very slowly for 2 to 3 minutes over low heat.

❊ PRESENTATION

Spoon the fava purée into the center of a warmed, deep plate. Pour the lobster and sauce on the purée. Sprinkle the black trumpets over the top.

STORING LOBSTERS: A good way to store live lobsters (for up to 3 days) is to wrap them tightly in several sheets of moistened newspaper and place them in the bottom of the refrigerator.

MAINE SEA SCALLOPS IN BLACK TIE

Serves 6 as an appetizer, 4 as a main course
Just a few ingredients, all of uncompromising quality, are combined in this elegant shellfish dish, which I
created for my first New Year's Eve dinner at Le Cirque in 1986 and which has since become a signature dish.
It is a harmonious combination of layered big, succulent sea scallops and dark diamonds of Perigord—
black truffles—both of which are encased in spinach and puff pastry. It can be assembled up to 4 hours in
advance, refrigerated, then baked and its sauce prepared 10 minutes before serving.

*2 black truffles, fresh or canned, golf ball size,
juice reserved*

*10 jumbo Maine sea scallops, very fresh
and firm*

Salt, freshly ground black pepper

*8 ounces spinach leaves, stems discarded,
leaves thoroughly washed*

1/2 pound puff pastry

1 egg whisked with 1 teaspoon water

1/4 cup dry white vermouth (Noilly Prat)

1/2 cup chicken jus (see page 371)

1 tablespoon sweet butter

✤ PREPARATION

Slice each truffle into 16 thin slices with a vegetable slicer or mandoline (you will need
about 3 slices of truffle per scallop). Save any juice, chop the trimmings, and set both
aside for the sauce.

Cut each scallop horizontally into 4 slices. Reconstruct each scallop by alternating the 4
slices of scallop with 3 slices of truffle. Season with salt and pepper and refrigerate until
needed.

Wilt the spinach in a steamer or in water for 1 to 2 minutes. Drain, cool under cold running water, and drain again. Carefully spread each spinach leaf open on a kitchen towel
and pat dry with a second towel.

Place a layered scallop in the center of a large spinach leaf and wrap the leaf tightly and
smoothly around the scallop. If the scallop is not totally enclosed in the spinach leaf, use
a second leaf to seal the scallop in. Repeat the same process for each layered scallop and
refrigerate until needed (discard or keep the remaining spinach leaves for other uses).

Sprinkle the counter and rolling pin with flour and roll out the puff pastry until very
thin, about 1/8 inch thick. Cut out 24 disks with a 1-1/2-inch round cookie cutter and 12
ribbons of puff pastry about 5 by 1-1/2 inches. Refrigerate the disks and ribbons on a
floured baking sheet for 15 minutes.

After the dough has rested, brush about 1 inch at one end of each ribbon with the egg wash. Place 1 spinach bundle on the other end of the ribbon and roll the ribbon around the bundle until it overlaps the brushed end to seal. Fold the pastry edges tightly over the top and bottom of the bundle. Brush 2 disks with the egg wash and place a disk on either side of the bundle. Press well to seal. Repeat the same steps to wrap each spinach bundle in the puff pastry.

Place the turnovers on a baking pan lined with parchment paper. Brush each pastry lightly with the remaining egg wash. Refrigerate until ready to cook.

Preheat oven to 450 degrees. Bake the turnovers for 5 to 8 minutes, depending on the size, or until golden (while baking, watch carefully that they do not burn).

Prepare the sauce while the turnovers are baking. Pour the vermouth into a small saucepan over high heat. Reduce to 1 teaspoon, about 10 minutes. Add the reserved truffle juice and the chicken jus. Reduce to 1/4 cup and stir in the butter. Add the reserved chopped truffle trimmings. Salt and pepper to taste and remove from heat.

✤ PRESENTATION

Split the turnovers in half from top to bottom with a sharp knife. Spoon 1 tablespoon of sauce on the bottom of 4 warmed plates if serving as a main course, 6 warmed plates if serving as an appetizer. Overlap 6 turnover halves (main course) or 4 halves (appetizer) like rose petals on top of the sauce. Serve immediately.

BUYING SEA SCALLOPS: Maine sea scallops are in bountiful supply from fall to spring. Look for firm, ivory-colored scallops, about 1-1/2 inches in diameter.

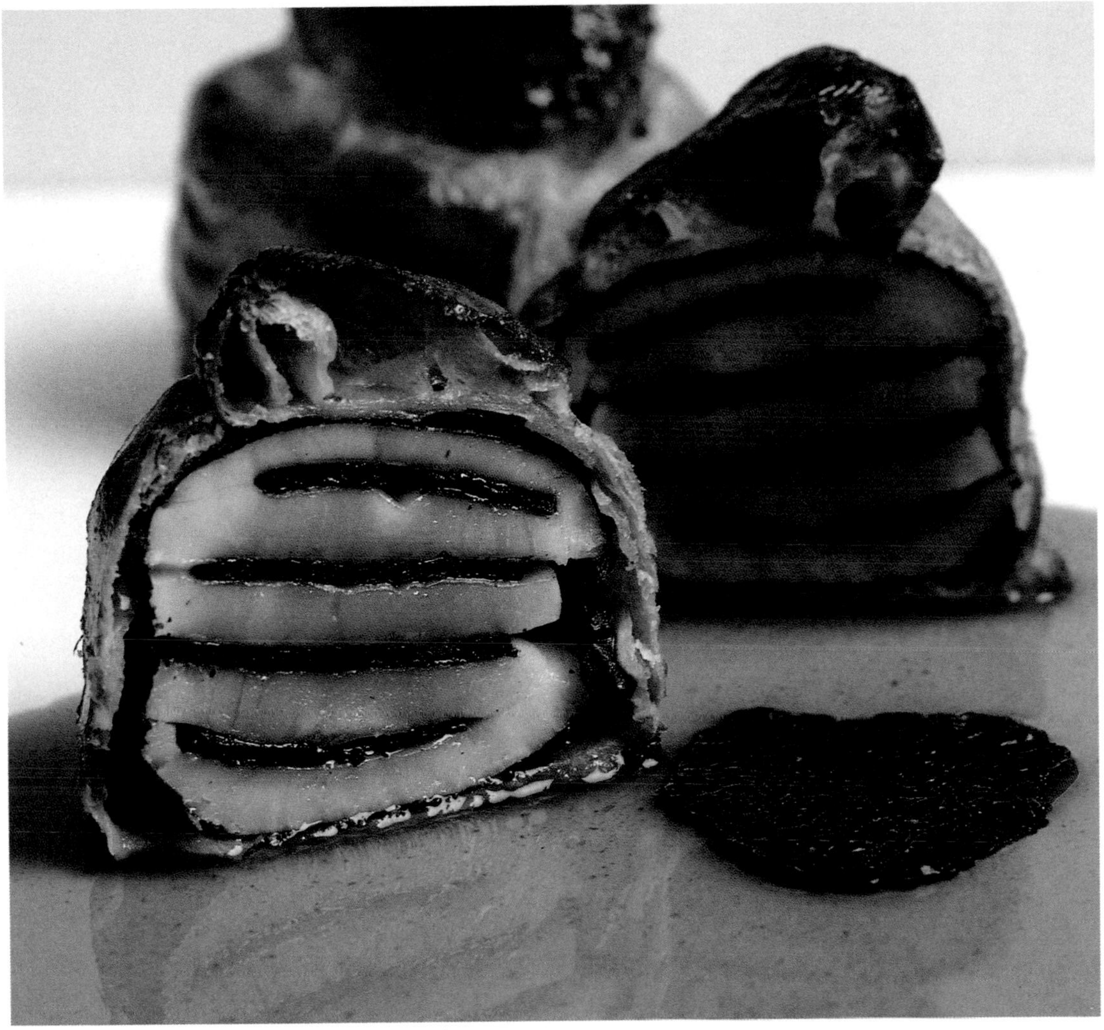

Sweet-Water Prawn and Chanterelle Casserole with Garlic

Serves 4 to 5

This hearty entrée is a fall version of paella, the lusty, rustic Spanish shellfish and rice dish.
The ingredients can be prepared up to 3 hours in advance, then cooked 25 minutes before serving.

3 tablespoons olive oil

1 small head garlic, cloves separated and peeled

2 sprigs fresh thyme

16 to 20 fresh-water prawns (about 2 pounds),
heads removed, tails shelled, leaving only
the shell at the end of the tail
(heads and shells reserved for the bouillon)

1/2 cup dry white wine

2 tablespoons sweet butter

1/3 cup white onions, peeled and finely chopped

1/2 cup carrots, finely chopped

1-1/2 cups converted rice

1 teaspoon salt

3 pinches of cayenne pepper

Salt, freshly ground black pepper

1/2 pound fresh chanterelles, split large,
or substitute any other seasonal mushroom

1-1/2 teaspoons garlic, peeled and chopped

2 tablespoons chives, minced

Preparation

Heat 2 tablespoons of the olive oil in a pan over medium heat. Add the whole garlic and the thyme and cook until the garlic is slightly colored, about 5 minutes. Add the prawn heads and shells, stir, and cook for 10 more minutes. Add the wine and reduce to 1 tablespoon. Add 5 cups water, bring to a boil, and boil for 15 minutes. Strain the bouillon into a bowl and set aside. Discard the rest of the solids.

Melt the butter in a large skillet or paella pan over medium heat. Add the onions and sweat for 3 to 4 minutes. Add the carrots and sweat for 3 minutes. Add the rice, 4 cups of the bouillon, 1 teaspoon salt, and 1 pinch of the cayenne pepper, and stir. Bring to a boil, reduce heat to medium, and cook for 20 minutes or until moisture is evaporated.

Salt and pepper the prawns. Add the 2 remaining pinches of cayenne pepper. Heat the remaining tablespoon olive oil in a large nonstick pan over high heat. Sauté the chanterelles for 5 minutes, add the prawns, and toss for 3 minutes. Add the chopped garlic, toss, and remove from heat.

When the rice is done, remove from heat, cover, and let set for 5 minutes.

Presentation

Garnish with the prawns and chanterelles, and sprinkle with the minced chives.

SEA SCALLOPS WITH MASHED POTATOES AND A RED ONION CONFIT

Serves 4

This earthy recipe features large scallops in a casual dish ideal for an informal fall gathering.
You can prepare the potato purée up to 2 hours beforehand, but the scallops should be cooked just before
serving. Shrimp can be substituted for the scallops in this recipe.

1 pound baking potatoes, peeled, in 1-inch dice

2 teaspoons salt

1/4 cup sweet butter, at room temperature

1/2 cup heavy cream, warmed

Salt, freshly ground black pepper

Pinch of freshly grated nutmeg

2 cups red onions, peeled and thinly sliced

3 tablespoons aged balsamic vinegar

16 jumbo sea scallops, cleaned and patted dry

1/4 cup flour (Wondra, if possible)

1/4 cup chicken stock (see page 370)

*4 sprigs fresh Italian parsley, leaves only,
coarsely chopped*

PREPARATION

Combine the diced potatoes in a pot over high heat with 2 quarts water and 2 teaspoons salt. Bring to a boil and boil until done, about 20 minutes. Drain and mash the potatoes through a sieve or food mill into the top of a double boiler. Add 2 tablespoons of the butter and the warm heavy cream and stir until smooth Add salt, pepper, and nutmeg. To keep the mashed potatoes warm until ready to serve, place the double boiler (with hot water in the bottom pot) over very low heat. Cover with plastic wrap to prevent drying.

Melt 1 tablespoon of the butter in a large pan over medium-low heat. Add the onions, salt, and pepper, and sweat until very soft. Add 2 tablespoons of the balsamic vinegar. Cook until the onions start to caramelize, about 10 to 15 minutes. When brown, remove and set aside.

Preheat a large nonstick pan over medium heat. Salt and pepper each scallop and dredge with flour, shaking off any excess. Add 1/2 tablespoon of the butter to the hot pan. Add the scallops and sauté them for 2 minutes on each side. Sprinkle on the remaining tablespoon vinegar, add the chicken stock, toss well, and cook for 2 minutes. Remove the scallops from the pan, reduce the sauce by half, and stir in the remaining 1/2 tablespoon butter. Test for seasoning and sprinkle with 1/2 of the chopped parsley.

PRESENTATION

Spread the onions on the bottom of a warmed shallow dish or serving plate. Spoon the mashed potatoes over the onions and place the scallops on top. Spoon the sauce over the scallops. Sprinkle with the rest of the chopped parsley.

Marinière of Littleneck Clams and Salmon with Champagne and Caviar

Serves 4
This is a great festive dish to serve at a special celebration.
It's also easy to prepare and the ingredients should be cooked just before serving—except for the clams,
which can be opened 15 to 20 minute s before finishing the dish.

24 littleneck clams, in the shell, well scrubbed

1 tablespoon shallots, peeled and finely chopped

1 cup dry champagne

*1/4 cup sweet butter, plus more
to grease the plates*

*2 tablespoons fresh Italian parsley,
leaves only, finely chopped*

*One 7-ounce salmon fillet, skin discarded,
the fillet cut horizontally into 4 thin slices*

Salt, freshly ground black pepper

2 ounces ossetra caviar

✤ Preparation

Preheat oven to 300 degrees. Put the clams in the bottom of a large, heavy pan. Add the shallots and the champagne and sprinkle with black pepper. Cover and warm on top of the stove over high heat. After a few minutes, remove any opened clams with a slotted spoon. When all the clams have opened and are removed, continue cooking the broth over high heat until reduced to about 1 cup. Strain with a Chinese strainer (a cone-shaped, fine-mesh strainer), and set aside until ready to serve. Remove the clams from their shells and set aside. Put 4 large half shells aside for the caviar and discard the rest.

When ready to serve, transfer the clam broth to a pot and boil over medium heat. Stir the butter and the parsley into the broth until blended and taste for seasoning. Add the clams to the warm broth and warm them for 1 minute.

Salt and pepper each slice of salmon. Lightly rub the bottom of 4 serving plates with a stick of butter. Place one slice of salmon on each plate and heat in the oven for 2 minutes.

Mix 1 tablespoon broth with the caviar in a cup at the last minute. (Do not heat the caviar or it will harden.) Divide the caviar evenly among the 4 reserved clam shells.

✤ Presentation

Divide the clams among the plates and arrange around the salmon. Place a caviar-filled clam shell on each piece of salmon. Pour the hot marinière over the clams. Serve warm.

Note: Buy littleneck clams live in the shell, with tightly closed valves. Avoid open, cracked, or broken shells. To serve clams on the half shell: Chill them in the freezer for 15 minutes (this makes it easier to open the clams), then hold the shell firmly, insert a clam-knife blade between the two valves, and cut the muscle.

STUFFED TOMATOES WITH CRAB AND FENNEL COULIS

Serves 4

When I get the chance to prepare a favorite summer meal for friends, it often includes stuffed tomatoes. This recipe is distinctly Provençal and is exquisite when served in its smooth, warm pool of fennel coulis flavored with olive oil. The ingredients can be assembled up to 2 hours in advance and refrigerated; just warm the tomatoes and the coulis 10 to 12 minutes before serving or 3 minutes in a microwave.

4 medium tomatoes, each about 2-1/2 inches in diameter, with a shallow incision 1 inch long in the shape of a cross on the bottom of each tomato

1-1/2 pounds fennel bulbs, trimmed, split, and sliced 1/4 inch thick

1 sweet red pepper, split, seeded, and cored

1 sweet yellow pepper, split, seeded, and cored

5-1/2 tablespoons olive oil

14 ounces fresh Maine or Maryland crabmeat

1/2 cup small black olives (Niçoise), pitted and diced

2 tablespoons chives, finely chopped

1 clove garlic, peeled and finely chopped

3 sprigs basil, large leaves chopped, small leaves reserved for garnish

Juice of 1 lemon

Salt, freshly ground black pepper

1/2 cup chicken stock (see page 370)

❧ PREPARATION

Bring 2 quarts water with 1/2 tablespoon salt to a boil in a medium-size pot over high heat. Plunge in the tomatoes and boil for 15 to 30 seconds, remove with a mesh skimmer, and cool under cold running water. Peel the tomatoes with a small knife. Cut a 1/4-inch cap from the top of the tomatoes. With a small spoon, carefully scoop out and discard the seeds and pulp, leaving the shell intact. Refrigerate the tomato shells with their caps on the side.

Return the same water used for the tomatoes to a boil, add the fennel, and cook until tender, about 10 minutes. Drain well and transfer to a blender or food processor. Purée and set aside.

Preheat broiler. Place the red and yellow peppers in a broiler pan skin side up. Broil until the skin turns black, about 8 to 10 minutes. Remove the peppers, cool under cold running water, and peel off the burnt skin. Dice the peppers into 1/4-inch pieces and set aside.

In a bowl, gently mix the crabmeat with 1/2 of the fennel purée, 1/2 of the sweet pepper dice, 1/2 of the Niçoise olives, all of the chives, 1-1/2 tablespoons of the olive oil, 1/2 of the chopped garlic, the chopped basil, lemon juice, salt, and pepper.

Salt and pepper each tomato shell and fill it with the crab mixture up to just above the rim. Cover with the cap and refrigerate until needed.

Mix the remaining fennel purée with the chicken stock and bring it to a boil in a pot over high heat. Pour into a blender, add the remaining chopped garlic, and blend. Add 3-1/2 tablespoons olive oil, one tablespoon at a time, and blend. Salt and pepper to taste and keep warm on the side.

Just before serving, drizzle the remaining 1/2 tablespoon olive oil over the tomatoes and warm them in the microwave for 2 minutes on high. (The tomatoes should not become too soft but the crab mixture should be hot.) If you do not have a microwave, cover the tomatoes with foil and warm them in a 375-degree oven for 10 minutes.

❧ PRESENTATION

Evenly divide the fennel sauce among 4 warm plates. Place one hot tomato on top of the sauce and sprinkle the remaining peppers and Niçoise olives all around. Decorate each tomato with a basil leaf.

SEA SCALLOPS WITH FRESH FENNEL AND CUMIN

Serves 4

The cumin and aniselike fennel that flavor the scallops in this winter dish give it a distinctive Middle Eastern character. Tender, sweet sea scallops—like those in this recipe—are best seared and left slightly undercooked, so that they retain as much of their natural juices as possible. To facilitate serving, cook the fennel and sauce up to 2 hours in advance, then reheat as needed; the scallops, however, should be cooked 5 minutes before serving.

1 medium sweet red pepper, split, cored, and seeded

2 quarts chicken stock (see page 370)

1 pound fennel bulbs, top and outer leaves trimmed, the bulbs quartered and each quarter cut into small wedges 1/2 inch thick (about 2 medium fennel bulbs)

3 tablespoons olive oil

Salt, freshly ground black pepper

1 teaspoon ground cumin

1 pound sea scallops, washed under cold running water to remove any sand, patted dry, and cut horizontally into 2 round halves (Refrigerate in a bowl covered with plastic wrap until needed.)

1 tablespoon all-purpose flour

2 tablespoons Spanish sherry vinegar

✤ PREPARATION

Preheat broiler. To remove the skin of the red pepper, place it skin side up in a broiler pan and broil until the skin turns black. Remove from heat, let cool, and peel off the skin under cold running water. Cut the red pepper into very thin strips and set aside.

Bring the chicken stock to a boil in a pot over medium heat. Add the fennel wedges and boil for 12 minutes, or until tender. Strain the stock with a Chinese strainer (a cone-shaped, fine-mesh strainer) into a bowl and set the cooked fennel wedges aside on a plate.

Pour 2 cups of the strained stock back into the pot (discard the rest), reduce it to 1/4 cup over medium heat, and set aside.

Heat 1 tablespoon of the olive oil in a nonstick pan over high heat. Add the cooked fennel wedges and sauté for 3 to 5 minutes or until lightly colored. Season with salt, pepper, and 1/2 teaspoon of the cumin powder, stir well, remove from heat, and keep warm on the side.

In the same very hot pan, add 1 tablespoon of the olive oil. Salt and pepper the scallops on both sides and dust them with flour and the remaining 1/2 teaspoon cumin. Quickly sear them, approximately 2 minutes on each side, over high heat, remove from heat, and keep warm on the side.

Add the sherry vinegar to the pan. Reduce by half over medium heat then add the reduced fennel bouillon. Whip in the remaining tablespoon of olive oil, remove from heat, strain, and set aside.

PRESENTATION

On a plate, arrange the fennel wedges in a circle, tips facing out like the petals of a flower. Place the scallops over the center and decorate with the red pepper strips. Spoon the sauce over all.

MARYLAND CRAB AND CARROT GRATIN WITH CORIANDER

Serves 4

This savory, easy-to-prepare gratin consists of a layer of sweet carrot purée covered with briny crab sautéed in lemon and topped with a glazed coriander cream. Assemble in a gratin dish up to 1 hour in advance, reheat slowly in the oven, and glaze just before serving.

3 tablespoons sweet butter

1/2 cup onions, peeled and chopped

8 coriander seeds, crushed

1 pound young spring carrots, peeled and sliced 1/4 inch thick

1 cup chicken stock (see page 370)

Salt, freshly ground black pepper

2 tablespoons chives, minced

2 sprigs coriander: 1 sprig leaves only, chopped, 1 sprig whole for garnish

1 pound Maryland crabmeat (jumbo lump quality)

Juice of 1/2 lemon

1/2 cup heavy cream, whipped

1 egg yolk

✿ PREPARATION

Melt 1 tablespoon of the butter in a medium-size pot over medium heat. Add the onions and coriander seeds and cook for 3 minutes while stirring. Add the carrots and sweat for another 5 minutes. Add the chicken stock, salt and pepper to taste, and bring to a boil. Lower heat to a simmer, cover with a lid, and cook for 30 minutes or until the carrots are tender when pierced with a knife. Add more chicken stock if needed to keep the carrots moist. Drain and transfer to a blender or food processor. Add 1 tablespoon of the butter, 1 tablespoon of the chives, 1/2 of the chopped coriander leaves, salt and pepper to taste, and purée until smooth. Spread the carrot purée evenly into a shallow gratin dish, about 8 inches round or square by 2 inches high, and keep warm on the side.

Melt the remaining tablespoon of butter in a pan over high heat. Add the crabmeat and the remaining tablespoon of chives and toss well for 2 minutes. Pour the lemon juice over, mix well, and remove from heat. Spoon the crabmeat evenly over the carrot purée. Warm the gratin dish in a 250-degree oven for 10 to 15 minutes.

Mix the whipped cream, egg yolk, and remaining chopped coriander leaves together in a bowl. Salt and pepper to taste.

Preheat broiler. When ready to serve, spread the coriander cream over the crab and broil for 1 minute until lightly colored.

✿ PRESENTATION

Garnish the center of the gratin with the sprig of coriander and serve immediately.

FISH

Spring   Summer   Autumn   Winter
❊   ⚜   🍃   ✤

Crisp Paupiette of Sea Bass in a Barolo Sauce ✤ page 164

Tuna Steak with Watercress and Yellow Wax Beans ⚜ page 166

Cold Brook Trout with Mint and Lemon ❊ page 167

Potato and Salted Cod Galettes with Caviar and Chives 🍃 page 169

Steamed Halibut with Cabbage and Rosemary ✤ page 171

Broiled Mackerel with Radicchio di Treviso
        and Sweet Peppers 🍃 page 173

Curried Grouper with Summer Vegetables ⚜ page 175

Peppered Tuna and Shoestring Potatoes with a Shallot Jus 🍃 page 177

Steamed Cod on a Beet and Mâche Salad ✤ page 179

Whole Red Snapper Baked with Dill and
        Cracked Peppercorns ❊ page 181

Black Sea Bass in a Lemon Broth with Asparagus ❊ page 183

Broiled Pompano with Condiments and Olive Oil ✤ page 185

Salmon in a Polenta Crust with Red Cabbage 🍃 page 186

Skate and Tomatoes in a Pistou Broth ⚜ page 188

Roasted Monkfish Biriatou 🍃 page 189

Lobster and Pompano Sottha Khunn ⚜ page 190

Black Sea Bass with an Herb Crust and Salsify ✤ page 192

Grouper with Fingerling Potatoes and Morels ⚜ page 194

Flounder Diable with Spinach and Salsify ✤ page 196

opposite page: Crisp Paupiette of Sea Bass in a Barolo Sauce

CRISP PAUPIETTE OF SEA BASS IN A BAROLO SAUCE

Serves 4

Paul Bocuse's *Rouget en Écailles de Pomme de Terre* inspired this exquisite dish of tender fish fillets wrapped in a crisp crust of sliced potatoes. But since those beautifully briny tiny red mullets from the Mediterranean are rarely available in this country, I suggest sea bass, which makes a superb substitute. For the sauce, I chose Barolo wine, one of the best wines of Piemonte (northwestern Italy), in honor of Sirio Maccioni, the owner of Le Cirque restaurant. I was duly flattered when Chef Bocuse sent the chefs from his restaurant at Epcot Center in Florida to Le Cirque to learn my adaptation of his recipe. You can assemble this dish up to 1 hour ahead of time and keep it refrigerated before cooking and serving it.

For the Paupiette of Sea Bass:

4 sea bass fillets, 7 ounces each, skinless, bones set aside for the sauce

Salt, freshly ground black pepper

3 sprigs fresh thyme: 1 sprig leaves only, chopped, and 2 sprigs halved for garnish

2 very large baking potatoes, peeled

3 tablespoons sweet butter

For the Leeks:

2 tablespoons sweet butter

2 leeks, white part only, thinly sliced

Salt, freshly ground black pepper

For the Sauce:

1 tablespoon oil, for cooking

1/2 cup shallots, peeled and chopped

1/2 cup white mushrooms, caps only, sliced

1/2 sprig fresh thyme

1 cup chicken stock (see page 370)

1 bottle (750 ml) of Barolo wine or other good red cooking wine

1 tablespoon heavy cream

1/2 cup sweet butter

Pinch of sugar

Salt, freshly ground black pepper

1 tablespoon chives, minced

❖ PREPARATION

For the Paupiette of Sea Bass:

Make each fillet as rectangular as possible (about 5 inches by 2 inches) by trimming off uneven edges with a sharp knife. Salt and pepper the fillets and sprinkle them with 1 teaspoon of the chopped thyme. Using a knife, shape each potato lengthwise by cutting off the rounded outer flesh to form 4 rectangular slices (do not cut off the tips of the potatoes). Cut each potato lengthwise into very thin, long slices with a vegetable slicer or mandoline. Each potato should yield about 16 slices (8 slices are needed to wrap 1 fish fillet). Do not rinse the potato slices as their starch will help the wrapped slices stick together. Toss the potato slices in 1 tablespoon of the butter, melted, and a pinch of salt.

Place a 10-inch-square piece of parchment paper on the counter. Choose 8 potato slices of approximately the same length. Place a fillet of fish horizontally at the top of the parchment paper so you can match the length of the potato wrap to the length of the fish. Place the first slice of potato perpendicular to the fish starting on the left side. Place a second slice overlapping the first one about 3/8 inch from the left edge. Continue overlapping the potato slices until you have covered an area equal to the length of the fillet of fish. Center the fish horizontally in the middle of the potato wrap and fold the edges of the potatoes over the fish to enclose it entirely. Repeat the same process for the remaining fillets and refrigerate.

For the Leeks:
Melt the butter in a pan over medium heat. Add the leeks and sweat until soft, about 4 minutes. Salt and pepper to taste. Keep warm on the side.

For the Sauce:
Heat the oil in a pot over high heat. Add the reserved sea bass bones, the shallots, mushrooms, and thyme sprig and roast for 8 to 10 minutes while stirring often. Add the chicken stock, bring to a boil, and cook until completely reduced. Add the Barolo wine, bring to a boil, and reduce by half. Remove and discard the fish bones with a mesh skimmer. Reduce the sauce to 2 tablespoons. Add the heavy cream, stir, and bring to a boil over low heat. Whip in the butter, sugar, and salt and pepper to taste. Strain the sauce with a fine mesh strainer and keep warm on the side. (If the sauce is too thick add a little water to thin it.)

To cook the paupiette of sea bass, preheat oven to 425 degrees. Melt the remaining 2 tablepoons butter in a large nonstick pan over high heat. Add the paupiettes of sea bass and sauté until golden brown, about 3 to 5 minutes on each side. If the fish is very thick, finish cooking in the oven for 4 to 5 minutes.

❖ PRESENTATION

Place a bed of leeks in the middle of 4 warm plates and ladle the sauce around the leeks (about 2 tablespoons per plate). Place a paupiette of sea bass on top of the leeks and garnish with 1/2 sprig of thyme. Sprinkle the plate with minced chives.

TUNA STEAK WITH WATERCRESS AND YELLOW WAX BEANS

Serves 4

The delicately sweet-sharp edge provided by the balsamic-dressed watercress, yellow wax beans, and shallots enhances the seared taste of the tuna in this warm-weather entrée. The ingredients for this dish can be prepared up to 2 hours in advance, the tuna and vegetables cooked 8 to 10 minutes before serving.

1 tablespoon tarragon, leaves only, chopped

3 tablespoons olive oil

Salt, freshly ground black pepper

2 center-cut tuna steaks (sushi quality), 8 ounces each, 1 inch thick

1/2 tablespoon balsamic vinegar

1 teaspoon red wine vinegar

1 tablespoon shallots, peeled and chopped

3/4 pound yellow wax beans, trimmed and cut into 2-inch pieces

8 medium shiitake mushrooms, stems discarded, caps finely sliced

4 bunches watercress, stems cut off just below the leaves and discarded, leaves refrigerated

❧ PREPARATION

Combine 1/2 tablespoon tarragon, 1/2 tablespoon olive oil, salt, and pepper in a small cup. Place the tuna steaks on a plate and brush both sides with the oil mixture. Cover with plastic wrap and marinate in the refrigerator for 5 to 10 minutes.

Prepare the dressing by mixing the vinegars, the shallots, the remaining 1/2 tablespoon tarragon, 2 tablespoons olive oil, salt, and pepper in a small cup. Set aside.

Bring 2 quarts water with 1/2 tablespoon salt to a boil in a pot over high heat. Add the beans and boil until tender, about 8 minutes. Drain and keep warm on the side.

Heat the remaining 1/2 tablespoon olive oil in a nonstick pan over high heat. Add the marinated tuna steaks and cook for 4 to 6 minutes on each side (4 minutes for rare). Remove the tuna from the pan and cut each steak into 4 slices 1 inch thick.

Add the sliced shiitakes, salt, and pepper to the pan over high heat and cook for 3 to 4 minutes. Remove from heat and set aside.

Mix the warm beans with 1/2 of the dressing. Warm the remaining dressing.

❧ PRESENTATION

Place the warm beans in the center of each plate with a bunch of watercress in the middle and 2 slices of tuna on each side. Sprinkle the remaining warm dressing over the watercress. Add the mushrooms on top. Serve warm.

COLD BROOK TROUT WITH MINT AND LEMON

Serves 4

Sweet, succulent, tender trout poached in a light, lemon-mint court bouillon, cooled and served with
a refreshing tabbouleh is perfect for a late spring or early summer alfresco lunch or dinner. The preparation—
all of which can be completed up to 6 hours before serving—is simplicity itself: poaching the fish,
preparing the dressing, steaming the couscous, and assembling the platter.

For the Poached Trout:

1 tablespoon salt

1 lemon, sliced

*10 to 12 sprigs fresh mint, 4 sprigs reserved
for garnish*

1 teaspoon freshly ground black pepper

1/2 tablespoon coriander seeds

1 small onion, peeled and sliced

1 clove

*4 brook trout, 14 ounces each, skinless, boneless,
and fins cut off (ask your fishmonger to debone
the trout for you or poach it with the bones and
carefully remove the trout fillet from the bone)*

Salt, freshly ground black pepper

For the Dressing:

Juice of 2 lemons

5 tablespoons olive oil

2 tablespoons chopped chives

1/2 tablespoon chopped mint leaves

Salt, freshly ground black pepper

For the Tomato and Cucumber Salad:

*1 European hothouse cucumber, peeled, split
lengthwise, seeded with a small spoon, in
1/4-inch dice*

*2 large ripe tomatoes, peeled, seeded, in 1/4-inch
dice*

1 lemon, peeled, seeded, and diced

For the Couscous:

1/2 cup instant couscous

Grated zest of 2 lemons

❀ PREPARATION

For the Poached Trout:

In a deep pan or fish poacher, combine 2 quarts water with the salt, the sliced lemon, 6
to 8 sprigs mint, the black pepper, coriander, onion, and clove and bring to a boil. Add
the trout and simmer gently for 3 minutes. Remove the pan from the heat and let the
trout poach in the broth. When cool, carefully transfer the poached trout to a tray and
discard the broth. Slice the trout gently from head to tail and cover it with plastic wrap
and refrigerate until needed.

For the Dressing:
Combine the lemon juice, olive oil, chives, chopped mint, and salt and pepper to taste in a cup and set aside.

For the Tomato and Cucumber Salad:
Sprinkle a little salt on the diced cucumber and tomatoes and set them in a colander for 20 minutes to drain. Mix the drained tomatoes and cucumber with 3 tablespoons of dressing and the diced lemon.

For the Couscous:
Bring 1 cup water to a boil and add the instant couscous. Mix, cover, and let the couscous absorb the water for 5 minutes. In a small pot over medium heat, boil the grated lemon zest for 8 minutes in 1 quart water. Strain out the zest and mix it into the couscous.

Mix 2 tablespoons of dressing with the couscous. Brush a small bowl (just large enough to hold all of the couscous) with olive oil and transfer the couscous to the bowl. Press to make sure the couscous is firmly packed in the bowl.

❋ PRESENTATION

Unmold the couscous in the center of a large oval platter. Place 2 trout on each side. Spoon the tomato and cucumber salad over the trout. Decorate with mint leaves. Serve extra dressing on the side.

BUYING BROOK TROUT: Brook trout is the best of the freshwater trout family. It is better to buy the fish whole, as boneless trout lose their freshness rapidly. Look for trout weighing 10 to 14 ounces each. They should be firm to the touch, slightly slimy, and with bright red gills.

POTATO AND SALTED COD GALETTES WITH CAVIAR AND CHIVES

Serves 4

These crisp, golden potato and cod patties with their chive-caviar cream sauce are an elegant version
of the renowned *brandade de morue*. The caviar is optional, but the best caviar for this dish is Russian ossetra
or American sturgeon. It is sweet with a touch of brininess. This recipe requires some assembly,
but is easy to accomplish and can be done a full day in advance. The creamy chive sauce can be made while
sautéeing the cod *galettes* 10 to 15 minutes before serving.

For the Potato Mixture:

2 large baking potatoes, about 3/4 pounds each

2-1/2 tablespoons sweet butter

1/2 cup onions, peeled and finely chopped

1 tablespoon minced chives

Salt, freshly ground black pepper

For the Codfish Mixture:

1 pound salted cod fillets (the thick part of
the fillet)

2 cups milk

1 sprig fresh thyme

2 cloves garlic, peeled

1 bay leaf

1/2 cup heavy cream

1 tablespoon minced chives

Salt, freshly ground black pepper

For the Galettes:

1/2 cup all-purpose flour (Wondra if possible)

1 tablespoon sweet butter

2 to 3 ounces ossetra or American sturgeon
caviar (optional)

For the Creamy Chive Sauce:

1/2 cup heavy cream

1 tablespoon minced chives

Salt, freshly ground black pepper

PREPARATION

To desalt the fish, place the cod in a very large bowl, cover with cold water, and refrigerate overnight. Three hours prior to cooking, drain the water and run cold water gently over the fish for a final rinse.

For the Potato Mixture:
Preheat oven to 375 degrees. Wrap the potatoes in aluminum foil and bake until done, about 45 minutes. Remove from oven and set aside.

Melt 1/2 tablespoon of the butter in a pan over medium heat. Add the onions and sweat until soft and translucent, about 5 minutes, and set aside.

Split the potatoes, place the flesh in a blender or food processor (discard the skin and foil), and purée. Transfer to a bowl and add the remaining 2 tablespoons butter, the sweated onions, chives, and salt and pepper to taste. Mix well and set aside.

For the Codfish Mixture:

Drain the fillets of cod. Bring the milk with the thyme, garlic, bay leaf, and a pinch of pepper to a boil in a medium pot over medium heat and boil for 3 minutes. Plunge in the fillets of cod and simmer for 6 to 8 minutes. Drain the fillets and discard the milk and spices. Break the warm cod into small flakes (discard any bones) with a fork and set aside.

Bring the cream to a boil in a pot over medium heat and boil for 5 minutes or until thickened. Add the chives, salt and pepper to taste, and the cod flakes. Set aside.

For the Galettes:

Line an 8-inch round or square pan with parchment paper. Spread 1/2 of the potato mixture evenly on the bottom of the lined pan. Evenly cover with the creamy cod mixture and then with the rest of the potato mixture. Cool in the freezer for 1 hour. Unmold the potato and cod cake on a cutting board. With a 4-inch-round cookie cutter, cut out 4 even, round *galettes*. Sprinkle flour on both sides.

Melt 1/2 tablespoon of the butter in a large nonstick pan over medium heat. Add the 4 cod *galettes*. Lightly brown and crisp for about 5 to 7 minutes. Turn them over, add the remaining 1/2 tablespoon butter, and cook for another 5 to 7 minutes, until golden and crispy (lower heat if necessary).

For the Creamy Chive Sauce:

Bring the heavy cream to a boil in a small pot and boil for 3 to 4 minutes. Add the chives and salt and pepper to taste, mix well, and keep warm on the side.

PRESENTATION

Pour 1 tablespoon of the creamy chive sauce in the middle of 4 warm plates. Place a *galette* on top and spoon equal measures of the caviar, if using, on top of each *galette*. Serve the remaining sauce on the side.

STEAMED HALIBUT WITH CABBAGE AND ROSEMARY

Serves 4

This entrée is remarkable for its simplicity and full flavor. Sweet savoy cabbage provides the bedding
for the halibut fillets steamed in a heady infusion of rosemary. Halibut is recommended for this
recipe, although other flat fish such as cod or salmon could also be used. The ingredients can be prepared up
to 2 hours in advance, but steam the fish and vegetables 10 minutes before serving.

*1 small head savoy cabbage,
halved lengthwise, thick stem removed and
discarded, leaves broken apart*

*2 sprigs rosemary: 1 sprig whole,
1 sprig leaves only, chopped*

1 lemon, quartered

1 teaspoon pink peppercorns, coarsely crushed

Salt, freshly ground black pepper

4 fillets of halibut, 7 ounces each, 3/4 inch thick

2 tablespoons olive oil

✤ PREPARATION

Bring 4 quarts water with 1 tablespoon salt to a boil in a pot over high heat. Add the cabbage leaves and boil for 6 to 8 minutes. Drain and cool the cabbage leaves in a colander under cold running water. Drain again and set aside.

Fill a fish steamer or a large pot into which a bamboo steamer will fit with 1 quart water. Add 1 teaspoon salt, the rosemary sprig, and 1/2 lemon and bring to a boil.

Place the cabbage leaves in the center of the steamer tray, sprinkle with 1/2 of the chopped rosemary, 1/2 of the crushed pink peppercorns, and a pinch each of salt and pepper. Season each fish fillet on both sides with salt, pepper, and the rest of the chopped rosemary and crushed pink peppercorns. Place the fish fillets over the cabbage and steam over high heat for 5 to 7 minutes or until done. Remove immediately from heat when done.

✤ PRESENTATION

Place the fillets of halibut in the center of a serving dish or on individual plates with the cabbage spread all around. Squeeze 1/2 lemon over the fillets and drizzle with the olive oil.

BROILED MACKEREL WITH RADICCHIO DI TREVISO AND SWEET PEPPERS

Serves 4

Rich, high-fat fish always benefit from a hint of bitterness. Consequently, mackerel is paired with sautéed radicchio di Treviso and arugula in this dish. The final garnish of deep-fried basil leaves provides a welcome crisp note. The ingredients can be prepared 1 hour in advance and the fish broiled 5 to 7 minutes before serving.

For the Mackerel:

2 small sweet peppers (one red, one yellow), quartered lengthwise, seeded, and cored

1/4 cup olive oil

2 tablespoons chopped garlic

1 pound radicchio di Treviso (or American radicchio), cut into 1-inch wedges, washed and drained

Salt, freshly ground black pepper

1/2 cup oil, for frying

2 bunches basil, leaves only

4 mackerels, 12 to 14 ounces each, filleted (each fillet should be about 3 ounces)

1/2 pound arugula, leaves only, stems discarded

Coarse sea salt

For the Dressing:

Juice of 2 lemons and grated zest of 1/2 lemon

1/4 cup tomatoes, split, seeded, in 1/4-inch dice

2 tablespoons chives, chopped

1 teaspoon crushed pink peppercorns

1 tablespoon small black olives (Niçoise), pitted and chopped

5 tablespoons olive oil

Salt, freshly ground black pepper

PREPARATION

For the Mackerel:

Preheat broiler. Place the red and yellow pepper quarters skin side up on a broiling pan. Brush the skin with a touch of oil and broil until the skin turns black, about 5 minutes. Remove from heat, let cool, and peel the skin off under cold running water. Halve each pepper quarter widthwise and set aside.

Heat 2 tablespoons of the olive oil in a large skillet over high heat. Add the chopped garlic and cook until golden while stirring with a wooden spoon to avoid burning. Add the radicchio, and salt and pepper to taste, stir well, cover with a lid, and cook for 3 minutes. Turn the radicchio over, add the sweet pepper, and cook for another 4 to 5 minutes. Remove and keep warm on the side.

Heat the frying oil to 325 degrees in a deep-fat fryer. Plunge the basil leaves in the hot oil, a few at a time, and turn them over while frying. Remove the basil leaves with a mesh skimmer after 10 seconds when almost translucent and drain them on a paper towel. Set aside.

For the Dressing:
Combine the lemon juice, lemon zest, tomatoes, chives, pink peppercorns, Niçoise olives, olive oil, and salt and pepper to taste in a small pot. Warm the dressing at very low heat for 2 to 3 minutes.

Brush the mackerel fillets with the remaining 2 tablespoons olive oil and season them with salt and pepper. Place the fillets on a broiling pan, skin side up. Broil them for 3 to 5 minutes, depending on the thickness of the fillets. Try to keep the mackerel slightly undercooked.

PRESENTATION

Arrange the arugula leaves, one next to the other like the petals of a flower, on the bottom of a round or oval plate. Place the warm radicchio and sweet pepper in the center with the broiled mackerel fillets on top. Spoon the lemon dressing over the fish and drizzle some over the arugula. Garnish the mackerel with the crispy basil leaves. Sprinkle a little coarse sea salt over the fish.

CURRIED GROUPER WITH SUMMER VEGETABLES

Serves 4

This wonderfully fragrant seared grouper, enhanced by a curried vegetable cream sauce and zucchini–
sweet pea garnish, supplies the perfect balance of hot and cool sensations to satisfy summer tastes.
Red snapper or black sea bass can be substituted for the grouper and basmati or white rice makes a nice
accompaniment. The sauce and vegetable garnish can be prepared up to 3 hours in advance,
then cooked with the fish 10 minutes before serving.

*4 fillets of grouper, 7 ounces each
(bones reserved for the sauce)*

1/4 cup shallots, peeled and chopped

1 sprig fresh thyme

1 small bay leaf

1 tablespoon sweet butter

3/4 cup carrots, peeled and sliced 1/4 inch thick

8 pearl onions, peeled and halved

*1/2 cup celery, trimmed, peeled, and cut
into 1/2-inch pieces*

1 clove garlic, peeled and finely chopped

*3/4 cup fresh fennel, greens and outer leaves
trimmed, the rest cut into 1/2-inch cubes*

1/2 cup tiny button mushrooms

*1 Golden Delicious apple, peeled and cored,
in 1/2-inch dice*

*1 tablespoon plus 1 pinch Madras
curry powder*

Pinch of saffron powder

Pinch of cayenne pepper

1/4 cup dry white wine

2 tablespoons port

1-1/2 cups heavy cream

2 teaspoons salt

1/2 cup zucchini, in 1/4-inch dice

*1/2 cup freshly shelled peas
(about 1 pound in the pod)*

1/2 tablespoon oil, for cooking

1 small bunch fresh coriander, leaves only

Salt, freshly ground black pepper

❧ PREPARATION

Bring 1 cup water with the reserved fish bones, shallots, thyme, and bay leaf to a boil in
a pot over high heat. Lower heat and simmer for 20 minutes. Skim the surface from
time to time while cooking. Strain the fish broth into a bowl, discard the solids, and
return the broth to the pot. Reduce to 1/4 cup over medium heat and set aside.

Melt the butter in a large pot over medium heat. Add the carrots, pearl onions, celery,
garlic, fennel, mushrooms, apple, 1 tablespoon of the curry powder, saffron, and
cayenne pepper, mix well, and sweat for 3 to 4 minutes (taking care not to brown the
vegetables). Season with 1 teaspoon salt. Pour in the white wine and the port, bring to a

boil, and stir well until totally evaporated. Add the fish broth, return to a boil, and reduce again until totally evaporated, stirring constantly. Add the heavy cream, stir well, and simmer for 20 minutes, making sure it does not boil. Remove from heat and taste for seasoning.

While the sauce is cooking, bring 1 quart water with 1 teaspoon salt to a boil in a pot over high heat. Plunge in the zucchini and peas and blanch for 2 minutes. Drain and keep warm on the side.

Heat the oil in a nonstick skillet over medium heat. Season the fish with salt, pepper, and a pinch of the curry powder. Sear the fish until the skin is crisp and has a light color, about 4 minutes. Turn the fish over and cook for another 3 minutes (or more if the fillets are very thick).

❧ PRESENTATION

Place the fish on the bottom of a large platter or plate. Spoon the creamy curry sauce with the vegetables over it. Sprinkle the peas and zucchini on top. Garnish with coriander leaves.

PEPPERED TUNA AND SHOESTRING POTATOES WITH A SHALLOT JUS

Serves 4

In this elegant version of steak/*pommes frites*, peppered tuna—used instead of beef—nests on a bed
of spinach flavored with a tart shallot jus and is topped with a stack of matchstick potatoes. The ingredients
for this dish can be prepared up to 2 hours in advance, but they will require last-minute cooking
10 minutes before serving.

*1 pound fresh spinach, stems discarded,
washed twice and drained*

2-1/2 tablespoons sweet butter

Salt, freshly ground black pepper

1 clove garlic, peeled and chopped

4 cups plus one tablespoon oil, for frying

*1 pound baking potatoes, peeled and
reserved in a bowl of cold water*

*Two 14-ounce tuna steaks (sushi quality),
1-1/2 inch thick (make sure the tuna you buy
is of a dark burgundy color with a
fresh translucent look; the fish should be firm
and not have a fishy smell)*

1/2 tablespoon crushed black peppercorns

1/2 cup shallots, peeled and sliced

2 tablespoons Spanish sherry vinegar

1/2 cup chicken jus (see page 371)

PREPARATION

Bring 2 quarts water with 1 tablespoon salt to a boil in a pot over high heat. Plunge in
the spinach leaves and boil for 3 minutes. Drain and cool the spinach under cold running water. Drain again and set aside.

Melt 1/2 tablespoon of the butter in a pan over high heat until light brown. Add the
spinach, and salt and pepper to taste and stir well. Add the garlic, toss for 2 minutes,
and keep warm on the side.

Heat the oil in a deep-fat fryer or deep skillet to 360 degrees.

Drain the peeled potatoes, cut each one lengthwise to 1/8-inch thickness, using a mandoline, food processor, or knife to obtain matchstick-size strips the length of the potato.
Reserve in cold water until ready to fry. Drain the matchstick potatoes and pat dry in a
towel. Carefully plunge them into the fryer one handful at a time. Stir until light gold-
en brown, about 3 minutes, remove with a mesh skimmer, drain on paper towels, and
sprinkle with a pinch of salt. Keep warm on the side.

Preheat oven to 250 degrees. Season the tuna steaks with salt and crushed black peppercorns. Heat 1 tablespoon oil in a skillet over high heat and sear the tuna for 2 to 5
minutes on each side. (The tuna will be rare if cooked for 2 minutes, medium if cooked
for 4 to 5 minutes.) Remove and keep warm in the oven for 3 to 5 minutes.

Melt 1 tablespoon of the butter in a pan over medium heat. Add the shallots and sweat for 3 to 4 minutes. Add the vinegar and reduce by half. Add the chicken jus and reduce by half. Stir in the remaining tablespoon of butter, salt and pepper to taste, and keep warm on the side.

PRESENTATION

Arrange a bed of spinach on the bottom of a warm platter or plate. Cut each tuna steak into 4 thick slices and place them over the spinach in a circle. Spoon the shallot sauce over the tuna and arrange the crispy matchstick potatoes in the middle in a dome, like a haystack.

STEAMED COD ON A BEET AND MÂCHE SALAD

Serves 4

The beautifully plump, firm-fleshed cod fillets featured in this dish pair perfectly with beet and mâche salad and a crisp, fried beet-chip garnish. A fine midwinter preparation when fresh cod, root vegetables, and mâche are readily available, it is also easy to prepare and can be made and then refrigerated up to 3 hours before serving, except for the beet chips. Steam the fish 8 minutes before serving and season the salad at the last minute.

8 beets (golf-ball size or slightly larger), greens discarded

1/2 tablespoon salt

1 tablespoon cornstarch

1/2 cup peanut oil

4 fresh cod fillets, 7 ounces each, boneless and skinless

Salt, freshly ground black pepper

3 tablespoons shallots, peeled and minced

2 sprigs of fresh tarragon, 1 sprig cut in half and 1 sprig leaves only, finely chopped

2 tablespoons red wine vinegar

2 tablespoons walnut oil

1/4 pound mâche, roots discarded

✤ PREPARATION

(Wear disposable gloves when handling beets to avoid unsightly beet stains.) Set 1 raw beet aside and boil the remaining ones in 2 quarts water with 1/2 tablespoon salt for 45 minutes to 1 hour (or until tender when pierced with a knife). Drain, let cool, and peel the beets by rubbing them with a paper towel (the skin should come off easily). Cover your cutting board with parchment or brown paper to avoid beet juice stains. Cut the 7 beets in 1/4-inch-thick sticks and set aside in a bowl.

Peel the remaining beet with a peeler and slice it paper thin with a vegetable slicer or mandoline. Dust the beet slices with cornstarch, then shake each slice to remove any excess. Warm 6 tablespoons of the peanut oil to 325 degrees. Plunge in the beet slices and fry them until crisp (do not color). Remove and drain the beet chips on a paper towels. Sprinkle them with a pinch of salt.

Add water to a pot into which a bamboo steamer or expandable steamer basket will fit and bring to a boil. Salt and pepper the cod on both sides. Place 1 tablespoon of the chopped shallots and 1/2 sprig tarragon on the bottom of the bamboo steamer or steamer basket. Place the fish over the shallots and tarragon and cover the fish with 1 tablespoon of the chopped shallots and another 1/2 sprig tarragon. Just before serving, place the steamer over the boiling water, cover, and steam for 5 to 8 minutes, depending on the thickness of the fish.

For the dressing, mix the vinegar with the remaining tablespoon shallots, the chopped tarragon, walnut oil, the remaining 2 tablespoons peanut oil, and salt and pepper. Add 2 tablespoons of dressing to the beet sticks and 1 tablespoon to the mâche lettuce.

❖ Presentation

Arrange a bed of beet sticks on each of 4 individual serving plates. Cover with a steamed cod fillet (discard the tarragon sprigs). Decorate the fish and plate with the mâche leaves and sprinkle the fillets with the beet chips. Serve the remaining dressing on the side.

Whole Red Snapper Baked with Dill and Cracked Peppercorns

Serves 4 to 6

In this recipe, a whole red snapper is completely covered with dill, lemon slices, and a sprinkling of sea salt and cracked black peppercorns both to impart flavor to the fish and to protect it from burning as it roasts. It could be served at a buffet with a vegetable salad accompaniment. The ingredients in this recipe can be prepared 2 to 3 hours in advance; the fish will need 35 to 45 minutes of cooking before serving.

2 large tomatoes

2 sweet red peppers, stems removed, quartered lengthwise, cored, and seeded

1 whole red snapper, 4 to 5 pounds, cleaned, with 2-inch-long incisions in the skin at 1-inch intervals on both sides from head to tail

1/2 tablespoon crushed black peppercorns

1/2 tablespoon coarse sea salt

2 cloves garlic, peeled: 1 sliced, 1 chopped

1/2 pound fresh dill, roots discarded: 4 stems with leaves chopped, the rest whole

1/2 cup plus 2 tablespoons olive oil

4 lemons: 2 sliced into 6 slices and 2 for juice

6 to 8 scallions, peeled and sliced 2 inches thick

2 medium zucchini, ends trimmed, sliced 1/4 inch thick

2 medium yellow squash, ends trimmed, sliced 1/4 inch thick

Salt, freshly ground black pepper

❋ Preparation

Bring 1 quart water to a boil in a medium pot over high heat. Blanch the tomatoes for 30 seconds, drain, and cool under cold running water. Peel and discard the skin. Split horizontally and discard the seeds. Chop the tomato flesh into small cubes and set aside.

Preheat broiler. Place the red pepper quarters skin side up on a broiler pan and broil until the skin turns black. Remove from heat, let cool, and rub the skin off under cold running water. Set aside.

Preheat oven to 450 degrees. Season the fish with crushed pepper and coarse salt on the skin and in the stomach cavity. Place the sliced garlic and 1/4 of the whole dill in the stomach cavity. Brush an oven pan with 1 tablespoon of the olive oil. Place 6 slices of lemon on the bottom. Spread another 1/2 of the whole dill over the lemon slices. Place the fish in the pan over the bed of dill. Cover the fish with 6 slices of lemon and the remaining whole dill. Sprinkle with 2 tablespoons of the olive oil and bake for 35 to 45 minutes (allow 10 to 12 minutes cooking time for each pound of fish).

Heat 2 tablespoons olive oil in a large pan over high heat. Add the scallions, zucchini, yellow squash, roasted red pepper quarters, chopped garlic, salt, and pepper. Toss well and cook for 8 to 10 minutes. Keep warm on the side.

To prepare the dressing, combine the tomato, the lemon juice, the chopped dill, the remaining 5 tablespoons olive oil, salt, and pepper in a small pot. Warm the dressing over very low heat for 2 to 3 minutes just before serving.

❀ Presentation

Serve the vegetables on the side in a dish on a large platter, present the red snapper in the middle with the lemon and dill (just the way it was cooked). Serve the warm sauce on the side. Carve the fish at the table. Push away and discard dill and lemon slices as you are carving the fish.

Buying Red Snapper: When buying red snapper, look for a bright, pink-skinned fish with bright red eyes and firmly attached scales. If you want the fish filleted, make sure your fishmonger does not skin it. The skin helps the flesh to stay moist while cooking.

BLACK SEA BASS IN A LEMON BROTH WITH ASPARAGUS

Serves 4

Light and luscious is a good way to describe this simple dish of seared black bass topped with
spring asparagus and lettuce and served in a scant pool of lemon broth. The ingredients of this recipe can be
prepared 1 to 2 hours in advance and the fish cooked 6 to 8 minutes before serving.

12 jumbo asparagus, stems peeled

*1 medium sweet red pepper, split lengthwise,
cored and seeded*

2 tablespoons shallots, peeled and minced

1 sprig thyme

Pinch of pepper

*8 ounces sea bass bones (ask for them
when you buy the fillets)*

Grated zest and juice of 1 lemon

3 tablespoons olive oil

Salt, freshly ground black pepper

4 fillets of black sea bass, 5 ounces each, skin on

1 head Boston lettuce, cut into 1/4-inch strips

*1 ounce chervil, leaves only,
reserved in ice water*

❀ PREPARATION

Bring 1 gallon water with 1 tablespoon salt to a boil in a tall pot over high heat. Blanch
the asparagus for 5 minutes. Drain, chill in ice water, and drain again. Cut off and discard 2 inches of the tough end of each stem and slice each asparagus spear into 1-inch
pieces. Set aside.

Preheat broiler. Place the pepper skin side up on a broiler pan and broil until the skin
turns black, about 8 to 10 minutes. Remove from heat, let cool, and rub the skin off
under cold running water. Dice and set aside.

In a saucepan, bring 1-1/2 cups water, with the shallots, thyme, and pepper, to a boil
over medium heat. Add the sea bass bones and simmer for 20 minutes. Carefully strain
with a fine-mesh strainer set over a bowl. Discard the solids and return the bouillon to
the saucepan. Reduce the bouillon to 1/3 cup over medium heat and set aside.

Bring 1 cup water to a boil in a small pot over high heat. Add the lemon zest, boil for 3
minutes, and strain out the zest.

To the bouillon add the blanched lemon zest, diced red pepper, lemon juice, 2 tablespoons of the olive oil, and salt and pepper to taste. Whisk well and set aside.

Heat the remaining tablespoon olive oil in a nonstick pan over high heat. Salt and pepper each sea bass fillet on both sides, place in the pan skin side down, and cook for 3 minutes on each side. Remove the fish from the pan and keep warm on the side. In the same pan, toss the asparagus and the lettuce strips for 3 minutes over medium heat. Season to taste.

❋ PRESENTATION

Place the sea bass fillets on a warm serving dish and cover with the asparagus and lettuce. Pour the warm lemon bouillon dressing on top. Drain and pat the chervil leaves dry and sprinkle them over the dressing. Serve immediately.

BROILED POMPANO WITH CONDIMENTS AND OLIVE OIL

Serves 4

This robust dressing of vegetables and condiments provides just the right sharp note to enliven broiled pompano fillets. Pompano is so low in fat that it tends toward dryness and requires particular attention during cooking. It is best to either pan-fry it briefly or broil it on a single side. The dressing can be prepared up to 2 hours in advance, the pompano broiled 6 to 8 minutes before serving.

1 sweet red pepper, split lengthwise, cored and seeded

2 tablespoons plus 1 teaspoon olive oil

2 scallions, white part only, minced

1/2 cup celery heart, trimmed and minced (keep 12 leaves aside for garnish)

1/2 cup zucchini, in 1/4-inch dice

1 tablespoon tiny French capers, drained

1 tablespoon cornichons, coarsely chopped

1/2 tablespoon freshly grated horseradish

2 lemons: 1 for juice, 1 peeled, the sections removed without membranes

4 fillets of pompano, 5 to 6 ounces each, skinless and boneless

1 sprig fresh thyme, leaves only, chopped

Salt, freshly ground black pepper

✤ PREPARATION

Preheat broiler. Place the pepper halves skin side up on a broiler pan and broil until the skin turns black. Remove from heat, let cool, and rub the skin off under cold running water. Dice the pepper into 1/4-inch cubes and set aside.

Heat 1-1/2 teaspoons of the olive oil in a pan over medium heat. Add the scallions and celery heart and sweat for 5 minutes. Add the zucchini and cook for 3 more minutes. Add the diced red pepper, capers, cornichons, horseradish, 1 tablespoon of the olive oil, lemon juice and lemon sections and mix well for 1 minute. Remove from heat and keep warm on the side.

Preheat broiler. Brush a broiling pan with 1 teaspoon olive oil and add the fish fillets. Brush the fillets with the remaining 1-1/2 teaspoons olive oil and sprinkle with thyme, salt, and pepper. Broil for 5 to 6 minutes on one side only. (If the fillets are very thick, turn them over and broil for 3 more minutes to avoid dryness on the other side.)

✤ PRESENTATION

Place the pompano fillets on a warm serving dish. Spoon the warm pickle garnish over the top, and decorate each fillet with 3 celery leaves.

SALMON IN A POLENTA CRUST WITH RED CABBAGE

Serves 4

A rich coating of crusty polenta over the salmon is complemented by a sweet-and-sour bed of
red cabbage and a light chive sauce. To guarantee the crust's integrity during its panfry, carefully spread the
polenta on the salmon then refrigerate it for at least 30 minutes before cooking. The ingredients can
also be prepared 1 to 2 hours ahead and the fish cooked 10 minutes before serving.

2 pounds red cabbage, stem discarded, leaves
sliced into 1/4-inch thick strips

2 tablespoons sweet butter

1 cup onions, peeled and finely chopped

Thumb-size piece fresh gingerroot

2 sprigs fresh thyme

1 clove garlic, peeled and finely chopped

Salt, freshly ground black pepper

6 tablespoons Spanish sherry vinegar

1 cup chicken stock (see page 370)

1/4 cup instant polenta

4 slices fresh salmon fillet, 6 to 7 ounces each,
2 inches wide and 1 inch thick, skinless

2 tablespoons sesame seeds, toasted for
1 minute under the broiler

2 tablespoons chives, cut into 1/4-inch lengths

1/2 tablespoon oil, for cooking

PREPARATION

Bring 2 quarts water to a boil in a large pot over high heat. Blanch the red cabbage for 3
minutes. Drain the cabbage leaves and set aside.

Melt 1 tablespoon of the butter in the same pot over medium heat. Add the onion, gingerroot, and 1 sprig of thyme and sweat for 3 to 4 minutes. Add the garlic and sweat for
2 more minutes. Add the blanched red cabbage, salt, and pepper and mix well. Cover
with a lid and cook slowly over low heat for 20 to 30 minutes. Stir occasionally. Add 3
tablespoons of the sherry vinegar and cook slowly for another 10 to 15 minutes. The
cabbage should be very soft but not colored. If the cabbage cooks too fast or begins to
color, add a few tablespoons of chicken stock. When done, taste for seasoning and keep
warm on the side. Discard the ginger and thyme.

Bring 2/3 cup of the chicken stock with a pinch of salt and pepper to a boil in a small
saucepan over medium heat. Add the polenta, stir well, and cook over low heat for 5 to
7 minutes. Add 1/2 tablespoon of the butter, remove from heat, and let cool until thick
but not firmly set.

Salt and pepper each salmon steak on both sides. Spread a 1/4-inch-thick layer of polenta on the top side of each steak. Evenly sprinkle the sesame seeds onto the polenta and
press lightly to fix the seeds into the polenta. Refrigerate until ready to cook.

Reduce the remaining 3 tablespoons sherry vinegar with the remaining thyme sprig by half over medium-high heat. Add the remaining 1/3 cup chicken stock, reduce by half, and whisk in the remaining 1/2 tablespoon butter. Strain the sauce and discard the thyme. Add the chives to the sauce, set aside, and keep warm.

Heat the oil in a nonstick pan over medium-high heat. Carefully place the salmon, polenta side down, in the hot pan. Gently cook for 5 minutes or until light brown. Carefully turn it over and cook for another 2 to 3 minutes. (If the salmon steak is less than 1 inch thick, reduce the cooking time by 2 minutes.) To be perfectly cooked, the salmon steaks should be slightly rare in the middle and moist.

PRESENTATION

Arrange a bed of cabbage, the size of the salmon steak, on the center of 4 warmed serving plates. Place the salmon steaks, polenta side up, over the cabbage. Spoon the chive-vinegar sauce on the plates, around the beds of cabbage.

Skate and Tomatoes in a Pistou Broth

Serves 4

Sparkling Mediterranean flavors permeate this easy summer dish of snow-white skate with its
perky red and yellow cherry tomatoes and fava bean garnish. The ingredients for this recipe can be prepared
up to 2 hours ahead, but the skate should be cooked 8 to 10 minutes before serving.

1 bunch basil, leaves only, coarsely chopped,
12 smallest leaves reserved for garnish

3 tablespoons plus 1 teaspoon olive oil

1 teaspoon chopped garlic

1 cup shelled fresh fava beans
(1-1/2 pounds in the pod)

1 cup yellow cherry tomatoes

1 cup red cherry tomatoes

1 tablespoon shallots, peeled and chopped

4 fillets of skate, 6 ounces each, cleaned

3 tablespoons dry white vermouth (Noilly Prat)

Juice of 1 lemon

Salt, freshly ground black pepper

❧ Preparation

Combine the chopped basil, 2 tablespoons olive oil, and the garlic in a food processor or
blender. Purée until very smooth and set aside.

Bring 2 quarts of water to a boil in a large pot over high heat. Blanch the beans and
tomatoes in the boiling water for 20 seconds, drain, cool under cold running water, and
drain again. Peel the tomatoes and fresh fava beans (pop them out of their skins after
making a little incision at one end of the bean with your finger). Set aside.

Preheat oven to 400 degrees. Brush a roasting pan with 1 teaspoon olive oil. Add the
shallots, skate, vermouth, tomatoes, beans, the remaining tablespoon olive oil, lemon
juice, salt, and pepper. Cover with aluminum foil and roast for 6 to 7 minutes or until
done.

❧ Presentation

Spoon 1/2 tablespoon of the blended basil oil on the bottom of a warm serving platter.
Place the skate fillets on the platter and the vegetables over the fish. Spoon a few tablespoons of cooking broth from the roasting pan over the fish and vegetables and sprinkle
with the rest of the basil oil. Garnish with the reserved basil leaves.

ROASTED MONKFISH BIRIATOU

Serves 4

Biriatou, a small French town in the heart of the Basque region, inspired this recipe.
Its colorful sweet peppers, garlic, and tomatoes—the basis of Basquaise *piperades*—are combined here with
prosciutto to create a delightfully sweet-salty garnish that harmonizes well with the roasted monkfish.
This fish is perfect for children and adults who are afraid of fish bones. When you roast a monkfish whole, the
only bone to remove is the center bone since there are no bones in the flesh itself. The vegetables can
be prepared up to 3 hours in advance, but the fish should be roasted 20 minutes before serving.
Steamed basmati rice is a suggested accompaniment for this dish.

*1 whole monkfish, about 3 pounds, tail,
skin, and membranes discarded*

Salt, freshly ground black pepper

Flour, for dredging

1/4 cup olive oil

2 cups onions, peeled and sliced 1/4 inch thick

*3 medium sweet peppers (1 green, 1 red,
1 yellow), split, seeded, cored, and thinly sliced*

5 cloves garlic, peeled and finely sliced

*1 jalapeño pepper, split, seeded, and chopped
(protect your hands by wearing
disposable gloves when handling jalapeños)*

2 bay leaves

2 sprigs fresh thyme

*3 ripe tomatoes or 6 plum tomatoes, peeled,
split, cored, seeded, and cut into chunks*

1/2 cup tomato juice

2 slices prosciutto, cut into thin strips

PREPARATION

Salt and pepper the fish and dredge it in the flour. Shake off any excess flour.

Heat the olive oil on top of the stove in a large oval or square roasting pan over high heat. Sauté the fish on both sides until lightly browned, about 3 to 4 minutes. Add the onions, sweet peppers, garlic, jalapeño pepper, bay leaves, and thyme around and under the fish. Gently stir with a spoon while sweating the vegetables until soft, about 5 to 7 minutes. Add the tomatoes, salt, and pepper. Mix well and reduce heat to medium. Turn the fish often while cooking for about 15 more minutes. Remove the fish and keep it warm on the side. Add the tomato juice to the vegetables and reduce liquid until slightly thickened, about 10 to 15 minutes.

PRESENTATION

Place the whole roasted monkfish in the center of a warm oval platter. Place the vegetables over and around the fish. Sprinkle the prosciutto over the top. Carve the fish at the table.

LOBSTER AND POMPANO SOTTHA KHUNN

Serves 4

Sottha Khunn was my right-hand man at Le Cirque and has been my friend for more than eight years. Originally from Cambodia, he has trained in France's greatest restaurants. In this recipe you can substitute large shrimp or prawns for the lobster. Keep in mind that shrimp and prawns need 3 to 4 minutes less cooking time than lobster. You can prepare the ingredients for this recipe 1 to 2 hours in advance. Just roast the lobster and the fish 30 to 35 minutes before serving.

2 live lobsters, 1-1/2 pounds each

Salt, freshly ground black pepper

2 tablespoons peanut oil

2 whole pompano, 1 pound each, cleaned

2 tablespoons cornstarch

12 scallions or spring onions, white part only, cut into 2-inch segments

1/2 tablespoon freshly grated gingerroot or 1 tablespoon lemongrass, finely chopped (reserve peel and scraps for the sauce)

3 sweet peppers (1 green, 1 yellow, 1 red), split, cored, and sliced into 1/4-inch strips

1/2 tablespoon chopped garlic

15 sprigs fresh coriander: 1/2 tied in a bunch, 1/2 leaves only, chopped

15 stems fresh mint: 1/2 tied in a bunch, 1/2 leaves only, chopped

1/4 teaspoon hot pepper flakes

3 tablespoons sweet butter

1/2 pound sugar snap peas, trimmed at both ends

3 tablespoons rice vinegar

1 clove garlic

1 cup chicken stock (see page 370) or water

1 cup coconut milk

1/4 cup toasted peanuts

❧ PREPARATION

Preheat oven to 450 degrees. Cut each raw lobster tail through the shell in 1-inch segments. Twist the claws off. Split the remaining shell in half lengthwise and rinse out the head and remove the guts. Season with salt and pepper and set aside.

Heat the peanut oil in a large (10 x 18 inch) deep roasting pan over high heat. Dust the fish with 1 tablespoon of the cornstarch, salt, and pepper. Place the fish in the roasting pan and arrange the lobster tail pieces and claws around them. Roast the fish on one side until golden brown, about 3 to 4 minutes. Turn the fish over and brown it on the other side, and turn the lobster pieces over. While the fish is roasting add the scallions, gingerroot or lemongrass, peppers, chopped garlic, coriander and mint bunches, hot pepper flakes, 2 tablespoons of the butter, and 3 pinches of salt. Mix well with the lobster around the fish and roast in the oven for 10 to 12 minutes. Remove all the lobster pieces and keep warm on the side, toss the vegetables, and add the sugar snap peas. Finish cooking the fish for another 10 minutes, remove the fish, and keep it warm on the side. Remove the vegetables to a small pan, discard the mint and coriander bunches, and keep warm on the side.

Transfer the roasting pan to the top of the stove, add the pieces of lobster head and shell to the pan, pour the vinegar over, and reduce to 1/2 tablespoon over high heat. Add the peel and scraps of ginger or lemongrass, garlic clove, and the remaining tablespoon of cornstarch. Whisk in 2 tablespoons of cold water and pour in the chicken stock. Bring to a boil, stir, and reduce for 8 to 10 minutes or until 1/3 cup liquid remains. Add the coconut milk, salt, pepper, 1/2 of the chopped coriander and 1/2 of the chopped mint, bring to a boil, and taste for seasoning. Stir in the remaining tablespoon of butter and strain into a small bowl. Discard the shells and ingredients remaining in the strainer.

PRESENTATION

Reheat the 2 pompano for 2 to 3 minutes in the center of a very large oval dish with the pieces of lobster all around. Heat the vegetables over high heat while tossing for 2 to 3 minutes and sprinkle them over the fish along with the toasted peanuts and remaining chopped mint and coriander. Bone the fish at the table by carefully lifting out the fillets; discard the bones in a separate bowl. (Each guest can remove the lobster meat from its shell by pulling the meat with a fork.)

BLACK SEA BASS WITH AN HERB CRUST AND SALSIFY

Serves 4

In this elegant recipe, black sea bass fillets are seared briefly, covered with a butter-based 6-herb coating, then broiled quickly to minimize moisture loss and to create a crisp, redolent crust. The fillets are then set atop a bed of tender, braised salsify. The ingredients for this recipe can be prepared up to 3 hours in advance, but the fish is roasted just before serving. Red snapper can be substituted for the black sea bass.

4 ounces of mixed fresh herbs, leaves only: chives (1 ounce), chervil (1/2 ounce), parsley (1 ounce), tarragon (1/2 ounce), rosemary (1 teaspoon), and basil (1 ounce)

2 slices white bread, trimmed of crusts

1/2 cup plus 2 tablespoons sweet butter, softened

Salt, freshly ground black pepper

1 pound salsify, peeled, 2 roots thinly sliced lengthwise for frying, the rest sliced at an angle into 1/4-inch pieces

1 cup corn oil

4 fillets of black sea bass, 7 ounces each

1 tablespoon vegetable oil

4 sprigs fresh chervil

❖ PREPARATION

Place the herb leaves in a blender or food processor and finely chop. Reserve 1 tablespoon of the herbs for the salsify. Add the bread to the herbs in the blender or food processor and finely chop. Add 1/2 cup of the butter, salt, and pepper and blend until smooth. Set aside in a small bowl.

Bring 2 quarts of water with 1 tablespoon salt to a boil in a pot over high heat. Add the 1/4-inch salsify slices and boil for about 5 to 7 minutes or until tender. Drain and toss the salsify in the remaining 2 tablespoons butter in a pan over medium heat for 3 to 4 minutes. Add the reserved tablespoon of fresh herbs, salt, and pepper to taste, and toss until well coated. Remove from heat and keep warm on the side.

Heat the corn oil in a deep-fat fryer or deep skillet to 350 degrees. Add the thinly sliced salsify and fry until golden crisp, drain on paper towels, and sprinkle with salt.

Salt and pepper the sea bass fillets. Heat the vegetable oil in a pan over high heat. Place the fish skin side down and sear for 2 minutes. Turn the fillets over and cook for another minute. Transfer the fillets to a broiling pan skin side up and let cool. Spread the bread and herb butter mixture evenly over the skin of each fillet. When ready to serve, preheat the broiler. Broil the fish for 2 minutes or until the herb crust has melted and starts to brown.

✤ PRESENTATION

Arrange the salsify and herb mixture on a warmed serving platter. Place the sea bass fillets over the salsify, and drizzle the melted butter from the broiler pan all around. Garnish with the sprigs of fresh chervil and the fried salsify.

GROUPER WITH FINGERLING POTATOES AND MORELS

Serves 4 to 6

For a dinner party, nothing surpasses a tender, juicy, roasted whole fish. This dish's festive look and inviting fragrance from a morel, pearl onion, new potato, and garlic garnish make it an impressive, hard-to-resist entrée. Oven roasting is an easy way to handle such a fish, but remember to baste it frequently to prevent dryness. You can substitute any other fish (such as red snapper or striped bass) of equal size. For serving ease, the ingredients can be prepared 3 hours in advance, but the fish should be roasted 35 to 45 minutes before serving.

2 cups pearl onions or small new onions, peeled, white part only

1 pound fingerling potatoes, thumb size, scrubbed (you can substitute Yukon gold or Yellow Finnish potatoes)

1 head garlic, broken into cloves and peeled

1 small whole grouper, about 4 pounds, guts, scales, and gills removed, washed and patted dry

3 sprigs fresh sage

1-1/2 teaspoons cracked black peppercorns

1-1/2 teaspoons coarse sea salt

2 tablespoons olive, peanut, or corn oil

1/4 pound fresh morels or 2 ounces dried (if using dried morels, presoak them for 3 to 4 hours in 2 cups warm water or overnight in cold water), stems discarded, caps throughly rinsed and patted dry, the largest ones halved

1 sprig fresh thyme, leaves only, chopped

Salt, freshly ground black pepper

3 tablespoons sweet butter

1 tablespoon red wine vinegar

❧ PREPARATION

Preheat oven to 450 degrees. Bring 3 quarts water with 1 tablespoon of salt to a boil in a pot over medium heat. Add the pearl onions and potatoes and boil for 5 minutes. Drain and set aside.

Crush 3 garlic cloves and stuff them into the cavity of the grouper with 2 sprigs of sage. Season the fish with the crushed peppercorns and coarse sea salt, inside the cavity and out.

Heat the oil until very hot in a large oven roasting pan on top of the stove over high heat. Add the fish to the pan and brown the skin on both sides. Add the potatoes, onions, morels, and remaining garlic cloves all around the fish. Sprinkle the vegetables with thyme and a pinch of salt and pepper. Add the remaining sprig of sage and 2 tablespoons butter, and place the pan in the oven for 25 to 30 minutes. Carefully toss the vegetables around the fish every 5 minutes with a spoon and brush the fish with the cooking butter. Transfer the fish to a large oval serving platter and keep warm. Discard the sage, add the remaining tablespoon of butter, and finish cooking the vegetables over low heat on the stove until lightly brown, about 6 to 10 minutes. Add the red wine vinegar and stir well for 2 minutes or until totally evaporated.

❋ PRESENTATION

Serve the whole fish on a warm oval serving platter. Spread the vegetables all around and spoon the cooking juice over the top. To carve the fish, use a fork and a wide knife. Run the blade of the knife along the middle of the fish from head to tail and carefully lift off the fillets on both sides. You can use a wide spreader or spatula to handle the fillets. To remove the dorsal bone, lift it from the tail side, break it at the head, and remove it to get to the 2 bottom fillets. Serve 1/2 a fillet per person with the vegetable garnish on top.

FLOUNDER DIABLE WITH SPINACH AND SALSIFY

Serves 4

The sharp, palate-piquing tang imparted by this dish's mustard *diable* gives the flounder the strong
shot of character that most lean, fine-fleshed fish need. Beds of spinach and salsify supply a nice, earthy touch
that subtly tempers the *diable's* spicy edge. You can prepare the ingredients for this recipe up to 2 hours in
advance but bake the fish 10 to 12 minutes before serving.

For the Garnish:

Juice of 1 lemon

*3/4 pound salsify, peeled and sliced at
an angle into 1/2-inch-by-1/4-inch pieces*

*1 pound spinach leaves, stems removed,
leaves washed and drained*

For the Sauce:

3 tablespoons Spanish sherry vinegar

2 tablespoons shallots, peeled and chopped

1 teaspoon crushed black peppecorns

1 small bay leaf

*2 cloves garlic: 1 peeled whole, 1 peeled
and finely chopped*

1/2 cup chicken jus (see page 371)

1/2 tablespoon sweet butter, softened

3 drops Tabasco

Pinch of salt

For the Flounder:

1-1/2 tablespoons sweet butter, softened

*4 fillets of flounder, 7 ounces each,
skinless and boneless*

Salt, freshly ground black pepper

1-1/2 teaspoon Colman's dry mustard

1/4 cup Dijon mustard

*4 slices white bread, crusts trimmed, ground into
fine crumbs in a blender or food processor*

✤ PREPARATION

For the Garnish:

Bring 2 quarts water with the lemon juice and 1 tablespoon salt to a boil in a pot over
high heat. Add the salsify and boil until tender when pierced with a knife, about 10 to
12 minutes. Drain and set aside.

Bring 2 quarts water with 1 tablespoon salt to a boil in a pot over high heat. Add the
spinach leaves, stir, and boil for 2 to 3 minutes. Drain and chill the spinach under cold
running water. Drain again, press well to extract any remaining water, and set aside.

For the Sauce:

Bring the vinegar to a boil in a small pot over medium heat with the shallots, crushed
peppercorns, bay leaf, and whole garlic clove and reduce to 1/2 tablespoon. Add the

chicken jus, and bring to a boil. Gently boil and reduce by half. Stir in the butter, Tabasco, and salt. Strain and keep warm.

For the Flounder:

Preheat oven to 450 degrees. Brush 1/2 tablespoon of the butter on the bottom of a roasting pan large enough to contain the 4 fish fillets. Season the fillets on both sides with salt, pepper, and dry mustard and place them in the greased pan. Spread a thin coat of Dijon mustard evenly over each fillet. Sprinkle the bread crumbs over the top of each fillet to cover the mustard. Melt 1/2 tablespoon of the butter and drizzle it over the coated fish.

Bake the fish in the oven for 5 to 6 minutes. Switch to the broiler and finish cooking until the crust is golden, about 3 minutes.

While the fish is baking, melt the remaining 1/2 tablespoon butter in a pan over medium heat. Add the chopped garlic, spinach, salsify, salt, and pepper. Toss well for 3 to 4 minutes and keep warm.

✤ Presentation

Place the spinach and salsify in the center of a large plate or platter. Place the fish on top and spoon the sauce around.

POULTRY

Spring   Summer   Autumn   Winter

❋   ⚜   🍃   ❄

Cured Duck Pot-au-Feu with an Herb Oil 🍃 page 200

Crispy Chicken Cooked Under a Brick with
    Garlic, Lemon, and Herbs ❄ page 202

Baby Chicken and Squash Casserole with Rosemary ❋ page 203

Chicken Casserole with Morels, Fava Beans, and
    Spring Potatoes ❋ page 204

Stuffed Quail with Fresh Figs and Swiss Chard Leaves ⚜ page 206

Crispy Duck with Spices, Spinach Purée, and
    Roasted Apricots ⚜ page 208

Broiled Squab and Endives with Cumin and Pine Nuts ❄ page 210

Gratin of Squab with Spring Vegetables ❋ page 212

Hot and Crusty Chicken My Way 🍃 page 214

Roasted Guinea Fowl in a Salt Crust Roger Vergé ❄ page 216

opposite page: Cured Duck Pot-au-Feu with an Herb Oil

CURED DUCK POT-AU-FEU WITH AN HERB OIL

Serves 4

Throughout France, the traditional Sunday meal during winter is *pot-au-feu*— literally "pot on the fire"— consisting of different cuts of meats and root vegetables boiled together in a broth. Depending on the region in which it's prepared, pot-au-feu may include pork, beef, veal, or poultry. This recipe features brine-cured lean Muscovy ducks, and is an adaptation from the more traditional pork cuts or beef pastrami. Be sure to soak the ducks for 48 hours in the recommended brine. This dish can be prepared up to 4 hours in advance, kept in a cool spot, then reheated for 15 to 20 minutes while you make the herb oil before serving.

For Curing the Duck:

6 quarts water

1-1/2 pounds coarse sea salt

1/2 pound sugar

2 female Muscovy ducks, 3 pounds each,
ready to cook , trussed

For Poaching the Cured Duck:

2 large carrots, peeled and split lengthwise

4 medium leeks, green parts split
lengthwise and tied in a bunch
with kitchen string,
white parts tied in a bunch,
reserved for the vegetable garnish

1 medium celeriac, about 1/4 pound,
peeled and quartered

1 medium onion, peeled and studded
with 1 clove

2 sprigs thyme

2 bay leaves

20 coriander seeds

10 peppercorns

For the Vegetable Garnish:

1 cup carrots, peeled and sliced 1/4 inch thick

12 pearl onions, peeled (see page 213)

1 medium celeriac, peeled and cut into
2-by-1/2-inch sticks

4 salsify roots, peeled and cut
into 1-inch segments

1/2 cup small turnips, peeled and sliced
1/4 inch thick

1/2 cup broccoli florets, 1 inch long

For the Herb Oil Dressing:

3 tablespoons chives, finely chopped

1 tablespoon fresh chervil, leaves only,
finely chopped, and 1 tablespoon fresh chervil
cut into small sprigs

1 tablespoon fresh tarragon, leaves only,
finely chopped

2 tablespoons shallots, peeled and finely chopped

1/2 teaspoon freshly ground black pepper

1/4 cup olive oil

Coarse sea salt

✒ PREPARATION

For Curing the Duck:
Bring the water to a boil in a large pot over high heat. Add the salt and sugar, stir well to dissolve, and remove from heat. When cool, pour into a large container (a clean plastic bucket, for example), add the ducks to the brine, and soak for 48 hours in the refrigerator. Just before cooking the ducks, drain them, and discard the brine.

For Poaching the Cured Duck:
Place the drained ducks in a large pot or stockpot, cover with water to about 3 inches above the ducks, and bring to a boil over high heat. Reduce the heat to a simmer and add the carrots, the green part of the leeks, the celeriac, onion, thyme, bay leaves, coriander seeds, and peppercorns. Skim the surface often with a spoon while cooking and simmer gently for 70 to 80 minutes or until the duck legs are fork tender. When done, carefully remove the ducks and set aside to cool on a cutting board. Strain and reserve the broth and discard the cooked vegetables.

For the Vegetable Garnish:
Pour the strained broth back into the pot. Bring to a boil, add the carrots, reserved white part of the leeks, and the pearl onions, and boil for 5 minutes. Add the celeriac and salsify and boil for 3 minutes. Add the turnips and boil for 8 minutes. Finally, add the broccoli and boil for another 3 minutes. Over a large bowl, drain the vegetables and set aside; keep 1 quart cooking broth and discard the rest.

Delicately remove the breasts and legs of the duck and place them in a shallow dish (discard the carcasses). Place the vegetables on top and cover with just enough cooking broth to keep the pot-au-feu moist. Keep warm until ready to serve.

For the Herb Oil Dressing:
Make the dressing by mixing together the chives, chopped chervil, tarragon, shallots, pepper, olive oil, and coarse sea salt to taste in a bowl.

✒ PRESENTATION

Garnish the warm pot-au-feu with the small sprigs of chervil. Serve the herb dressing on the side along with some coarse salt for guests to spoon over their cured duck and vegetables.

STORING FRESH HERBS: Most fresh herbs will keep well if they are wrapped in a moistened paper towel and then covered loosely with plastic wrap or placed in an open plastic bag in the refrigerator.

CRISPY CHICKEN COOKED UNDER A BRICK WITH GARLIC, LEMON, AND HERBS

Serves 4

Olive oil with thyme, lemon, garlic, and chives accents this incredibly tasty version of the traditional *pollastrino al mattone:* chicken crisped under a brick. A *mattone* is the earthenware brick used in the Lucca region of Italy, and it is essential, as its weight is the main reason the chicken develops its tantalizingly crisp crust. Marinate the chicken overnight with the flavoring ingredients. The chicken needs 40 to 45 minutes of cooking before serving.

2 free-range chickens, 2-1/2 pounds each, halved (split each chicken along the backbone and cut between the breasts to halve them), giblets and excess fat discarded, chicken halves flattened on skin side with a meat pounder or heavy skillet; or 4 cornish hens prepared the same way

4 cloves garlic, peeled and quartered lengthwise

3 sprigs fresh rosemary

3 sprigs fresh thyme

Salt, crushed black peppercorns

3 lemons: 2 sliced in 1/4-inch slices and 1 for juice

6 tablespoons olive oil

1/4 cup chives, cut into 1/2-inch sticks

❖ PREPARATION

Stud each chicken breast with 2 pieces of garlic and do the same with each chicken leg. Stud each breast and leg with a piece of rosemary and thyme. Season the chicken with salt and crushed black peppercorns. Marinate the chicken in a bowl with the lemon slices, 1/4 cup of the olive oil, and the remaining thyme and rosemary. Cover and refrigerate for at least 5 to 6 hours, preferably overnight.

Preheat oven to 475 degrees. Heat 1 or 2 cast-iron skillets large enough to fit all 4 chicken halves on the stove over high heat. When very hot, add 1 tablespoon of the olive oil and the chicken halves skin side down with the lemon slices and the herbs. Wrap 2 bricks or flat heavy stones in aluminum foil and place them over the chicken halves to press them down in the pan and cook for 8 to 10 minutes or until the skin turns uniformly golden. Place the weighted-down chickens in the oven and roast for another 20 minutes. Remove the bricks, turn the chickens over, and cook for another 10 to 15 minutes or until done.

❖ PRESENTATION

Place the chicken on a large platter. Garnish with the lemon and herbs. Sprinkle with the lemon juice, the remaining tablespoon olive oil, and the chives. Serve immediately.

BABY CHICKEN AND SQUASH CASSEROLE WITH ROSEMARY

Serves 4

This light and quick chicken fricassée creates a savory and wholesome dish. The ingredients can be prepared up to 2 hours in advance, then cooked with the chicken 20 to 25 minutes before serving

4 baby chickens, 1 pound each, halved
Salt

Cayenne pepper

Sugar

5 tablespoons olive oil

16 cloves garlic, peeled

1/2 pound yellow squash,
cut into 1/2-inch slices

1/2 pound zucchini,
cut into 1/2-inch slices

1 bay leaf

1 sprig fresh rosemary

Zest of 1/2 lime cut in julienne (matchstick size)
and juice of 1 lime

2 cups plum tomatoes, cut into 1/2-inch slices

1/4 cup chicken stock (see page 370) or water

❀ PREPARATION

Preheat oven to 450 degrees. Season the chicken with salt, cayenne pepper, and a pinch of sugar. Heat 2 tablespoons of the olive oil in a large roasting pan over high heat. Add the chickens, skin side down, and sauté until golden, about 4 to 6 minutes. Turn them over and add the garlic, squash and zucchini slices, bay leaf, rosemary, lime zest, and salt. Drizzle 1 tablespoon of the olive oil over the casserole and carefully toss. Place the pan in the oven and roast for 15 to 20 minutes, tossing 2 or 3 times.

Place the tomato slices in a bowl. Season with salt, a pinch of cayenne pepper, and sugar. Toss them in 1 tablespoon of the olive oil and the lime juice and spread them over the chicken-squash casserole. Cook for 5 to 7 minutes more. Discard the bay leaf and rosemary sprigs, transfer the chicken and garnish to a large serving platter, and keep warm. Add the stock or water to the pan drippings and simmer for 3 to 4 minutes over medium heat. Add the remaining tablespoon olive oil, mix well, and strain the sauce.

❀ PRESENTATION

Place the chickens on a platter. Arrange the vegetables over them. Spoon the sauce evenly over the warm dish.

STORING FRESH CHICKEN: The best way to store a fresh chicken is to wash it in cold water, pat it dry, and lightly sprinkle it with salt (inside and outside). Then wrap the chicken in a cotton kitchen towel or waxed paper, place it on a plate, and keep in the coldest spot of your refrigerator.

CHICKEN CASSEROLE WITH MORELS, FAVA BEANS, AND SPRING POTATOES

Serves 4

This chicken casserole is a celebration of spring with the delicate taste of fresh morels, tender fava beans, and new spring potatoes scented with a chive jus. The ingredients of this dish can be prepared up to 2 hours in advance, the casserole assembled and cooked 40 to 45 minutes before serving.

2 cups shelled fresh fava beans
(about 3 pounds fava with pod)

1 tablespoon plus 1-1/2 teaspoons olive oil
or canola oil

1/2 pound fresh morels, caps only, washed twice,
drained and sliced 1/2 inch thick

Salt, freshly ground black pepper

1 cup chicken stock (see page 370)

One 3-1/2-pound free-range chicken,
cut into 10 pieces: 2 legs, 2 thighs, 2 wings, and
2 breasts cut in half widthwise (Cut off the legs
and remove the thighs at the joint. Remove

the tips of the drumsticks. Remove the breasts
and cut them in half. Remove the wings and
discard the tips. Discard the carcass.)

16 cloves garlic, unpeeled

1 bay leaf

1 sprig fresh thyme, leaves only, chopped

1/2 pound new potatoes (golf ball size),
scrubbed, split in half

8 small shallots or spring onions,
peeled and halved

3 tablespoons chives, minced

❁ PREPARATION

Bring 1 quart water to a boil in a pot over high heat. Plunge in the fava beans for 1 minute, drain, and cool under cold running water. Drain again, make a small incision in the skin with your thumbnail, and pop the bean out. Discard the skins and refrigerate the beans until needed.

Heat 1-1/2 teaspoons oil in a skillet over high heat. When very hot, add the morels, salt, and pepper and toss for 2 to 3 minutes. Add the chicken stock, bring to a boil, boil for 3 minutes, and set aside until needed.

Preheat oven to 425 degrees. Pat the chicken pieces dry and then salt and pepper them. Heat the remaining tablespoon oil in a very large cast-iron pot or in a large roasting pan on the stove over high heat. Add the chicken skin side down and sauté for 5 to 7 minutes or until golden brown. Turn the chicken pieces over and add the garlic cloves, bay leaf, chopped thyme, potatoes, shallots, salt, and pepper. Toss well, transfer to oven, and roast for 15 minutes. Pour the morels and chicken stock over the pieces of chicken, mix well, and roast for another 25 to 30 minutes in the oven. Remove from the oven and keep warm on the stove over medium heat. Add the fava beans and 1/2 of the chives and cook for 3 to 4 minutes.

❋ PRESENTATION

Present this dish in the roasting pot or arrange the pieces of chicken with the vegetables on top in a warmed deep dish. Sprinkle with the remaining chives.

Stuffed Quail with Fresh Figs and Swiss Chard Leaves

Serves 4

This elegant and original recipe shows off perfectly the great combination of meat and fruit often used with birds or game. Here boneless quails are stuffed with whole fresh figs wrapped in prosciutto, roasted, and served on Swiss chard and couscous. The ingredients of this recipe can be prepared 2 to 3 hours in advance and cooked 15 to 20 minutes before serving.

12 small mission figs (just ripe)

2 slices thin prosciutto, cut into 8 equal pieces

Salt, freshly ground black pepper

Ground cardamom

8 quails, boneless

Juice of 1 lemon and zest of 1 lemon cut into julienne (matchstick size)

1 pound Swiss chard, leaves only

2 cups chicken stock (see page 370)

1 cup instant couscous

1/4 cup olive oil

1/2 cup onions, peeled and sliced

2 tablespoons sliced almonds, lightly toasted

❧ Preparation

Wrap 8 figs with the pieces of prosciutto. Season each fig with salt, pepper, and a pinch of cardamom. Stuff each boneless quail with 1 wrapped fig and squeeze the quail lightly on its sides to give it an oblong shape. Season each quail with salt, pepper, and a pinch of cardamom and set aside.

Bring 3 cups water to a boil in a small pot over high heat. Add the lemon zest and boil for 10 minutes. Strain out the zest and finely chop half of the zest. Set aside.

Bring 3 quarts water with 2 tablespoons salt to a boil in a pot over high heat. Blanch the Swiss chard for 4 to 5 minutes, until the leaves are tender. Drain and cool under cold running water. Drain well again and set aside.

Bring the chicken stock to a boil in a pot over high heat. Remove from heat and add the couscous, the chopped lemon zest, a pinch of cardamom, salt, and pepper. Mix well, cover, and let sit for 5 minutes.

Preheat oven to 475 degrees. On top of the stove, heat 1 tablespoon of the olive oil in a roasting pan over high heat. When hot, place the quails breast side down in the pan and brown the skin. Turn and roast them in the oven for 12 to 15 minutes. Add the 4 remaining figs during the last 3 to 4 minutes of roasting.

Heat 1 tablespoon of the olive oil in a pan over high heat. Add the onions and sweat for 2 minutes. Add the blanched Swiss chard, salt, pepper, and a pinch of cardamom and toss well for 3 to 5 minutes. Remove from heat and set aside.

Mix the lemon juice and the remaining 2 tablespoons olive oil into the couscous.

 PRESENTATION

Arrange the Swiss chard in a dome shape in the center of a large platter. Place the quails around the Swiss chard and then arrange the couscous around the quails and out to the rim of the platter. Sprinkle with the toasted almonds.

Crispy Duck with Spices, Spinach Purée, and Roasted Apricots

Serves 4

Firm, ripe apricots and an intensely tasty spinach purée provide the sweet and rich flavors to counterbalance spicy roasted duck. You can prepare the spinach purée up to 3 hours in advance and roast the duck 40 to 45 minutes before serving.

2 female Muscovy ducks, 3 pounds each, oven ready (or 1 large duck 4 to 4-1/2 pounds)

Salt, freshly ground black pepper

Three 1/2-inch slices gingerroot, 1 slice peeled and grated

Juice of 1 orange and grated zest of 1/2 orange, peel and pulp reserved

Juice of 2 lemons, peel and pulp reserved

1 tablespoon oil, for cooking

1-1/2 teaspoons ground coriander seeds

1 teaspoon freshly ground black pepper

1 teaspoon cinnamon

2 tablespoons apricot preserves

1/4 cup sweet butter

1/2 cup onions, peeled and finely sliced

2 pounds spinach, leaves only, thoroughly washed

8 small apricots, ripe but firm

2 teaspoons sugar

❧ Preparation

Place the ducks in a large stockpot and cover with water approximately 2 inches above the ducks. Bring to a boil over high heat and boil for 3 minutes. Drain the ducks thoroughly and discard the cooking water. Air dry the ducks for about 15 minutes, or pat dry with towels if necessary, then salt and pepper each one inside and out and stuff them both with a piece of gingerroot and the reserved orange and lemon peels and pulp.

Preheat oven to 450 degrees. Place the oil and the ducks in a roasting pan and put in the oven. Combine the grated gingerroot, coriander, black pepper, cinnamon, orange zest and juice, lemon juice, and apricot preserves in a bowl. Brush this mixture on the ducks every 5 minutes as they roast. The ducks will need no more than 30 to 35 minutes of roasting for pink meat. When done, transfer the ducks to a cutting board, remove the legs and breasts, and cut them into serving pieces. Place the pieces of duck on a large serving platter and keep warm in a 250-degree oven. Discard the carcasses.

While the ducks are roasting, prepare the spinach purée and roasted apricots. Melt 1/2 tablespoon of the butter in a small pan over medium heat. Add the onions and sweat until soft, about 5 minutes. Set aside.

Bring 5 quarts water with 1 tablespoon salt to a boil in a large pot over high heat. Add the spinach and boil until tender, about 3 to 5 minutes. Drain well and transfer to a blender or food processor along with the sweated onions. Cook 2-1/2 tablespoons of the butter until light brown in a small pot over medium heat. Pour the brown butter over the spinach. Purée until very smooth and taste for seasoning. Transfer to a serving dish and keep warm in the oven next to the duck.

Combine the whole apricots with the remaining tablespoon butter and the sugar in a small pan over medium heat and sauté until slightly soft, about 10 to 15 minutes.

PRESENTATION

Place the warm apricots over the pieces of duck. Serve the warm spinach purée on the side. Warn your guests about the apricot pits!

FOR CRISP DUCK SKIN: Prepoaching duck before it is roasted allows the release of fat and guarantees a very crisp skin when baked.

Broiled Squab and Endives with Cumin and Pine Nuts

Serves 4

One of the best ways to prepare a squab is to split, flatten, and broil it. The squabs in this recipe are flavored with honey, lemon juice, and cumin for a deliciously glazed skin. The ingredients can be prepared up to 2 hours in advance and the squabs broiled 15 to 20 minutes before serving. You can substitute baby chickens for squabs in this recipe, but cook the chickens 10 to 15 minutes more under the broiler.

4 squabs, trimmed and cleaned, wings and necks reserved. (Split each squab carefully along the back side halfway through the breastbone so that the squab halves remain attached. Remove the backbones and set aside. Flatten the squabs by pounding on the skin lightly with a large flat knife or a meat mallet.)

2 teaspoons ground cumin

2 cloves garlic, peeled and sliced

Pinch of cayenne pepper

2 tablespoons olive oil

1/2 cup onions, peeled and sliced

1/2 cup sweet red pepper, split, cored, seeded, in 1/4-inch dice

Zest of 1 lemon

1 tablespoon honey mixed with juice of 1/2 lemon

1 pound small endives, quartered lengthwise

Salt, freshly ground black pepper

1/2 cup chicken stock (see page 370)

1 tablespoon sweet butter plus 1 teaspoon melted

2 tablespoons white raisins soaked for 2 hours in 1 tablespoon port wine

2 tablespoons pine nuts, lightly toasted

2 tablespoons chives, minced

✤ Preparation

Place the squabs, 1 teaspoon of the cumin, 1 sliced garlic clove, the cayenne pepper, 1 tablespoon of the olive oil, and salt to taste in a large bowl. Mix well, cover, and marinate in the refrigerator for 3 to 4 hours.

Drain the squabs and discard the marinade. Heat the remaining olive oil in a roasting pan over medium heat. Add the reserved squab wings, necks, and backbones and roast for 3 minutes. Add the sliced onions, the diced red pepper, the remaining sliced garlic clove, the lemon zest, the remaining teaspoon cumin, 1 teaspoon of the honey-lemon mixture, and sweat for 3 to 4 minutes. Add the endives, salt, and pepper, mix well, and sweat for 7 to 10 minutes (do not let the endive color too much while sweating). Add the chicken stock and cook slowly for 15 minutes, tossing from time to time.

Preheat broiler. Cover the vegetables completely with the 4 flat squabs skin side up (this will keep the vegetables from burning under the broiler). Brush the squabs with the melted butter and broil on the lowest level of the broiler. Cook for about 12 to 15

minutes, turning the pan around often for even cooking. Brush the squabs with the remaining two teaspoons honey-lemon mixture several times while broiling. When the skin is brown pour the soaked raisins over and cook for 3 more minutes for rare. If you prefer the meat cooked medium, cook 3 to 4 more minutes under the broiler. Remove from the broiler and discard the necks, wings, and backbones. Transfer the squabs to a large platter. Arrange the vegetables over and around the birds and keep warm.

Reduce the juice in the pan to 1/4 cup over medium heat, mix in the remaining table-spoon butter, and season to taste.

✤ PRESENTATION

Spoon the cooking juice over the birds and vegetables and sprinkle with the toasted pine nuts and the chives.

GRATIN OF SQUAB WITH SPRING VEGETABLES

Serves 4

A gratin is the golden crust that forms on the surface of a dish that is cooked in the oven or under a broiler, often sprinkled with cheese, eggs, or bread crumbs. In this gratin, polenta and Parmesan are used to top the layered mosaic of baby artichokes, carrots, turnips, pearl onions, and lightly crisp roasted breasts of squab. This beautiful dish, which can be prepared up to 1 hour beforehand, is great for casual entertaining. It's simple to assemble and cook; just reheat and broil it before serving.

4 squabs, 1 pound each, oven ready (livers reserved)

Salt, freshly ground black pepper

1 tablespoon oil, for cooking

1/2 cup spring onions or pearl onions, peeled and sliced (see note)

12 baby carrots, peeled and greens discarded

12 baby turnips, stems removed, peeled with a knife and split in half if too large

6 baby artichokes, leaves removed, hearts trimmed and quartered

1 stalk celery, cut into 1/4-inch slices

4 cloves garlic, peeled and sliced

1 sprig fresh thyme, leaves only, finely chopped

2 cups chicken stock (see page 370)

8 to 10 seasonal mushrooms (morels, oyster, or shiitake), caps only, cleaned

8 asparagus spears, 3-inch tips only

1/4 cup fresh peas (about 1/2 pound in the pod)

3 tablespoons sweet butter

1/2 cup instant corn polenta

3 tablespoons freshly grated Parmesan cheese

❀ PREPARATION

Preheat oven to 450 degrees. Salt and pepper the squabs inside and out. Heat the oil in a large roasting pan on top of the stove over high heat. Place each squab with one side of its breast down in the pan and brown the skin for 2 to 3 minutes, then shift each squab onto the other side of its breast and brown the skin for 2 minutes. Turn the squabs on their backs and spread the onions, carrots, turnips, artichokes, celery, garlic, and thyme evenly around the birds. Salt and pepper the vegetables and place the roasting pan in the oven. Toss the vegetables often while the squabs are cooking and if they seem about to dry out or burn, add chicken stock 1 tablespoon at a time to moisten them again. For a perfect medium-rare, roast the squabs for 15 to 18 minutes. For well done, add 10 to 15 minutes more of cooking. Remove the squabs from the pan and set aside to cool.

Reduce the oven temperature to 325 degrees and add the mushrooms, asparagus, peas, squab livers, 1 tablespoon of the butter, and 1 tablespoon of the chicken broth to the roasted vegetables. Toss well and roast for another 10 minutes, stirring occasionally and adding more chicken stock if the vegetables are drying out. Remove from heat and keep warm on the side.

While the squabs and vegetables are cooking, bring 1-1/2 cups of the chicken stock to a boil in a pot over high heat. Add the polenta, lower heat to medium-low, and cook while stirring for another 10 to 15 minutes. When the polenta starts to thicken, add the remaining 2 tablespoons butter, 1 tablespoon of the Parmesan cheese, salt, and pepper and cook until the polenta has a very soft consistency. Remove from heat and keep warm on the side.

Carve the breasts off the squab and shape them nicely by cutting off uneven edges. Dice the leg meat and add it to the vegetables and liver.

Preheat broiler. Arrange the warm vegetable and liver mixture in a warmed shallow gratin dish about 14 by 7 inches and cover evenly with the warm polenta. Sprinkle the remaining 2 tablespoons Parmesan evenly over the polenta and arrange the breasts of squab skin side up in a nice design (like the petals of a flower). Press the breasts into the polenta until it reaches the skin and broil for 1 or 2 minutes or until the cheese turns golden brown.

❀ PRESENTATION

This dish should be served at the table right from the gratin dish.

PEELING PEARL ONIONS: When peeling pearl onions, place them in a bowl of lukewarm water for 10 minutes. This will make it easier to remove the skins.

HOT AND CRUSTY CHICKEN MY WAY

Serves 4

This is one of my favorite, year-round ways of preparing chicken; it's a snap to cook, powerfully aromatic, and full of flavor. Wasabi, ginger, garlic, and coriander create a definitive Far Eastern accent that sparkles when paired with mesclun salad. You can bread and refrigerate the chicken and prepare the salad dressing 1 hour in advance, but the chicken is best when baked 30 to 40 minutes before serving.

For the Chicken:

2 chickens, 2-1/2 pounds each, each chicken cut into 10 serving pieces: 2 breasts split in half widthwise, 2 legs with the tips of the drumsticks trimmed, 2 thighs, and 2 wings with the tips removed

Salt

Pinch of cayenne pepper

1 teaspoon wasabi paste (Japanese horseradish); if not available substitute 2 teaspoons Colman's dry mustard

Juice of 1/2 lemon

1 teaspoon ground coriander

1 tablespoon gingerroot, grated

1 teaspoon chopped garlic

1-1/2 teaspoons honey

2 tablespoons olive oil

3 eggs

1-1/2 teaspoons soy sauce

Freshly ground black pepper

2 cups fresh bread crumbs

1/2 cup all-purpose flour

1 teaspoon sweet butter, for greasing the roasting pan

1 sprig fresh coriander, leaves only

For the Dressing:

3 sprigs fresh coriander, leaves only, finely chopped

1 teaspoon grated gingerroot or ground ginger

1 teaspoon soy sauce

Dab of wasabi paste

Juice of 1/2 lemon

3 tablespoons olive oil

Salt, freshly ground black pepper

For the Salad:

1 pound mesclun (assorted greens and herbs) or 1 head curly chicory

2 heads Lollo Rossa or radicchio

1 bunch arugula

✐ PREPARATION

For the Chicken:

Season the pieces of chicken with salt, the cayenne pepper, wasabi paste, lemon juice, ground coriander, grated gingerroot, garlic, honey, and 1 tablespoon of the olive oil. Toss well, cover, and marinate for 3 to 4 hours in the refrigerator.

Preheat oven to 400 degrees. In a bowl, mix the eggs with 1-1/2 teaspoons of the olive oil, soy sauce, and salt and pepper. Spread the bread crumbs in a pan. Dredge each piece of chicken in the flour, shake off excess flour, dip well into the egg mixture, and roll in the bread crumbs (press firmly to attach the crumbs to the chicken). Set the breaded chicken pieces aside in a large buttered roasting pan. Drizzle the remaining 1-1/2 teaspoons olive oil on the pieces of chicken and bake in the oven for 30 to 40 minutes or until golden brown, turning the pieces over halfway through the cooking time.

For the Dressing and Salad:
While the chicken bakes, prepare the salad dressing in a salad bowl. Mix the coriander, gingerroot, soy sauce, wasabi paste, lemon juice, and olive oil together. Add salt and pepper to taste and set aside. Add the assorted salad and toss just before serving.

PRESENTATION

Place the crispy chicken on a warmed platter and sprinkle with the fresh coriander leaves. Serve the mixed greens salad tossed with the ginger and soy sauce dressing in a salad bowl on the side.

ROASTED GUINEA FOWL IN A SALT CRUST ROGER VERGÉ

Serves 4 to 6

This dish is a traditional and favorite way of cooking poultry from master chef Roger Vergé, my mentor and friend, when he entertains at home in Mougins on the Riviera. Cooking meat, poultry, or fish in a special clay container or a salt crust produces enticingly juicy and flavorful flesh. The crust hardens into a shell to trap the fragrant herbs in the bird and give a slight briny taste to the meat. You can assemble this dish up to 3 hours beforehand and cook it 60 minutes before serving.

For the Salt Crust:

8 cups all-purpose flour

3-1/2 cups water

2 cups coarse sea salt

1-1/2 teaspoons chopped fresh sage

1-1/2 teaspoons chopped fresh thyme

1-1/2 teaspoons crushed black peppercorns

For the Roasted Fowls:

1 tablespoon oil, for cooking

2 guinea fowls, 2 pounds each, trussed
and ready to roast

2 slices bacon

4 cloves garlic, peeled

2 sprigs fresh thyme

2 sprigs fresh sage

1 small onion, peeled and split

1 teaspoon crushed black peppercorns

For the Roasted Vegetables:

4 slices bacon, cut into 1-inch pieces

1/2 cup carrots, peeled and sliced 1/4 inch thick

1/2 cup turnips, peeled and cut into wedges
1/2 inch thick

1/2 cup celeriac, peeled and cut into
1/2-inch cubes

1/2 cup onions, peeled and cut into
wedges 1/4 inch thick

1/2 cup small shiitake mushrooms,
caps only, cleaned

6 cloves garlic, peeled and split

1 sprig fresh thyme

1 sprig fresh sage

Salt, freshly ground black pepper

Green leaves for garnish

❖ PREPARATION

For the Salt Crust:

In a bowl, combine the flour, water, salt, sage, thyme, and peppercorns. Use a food processor (hook attachment at low speed) or your hands to knead the dough until all ingredients are well combined. If too soft, add a little flour while kneading (it will be more difficult to seal the birds if the dough is too soft).

Split the dough evenly and with a rolling pin on a floured counter roll each half to about 1/2 inch thick, in a rectangle roughly 10 by 20 inches. Store the 2 sheets of rolled dough between 2 sheets of 10-by-20-inch parchment paper. Refrigerate both sheets of dough for an hour or until needed.

For the Roasted Fowls:
Heat the oil in a roasting pan on top of the stove over high heat. Place both birds in the pan on one side of their breasts and brown the skin, about 4 to 5 minutes. Shift the guinea fowls to the other side of their breasts and brown for the same length of time. When done, turn the birds on their backs and cook for another 4 to 5 minutes. Remove the birds from the pan and set aside to cool.

Stuff each bird with 1 slice bacon, 2 cloves garlic, 1 sprig each thyme and sage, 1/2 of the small onion, and 1/2 teaspoon black pepper.

Preheat oven to 450 degrees. Remove the top parchment paper from each piece of dough. Place each bird along the width of a piece of dough, 1-1/2 inches away from the edge. Brush a little water on the dough to help seal it and flip the dough over the birds delicately and evenly. Firmly press the dough on and around the birds to seal them in completely. Place both birds in a roasting pan and bake in the oven for 1 hour. Remove from oven, transfer the birds to a plate, and keep warm.

For the Vegetables:
Reduce oven to 375 degrees. Remove the fat from the pan used to brown the birds. Add the bacon and cook it for 3 minutes over medium heat on the stove. Add all the vegetables, garlic, sprigs of thyme and sage, salt, and pepper, and toss for 3 to 5 minutes.

Place the pan in the oven and gently roast the vegetables for 30 to 40 minutes. Remove from heat and transfer to a warmed serving dish.

❖ PRESENTATION

Present the 2 birds in their crusts on a large tray decorated with the green leaves. Cut the crust all around the base of each bird with a strong knife. Lift the salt crust from the birds and discard. Carve the birds at the table and serve the roasted root vegetables on the side.

Meat and Game

Spring   Summer   Autumn   Winter
❄   ⚜   🍃   ✤

Rib-Eye Steak with Stuffed Marrow Bones and Turnips 🍃 page 220

Short Ribs Miroton ✤ page 222

Sirloin Napoleon with Black Olives and Zucchini ⚜ page 223

Hanger Steak with Scallions and Shredded Corn Crêpes ⚜ page 224

Beef Tenderloin with Glazed Onions in Balsamic Vinegar ❄ page 225

Veal Chops with Ginger and Swiss Chard Strudel ⚜ page 227

Calf's Liver with Fresh Pea Croquettes ❄ page 230

Crusty Sweetbreads with Hot Mustard, Bacon, and a
        Shallot Jus 🍃 page 232

Braised Veal Shank with Lemon, Dried Apricots, and Thyme ✤ page 234

Lamb Chops Champvallon ✤ page 236

Braised Leg of Lamb Cleopatra ❄ page 237

Leg of Baby Lamb with Lemon, Tomatoes, Artichokes,
        and Olives ❄ page 239

Eggplant and Lamb Cake with a Garlic Jus ⚜ page 241

Pig Knuckles with Endives, Lentils, and Oregano ✤ page 243

Roast Loin of Pork with Curried Cauliflower and Apple Purée 🍃 page 246

Suckling Pig with Snow Peas, Radishes, and Rosemary ❄ page 248

Leg of Venison with Stuffed Mini-Pumpkins 🍃 page 251

Pheasant Salad with Walnuts, Crisp Celery, and Artichokes 🍃 page 254

Wild Partridge with a Red Cabbage Confit and
        Fall Fruit Chutney 🍃 page 256

Tomatoes Stuffed with a Ragout of Rabbit, Chanterelles,
        and Rosemary ⚜ page 258

Creamy Rabbit Casserole with Nine Spring Herbs ❄ page 260

Braised Rabbit with Pappardelle Pasta and Sage 🍃 page 262

opposite page: Beef Tenderloin with Glazed Onions in Balsamic Vinegar

RIB-EYE STEAK WITH STUFFED MARROW BONES AND TURNIPS

Serves 4

Smooth-textured, lightly flavored, and highly nutritious, marrow is used to garnish these seared rib-eye steaks, a variation of the Burgundian *côte de boeuf à la moelle*. You can prepare the marrow bones and vegetables up to 3 hours in advance but the steak should be cooked 15 to 20 minutes before serving.

8 very large marrow bones, each 2 inches long (hollow part 1-1/2 inch in diameter)

2 pounds turnips (golf-ball size), peeled

Salt, freshly ground black pepper

Pinch of sugar

2 tablespoons sweet butter

2 sprigs rosemary

1/2 cup chicken jus or beef jus (see page 371)

1 cup shallots, peeled and chopped

1 bottle full-bodied red wine

1 pound assorted mushrooms (white, shiitake, chanterelles), cut into 1/2-inch pieces

1/4 cup Italian parsley, leaves only, chopped

2 rib-eye steaks, 1 pound each, trimmed of fat and tendons

1/2 tablespoon crushed black peppercorns

1 tablespoon oil, for cooking

Mustard

PREPARATION

To remove the marrow from the bones, rub 1 teaspoon salt on each end of the bone and place the bones in the refrigerator overnight. The marrow will pop out easily the next day. If you do not have time to refrigerate the bones overnight, poach the whole bones in boiling water for 2 minutes, drain, and let them cool a few minutes before pushing the marrow out.

Cut the marrow into 1/4-inch-thick slices and set 4 slices aside to be cooked with the turnips. Soak the rest of the marrow in cold water and refrigerate until needed.

Preheat oven to 425 degrees. Place the whole turnips, salt, pepper, sugar, 1 tablespoon of the butter, the rosemary, the 4 marrow slices, and the beef stock in a roasting pan. Cover with parchment paper and roast in the oven for 45 minutes to an hour. When done (tender to the knife), lower the temperature to 350 degrees, discard the parchment paper, and finish roasting the turnips until lightly brown. Set aside.

While the turnips are roasting, poach the bones for 5 minutes in boiling water, rinse, and set aside in a bowl of clean water until needed.

Melt the remaining tablespoon butter in a large pan over medium heat. Add the shallots and sweat for 5 minutes. Pour the red wine over the shallots and cook until the wine totally evaporates, about 30 to 40 minutes. Add the mushrooms, salt, and pepper.

Toss well and cook until the mushrooms release their liquid and it evaporates, about 15 minutes. Remove from heat and set aside to cool.

When cool, coarsely chop the mushroom mixture in a blender or food processor, taste for seasoning, and mix in 1/2 of the parsley.

Bring 1 quart water to a boil in a pot over high heat, plunge in the remaining slices of marrow, and cook for 1 to 2 minutes. Drain, season with salt and pepper, and set aside.

Drain the marrow bones and stand them upright. Stuff each one halfway with the mushroom mixture. Add 2 slices of marrow to each bone and finish stuffing with the mushroom mixture. Place the remaining marrow on top. Keep warm until ready to serve.

Season the steaks with salt and the crushed black peppercorns on both sides. Warm the oil in a skillet or heavy-bottom roasting pan on the stove over high heat. Sear the steaks for 3 to 4 minutes on each side for very rare. For rare steaks sear for 6 to 7 minutes on each side, for medium-rare 9 to 10 minutes on each side, for medium 11 to 12 minutes on each side, and for well-done 13 to 14 minutes on each side. Immediately remove to a cutting board and slice each steak into 6 pieces.

PRESENTATION

Arrange the steak slices in the center of a large, warmed serving platter with the warm marrow bones on top and the roasted turnips around. Serve with a good-quality mustard on the side.

Short Ribs Miroton

Serves 4

This is an updated version of *miroton parmentier*, an ancient French dish of fork-tender braised beef that's rich in onions and—in this recipe—soft potatoes that absorb the delicious taste of the stew while cooking. When braising, remember to use a pot that has a tightly fitting lid, which reduces the amount of liquid needed for cooking and results in more concentrated flavors. You can prepare this winter dish up to 3 hours in advance; just add extra liquid if needed and reheat 15 to 20 minutes prior to serving.

3 pounds beef short ribs (about 2 inches thick), cut in pairs, fat removed

1 bottle dry white wine (a Mâcon white, for example)

1/2 pound onions, peeled and cut into large wedges

1/4 pound bacon cut into 1/2-inch cubes

Salt, crushed black peppercorns

2 sprigs fresh thyme

6 sprigs parsley, leaves chopped and reserved, stems set aside

1 bay leaf

2 tablespoons sweet butter

2 tablespoons all-purpose flour

2 pounds medium red or white potatoes (about the size of a lemon), scrubbed and halved

✤ Preparation

Marinate the short ribs in a nonreactive bowl (porcelain or stainless steel) with the wine, onions, bacon, 1 teaspoon each salt and peppercorns, and a bouquet garni made of the thyme sprigs, parsley stems, and bay leaf tied together with kitchen string. Mix well, cover, and refrigerate overnight (or a minimum of 8 hours). When marinated, drain in a colander set over a bowl. Set both the drained ingredients and the marinade aside. (If you don't have time to marinate the meat, start with the next step of this recipe.)

Preheat oven to 425 degrees. In a roasting pan on top of the stove, melt the butter over high heat. Add the ribs and bacon and sauté on both sides, about 10 to 12 minutes, or until lightly browned. Add the marinated onions and bouquet garni, mix well, and sweat for 10 more minutes. Sprinkle with the flour and bake in the oven for 5 to 7 minutes. Return the roaster to the stove over medium heat, toss well for 3 minutes, and add the marinade, potatoes, salt, and pepper. Mix, cover, and bake in the oven for 45 to 75 minutes, depending on the thickness of the meat and potatoes. Mix well every 15 minutes while cooking.

✤ Presentation

Remove and discard the herbs. Sprinkle with chopped parsley and serve the *miroton* in the cooking pot.

SIRLOIN NAPOLEON WITH BLACK OLIVES AND ZUCCHINI

Serves 4

The thin slices of sirloin in this dish are seared on only one side. This keeps them slightly rare and the taste of the olives fresh. You can prepare the zucchini and tapenade up to an hour before serving, but the sirloin requires a last-minute sauté and assembly.

1/4 cup olive oil

*3 cloves garlic: 2 peeled and sliced,
1 peeled and chopped*

Salt, freshly ground black pepper

*3 zucchinis, about 6 inches long, ends trimmed,
cut lengthwise in 1/4-inch slices
(12 large slices)*

1 cup small black olives (Niçoise), pitted

*12 very thin slices of sirloin, 1/4-inch thick,
cut horizontally (about 2-1/2 ounces each)
trimmed; or four 8-ounce sirloin steaks,
each split into 3 horizontal slices*

*4 ripe plum tomatoes, split, seeded, in
1/4-inch dice*

3 tablespoons chives, chopped

3 tablespoons chervil, leaves only

❧ PREPARATION

Preheat the broiler. Brush a broiler pan with 1/2 tablespoon of the olive oil. Add a few slices garlic and salt and pepper. Place the zucchini slices side by side on the garlic. Brush 1/2 tablespoon of the olive oil on the slices, add the remaining garlic and salt and pepper. Broil the zucchini until light brown, about 5 minutes. Turn the slices over and repeat the process. Remove and keep warm.

Purée the pitted Niçoise olives in a blender or food processor. Add the chopped garlic and 1 tablespoon of the olive oil. Process again until smooth and set aside.

Fold 2 sheets of aluminum foil in 2 double-layered 8-inch squares. Brush each with olive oil. Brush the sirloin on one side with the olive purée. Place 6 slices of sirloin, olive side down, on each foil square. Brush the top of the sirloin with olive oil. Heat a large non-stick pan over high heat. When the pan is very hot, flip one square of the foil, sirloin side down, onto the pan. Keep the foil on while cooking. For rare, cook 1 minute, medium-rare 1-1/2 minutes, well-done 2 minutes. Flip the sirloin (foil side down) onto the counter. The steak will be cooked on only one side and the olive purée will be warm. Repeat the process with the remaining sirloin.

When the meat is cooked, add the tomatoes to the pan with 1 tablespoon olive oil, the chives, salt, and pepper. Toss for 2 minutes or until the tomatoes are warmed.

❧ PRESENTATION

Alternate 3 slices of steak with 3 slices of zucchini on each of 4 warmed serving dishes. Spoon the tomatoes over the top and garnish with the chervil leaves.

HANGER STEAK WITH SCALLIONS AND SHREDDED CORN CRÊPES

Serves 4

The full, beefy flavor of seared hanger steak goes well with robust corn salsa and crêpes in this recipe. Hanger steak is also called *bavette* in French and is a favorite cut served in French bistros. You can prepare the salsa and crêpes in this recipe up to 2 hours before serving, but sauté the beef at the last moment.

2-1/2 tablespoons olive oil, plus more for frying

2 cups corn kernels (about 6 medium fresh ears)

Salt, freshly ground black pepper

1/4 cup all-purpose flour

4 eggs

1 cup milk

Pinch of freshly grated nutmeg

3 tablespoons chives, finely chopped

1 pound hanger steak, trimmed of fat and cut into 1/2-inch strips on a bias across the grain

1/2 cup scallions, trimmed, and sliced 1/4 inch thick

1 small jalapeño pepper, split, cored, and finely chopped, or 1 teaspoon hot pepper flakes

1 clove garlic, peeled and chopped

1 cup tomatoes, cored, seeded, in 1/4-inch dice

❧ PREPARATION

Heat 1/2 tablespoon of the olive oil in a pan over medium heat. Add the corn, salt, and pepper, cover, and cook for 2 to 3 minutes, tossing twice. Transfer to a blender or food processor and set aside to cool. When cool, add the flour, eggs, milk, nutmeg, salt, and pepper. Blend until smooth and pour into a bowl. Add 1/2 of the chives and mix.

Brush a nonstick 6-inch pan over medium heat with olive oil. Add 2 or 3 tablespoons of the batter and tilt the pan so that it runs evenly to all edges. Cook for 1 to 2 minutes and flip the crêpe over. Cook for another 1 to 2 minutes. Remove to a large plate and set aside to cool. Repeat the process until you have cooked all of the batter (yields about 10 to 12 crêpes). Cut the crêpes into strips 1-inch wide and set aside.

Season the meat with salt and pepper. Warm the remaining 2 tablespoons olive oil in 1 very large skillet over high heat. Place the meat in the hot pan and sear for 1 minute. (This cooking time is for rare, which is best for this recipe. If you prefer medium, add 3 minutes.) Turn the meat over, spread the scallions, jalapeño, and garlic over each piece, and toss well for 1 minute. Add the crêpe strips and toss quickly for 1 minute to reheat the crêpes. Remove the meat and crêpes to a warm oval dish. Toss the tomato dice in the hot pan for 30 seconds over high heat and season with salt and pepper.

❧ PRESENTATION

Sprinkle the diced tomatoes and the remaining chives over the meat and crêpes.

BEEF TENDERLOIN WITH GLAZED ONIONS IN BALSAMIC VINEGAR

Serves 4

Balsamic vinegar imparts a wonderfully sweet/sour edge to this oven-roasted beef tenderloin garnished with onions, mushrooms, and artichokes. You can prepare the vegetables up to 2 hours in advance, but roast the beef just 20 minutes before serving.

8 medium artichokes

1 lemon, split

2 tablespoons olive oil

1/2 pound assorted fresh mushrooms (e.g., morels, chanterelles, or white mushrooms), caps only for morels and domestic mushrooms, cut in half if too large

2 sprigs fresh thyme

10 coriander seeds, crushed into a powder

Salt, freshly ground black pepper

1 clove garlic, peeled and finely chopped

2 pounds beef tenderloin, center cut, 3-inch diameter (ask your butcher to remove any skin and fat and to tie the roast with a string)

2 tablespoons sweet butter

2 pounds large spring or regular onions, peeled and cut into 1-inch wedges

1/2 cup balsamic vinegar (see note)

3 sprigs parsley, leaves only, finely chopped

Aged balsamic vinegar (25 years or more), for sprinkling on the cooked meat (optional)

❋ PREPARATION

Remove and discard the leaves of the artichokes. Shape the hearts with a knife until round and smooth and scoop out the chokes with a spoon. Rub each artichoke with a lemon half. Cut each heart into 6 wedges and squeeze the remaining piece of lemon over them.

Heat the olive oil in a large pan over medium heat. Add the artichokes, mushrooms, 1 sprig of thyme, and the coriander powder. Toss often and add salt and pepper. When the artichokes are fork tender, about 12 to 15 minutes, add the chopped garlic, discard the thyme, and taste for seasoning. Remove from heat and keep warm on the side.

While the vegetables are cooking, start preparing the meat.

Preheat oven to 425 degrees. Season the meat with salt and pepper. Melt the butter in a roasting pan on top of the stove over medium heat. Brown the beef tenderloin on all sides, about 7 to 8 minutes. Add the onions and the remaining thyme sprig. Mix well and place in the oven. Turn the beef and onions over and baste the meat with 1 table-spoon of the balsamic vinegar every 5 minutes using about 3 tablespoons total. For rare meat, cook 10 to 15 minutes, for medium-rare, 20 minutes, and for well-done, 25 to 35 minutes. Remove the tenderloin to a cutting board.

Add the remaining vinegar to the roasting pan and stir the onions a few times while cooking. Remove from oven when the vinegar has evaporated and the onions start to caramelize.

❋ PRESENTATION

Slice the tenderloin into 1/2-inch-thick slices and arrange them in the center of a warmed, oval serving platter. Spread the caramelized onions over the beef and arrange the mushrooms and artichokes around the edges. Sprinkle with parsley. Serve the aged balsamic vinegar, if using, on the side for guests who wish to add a few drops to flavor the meat.

Note: If you do not have any balsamic vinegar, reduce 1 cup of red wine vinegar with 2 cups of port wine to 1/4 cup in a small saucepan over medium heat (about 20 minutes). The flavor will not be the same as if using balsamic vinegar, but you will obtain a sweet-and-sour taste almost as rich.

ENSURING JUICY ROASTS: After roasting, let meat or poultry rest for a few minutes before carving. This will allow an even distribution of the juices throughout the roast and ensure more tender meat.

VEAL CHOPS WITH GINGER AND SWISS CHARD STRUDEL

Serves 4

Glistening candied ginger and a crispy Swiss chard–and–Parmesan-filled pastry create a delectable garnish
for the roasted veal chops in this recipe. A summer favorite, the strudel takes time—rather than skill—to prepare
its filling, roll, and bake, but it is well worth the effort. For easy serving, plan to assemble the strudel and candy
the ginger up to 8 hours beforehand and keep refrigerated. The strudel can be baked and
the veal roasted 20 minutes before serving.

For the Veal Chops and Juice:

2 tablespoons olive oil

4 veal chops, about 8 to 10 ounces each, fat
trimmed, 1 pound bones and trimmings from
the veal chops reserved

1/2 cup shallots, peeled and thinly sliced

1/4 cup carrots, peeled and sliced 1/4 inch thick

1/4 cup celery, sliced 1/4 inch thick

4 cloves garlic, peeled and crushed

1/2 cup dry white wine

Juice of 1 lemon

Salt, freshly ground black pepper

For the Candied Ginger:

3 ounces gingerroot (1 large root), peeled and
julienned (matchstick size), peel reserved

2 tablespoons sugar

For the Swiss Chard Strudel:

1-1/2 pounds Swiss chard, leaves only

1 pound spinach, leaves only

2 tablespoons olive oil

1/2 cup onions, finely chopped

1/2 cup white mushrooms, caps only,
thinly sliced

1 clove garlic, peeled and finely chopped

Salt, freshly ground black pepper

Pinch of freshly grated nutmeg

3 tablespoons mascarpone cheese

1/4 cup freshly grated Parmesan cheese

3 sheets phyllo dough
(14 by 18 inches each)

❧ PREPARATION

For the Veal Juice:

Preheat oven to 400 degrees. Heat 1 tablespoon of the olive oil in a roasting pan on top
of the stove over high heat. Add the bones and trimmings and sauté for 4 to 5 minutes.
Transfer the roasting pan to the oven and roast the bones for 10 minutes. Add the shallots, carrots, celery, garlic, and reserved ginger peel, toss well, and roast for 15 minutes
more, tossing from time to time. Add the white wine and cook for another 15 minutes.

Add 1 cup water, mix well, and cook for another 15 minutes. Strain the veal juice with a fine-mesh strainer into a small bowl, discard the bones and vegetables, and set the veal juice aside.

For the Candied Ginger:
While the bones are roasting, place the ginger in a small casserole with 1 cup water and the sugar. Boil gently for about 20 minutes until reduced to 1 tablespoon of heavy syrup. Drain through a strainer into a small bowl, reserve the syrup, and air-dry the ginger in the strainer.

For the Swiss Chard Strudel:
Bring 4 quarts water with 1 tablespoon of salt to a boil. Add the Swiss chard and boil for 3 to 4 minutes. Add the spinach leaves and boil for another 3 to 4 minutes, drain in a colander, and chill under cold water. Firmly press the greens inside the colander with your hands to remove any excess water and then chop them roughly. Set aside.

Heat 1 tablespoon of the olive oil in a large pan over high heat. Add the onions and toss for 3 minutes. Add the mushrooms and garlic, toss well, and cook until all moisture has evaporated, about 5 to 7 minutes. Add the greens, salt, pepper, and nutmeg and toss well. Remove from heat and set aside to cool.

When cool, transfer the greens, onion, and mushroom mixture to a blender or food processor and finely chop. Add the mascarpone and 2 tablespoons of the Parmesan and mix until well combined. Taste for seasoning and set aside.

Spread a slightly damp cotton kitchen towel on the counter. Unfold a sheet of phyllo dough on the towel and brush it with a light coat of olive oil. Sprinkle the dough with 1/2 tablespoon of the Parmesan. Place a second sheet of phyllo over the first one, brush it with olive oil, and sprinkle it with another 1/2 tablespoon Parmesan. Repeat the same process with a third sheet of phyllo dough.

Preheat oven to 400 degrees. Spoon the smooth green mixture along the longest side of the dough, 1 inch from the edge and sides. The green stuffing should be approximately 2 inches wide and 12 to 14 inches long. Roll the dough lengthwise around the green stuffing starting with the 1-inch-long side edge and close the ends by pressing down on the dough with your fingers.

Carefully transfer the strudel onto a baking sheet, brush the strudel on all sides with olive oil, and evenly sprinkle it with the remaining 1/2 tablespoon Parmesan. Bake the strudel for 12 to 15 minutes or until golden brown. Remove from heat and keep warm. Cut the strudel in 2-inch pieces with a serrated or electric knife just before serving.

For the Veal Chops:
Cook the veal chops when you are ready to bake the strudel. Heat 1/2 tablespoon of the olive oil in a hot pan over medium heat. Salt and pepper the veal chops on both sides

and sauté them for 5 to 7 minutes or until golden, then turn the chops over and cook for another 5 minutes or until golden. Remove the chops to a roasting pan and finish cooking them in the oven for another 8 to 10 minutes. Transfer the chops onto a warm serving platter and keep warm on the side.

Add 1/2 tablespoon of the ginger syrup to the hot pan used to cook the veal chops. Add the lemon juice, stir well, and cook for 1 minute on top of the stove. Add the veal juice, stir, and bring to a boil. Reduce the sauce to about 1/4 cup and stir in the remaining 1/2 tablespoon olive oil. Add seasoning to taste and strain over the veal chops.

❧ PRESENTATION

Sprinkle the warm veal chops with the candied ginger. Serve the strudel on the side.

Calf's Liver with Fresh Pea Croquettes

Serves 4
Highly nutritious calf's liver is presented with pea croquettes for a filling spring lunch.
You can prepare the pea croquettes 3 to 4 hours in advance.

2 slices bacon

3-1/2 cups freshly shelled peas (about 3-1/2 pounds unshelled)

2 tablespoons sweet butter

1/4 cup heavy cream

Salt, freshly ground black pepper

3 tablespoons all-purpose flour, sifted

2 eggs, beaten

1/2 cup fresh bread crumbs

2 tablespoons oil, for cooking

4 slices calf's liver, 1/2 inch thick, about 6 ounces each

1 cup onion, thinly sliced

2 tablespoons Spanish sherry vinegar or red wine vinegar

❀ Preparation

Preheat oven to 375 degrees. Place the bacon on a baking sheet with sides and crisp it in the oven until brown, about 15 minutes, or in the microwave for about 3 to 4 minutes. Cut the bacon slices into 1/2-inch segments and set aside.

Bring 2 quarts water with 1/2 tablespoon salt to a boil. Add the fresh shelled peas and boil for 8 to 10 minutes. Drain well in a colander, pressing lightly to extract any extra water. Transfer the peas to a blender or food processor, add 1 tablespoon of the butter, the heavy cream, a pinch of salt, and pepper and purée until smooth. Place a 10-inch square of waxed paper or plastic wrap on a baking sheet. Pour the pea purée evenly on the paper to form a 6-inch square 1/2 inch thick. Cover with a second sheet of paper or plastic, let cool, and freeze for 1 hour. Remove from freezer, discard both sheets of waxed paper, and place on a cutting board. Cut into 8 equal triangles by making diagonal cuts from corner to corner, and then a cross in the middle of the square. Prepare 3 bowls: one with the flour, one with the beaten eggs, and one with the bread crumbs. Dip each triangle on both sides first in the flour, then in the eggs, and finally in the bread crumbs, shaking each time to remove any excess. Refrigerate the breaded pea triangles until needed.

Heat 1 tablespoon of the oil in a large nonstick pan over medium heat. Add the pea croquettes and cook until golden brown, about 2 minutes on each side, turning them carefully. Remove from the pan with a spatula and keep warm.

Season the calf's liver with salt and pepper and dredge each slice in flour until lightly coated, shaking off any excess. Wipe the pan, add the remaining tablespoon oil, and heat over high heat until hot. Add the liver and cook for 3 minutes on each side for medium-rare (if slices are thin cook for 2 minutes per side). Remove the liver to a warm serving dish and add the remaining tablespoon butter to the pan. Add the onions and toss for 2 minutes. Add the vinegar and cook for 1 or 2 minutes or until most of the liquid has evaporated.

❀ PRESENTATION

Arrange the slices of liver overlapping one another in the center of a serving dish. Spread the onion butter sauce over the liver and place the pea croquettes all around, then sprinkle with the bacon.

CRUSTY SWEETBREADS WITH HOT MUSTARD, BACON, AND A SHALLOT JUS

Serves 4

One of my favorite ways to prepare sweetbreads is to coat them with a hot mustard crust and quickly sauté
to create a crunchy crust around this sweet and tender organ meat. For serving ease,
prepare the vegetables and bread the sweetbreads up to 3 hours in advance, refrigerate, and then
cook them 10 to 15 minutes before serving.

*1-1/2 pounds sweetbreads (3 pieces)
(Buy large pink and rounded sweetbreads and
avoid those with bruises or blood stains.)*

1 teaspoon salt

*Bouquet garni: 1 bay leaf, 1 sprig thyme,
2 sprigs parsley, and 1 stalk celery, tied together
with kitchen string*

3 cloves garlic, peeled and split

10 black peppercorns

1 small onion, peeled and studded with a clove

Salt, freshly ground black pepper

5 tablespoons all-purpose flour

*2 tablespoons Dijon mustard mixed with
1 teaspoon Colman's dry mustard*

*6 slices white bread, trimmed of crusts
and finely chopped*

1 tablespoon olive oil

*1/4 pound fresh chanterelle mushrooms or
seasonal mushrooms*

2 tablespoons sweet butter

3 tablespoons shallots, peeled and finely chopped

1 tablespoon parsley, leaves only, finely chopped

*5 endives (1/4 pound), ends trimmed, sliced
1 inch thick*

Pinch of sugar

1/2 tablespoon oil, for cooking

*2 tablespoons dry white Vermouth
(Noilly Prat) or port*

1/4 cup chicken stock (see page 370) or beef stock

*2 slices bacon, crisped under the broiler
or in the microwave*

✒ PREPARATION

Soak the sweetbreads in ice-cold water and refrigerate overnight or for at least 5 to 6
hours. Drain when ready to use.

Place the sweetbreads in a casserole and add cold water to cover. Add 1 teaspoon salt,
the bouquet garni, garlic, peppercorns, and onion and bring to a boil. Poach for 3 minutes at a low boil. Drain, discard the vegetables and bouquet garni, and set the sweetbreads on a cutting board to cool. Peel off the thin membrane and remove any fat and
nerves from the sweetbreads. Slice each sweetbread into 1/3-inch-thick slices (try to have
an equal number of slices per serving). Season with salt and pepper and sprinkle flour
on both sides of the sliced sweetbreads. Brush them with the mustard on one side and

place them mustard side down on the bread crumbs in a shallow dish. Brush the other side with mustard and cover with bread crumbs. Press gently to make the crumbs stick and transfer to a baking sheet or platter and refrigerate until ready to cook.

Heat 1/2 tablespoon of the olive oil in a large nonstick pan over high heat. Add the mushrooms and toss for 4 to 5 minutes. Add salt, pepper, 1/2 tablespoon of the butter, 1 tablespoon of the shallots, and 1/2 tablespoon of the parsley and toss for 2 minutes. Remove from the pan and keep warm on the side.

Wipe the pan clean and heat the remaining 1/2 tablespoon oil over high heat. Add the endive, salt, pepper, and sugar, cover with a lid, and cook for 2 minutes. Remove the lid and toss for 5 minutes with 1/2 tablespoon of the butter. When lightly caramelized, remove and keep warm.

Wipe the pan clean and heat the cooking oil over medium heat. Add the breaded sweetbreads and cook for 5 to 6 minutes or until golden brown. Add 1/2 tablespoon of the butter in small pieces and turn the sweetbreads over to cook for another 5 to 6 minutes. Remove the sweetbreads and keep warm. Wipe the pan clean, add the remaining 2 tablespoons shallots, and toss for 1 minute over medium heat. Add the vermouth and reduce to 1/4 cup. Add the chicken or beef stock and reduce to 4 tablespoons. Add the remaining 1/2 tablespoon butter and the remaining 1/2 tablespoon parsley. Taste for seasoning.

PRESENTATION

Place the endives in the center of a large warm platter or plate in a dome shape. Arrange the slices of sweetbread around them. Sprinkle with the mushrooms and the bacon and nap with the jus.

BRAISED VEAL SHANK WITH LEMON, DRIED APRICOTS, AND THYME

Serves 4

Sumptuous, festive, and inviting is the best way to describe these braised and glazed veal shanks with their lemony vegetables and dried apricots. This recipe can be prepared up to 3 hours before serving.

2 small veal shanks, about 2 pounds each (ask your butcher to trim the top and bottom bones and to remove any fat)

Salt, freshly ground back pepper

2 tablespoons all-purpose flour

1/4 cup olive oil

12 whole shallots, peeled

4 large carrots, peeled and sliced in 1/2-inch diagonal slices

8 medium turnips, peeled

8 cloves garlic, peeled

2 cups button mushrooms (about 1/2 pound)

3 sprigs thyme: 2 whole, 1 leaves only, finely chopped

1 bottle dry white wine

4 lemons: zest cut into julienne (matchstick size), and juice reserved

1 tablespoon sugar

1 cup apricot nectar (unsweetened if possible) or orange juice

16 dried apricot halves, presoaked for 1/2 hour in 1 cup warm water with the juice of 1 lemon (if you prefer to use fresh apricots, split them, remove the pits, and toss them in a hot pan with a touch of butter and sugar for 3 to 5 minutes before adding to the sauce and vegetables)

✤ PREPARATION

Preheat oven to 400 degrees. Salt and pepper the veal shanks and dredge them in the flour. Heat 3 tablespoons of the olive oil in a Dutch oven or other roasting pan on top of the stove over medium heat. Add the shanks and brown all sides gently until golden, about 10 minutes. Add the shallots, carrots, turnips, garlic, mushrooms, and 1 whole thyme sprig, place the pan in the oven, and roast, uncovered, for 20 minutes. Turn the meat over and toss the vegetables every 5 minutes. Add the white wine, cover with a lid, and cook for 30 to 40 minutes.

While the shanks are cooking, bring 2 quarts water to a boil. Add the lemon zest and boil for 15 minutes. Strain out the zest, rinse, and set aside.

Heat the sugar with 1 teaspoon water in a medium saucepan over high heat until brown (but not too dark). Remove from heat and pour the remaining lemon juice over, taking care not to get splattered. Stir the lemon juice to dilute the caramel and reduce by half over high heat. Add the apricot nectar or orange juice and stir until boiling rapidly.

Remove the roasting pan from the oven. Remove the vegetables from around the shanks with a skimmer or slotted spoon, and set them aside. Pour the lemon-apricot juice over the meat, mix well, cover, and cook for another 30 to 40 minutes. When done, the meat should be firm but easily pierced with a fork.

Remove the shanks, place them in a deep dish, and keep warm. Strain the sauce into the medium saucepan and discard the thyme sprig. You should have about 1-1/2 cups sauce. If you have less, add water to make up the difference. If you have more than 1-1/2 cups sauce, reduce over medium heat.

Drain the apricots well. Add them to the sauce with the blanched lemon zest and the vegetables. Reheat gently over medium heat and stir in the remaining tablespoon olive oil. Test for seasoning—the sauce should have a distinctive lemon flavor. If the sauce is not sour enough, you can add the juice of 1/2 lemon. If the taste of lemon is too strong, add 1 or 2 tablespoons sweet butter.

✤ PRESENTATION

Place the veal shanks in a deep serving dish. Spoon the vegetables and the sauce over the top. Sprinkle with the chopped thyme, sticking a few pieces of thyme sprig into the bone marrow.

Lamb Chops Champvallon

Serves 4

Braised lamb chops, onions, and potatoes perfumed with thyme make a classic, soul-satisfying winter dish. This recipe was created by one of King Louis XIV's mistresses to gain his favor. You can prepare this regal version up to 3 hours in advance then reheat it slowly 15 to 20 minutes before serving.

12 lamb chops, 1/2 inch thick, trimmed of all fat

Salt, freshly ground black pepper

1 tablespoon oil, for cooking

4 tablespoons sweet butter (2 tablespoons of it melted)

2 large onions, peeled and sliced 1/8 inch thick

2 cloves garlic, peeled and finely chopped

2 sprigs fresh thyme

2 bay leaves

3 pounds baking potatoes, peeled and sliced 1/8 inch thick

3 cups chicken stock (see page 370)

2 sprigs parsley, leaves only, minced

✤ Preparation

Preheat oven to 350 degrees. Use a thick copper pot about 4 inches deep and 14 inches in diameter, or a large roasting pan that fits all the chops. Salt and pepper the chops, heat the oil in the pan over high heat and brown on both sides for 3 to 4 minutes. Remove the chops and set aside.

Add 2 tablespoons of the butter, the onions, garlic, thyme, and bay leaves to the same roasting pan and sweat for 8 to 10 minutes (making sure the onions do not color).

Put the potatoes in a bowl. Add the salt, pepper, onions, garlic, and herbs. Mix well.

Brush the inside of the pan with 1 tablespoon of the melted butter. Spread 1/2 of the potato/onion mixture evenly on the bottom of it, about 1/4 inch thick and include 1 bay leaf and 1 thyme sprig. Fit all the chops side by side over the potato layer. Cover with the rest of the potato/onion mixture. The top layer will also be 1/4 inch thick and include 1 bay leaf and a thyme sprig. Press down on the top layer with a spatula. Pour in the chicken stock until it reaches the top layer of potatoes. Cut a piece of parchment paper the size of the inside of the pan to use as a lid. Brush it with the tablespoon melted butter and place it butter side down, covering the entire surface of the potatoes.

Bake for about 75 to 90 minutes. The top layer should be light brown and the inside moist, with 1/3 of the chicken stock left. Discard the parchment, bay leaves, and thyme.

✤ Presentation

Sprinkle the dish with parsley, and serve from the pan.

BRAISED LEG OF LAMB CLEOPATRA

Serves 6 to 8

This richly aromatic dish is inspired by the one served at our wedding rehearsal dinner in Cannes by the chef of our long-standing Egyptian friends, the El Maghrabys. Rubbing the leg of lamb with a combination of 11 spices—including cumin, allspice, cayenne, cardamom, fennel, and coriander—then baking it slowly for about 3 hours with a vegetable garnish produces an exquisitely tender and aromatic dish.

For the Leg of Lamb:

1 whole leg of lamb (approximately 5 to 6 pounds), fat and hipbone removed, oven ready

8 cloves garlic: 5 peeled and sliced, 3 peeled and each cut lengthwise into 6 sticks

Salt, freshly ground black pepper

1/4 cup olive oil

3 cups onions, peeled and coarsely chopped

4 cups carrots, peeled and coarsely chopped

3 cups celery, coarsely chopped

2 cups fresh fennel, trimmed and coarselychopped

1 small jalapeño pepper, halved, seeds discarded, and minced (wear disposable gloves when handling jalapeños)

4 cups tomatoes, cored, peeled, and coarsely chopped

6 cups chicken stock (see page 370)

1/4 cup Italian parsley, leaves only, chopped

For the Spice Mix:

Combine the following in a bowl but reserve 1 tablespoon of the spice mix for the vegetables 1/2 tablespoon for the couscous: 3 tablespoons ground cumin; 2 teaspoons cinnamon; 1 teaspoon ground allspice; 1 tablespoon ground coriander; 1/2 teaspoon freshly grated nutmeg; 1/2 tablespoon ground fennel seeds; 1 tablespoon ground cardamom; 1 teaspoon ground ginger; 1/2 teaspoon ground star anise; pinch of ground cloves; 1 teaspoon cayenne pepper

For the Couscous:

1 pound instant couscous

2 cups chicken stock

1 teaspoon honey

1/4 cup small golden raisins

3 tablespoons sweet butter

1/4 cup pine nuts, toasted

2 tablespoons fresh coriander leaves, finely chopped

❊ PREPARATION

For the Leg of Lamb:

Preheat the oven to 375 degrees. Make 18 deep incisions all around the leg of lamb with a small knife. Push a garlic stick into each incision. Season the meat with 4 tablespoons of the spice mix, salt, and pepper. Rub the leg to help the meat absorb the seasoning.

On top of the stove, heat 3 tablespoons of the olive oil in a deep roasting pan over high heat and brown the leg of lamb on all sides, about 15 minutes.

Add the sliced garlic, onions, carrots, celery, fennel, and jalapeño pepper and stir well for 10 minutes over medium heat. Add the tomatoes and sprinkle the reserved tablespoon of spice mix and 1 teaspoon salt over the vegetables. Cover with a lid or aluminum foil and roast in the oven for 1 hour. Turn the vegetables and lamb every 10 to 15 minutes.

Bring the chicken stock to a boil, add to the roasting pan, and tightly cover again. Lower the temperature to 300 degrees and cook for another 2-1/2 hours. Turn the lamb every 15 to 20 minutes and stir the vegetables around while cooking. The lamb should be very tender when cooked and there should be 1-1/2 to 2 cups of sauce left.

Remove the pan and carefully transfer the leg of lamb to a large and deep warmed serving dish. Spoon the vegetables all around the lamb and keep warm.

To finish the sauce, add the parsley, remaining tablespoon olive oil, salt, and pepper to taste and stir.

For the Couscous:
Spread the couscous into a small casserole. Bring the chicken stock to a boil and dissolve the honey and 1/2 tablespoon of the spices in the stock. Add the couscous, then add the raisins, mix well, and cover tightly with foil. Keep warm in the oven for 10 to 15 minutes at 250 degrees. Remove from the oven, discard the foil, add the butter, and mix with a fork. Transfer the couscous to a warm serving bowl and sprinkle with the toasted pine nuts and coriander leaves. Keep warm until ready to serve.

❀ PRESENTATION

Pour the sauce over the meat and vegetables. Serve the couscous on the side and carve the meat at the table.

GETTING THE MOST OUT OF SPICES: Toasting whole spices (cumin seeds, coriander seeds, cinnamon sticks, cloves, peppercorns) in a dry pan for a minute or two over low heat brings out their natural oils and flavor. They can then be ground and will have a much fresher flavor than preground spices. Always store spices away from heat and light. As they will lose their flavor over time, buy them only as needed or in small quantities.

Leg of Baby Lamb with Lemon, Tomatoes, Artichokes, and Olives

Serves 4 to 6

By combining lemons, tomatoes, artichokes, thyme, and olives, this recipe for lamb uses ingredients familiar to the Riviera. Spring is traditionally the best time for baby lamb and for lemons. This refreshingly light dish is easy to assemble and can be prepared up to 2 hours in advance and finished 35 to 40 minutes before serving.

3 lemons: zest cut into a thin julienne (matchstick size), the juice of 2 lemons, and the filleted sections of one (white inner skin and membranes removed with a paring knife)

16 baby artichokes

2 legs of baby lamb, about 2-1/2 pounds each (ask your butcher to remove the hipbones and make the legs oven-ready)

1 teaspoon crushed black peppercorns

3 tablespoons olive oil

2 sprigs fresh thyme

1 bay leaf

1/2 cup onions, peeled and coarsely chopped

2 cloves garlic, peeled and chopped

Salt, freshly ground black pepper

1 teaspoon honey

8 plum tomatoes, cored, peeled, halved lengthwise, seeds discarded

1/4 cup small black olives (Niçoise)

3 sprigs Italian parsley, leaves only, chopped

❋ Preparation

Bring the julienne of lemon zest to a boil in a quart of water for 8 to 10 minutes; drain, add another quart of fresh water, and bring to a boil again. Strain out the zest and set aside.

Remove the outer leaves of the baby artichokes, cut off the tips of the leaves 1 inch above the hearts, and trim the bottoms until round and smooth with a small paring knife. Halve the artichokes lengthwise and toss them in the juice of 1/2 lemon. Set aside.

Preheat oven to 425 degrees. Season the baby lamb with the crushed black peppercorns and salt. On top of the stove, heat 2 tablespoons of the olive oil in a large roasting pan over high heat. Brown the lamb on all sides, about 5 to 7 minutes. Add the thyme, bay leaf, onions, garlic, and baby artichokes, and stir well. Add a touch of salt and pepper and roast in the oven for 25 to 30 minutes, turning the roasts and tossing the vegetables every 6 to 8 minutes.

Brush the legs with the honey, pour the remaining juice of 1-1/2 lemons over the top, and add the cooked lemon zest. Mix well and roast for 5 minutes. Add the tomato halves and roast for another 12 to 15 minutes. Remove from the oven when done.

To check doneness, use a meat thermometer. For rare, the thermometer should read 130 to 140 degrees. For medium-rare, 145 to 155 degrees, and for well-done, above 170 degrees.

Transfer the legs of lamb to a cutting board, cover loosely with foil, and let them rest for 10 minutes. Add 2 tablespoons water to the vegetables and mix. Taste for seasoning.

Pit the Niçoise olives by placing them in a zip-lock bag and lightly crushing them with a mallet or the flat side of a large knife. Remove the olives, discard the pits, and set aside.

❊ PRESENTATION

Carve the legs of lamb into thin slices on an angle from the plump side of the shank. Place one bone in the middle of a large oval serving dish with the sliced meat resting on each side of the bone. Arrange the vegetables over and around the meat and bone. Drizzle the remaining tablespoon olive oil over the meat and vegetables. Sprinkle the lemon fillets with the Niçoise olives and parsley.

Eggplant and Lamb Cake with a Garlic Jus

Serves 4 to 6

In this elegant interpretation of moussaka, eggplant is cut into thin lengthwise slices, roasted, then used to line a low, round mold. Separate layers of sautéed mushrooms, tomatoes, lamb medallions, and spinach are packed inside and the assembly is baked and served with a fragrant garlic, cumin and coriander jus. This cake can be prepared up to 6 hours in advance, refrigerated until needed, then baked for 15 minutes before serving.

For the Lamb Medallions:

12 lamb chops, about 3 pounds total
(Ask your butcher to separate the chops if on a rack, cut out the 12 medallions of lamb from the bones, and trim the meat and bones of fat and tendons. Reserve the trimmed bones for the jus.)

Salt, freshly ground black pepper

1 tablespoon olive oil

For the Lamb Jus:

3 cloves garlic, peeled and thinly sliced

2 sprigs fresh thyme

1/4 cup onions, peeled and coarsely chopped

1 teaspoon ground cumin

10 coriander seeds

2 teaspoons tomato paste

1 cup dry white wine

For the Vegetables:

5 tablespoons olive oil

3 large eggplants, peeled, ends trimmed, and sliced lengthwise into 1/4-inch-wide strips

Salt, freshly ground black pepper

2 large tomatoes, cored, peeled, and sliced 1/4 inch thick

2 cups white mushrooms, caps only, sliced

1 cup onions, peeled and thinly sliced

2 pounds spinach leaves, stems removed, thoroughly washed and drained

2 cloves garlic, peeled and chopped

❦ Preparation

For the Lamb Medallions:
Place the lamb medallions side by side on a cutting board. Cover them with parchment paper and flatten them slightly with a mallet or with the palm of your hand. Discard the parchment paper and salt and pepper the medallions on both sides.

On top of the stove, heat the olive oil over high heat in a large roasting pan. Add all of the lamb medallions and brown 1 to 2 minutes on each side for rare, 3 to 4 minutes for medium, and 5 to 7 minutes for well-done. Remove the lamb and set aside to cool.

For the Lamb Jus:
Preheat oven to 425 degrees. Add the reserved lamb bones to the roasting pan and roast in the oven for 35 to 40 minutes. Add the garlic, thyme, onions, cumin, and coriander seeds and roast for another 10 minutes. Remove from the oven and place the pan on the

stove. Add the tomato paste, stir well, add the white wine, and reduce over high heat until all the moisture is evaporated. Add 1 cup water, simmer gently, and reduce to 1/3 cup. Strain over a small bowl and set the sauce aside. Discard the bones and herbs.

For the Vegetables:

Preheat oven to 425 degrees. Brush a baking pan with olive oil. Place the eggplant strips side by side in the pan. Brush the top of each with olive oil, then salt and pepper them. Bake the eggplant in the oven until soft, lightly roasted, and golden, about 20 minutes. Finish cooking under the broiler if necessary. Remove the eggplants with a spatula and set aside to cool.

Brush the pan used to cook the eggplant with olive oil. Sprinkle it with salt and pepper. Put the tomato slices in the pan and roast them in the oven for about 20 minutes or until baked and lightly dried.

While the eggplants and tomatoes are roasting in the oven, heat 1/2 tablespoon of the olive oil in a large skillet over high heat and sauté the mushrooms for 5 minutes. Add the onions and cook for another 5 minutes. Sprinkle with salt and pepper and transfer the mushroom mixture to a plate.

To assemble the cake, line the bottom of an 8-inch springform cake pan (or a regular cake pan lined with parchment paper) with the cooked slices of eggplant in the following way: Place the narrow end of an eggplant slice at the center of the mold (like the hand of a clock) with the wider end resting over the rim of the mold. Slightly overlap the next slice on the first one and continue lining the mold clockwise with the rest of the eggplant slices.

Next, spread the mushroom mixture over the eggplant-lined cake mold. Press with a spoon to flatten the surface. Place the baked tomatoes over the mushrooms and flatten again using a spoon. Place the lamb medallions over the tomatoes and flatten. Place the spinach over the lamb and flatten. Close the cake by folding the large-ends of eggplant slices over the spinach. Press down very firmly over the surface with a board or plate.

Twenty minutes before serving, reheat the cake in a 350-degree oven for 15 to 20 minutes. Bring the lamb jus to a boil and stir in 1/2 tablespoon olive oil. Taste for seasoning.

❧ Presentation

Invert the eggplant cake on a round platter and unmold it. Serve the warm lamb jus on the side. You can slice the cake with an electric or serrated knife, or serve it with a spoon, cutting around the small chops.

PIG KNUCKLES WITH ENDIVES, LENTILS, AND OREGANO

Serves 4

With its full-bodied fresh pork flavor and rich, lusty sauce, this braised knuckle is a casual midwinter dinner entrée. Slightly bitter endive provides a nice contrast to the somewhat sweet pork and earthy lentils in this dish, which requires overnight marinating. You can prepare this recipe up to 5 hours in advance, then reheat as needed.

For the Knuckles and Endives:

4 fresh pig knuckles, about 1 pound each and 2-1/2 to 3 inches in height

2 tablespoons coarse salt

2 tablespoons mixed seasonings:
Combine in a cup 2 teaspoons freshly ground black pepper, 2 teaspoons minced garlic, and 2 teaspoons ground coriander

4 whole sprigs fresh oregano or 2 tablespoons dried leaves

2 bay leaves

2 cups carrots, peeled and sliced at an angle 1/3 inch thick

1 cup onion, peeled and sliced

8 medium Belgian endives, hard ends and wilted outer leaves discarded

Salt, freshly ground black pepper

4 slices bacon, halved widthwise

1 teaspoon honey

2 tablespoons Spanish sherry vinegar

For the Lentils:

1-1/2 cups green lentils

1 bay leaf

1 sprig fresh thyme

1 small onion, peeled

1 carrot, peeled

1 stalk celery

1 tablespoon salt

1 tablespoon sweet butter

Dijon mustard, for serving

✤ PREPARATION

For the Knuckles and Endives:
Rub the pig knuckles with the coarse salt and 1 tablespoon of the mixed seasonings a day in advance or at least 8 to 10 hours prior to cooking. Cover with plastic wrap and refrigerate until ready to cook.

Place the pig knuckles in a deep pot and cover with water. Add 2 sprigs oregano, 1 bay leaf, 1 cup of the carrots, and 1/2 cup of the onions. Bring to a boil over high heat, reduce heat, and simmer for 1-1/2 to 2 hours. Skim the surface from time to time. Remove the knuckles with a slotted spoon to a plate. Strain and set aside 4 cups of the cooking liquid, discarding the rest with the vegetables and aromatic herbs.

Preheat oven to 400 degrees. Salt and pepper the endives and wrap each one in a slice of bacon. On top of the stove, sauté the wrapped endives on all sides in a large Dutch oven or roasting pan over medium heat until the bacon fat melts. Add the remaining cup carrots and the remaining 1/2 cup onion, the remaining 2 sprigs oregano, 1 bay leaf, and 1 tablespoon ground seasoning mix, and toss for 3 minutes. Add the pig knuckles to the pot around the endives and a pinch of salt and pepper. Cover with a lid, transfer to the oven, and braise for 30 to 40 minutes. Turn the endives and meat every 10 to 12 minutes, adding 1/2 cup of the strained cooking liquid at a time if the ingredients become too dry.

For the Lentils:

While the pig knuckles are cooking with the endives, cook the lentils. Place the lentils in a pot with 8 cups cold water. Bring to a boil, add the bay leaf, thyme, onion, carrot, and celery with the tablespoon of salt. Return to a boil, skim the surface, and simmer for 35 to 45 minutes or until tender. Drain and discard the vegetables, bay leaf, and thyme. Toss the warm lentils with the butter and keep warm.

Mix the honey and vinegar together in a small bowl. Remove the casserole from the oven. Place the pig knuckles in a pan and brush them with the honey-vinegar mixture. Return the pan to the oven and cook until the skin caramelizes lightly (turn them often).

Remove the bacon from the endives and discard. Discard the oregano and bay leaf.

✣ PRESENTATION

Spread the lentils over the bottom of a deep warmed serving dish or serve in the roasting casserole. Place the pig knuckles on top, in the center, and arrange the endives, carrots, and onion over and around the knuckles. Pour the cooking juice around. Serve
with Dijon mustard on the side.

Roast Loin of Pork with Curried Cauliflower and Apple Purée

Serves 4 to 6

This beautifully bronzed, curried roast pork loin is as tender and delicate as it is handsome and fragrant. Here it is served with a thick, creamy cauliflower and apple purée, a splendid counter to the rich, dense roast. To facilitate serving, this pork loin can be cooked 1 hour before serving and kept warm, and the accompanying purée can be prepared up to 2 hours in advance. You can also use pork chops if you do not have the time to cook the loin.

For the Roast Loin of Pork:

3-1/2 pounds of pork loin, boned and oven ready, chine and rib bones reserved for the jus

Pinch of cayenne pepper

1/2 tablespoon Madras curry powder

Pinch of saffron (powder or threads)

Salt, freshly ground black pepper

1 tablespoon lard (or sweet butter)

1 cup onions, peeled and cut into 1-inch-thick wedges

1 cup carrots, peeled and sliced into 1/2-inch segments

1 tablespoon garlic, peeled and sliced

1 bay leaf

3 sprigs fresh coriander, leaves chopped, stems reserved

2 sprigs Italian parsley, leaves chopped, reserved

1/2 cup dry white wine

2 cups chicken stock (see page 370)

For the Cauliflower and Apple Purée:

3 cups cauliflower florets (about 1-1/2-pound head)

1/2 tablespoon sweet butter

1 cup onion, peeled and thinly sliced

2 Golden Delicious apples, peeled, split, cored, in 1/2-inch dice, peels and scraps reserved

1/2 tablespoon Madras curry powder

Pinch of saffron (powder or threads)

Pinch of cayenne pepper

Salt

3/4 cup heavy cream

1/2 tablespoon sweet butter

🖎 Preparation

For the Roast Loin of Pork:

Preheat oven to 350 degrees. Season the pork with the cayenne pepper, curry powder, saffron, salt, and black pepper. Melt the lard in a Dutch oven or roaster on top of the stove over high heat. Add the roast, chine, and rib bones and brown the meat on all sides, about 10 minutes. Add the onions, carrots, garlic, bay leaf, reserved apple scraps and peels, and the coriander and parsley stems. Stir well for 2 to 3 minutes and place the casserole in the oven. Turn the roast over every 10 minutes. After 1/2 hour of roasting, add the white wine, cover with a piece of aluminum foil, and roast for another 1/2 hour. Add the chicken stock, stir well, and cook for another 30 to 40 minutes. Turn the roast every 15 minutes while it's cooking. When the meat is tender and done, transfer the casserole to the stove top. Remove the loin of pork to a cutting board and wrap with foil to keep it warm. Reduce the cooking liquid to about 1/4 cup over medium-high heat, or add a touch of water to make 1/4 cup liquid. Strain the liquid into a small saucepan, discard the bones and vegetables, and set aside.

For the Cauliflower and Apple Purée:
Bring 2 quarts water with 1/2 tablespoon salt to a boil over high heat. Add the cauliflower florets and boil for 6 to 8 minutes or until tender when pierced with a knife. Drain and set aside.

Heat the butter in a casserole over medium heat. Add the sliced onions, apple dice, curry powder, saffron, cayenne pepper, and a pinch of salt. Reduce heat to low and sweat until soft for about 15 minutes (making sure not to color the onions). Add the cooked cauliflower and mix well. Pour in the heavy cream, bring to a boil, and simmer gently for another 15 minutes. Pour the mixture into a blender or food processor and purée. Spoon the purée into a warmed serving bowl. Keep warm until needed.

Just before serving, carve the loin of pork into thin slices. Over low heat, stir 1/2 tablespoon butter into the jus and add the chopped coriander and parsley leaves.

PRESENTATION

On a warm serving platter, arrange the slices of pork in a rosette shape (overlapping in a circle). Spoon on the hot jus. Serve the cauliflower and apple purée on the side.

SUCKLING PIG WITH SNOW PEAS, RADISHES, AND ROSEMARY

Serves 12 to 15

Edible from head to toe, roast suckling pig is one of the most succulent dishes in Western cuisine.
This version is precut to facilitate its cooking and serving. A full day of marinating is needed to flavor the meat.
The vegetables can be prepared 2 to 3 hours in advance but should be cooked at the last minute.
The meat will require 1 hour of cooking before serving.

For the Suckling Pig:

3 tablespoons garlic, peeled and chopped

1 teaspoon hot pepper flakes

2 sprigs rosemary, leaves only, finely chopped

8 juniper berries, crushed and finely chopped

12 coriander seeds, crushed

1/2 cup shallots, peeled and sliced

2 teaspoons freshly ground black pepper

3 tablespoons olive oil

1 suckling pig, approximately 15 pounds
(Ask your butcher to cut the pig into pieces:
2 back legs with hipbone removed; 1 saddle;
2 shoulders, deboned, tied, and ready to roast;
2 sets of short ribs, and 2 racks.
Have the bones split in small pieces for the
sauce. Liver and kidneys are optional—
you can roast them with the rest of the meat for
about 20 minutes. Head, neck, and feet
can be reserved to make headcheese pâté,
otherwise discard.)

Salt

5 tablespoons red wine vinegar

For the Sauce:

2 tablespoons olive oil

1 cup carrots, peeled and coarsely chopped

1 cup onions, peeled and coarsely chopped

1/2 cup celery, ends trimmed, coarsely chopped

2 sprigs rosemary

1 head garlic, split in half horizontally

8 juniper berries

1/4 teaspoon hot pepper flakes

1/4 cup red wine vinegar

2 cups dry white wine

1 cup tomatoes, coarsely chopped

Salt, freshly ground black pepper

1 tablespoon sweet butter

For the Garnish:

4 bunches small pink radishes
(about 40 to 50 radishes), top greens and
rootlets discarded, scrubbed

2 pounds fresh snow peas or sugar peas, ends
trimmed

1 tablespoon olive oil

2 tablespoons sweet butter

12 scallions, white part only

1/2 cup carrots, peeled and cut into small strips

1/2 cup celery, cut into 1/8-inch slices

2 sprigs rosemary, leaves only, finely chopped

1 tablespoon garlic, peeled and finely chopped

Salt, freshly ground black pepper

❊ PREPARATION

For the Suckling Pig:

In a bowl, mix together the garlic, hot pepper flakes, rosemary, juniper berries, crushed coriander seeds, shallots, pepper, and olive oil. Rub each piece of meat with the mixture. Place the seasoned pieces of meat in a container and cover with plastic wrap. Marinate the suckling pig in the refrigerator for 24 hours.

Preheat oven to 425 degrees. Place the pieces of marinated meat, skin side up (leaving a bit of space between the pieces), in 1 or 2 roasting pans (the largest size that will fit in your oven). Wipe off the seasoning from the skin with a paper towel to avoid burning when roasting. Sprinkle 1 tablespoon salt evenly over the skin and rub it in with your fingers. Let the skin dry at room temperature for 1 hour before cooking (this will insure a crispy roasted skin).

Place the pan in the oven and roast for 30 minutes. Remove from heat, brush each piece of meat with a little red wine vinegar, and cook in the oven for another 10 minutes. Remove the pan from the oven, transfer the racks and short ribs to a cutting board after a total of 40 minutes of roasting. Baste the rest of the meat again with vinegar, return the pan to the oven, and cook for another 10 minutes.

Remove the pan from the oven and transfer the saddle to the cutting board after a total of 50 minutes of roasting. Baste the rest of the meat again with vinegar and cook for another 10 minutes.

Remove the pan from the oven and transfer the shoulders to the cutting board after a total of 1 hour of roasting. Return the pan to the oven and roast the legs for 10 to 15 minutes more (for a total of 70 to 75 minutes). Each cooked piece of meat should reach an internal temperature of 170 degrees to 180 degrees. Let the meat rest for 10 to 15 minutes before carving.

For the Sauce:

Prepare the sauce while the suckling pig is roasting. Heat 1 tablespoon of the olive oil in a large cast-iron pot oven medium heat. Add the reserved bones and color for 13 to 20 minutes. Add the carrots, onions, celery, rosemary, garlic, juniper berries, and hot pepper flakes and stir for another 10 minutes. Add the red wine vinegar and cook for 5 minutes. Add the white wine and the tomatoes, bring to a boil, and boil for 10 minutes. Add 3 cups water, return to a boil, and simmer for 1 hour. You should have approximately 1 1/2 cups sauce left. Strain the sauce over a bowl. Discard the bones and vegetables and transfer the sauce back into the cooking pot on the stove top. Reduce the sauce to 1 cup over medium heat if needed. Salt and pepper to taste and stir in the remaining tablespoon olive oil and the butter.

For the Garnish:

Bring 4 quarts water with 1 tablespoon salt to a boil. Add the pink radishes and boil for 3 minutes. Add the snow peas and boil for 3 to 4 minutes. Drain and chill under cold running water. Drain again and set aside.

In each of 2 pans over medium heat, heat 1/2 tablespoon of the olive oil and 1 tablespoon of the butter. Put 1/2 of the scallions, carrots, celery, and rosemary in each pan and sweat for 5 minutes (do not color). Add 1/2 of the pink radishes, 1/2 of the snow peas, salt, and pepper to each pan and cook for about 10 minutes while tossing often. Add the garlic, toss well, combine in 1 pan, and keep warm until ready to serve.

❊ Presentation

Carve the legs, shoulders, and saddle into thin slices. Cut the chops and ribs through the rib bone. Arrange the meat on a large platter or roasting pan. Spoon the hot jus over the top. Serve the vegetables on the side in a serving bowl.

LEG OF VENISON WITH STUFFED MINI-PUMPKINS

Serves 6 to 8

This elegant fall dish combines gamy venison marinated for 48 hours prior to cooking with
mini-pumpkins stuffed with nutritious spiced sweet potato and banana purée, salsify, and chestnuts.
The ingredients for the mini-pumpkins can be prepared up to 2 hours in advance.
The venison should be roasted about 1 hour before serving.

For the Leg of Venison:

*1 leg of young venison, about 6 to 8 pounds
(or 1/2 of a large leg), boneless, trimmed,
and ready to roast*

*1 cup onions, peeled and cut into
1/2-inch wedges*

1/2 cup carrots, peeled and sliced 1/2 inch thick

1/2 cup celeriac, peeled, in 1/2-inch dice

5 cloves garlic, peeled

1 tablespoon juniper berries, crushed

2 bay leaves

1/2 tablespoon crushed black peppercorns

1 bottle red wine (strong bodied for cooking)

Salt, freshly ground black pepper

2 tablespoons oil, for cooking

2 pounds venison bones, broken into pieces

2 tablespoons all-purpose flour

1 tablespoon sweet butter

For the Stuffed Mini-Pumpkins:

*8 mini-pumpkins, about 3 to 4 inches wide,
scrubbed*

2 tablespoons sweet butter

1/4 cup onions, peeled and finely chopped

*1 cup apples, peeled, split, cored,
in 1/4-inch dice*

1 cup sweet potatoes, peeled, in 1/4-inch dice

1/4 cup bananas, peeled and sliced

1 teaspoon ground cinnamon

1 cup heavy cream

Salt, freshly ground black pepper

Juice of 1 lemon

*6 cups salsify root (about 1 pound), peeled
and cut into 3-inch segments*

1 cup oil, for frying

16 chestnuts, skin slit on the dome side

*16 spinach leaves, stems discarded, thoroughly
washed and patted dry*

✍ PREPARATION

For the Leg of Venison:
Place the leg of venison in a porcelain or other nonreactive baking dish and spread the
onions, carrots, celeriac, garlic, juniper berries, bay leaves, and black peppercorns over
the top and all around. Add the red wine. Cover and marinate in the refrigerator for at
least 48 hours.

Preheat oven to 425 degrees. Remove the venison from the marinade and pat it dry with a paper towel. Strain the vegetables and set the wine and vegetables aside separately. Salt and pepper the venison leg.

Heat the cooking oil in a large roasting pan on top of the stove over high heat. Add the venison leg and brown on all sides. Place the bones all around the leg, the marinated vegetables over the bones, mix, and roast in the oven for 15 to 20 minutes. Turn the leg over, stir the bones, and sprinkle the flour over the bones and vegetables. Mix well and roast for 10 minutes more. Add the red wine marinade, stir well, and cook for 20 to 30 minutes more or until the internal temperature of the venison has reached 130 degrees for rare to 150 degrees for medium. Transfer the roasting pan to the stove top and remove the leg to a cutting board, keeping it warm under a tent of aluminum foil. You should have approximately 2 cups sauce left in the pan. If you have less sauce, add 1/4 cup of water. Reduce the sauce to 1 cup over medium heat, about 15 minutes, add salt and pepper, and strain over a small saucepan. Discard the bones and vegetables. When ready to serve, stir the butter into the warm sauce.

For the Stuffed Mini-Pumpkins:
Preheat oven to 350 degrees. Place the whole pumpkins in a roasting pan, cover with a piece of aluminum foil, and bake them for 30 to 40 minutes or until easily pierced with a knife. Set aside to cool, then cut off, and discard the top section, about a 1/4-inch cap. Scoop out and discard the seeds with a small spoon. Scoop out the flesh and set aside. Set the hollow pumpkin shells aside.

Melt 1 tablespoon of the butter in a large skillet over medium heat. Add the chopped onions, apple and sweet potato dice, bananas, and cinnamon and sweat for 8 to 10 minutes. Add the heavy cream and simmer gently for 15 to 20 minutes until the sweet potatoes are cooked. Transfer the sweet potato and banana mix to a blender or food processor, add the pumpkin flesh, salt, and pepper and blend until finely puréed. If too thick, add a few drops of water. Stuff each pumpkin shell with the purée (not quite to the rim) and keep warm.

Bring 2 quarts water with 1 teaspoon salt and the lemon juice to a boil. Add the salsify and boil for 15 minutes or until tender when pierced with a knife. Drain, cool, quarter each piece lengthwise, and set aside.

Heat the frying oil to 350 degrees in a large heavy-bottom pan. Fry the chestnuts for about 3 to 4 minutes. Remove, drain on a paper towel, and peel while warm. Set aside with the salsify. Fry the spinach leaves a few at a time for about 1 minute. Drain on paper towels and add a pinch of salt.

Melt the remaining tablespoon butter in a pan over medium heat. Add the salsify pieces and the chestnuts and toss for 2 to 3 minutes. Salt and pepper to taste.

Garnish each stuffed pumpkin with 6 to 8 pieces of salsify. Place 2 chestnuts side by side on the edge of each pumpkin, and stick 2 fried spinach leaves between the chestnuts.

🌿 PRESENTATION

Carve the leg of venison into thin slices. Arrange the slices, slightly overlapping, around a large platter. Place the stuffed mini-pumpkins in the middle of the platter. Pour 1/2 of the hot sauce over the meat and the rest into a gravy boat to be served on the side.

Pheasant Salad with Walnuts, Crisp Celery, and Artichokes

Serves 4

This elegant warm autumn salad combines delicate woodsy flavors with crunchy textures.
If pheasant is not available, guinea fowl, quail, or squab will work well as substitutes. You can prepare the salad
and vegetables 2 to 3 hours in advance and refrigerate. Just season and toss the salad right before serving and
cook the meat and vegetables 1 hour before serving.

For the Pheasants:

*2 pheasants (hens), 2 pounds each, trussed
and ready to roast*

Salt, freshly ground black pepper

2 tablespoons oil, for cooking

For the Vegetables:

4 artichokes, rinsed

1 cup plus 1 tablespoon oil, for frying

*1 cup celeriac, peeled and cut in a julienne
(3-inch matchsticks)*

3 cups seasonal wild mushrooms, sliced

*1 tablespoon balsamic vinegar
(aged balsamic, if possible)
or red wine vinegar*

*1/2 tablespoon Spanish sherry vinegar or
1 tablespoon red wine vinegar*

2 tablespoons olive oil

2 tablespoons walnut oil

2 tablespoons coarsely chopped walnut halves

2 tablespoons chives, minced

Salt, freshly ground black pepper

*1 pound assorted fresh greens
(mâche, curly chicory, escarole)*

Preparation

For the Pheasants:

Preheat oven to 450 degrees. Salt and pepper the pheasants inside and out. Heat
1 tablespoon of the oil in a roasting pan on top of the stove over high heat. Add the
pheasants and brown on all sides, approximately 5 to 6 minutes altogether. Set the birds
on their backs and roast in the oven for 20 to 25 minutes. Remove from heat and set
aside on a cutting board to cool. Remove the breasts with a sharp knife and set aside.
Remove the leg meat and cut it into small cubes. Discard the bones.

Heat the remaining tablespoon oil in a pan over high heat. Add the diced leg meat cubes
and sauté until crisp, about 10 to 12 minutes. Transfer the leg meat to a paper towel to
drain and sprinkle with a pinch of salt.

For the Vegetables:

Peel the outer leaves of each artichoke, cut off the stem below the heart, and shape the
bottom with a paring knife until round and smooth. Cut off the tips of the leaves to
within 1/2 inch of the hearts and core the hearts. Finely slice with a mandoline or
vegetable slicer.

Heat the cup of oil in a large pot to 350 degrees and fry the artichoke slices until golden. Remove to a paper towel to drain and sprinkle with a pinch of salt.

Fry the celeriac in the same hot oil until light golden brown. Remove to a paper towel to drain and sprinkle with a pinch of salt.

Heat 1 tablespoon of the oil in a pan over high heat. Sauté the mushrooms until cooked and lightly colored, about 5 to 7 minutes. Set aside.

Preheat broiler. Make the dressing by mixing the vinegars with the oils, walnuts, chives, salt, and pepper.

Just before serving, warm up the pheasant breasts under the broiler for 2 to 3 minutes. Cut them into thin slices and pour 1 tablespoon dressing over the warm breasts.

Toss the mixed greens with the rest of the dressing just before serving.

PRESENTATION

Place half of the tossed greens on the bottom of a large serving dish. Arrange the warm slices of breast over the salad greens. Arrange the rest of the greens in a bunch in the middle. Sprinkle with the crisp pieces of leg meat, warm mushrooms, and artichoke and celeriac chips. Serve warm.

BUYING PHEASANT: If you are cooking an imported pheasant from Scotland (its meat is darker and tastier than that of domestic-bred pheasants), look for and remove the shot while carving the bird. If you buy farm-raised pheasants, make sure they're free-range—raised under nets in large open areas where they can feed on a variety of foods. Battery-raised pheasants will taste like chicken.

Wild Partridge with a Red Cabbage Confit and Fall Fruit Chutney

Serves 4

The mild gamy taste of roasted partridge in this recipe is highlighted with sweet and sour garnishes. The cabbage confit and fall fruit chutney are sweetened with orange juice, sugar, and a splash of vinegar and flavored with spices. You can substitute squab or baby pheasant in this dish. Prepare the cabbage and the chutney up to 4 hours in advance. The partridge is best when cooked just before serving.

For the Partridges:

4 partridges, about 16 to 18 ounces each, trussed and ready to roast

Salt, freshly ground black pepper

4 slices bacon

Four 1/2-inch pieces orange zest

4 sprigs marjoram

4 cloves garlic, peeled

1 tablespoon oil, for cooking

1/2 cup onions, peeled and coarsely chopped

1 tablespoon Grand Marnier or brandy

1/3 cup chicken stock (see page 370)

For the Red Cabbage Confit:

3 pounds red cabbage (about 1 large head or 2 small), split into 6 wedges, the thick stem cut off and discarded, each cabbage wedge broken into small leaves

2 tablespoons sweet butter

1 cup onions, peeled and finely sliced

1 teaspoon chopped garlic

Salt, freshly ground black pepper

1/2 tablespoon sugar

Juice of 1 orange

3 tablespoons red wine vinegar

For the Fall Fruit Chutney:

1 tablespoon sweet butter

1/2 cup onions, peeled, in 1/2-inch diced

1 stick of cinnamon

Peel and juice of 1 orange

1-1/2 teaspoons of mixed spices: Combine in a cup 1/2 teaspoon Madras curry powder, 2 pinches of ground ginger, 2 pinches of ground star anise, 4 pinches of coriander powder

1/2 cup red or black plums, pitted and cut into 1/2-inch pieces

1/2 cup apples, peeled, cored, in 1/2-inch dice

1/2 cup pears, peeled, cored, in 1/2-inch dice

1 tablespoon sugar

3 tablespoons Spanish sherry vinegar or white vinegar

1/2 cup fresh cranberries

Salt, freshly ground black pepper

Preparation

For the Partridges:
Preheat oven to 450 degrees. Salt and pepper the partridges inside and out. Wrap each partridge with 1 slice bacon. Put 1 piece orange zest, 1/2 sprig marjoram, and 1/2 garlic clove inside each partridge.

Heat the cooking oil in a large roasting pot or pan on top of the stove over high heat. Sauté the partridges for about 5 minutes on each side of their breasts, then turn them on their backs, add the onions, remaining 2 cloves garlic, and remaining 2 marjoram sprigs and roast in the oven for 15 minutes. Remove any fat from the pan, add the Grand Marnier, and cook for about 1 minute until the liqueur has evaporated. Add the chicken stock and roast for another 5 minutes. Remove the pan from the oven, drain the partridges of their juices over the pan, and keep the birds warm on the side. Boil the cooking juices in the pan on the stove top until reduced to 1/4 cup. Strain and set aside.

For the Red Cabbage Confit:
Preheat oven to 450 degrees. Bring 4 quarts water with 1 tablespoon salt to a boil in a pot over high heat. Add the cabbage leaves, boil for 6 to 8 minutes, and drain.

Melt the butter in a large roasting pan or casserole on the stove over medium heat. Add the onions and garlic and sweat for 3 to 4 minutes. Add the blanched cabbage leaves, toss well for another 5 minutes, and season with salt, pepper, and the sugar. Add the orange juice and roast in the oven for 20 minutes, tossing the cabbage from time to time. Sprinkle with the vinegar and cook for another 10 to 15 minutes until the cabbage leaves are soft and still slightly moist. Remove from the oven and keep warm.

For the Fall Fruit Chutney:
Melt the butter in a large, heavy-bottom pan over medium heat. Add the onions, cinnamon stick, orange peel, and mixed spices and sweat for 3 to 5 minutes (stir well while cooking). Add the plums, apples, pears, and sugar and sweat for another 10 minutes until the fruit have softened and are lightly glazed. Add the vinegar, orange juice, the cranberries, and salt and pepper to taste, mix, and cover with a lid. Simmer gently over low heat for 20 to 30 minutes or until all moisture has evaporated. Once cooked, discard the cinnamon and the orange peel.

Presentation

Place the red cabbage leaves in a dome shape in the center of a large round platter or roasting pan. You can serve the partridges either whole or carved. Lean the whole or carved partridges all around the cabbage. Spoon the chutney around the partridges. Serve the hot jus on the side.

Tomatoes Stuffed with a Ragout of Rabbit, Chanterelles, and Rosemary

Serves 4

A couple of years ago I created an all-tomato dinner at New York's James Beard House, a foundation that fosters gastronomy in America, and this dish was part of the 8-course menu served that evening. To ensure that the tomatoes maintain their integrity when baked, select medium-size ones that are ripe yet still firm to the touch. The ingredients can be prepared and the rabbit cooked 2 to 3 hours in advance, the stuffed tomatoes baked 15 to 20 minutes before serving.

4 ripe tomatoes, 12 ounces each

1 whole rabbit, about 2 pounds, liver and kidneys reserved (ask your butcher to cut the rabbit into 8 serving pieces)

Salt, freshly ground black pepper

3-1/2 tablespoons olive oil

2 sprigs fresh rosemary: 1 whole, 1 leaves only, finely chopped

1/2 cup white onions, peeled, in 1/4-inch dice

1/4 cup carrots, peeled, in 1/4-inch dice

1/4 cup celery, trimmed, in 1/4-inch dice

1/4 pound fresh chanterelle mushrooms, cleaned,

stems sliced and caps whole, reserved separately (if chanterelles are not available, you can substitute any other seasonal mushroom)

2 teaspoons chopped garlic

2 teaspoons all-purpose flour

1 teaspoon tomato paste

1 cup dry white wine

1-1/2 cups chicken stock (see page 370)

2 slices dried white bread, crusts trimmed, cut into 1/4-inch cubes

2 tablespoons freshly grated Parmesan cheese

1 tablespoon shallots, peeled and chopped

❧ Preparation

Bring 2 quarts water to a boil in a pot over high heat. Plunge in the tomatoes for 30 seconds, remove, and cool under cold water. Peel off and discard the skin. Cut a 1/4-inch cap off the top of each tomato and set aside. Scoop out and discard the seeds. Delicately scoop out the flesh of the tomatoes, dice, and set aside. Set the carved tomatoes aside with the caps.

Salt and pepper the 8 pieces of rabbit. Heat 2 tablespoons of the olive oil in a large Dutch oven or a braising pan on the top of the stove over high heat. Add the pieces of rabbit and sprinkle with 3/4 of the chopped rosemary. Add the onions, carrots, celery, and chanterelle stems, and roast for 5 minutes. Turn the pieces of rabbit over, add the garlic and the flour, stir well, and roast for another 2 to 3 minutes. Add the tomato paste, toss well for 2 minutes, add the white wine and the fresh tomato dice, cover, and cook for 10 minutes over medium heat. Add the chicken stock, cover, and cook for another 20 to 30 minutes or until well done (the meat should come off the bones easily).

Remove the rabbit pieces to a cutting board. Place the pot with the vegetables and sauce on the stove over medium-low heat and reduce the sauce to 1/2 cup. Set aside.

When cool, remove and shred the rabbit meat from the bones with your fingers or a fork and discard the bones. Place the shredded meat in a bowl, add the diced bread, 1/2 of the sauce with the vegetables, 1 tablespoon of the grated Parmesan, salt, and pepper and toss well.

Preheat oven to 400 degrees. Salt and pepper the carved tomatoes and evenly drizzle 1/2 tablespoon of the olive oil in the cavities. Fill the tomatoes to the top with the rabbit mixture and cover with the caps. Place the stuffed tomatoes on an oiled baking sheet, drizzle with 1/2 tablespoon of the olive oil, and sprinkle with the remaining tablespoon grated Parmesan cheese.

When ready to serve, place the tomatoes in the oven for 8 to 10 minutes. During the last 3 minutes of roasting, add the reserved liver and kidneys and a pinch of salt and pepper to the pan.

While the tomatoes are roasting, heat the remaining 1/2 tablespoon olive oil in a pan over high heat. Add the chanterelle caps and toss them for 3 to 5 minutes. Add salt, pepper, the shallots, and the rest of the chopped rosemary, and toss for 2 minutes. Add the remaining sauce with vegetables, boil for 2 minutes, and set aside.

❦ PRESENTATION

Spoon the chanterelle caps with the vegetables onto the bottom of a large warmed platter and arrange the tomatoes over the mushrooms. Decorate each tomato cap with a piece of rosemary sprig. Slice the liver and kidneys and scatter them around the stuffed tomatoes.

BUYING RABBIT: Rabbit meat is very lean and tender with a delicate flavor. Usually sold whole, look for meaty rabbits with pink flesh. A young rabbit weighs 2 to 3 pounds. A rabbit over 4 pounds is best stewed. Before cooking, remove any remaining fat and glands.

CREAMY RABBIT CASSEROLE WITH NINE SPRING HERBS

Serves 4

Although it has its own delicate taste, rabbit is especially good at carrying other flavors, notably rosemary, thyme, garlic, or mustard. In this recipe, 9 herbs and greens are combined to create a delightfully pungent emerald sauce that enriches the braised rabbit beautifully. You can prepare this dish up to 1 hour in advance, then reheat and finish before serving.

For the Rabbit:

1 young rabbit, 3-1/2 pounds (ask your butcher to cut the rabbit into 8 serving pieces)

Salt, freshly ground black pepper

1 tablespoon oil, for cooking

12 pearl onions, peeled (see page 213)

1 cup button mushrooms

1 cup carrots, peeled and sliced 1/4 inch thick

1 bouquet garni: 1 bay leaf, 1 stalk celery, 10 sprigs parsley, and 2 sprigs thyme tied together with kitchen string

1 clove garlic, peeled and chopped

1/4 cup dry white vermouth (Noilly Prat)

3 cups chicken stock (see page 370)

1 cup basmati rice

1 bay leaf

1/2 cup heavy cream

3 egg yolks

Mix together the following fresh herbs: 1 small bunch watercress, leaves only; 2 ounces fresh sorrel, leaves only, chopped; 2 sprigs tarragon, leaves only; 3 tablespoons chives, cut into 1/2-inch lengths; 3 tablespoons chervil, leaves only; 1 tablespoon dill, leaves only; 3 sprigs Italian parsley, leaves only, coarsely chopped; 1 sprig basil, leaves only, cut into wide strips; 2 tablespoons coarsely chopped celery heart leaves

❈ PREPARATION

Sprinkle the pieces of rabbit with salt and pepper. Heat the oil in a large Dutch oven over medium heat on top of the stove. Add the rabbit pieces and brown lightly on all sides. Add the pearl onions, mushrooms, carrots, and bouquet garni and sweat for 5 minutes. Add the garlic and toss well for 4 minutes. Add the vermouth and cook for 5 more minutes or until the alcohol has evaporated. Add 1 cup of the chicken stock, cover, and cook at low heat for 20 minutes.

Discard the bouquet garni and remove the pieces of rabbit and vegetables with a slotted spoon. Set aside. Reduce the cooking liquid to 1/2 cup over medium heat, strain, and set aside in a medium saucepan.

While you are cooking the rabbit, prepare the rice. Bring the remaining 2 cups chicken stock with 1 bay leaf to a boil in a pot over high heat. Add the basmati rice and a pinch of salt, cover, reduce heat to a low simmer, and cook for 15 minutes. Remove from heat and keep warm on the side.

When ready to serve, mix the heavy cream with the egg yolks in a bowl. Bring the cooking liquid from the rabbit stew to a boil over medium heat. Whip in the heavy cream–egg mixture. When warm, add the 9-herb mixture, salt, and pepper. Stir the sauce with a wooden spoon until very warm (do not boil, otherwise the sauce might curdle). If the sauce becomes too thick, add a touch of chicken stock or water to dilute it.

❋ PRESENTATION

Place the pieces of rabbit and the vegetables in a warmed deep dish. Pour the herb cream sauce over and serve the basmati rice on the side.

BRAISED RABBIT WITH PAPPARDELLE PASTA AND SAGE

Serves 4

In this wonderfully homespun dish fit for casual entertaining, pappardelle, a large ribbon pasta,
is served with a rich sauce of rabbit morsels braised with diced vegetables that are flavored with sage. The rabbit
can be braised up to 5 hours in advance but the pasta should be cooked 5 minutes before serving.

2 medium onions, peeled

2 medium carrots, peeled

1 small celeriac, peeled

1/2 cup white mushrooms, caps only

6 cloves garlic, peeled

2 sprigs fresh sage leaves, finely chopped

*1 young rabbit, about 3 pounds, kidneys and
liver cut in small pieces and reserved
(ask your butcher to cut the rabbit
into 8 serving pieces)*

Salt, freshly ground black pepper

3 tablespoons plus 1 teaspoon olive oil

1-1/2 teaspoons tomato paste

1-1/2 teaspoons all-purpose flour

1 cup dry white wine

1/2 cup tomato, peeled, split, seeded, and diced

2 cups chicken stock (see page 370)

*1/2 pound dried pappardelle pasta
or 1 pound fresh*

1 tablespoon sweet butter

1/4 cup freshly grated Parmesan cheese

✒ PREPARATION

Chop the onions, carrots, celeriac, mushrooms, garlic, and half of the sage into large
pieces.

Preheat oven to 400 degrees. Sprinkle the pieces of rabbit with salt and pepper. On the
stove, heat 2 tablespoons of the olive oil in a large casserole with a tight-fitting lid over
high heat. When hot, add the rabbit pieces and cook uncovered until browned on all
sides, about 8 to 10 minutes. Add the chopped vegetables and mix well with a wooden
spoon. Reduce the heat to medium and sweat the vegetables for 10 minutes while stirring often. Add the tomato paste, mix well, and sprinkle with flour.

Place in the oven for 8 to 10 minutes, until the flour browns. Pour the white wine over,
add half of the tomatoes, mix well, cover tightly, and braise for 15 minutes. Add the
chicken stock, salt, and pepper and braise for another 35 to 40 minutes. Stir every 10
minutes. The rabbit is cooked when the meat in the rear leg is tender to the bone when
pierced with a small knife. Remove from oven when done.

Carefully remove the rabbit pieces with a slotted spoon to a cutting board. Place the
casserole on top of the stove and reduce the sauce with the vegetables to 1 cup over
medium heat. Stir in the remaining diced tomatoes, cook for 2 minutes more, season to
taste, and keep warm on the side.

When the rabbit is cool enough to handle, detach the meat with your fingers and shred it (don't bother removing the meat from the neck and rib cage). Discard all bones.

Bring 4 quarts water with 1 tablespoon salt to a boil in a large pot over high heat. Add the pappardelle and cook for 6 minutes if for dried pasta, 3 minutes for fresh. Drain the pasta and pour it into a large warm serving bowl. Toss with 1 tablespoon olive oil.

Add the shredded meat to the warm vegetable sauce with the butter and the remaining chopped sage, mix well, and keep warm.

Heat a small pan over high heat with the remaining teaspoon of oil. Season and toss the liver and kidneys for 2 minutes.

PRESENTATION

Pour the rabbit and vegetable sauce over the hot pappardelle and sprinkle with the liver and kidney mixture. Serve very hot with grated Parmesan on the side.

Side Dishes

Spring   Summer   Autumn   Winter
❁   ⚜   🍃   ❖

Morel Custard with a Shallot Jus ❁ page 266

Gratin of Cardoon Francine ❖ page 267

Roasted Baby Beets with Szechuan Pepper ⚜ page 268

Gratin of Celery Heart ❁ page 269

Zucchini and Eggplant Rosace with Thyme ⚜ page 270

Zucchini with Orange Zest and Rosemary ❁ page 271

Roasted Baby Artichokes with Bacon ❁ page 272

Cabbage Stuffed with Apples and Cranberries 🍃 page 273

Caramelized Turnips with Rosemary and Honey ❖ page 275

Sweet Potato Purée with Fruits and Spices ❖ page 276

Baked Potatoes on a Bed of Sea Salt with Fresh Truffles 🍃 page 277

Roasted Endives Wrapped in Bacon with Juniper and Orange ❖ page 278

Vegetable Cake Provençal ⚜ page 279

Broccoli Purée with Ginger ❖ page 282

Spring Vegetable Casserole with Rosemary and Chives ❁ page 283

Summer Vegetable Casserole with Basil and Black Olives ⚜ page 285

Fall Vegetables Roasted with Juniper Berries and Walnuts 🍃 page 288

Winter Vegetable Casserole with Spices and Orange Zest ❖ page 290

MOREL CUSTARD WITH A SHALLOT JUS

Serves 4

The deep, woodsy flavor and melting texture of these morel timbales with their pleasantly piquant shallot sauce are ideal complements to such meats as sautéed chicken breast with sage or veal medallions. You can prepare this recipe up to 2 hours beforehand, and then warm the timbales slowly before serving.

2 tablespoons sweet butter

4 large shallots, peeled and thinly sliced

1 sprig sage

1 large clove garlic, peeled and chopped

*1/2 pound fresh morels, caps only, split;
or 2 ounces dried morels soaked in 2 cups warm
water for 3 to 4 hours, drained,
caps only, split*

1 cup white mushrooms, caps only

Salt, freshly ground black pepper

1/2 cup chicken stock (see page 370)

1 cup heavy cream

2 whole eggs

1/2 tablespoon sugar

1 tablespoon vinegar

❀ PREPARATION

Melt 1 tablespoon of the butter in a large pan over medium heat. Add 1 tablespoon of the sliced shallots, 1/2 sprig of sage, and the garlic, and sweat for 2 to 3 minutes. Add the morels, the mushrooms, salt and pepper and sweat until all moisture has evaporated, about 10 minutes (do not color). Add 1/4 cup of the chicken stock, bring to a boil, and boil for 2 minutes. Drain the mushroom mixture, discard the sage, and set 4 pieces of morel aside. Put the mushroom mixture back into the pan, add the cream, mix well, bring to a boil, and simmer for 3 minutes. Add salt and pepper, remove from heat, cool for 4 minutes, and pour into a food processor. Add the eggs and blend until smooth.

Preheat oven to 350 degrees. Butter 4 soufflé cups or round molds (2-1/2 inches in diameter by 1 inch high) and spoon the mushroom mixture evenly into each one. Place the timbales in a deep baking pan and fill the pan with 1 inch warm water. Place the pan on the oven's middle rack and bake for about 35 to 40 minutes or until the custard is set.

As the custard cooks, melt the remaining tablespoon butter over medium heat. Add the remaining shallots and 1/2 sprig of sage and sweat for 6 to 8 minutes or until lightly colored. Add the sugar and cook the shallots until lightly caramelized. Add the vinegar and cook until it has evaporated. Add the remaining 1/4 cup chicken stock, and boil for 2 minutes. Remove from heat, salt and pepper to taste, discard the sage, and set aside.

❀ PRESENTATION

Unmold the warm custards onto a warm serving plate. Top each custard with a reserved piece of morel. Spoon the shallot jus around.

GRATIN OF CARDOON FRANCINE

Serves 4 to 6
This is an adaptation of my grandmother's recipe served during the winter with roasted fowl.
This Lyonnais dish is a Christmas tradition. The cardoon is a vegetable that looks like celery but tastes like
artichokes and is popular in Southern France, Italy, and Greece.

1 tablespoon salt

*3 bunches of cardoon, outer leaves and ends
trimmed, stalks sliced into 2-inch-long segments,
each segment halved and stringy skin pulled
off with a small paring knife (immediately
plunge cardoon into 3 quarts water mixed with
juice of 2 lemons to avoid browning)*

1-1/2 cups chicken stock (see page 370)

2 ounce fresh beef marrow, sliced

1-1/2 tablespoons all-purpose flour

Salt, freshly ground black pepper

*1 cup Gruyère or Emmenthal cheese,
freshly grated*

✤ PREPARATION

Add the salt to the cardoon and lemony water and bring to a boil in a large pot over high heat. Simmer the cardoon for 40 to 50 minutes or until tender. Drain well.

Preheat oven to 425 degrees. Bring chicken stock to a boil in a small pan. Place the marrow in a large pan and melt over medium heat. Add the flour and whisk for 3 to 5 minutes. Add the boiling chicken stock, stir, and cook for 5 minutes. Add the cooked cardoons, salt and pepper to taste, and toss well.

Transfer to a buttered shallow baking dish and sprinkle the top with grated cheese. Bake for 15 to 20 minutes, or until golden brown.

✤ PRESENTATION

Serve warm from the gratin dish.

ROASTED BABY BEETS WITH SZECHUAN PEPPER

Serves 4

With their deep, earthy flavor and delicate peppery seasoning, these baby beets provide an excellent contrast to such substantial meats as sautéed pork chops, roasted short ribs, or grilled sirloin steak. Baby beets come in bunches, from 8 to 12 beets per bunch. Although they vary in color (red, yellow, striped) they are very similar in size and taste. Mild but fragrant Szechuan peppercorns are found in Chinese markets and specialty stores. This recipe can be prepared up to 4 hours in advance; just peel and toss the beets in butter before serving.

2 tablespoons oil, for cooking

*28 to 32 baby beets
(3 different-colored bunches, if possible),
stems cut 1/2 inch above the beets and discarded,
rootlets removed with a paring knife and
discarded, dirt scraped off around the stem area,
beets scrubbed*

1 cup onions, peeled and split into 6 wedges

1 head garlic, unpeeled, split horizontally

1 tablespoon whole Szechuan peppercorns

1 teaspoon sugar

Coarse sea salt, freshly ground black pepper

1/2 cup dry white wine

1 tablespoon sweet butter

2 cloves garlic, peeled and finely chopped

2 teaspoons finely ground Szechuan pepper

*1 tablespoon fresh Italian parsley, leaves only,
finely chopped*

❧ PREPARATION

Preheat oven to 400 degrees. Place the oil, beets, onions, split garlic head, Szechuan peppercorns, sugar, 3/4 teaspoon coarse sea salt, and black pepper in a roasting pan. Mix well, place the pan in the oven, and roast for about 1 hour. Toss several times while cooking. After 30 minutes of roasting, add 2 tablespoons of the white wine. Add 2 more tablespoons white wine after every 10 to 12 minutes of cooking (using 1/2 cup in all). Remove the pan from the oven when the beets are fork-tender. Set the beets aside to cool and discard the other roasted ingredients.

Place a piece of parchment paper on your cutting board and wear disposable gloves to avoid beet stains. Remove the beet skins by rubbing them off with your fingers. On top of the stove, melt the butter in a pan over medium heat. Add the beets and cook them for 5 to 7 minutes. Add the chopped garlic, ground Szechuan pepper, salt, and pepper and toss for 1 minute. Transfer to a warmed serving dish.

❧ PRESENTATION

Sprinkle the beets with chopped parsley.

GRATIN OF CELERY HEART

Serves 4

Smoky bacon and tangy mustard accent the cool, verdant flavor of braised celery hearts in this recipe—
a side dish suitable for roasted poultry, lamb, or beef. You can prepare this gratin up to 3 hours beforehand,
but bake it just before serving.

3 tablespoons sweet butter

2 slices bacon, cut into 1/2-inch pieces

1/3 cup carrots, peeled and sliced 1/4 inch thick

1/3 cup onions, peeled and sliced 1/4 inch thick

2 sprigs thyme, leaves only, finely chopped

3 bunches celery, outer stalks cut off and reserved for another use, leaving three 6-inch-long celery hearts,

trimmed if necessary and quartered lengthwise, a few celery leaves reserved for garnish

4 cups chicken stock (see page 370)

Salt, freshly ground black pepper

1/4 cup Dijon mustard

1/2 cup fresh white bread crumbs (5 slices trimmed of crust and chopped finely in a blender or food processor)

❀ PREPARATION

Preheat oven to 350 degrees. Melt 1 tablespoon of the butter and cook the bacon in a large and deep roasting pan on top of the stove over high heat. Color the bacon lightly, add the carrots, onions, and thyme and sweat for 3 to 4 minutes. Spread the ingredients evenly in the pan and cover with the pieces of celery heart, side by side. Add the chicken stock to the level of the celery and season with salt and pepper. Cover with a piece of parchment paper cut the size of the pan and braise in the oven for 45 minutes to 1 hour, or until fork-tender.

Remove from heat and carefully drain any remaining juices (hold a lid on top of the vegetables to keep them in place while draining).

Fifteen minutes before serving, either transfer the vegetables and celery to a nice gratin dish or keep them in the roasting pan. Brush a 1/4-inch-thick layer of Dijon mustard on the celery and sprinkle evenly with the bread crumbs. Melt the remaining 2 tablespoons butter and drizzle over the bread crumbs.

Raise the oven temperature to 475 degrees. Bake the gratin of celery until the bread crumbs become light brown and crusty, about 10 to 12 minutes.

❀ PRESENTATION

Serve the warm gratin of celery in the gratin dish and decorate with a few reserved celery leaves.

ZUCCHINI AND EGGPLANT ROSACE WITH THYME

Serves 4

Alternating slices of zucchini and eggplant in a circular pattern form a very elegant *rosace*, which is flavored with olive oil, garlic, and thyme and topped with warm tomatoes. Serve it with broiled fish, shrimp, or chicken. You can prepare the ingredients up to 3 hours in advance and cook them just before serving.

3 tablespoons olive oil

1 zucchini, about 7 inches long by 1-1/2 inches in diameter, cut into about 40 thin slices at an angle (about 2-1/2 inches long and 1/8 inch thick) with a mandoline or vegetable slicer

1 eggplant, about 6 inches long by 3 inches in diameter, peeled, split lengthwise, each half cut (across the width) into thin slices about the same size as the zucchini slices

Salt, freshly ground black pepper

1 sprig fresh thyme, leaves only, finely chopped, or 1 teaspoon dried leaves

1 teaspoon garlic, peeled and finely chopped

2 large ripe tomatoes, cored, split, seeded, and coarsely chopped

2 sprigs basil, leaves only, finely chopped

❧ PREPARATION

Fold 4 sheets of aluminum foil into double-thick 7-inch squares. Brush each foil square with 1 teaspoon olive oil.

To build the rosace, lay 1 square of foil flat on the counter. Place 1 piece of zucchini on the foil close to the edge. Overlap the zucchini with a piece of eggplant; 3/4 inch of the zucchini should be visible under the eggplant slice and then 3/4 inch of the eggplant should be visible under the next zucchini, and so on. Continue overlapping the zucchini slices with the eggplant slices until you have completed a full circle. To fill the hole in the middle of the rosace, cover with a few alternating slices of zucchini and eggplant. Repeat the same process for all 4 rosaces. Refrigerate until ready to broil.

Preheat broiler. Brush each rosace with a light coating of olive oil. Salt, pepper, and sprinkle with fresh thyme. Place the 4 foils with the rosace on a baking sheet and broil until lightly colored and cooked, about 8 to 10 minutes. Remove from heat and set aside.

Heat 2 teaspoons of the olive oil in a pan over high heat. Add the garlic, the tomatoes, basil, salt, and pepper and toss quickly. Remove from heat when warm.

❧ PRESENTATION

To remove the rosace from the foil, just place the foil on the edge of the serving plate and slide the rosace down with a spatula onto the plate while pulling the foil out from under. Place the broiled fish, shrimp, or chicken over the zucchini and eggplant and spoon the warm tomatoes over the top.

Zucchini with Orange Zest and Rosemary

Serves 4

With its sunny Mediterranean flavors, this dish is an ideal accompaniment to broiled chicken, fish, or shrimp that have been marinated with orange slices and rosemary. Prepare the ingredients for this recipe up to 2 hours before serving and then cook them as needed.

Juice and zest of 1 orange, zest cut into julienne (matchstick size)

2 tablespoons olive oil

3 cups zucchini, ends trimmed, in 1/4-inch slices

2 tablespoons rosemary, leaves only, chopped

Salt, freshly ground black pepper

❋ Preparation

Bring 1 quart water to a boil in a small pot over high heat. Plunge in the orange zest, cook for 2 minutes, and drain. Bring a fresh quart of water to a boil in the same pot and cook the zest for 5 to 7 minutes more. Strain out the zest and set aside.

Heat the olive oil over high heat in a large pan. Add the zucchini, rosemary, salt, and pepper. Toss often while cooking for about 6 to 8 minutes (reduce heat if necessary to avoid coloring the zucchini). Pour in the orange juice and cook until totally evaporated. Add the orange zest, toss, and taste for seasoning.

❋ Presentation

Arrange the sliced zucchini in a bowl with some of the orange zest on top. Serve warm.

Zesting Fruit: If you don't have a zester, you can remove the zest of any citrus fruit with a standard swivel peeler. Guide the peeler against the fruit and use a sawing motion to remove a section of zest. To julienne the zest, first trim it until square or rectangular depending on its shape and then cut it matchstick size.

Roasted Baby Artichokes with Bacon

Serves 4

Roasted artichokes and bacon have a pleasant affinity for one another and here they are further enhanced with thyme, bay leaves, and olive oil. This side dish, which can be prepared up to 3 hours beforehand then reheated as necessary, is superb with sautéed or roasted veal or lamb.

16 to 20 baby artichokes

Juice of 1 lemon

3 slices bacon, cut into 1-inch segments

3 tablespoons olive oil

1 cup onions, peeled and cut into 1/2-inch wedges

6 cloves garlic, peeled

1 sprig thyme

1 bay leaf

Salt, freshly ground black pepper

❀ Preparation

Pull off the outer leaves of each artichoke. Cut off the stem at the base of each artichoke, as well as the tip of the leaves, 1 inch above the heart. With a paring knife, shape the hearts until round and smooth. Discard any trimmings. Split each artichoke and soak them in 2 quarts water mixed with the lemon juice.

Preheat oven to 400 degrees. Drain the artichokes. Heat a roasting pan or casserole on top of the stove over medium heat. Add the bacon and cook for 4 to 5 minutes. Add the olive oil, onions, garlic, thyme, bay leaf, and the artichokes and sweat for 2 to 3 minutes, tossing often. Add salt and pepper and roast in the oven for 35 to 40 minutes, tossing every 6 to 10 minutes. Add 2 tablespoons water from time to time, if necessary, to keep the artichokes moist while roasting.

❀ Presentation

Discard the thyme and bay leaf and transfer to a warm serving bowl.

CABBAGE STUFFED WITH APPLES AND CRANBERRIES

Serves 4

These little packages of savoy cabbage are bursting with a wonderfully bright, sweet-tart filling. This is a particularly good side dish to accompany game, and can be assembled up to 2 hours in advance and cooked before serving.

One 1-1/2-pound head savoy cabbage, cored, 2 to 3 outer leaves discarded, 12 nice, whole, loose leaves reserved, the rest quartered and cut into 1/2-inch-wide strips

2 tablespoons sweet butter (1 tablespoon melted)

1 cup onions, peeled, in 1/4-inch dice

One 1-inch stick of cinnamon or a pinch of ground cinnamon

2 Golden Delicious apples, peeled, cored, in 1/4-inch dice

1/2 cup chicken stock (see page 370)

Salt, freshly ground black pepper

1/2 cup fresh cranberries

2 teaspoons maple syrup

1/4-inch slice fresh gingerroot, unpeeled

PREPARATION

Bring 3 quarts water with 1 tablespoon salt to a boil. Plunge the whole cabbage leaves into a boiling water for 3 to 4 minutes. Remove them with a slotted spoon or a skimmer and cool under cold running water taking care not to damage the leaves. Drain, pat the leaves dry, and set them aside.

Plunge the cabbage slices into the same boiling water and boil for 3 to 4 minutes. Drain and cool under cold running water. Drain again, squeezing out any excess water, and set aside.

Melt 1 tablespoon butter in a casserole over medium heat. Add the onions and cinnamon and sweat for 3 to 4 minutes. Add the apples, the blanched cabbage slices, 1/4 cup of the chicken stock, salt, and pepper, cover with a lid, and cook for another 15 to 20 minutes or until the cabbage is soft and tender. Reduce heat and add more stock if necessary to keep the cabbage moist while cooking. Remove from heat, discard the cinnamon, drain off any leftover liquid, and set aside to cool.

Warm a pan over medium heat. Add the cranberries, maple syrup, and gingerroot. Cover and cook for 2 to 3 minutes. Remove the lid and toss until all moisture has evaporated, about 2 minutes. Discard the gingerroot and set the cranberries aside to cool.

Preheat oven to 425 degrees. Arrange the blanched cabbage leaves in 4 circles about 6 inches in diameter (3 leaves per circle), the top of each leaf overlapping in the center of the circle to form a nest. Cut off and discard the bottom edges and thick ribs of the leaves. Brush the cabbage circles with 2 teaspoons of the melted butter and season with salt and pepper. Divide the apple and cabbage mixture among the 4 circles and place in the center of each nest. Spoon 3/4 of the cranberries evenly into the cabbage nests. Fold the leaves over tightly (trim them if necessary) to enclose the stuffing.

Place a cabbage package in the center of a cotton kitchen towel. Wrap, twist, and squeeze the towel tightly around the stuffed cabbage. Remove the firm, stuffed cabbage from the towel and place in a shallow baking dish. Repeat the same process with the other 3 cabbage packages.

Brush the stuffed cabbages in the baking dish with the remaining teaspoon melted butter and pour in the remaining 1/4 cup chicken stock. Bake in the oven for 15 minutes.

PRESENTATION

Spoon the remaining cooked cranberries over the cabbage and serve hot in a shallow dish.

SIDE DISHES

CARAMELIZED TURNIPS WITH ROSEMARY AND HONEY

Serves 4

Small turnips are cooked with rosemary and honey until they are tender, lightly herbed, and delicately glazed, which makes them a particularly good accompaniment for a full-flavored roast pork or duck. The turnips can be prepared up to 2 hours in advance and reheated just before serving.

1-1/2 cups chicken stock (see page 370)

2 tablespoons sweet butter

3 sprigs fresh rosemary: 2 whole, 1 leaves only, finely chopped

2 pounds small and very firm turnips, peeled with a small knife (a 1/8-inch-thick layer

of skin removed) and sliced 1/8 inch thick

1 tablespoon rosemary honey or blossom honey

Salt, freshly ground black pepper

1 tablespoon white vinegar

✤ PREPARATION

In a small pan, begin heating the chicken stock. Melt the butter in a pan over medium heat. Add the chopped rosemary, turnips, honey, salt, and pepper and toss while cooking for 5 to 7 minutes or until lightly colored. Add the vinegar and let evaporate (about 30 seconds). Add the warm chicken stock, 1/4 cup at a time, tossing often, and cook until the turnips are tender when pierced with a knife and the stock has totally evaporated, about 25 to 40 minutes.

Toss the turnips over high heat until lightly brown and caramelized. Remove from heat.

✤ PRESENTATION

Serve the warm carmelized turnips in a serving dish with pieces of the rosemary sprigs placed around the perimeter for decoration.

Sweet Potato Purée with Fruits and Spices

Serves 4 to 6

Buttery-smooth and rich in fall aromas and flavors, this cranberry-capped, golden, fruit-flavored purée provides an appealing contrast to roast game—venison or pheasant—or even a grilled pepper steak. It can be prepared up to a day in advance, carefully stored in the refrigerator, then heated before serving.

2 pounds sweet potatoes, peeled, and cut into 1/2-inch cubes

1 Golden Delicious apple, peeled, cored, in 1/4-inch dice

2 oranges: peel and juice of 1 orange, 1 orange thinly sliced for garnish

1 small banana, peeled and sliced 1/2 inch thick

Two 1-1/2-inch sticks cinnamon

2 tablespoons sugar

1 bay leaf

3/4 cup heavy cream

1 small onion, peeled and studded with 2 cloves

Salt, freshly ground black pepper

2 tablespoons sweet butter

12 fresh cranberries

❖ Preparation

Place the sweet potatoes in a large pot. Add enough water to cover by 1 inch, a pinch of salt, 1/2 of the orange peel, 1 cinnamon stick, the bay leaf, and onion studded with cloves. Bring to a boil and simmer for about 20 to 25 minutes or until fork tender.

While the sweet potatoes are cooking, prepare the fruit. Melt 1 tablespoon of the butter in a heavy-bottom pan over medium heat. Add the apple, banana, the rest of the orange peel, and the remaining stick of cinnamon and sweat until lightly caramelized, tossing often, about 7 to 10 minutes. Transfer the fruits to a plate with a slotted spoon. Add 1 tablespoon of the sugar to the pan, cook to a light brown caramel, carefully add the orange juice, and reduce to 1 tablespoon. Add 3/4 of the heavy cream and boil for 3 to 4 minutes. Return the cooked fruit to the pot, mix well, and simmer for 3 to 4 minutes. Remove from heat and discard the orange peel and cinnamon stick. Keep warm.

When the sweet potatoes are done, drain them and discard the orange peel, cinnamon stick, bay leaf, and onion. Transfer the warm sweet potatoes to a food processor. Add the fruit, salt and pepper, and purée. Mix in the remaining cream if the purée is too thick, and taste for seasoning. When ready to serve, toss the cranberries in the remaining tablespoon butter and the remaining tablespoon sugar in a small pot over high heat for 4 minutes or until tender.

❖ Presentation

Transfer the purée into a deep, warm bowl. Decorate the sides with the orange slices and place the cranberries on top of the purée.

BAKED POTATOES ON A BED OF SEA SALT WITH FRESH TRUFFLES

Serves 4

This festive dish combines a Frenchman's favorite foods: potatoes and truffles. You can use the aromatic, white *tartufi d'Alba*, available in autumn, or the earthy black truffles from Perigord, available in winter. Few foods are as sumptuous as truffles, and it is best to serve this dish as an appetizer. Prepare just before serving, although the potatoes may be baked up to 20 minutes in advance, then kept warm until needed.

1 cup coarse sea salt

4 large baking potatoes, about 14 ounces each, scrubbed and dried

5 tablespoons sweet butter: 4 tablespoons softened and 1 tablespoon melted

Salt, freshly ground black pepper

1 ounce white truffles (about 1 or 2 firm white truffles) or 2 ounces black truffles (about 2 or 3 firm black truffles), cleaned of dirt, thinly sliced with a truffle slicer, adjustable vegetable slicer, or peeler, scraps reserved

PREPARATION

Preheat oven to 425 degrees. Spread the coarse sea salt evenly on the bottom of a roasting pan large enough to hold the potatoes. Place the potatoes over the salt and bake in the oven for 40 to 50 minutes or until easily pierced with a small knife. Every 15 minutes, give the potatoes a 1/4 turn to allow them to cook evenly and pick up the flavor of the sea salt. When done, remove the potatoes from the oven, brush any sea salt off the skins, and set aside to cool for 5 minutes. Reserve the salt to decorate the serving plates.

Cut off a 1/2-inch cap along the length of each potato using the flattest part of the potato as the cap. Scoop the potato flesh out of each cap into a bowl and discard the caps. Carefully scoop the potato flesh out of each potato bottom, leaving a 1/4-inch-thick shell. Place the potato flesh in a medium bowl and set the potato shells aside.

Add the 4 tablespoons softened butter to the potato flesh along with salt and pepper to taste, and 6 to 8 very thin white truffle shavings or twice as much black truffle, along with the truffle scraps. Mash with a large fork and taste for seasoning.

Refill each potato shell evenly with the potato and truffle mixture. Reheat the potatoes for 3 to 4 minutes in the oven or for 45 seconds in a microwave set on high.

PRESENTATION

Arrange a bed of coarse sea salt on the bottom of 4 serving plates. Place one potato on each plate. Cover each potato with the remaining thin truffle slices. Press lightly on the truffle slices to secure them in the potato stuffing. Combine the tablespoon of melted butter with a pinch of salt and pepper and sprinkle evenly over each potato.

Roasted Endives Wrapped in Bacon with Juniper and Orange

Serves 8

With its bittersweet flavor, this bacon-wrapped endive is a superb complement to roast beef, pork, or game.
You can prepare this dish up to 3 hours in advance and broil just before serving.

*8 large Belgian endives,
wilted outer leaves discarded*

Salt, freshly ground black pepper

Sugar

8 slices bacon, at room temperature

1 cup onions, peeled and thickly sliced

1 cup carrots, peeled and thickly sliced

5 cloves garlic, peeled and crushed

1 orange, halved and cut in thick slices

1/2 tablespoon juniper berries

✤ Preparation

Preheat oven to 375 degrees. Carefully open a few leaves at the tip of each endive. Add a pinch of salt, pepper, and sugar in between the leaves and close the leaves back as tightly as possible. Place the bacon slices side by side between 2 sheets of plastic wrap and pound with a meat mallet to flatten and lengthen them as much as possible. Discard the plastic wrap and completely wrap each endive evenly and tightly with a slice of bacon from top to bottom in a spiral.

Spread the onions, carrots, garlic, orange pieces, and juniper berries in a deep roasting pan. Season with salt and pepper and place the endives on top side by side. Place the pan in the oven on the middle rack and roast for about 75 to 90 minutes. Turn the endives every 15 minutes to roast evenly. They will be done when fork tender. Add a few tablespoons water and cover with a layer of greased parchment paper if the vegetables brown too fast or become too dry. Remove the pan and discard the juniper berries and pieces of orange. Transfer the onions and carrots to a plate with a slotted spoon and carefully pour off the melted bacon fat into a cup.

Preheat broiler. Just before serving, place the pan with the endives under the broiler. Broil the bacon for a few seconds, rotating the endives until all the bacon is crisp.

✤ Presentation

Serve the endive with or without the vegetable garnish. Place the hot endives on a serving plate. Lightly drizzle the melted bacon fat over the top and serve immediately.

Vegetable Cake Provençal

Serves 8 to 10

Colorful, festive, and full of intense Mediterranean flavors, this seven-layer cake could be an entrée in a vegetarian feast or an accompaniment to roasted rack of lamb or veal. It takes some time to prepare, since each vegetable requires separate cooking before assembly, but this can be done up to a full day in advance; warming is all that's then needed before serving.

6-1/2 tablespoons olive oil

Salt, freshly ground black pepper

Sprig of fresh rosemary, leaves only, chopped

Two 7-inch-long zucchinis, ends trimmed, cut lengthwise into 1/8-inch slices with a vegetable slicer or mandoline

3 medium sweet red peppers, cut into 3 equal pieces lengthwise, stem and seeds discarded

1 medium eggplant, peeled, ends trimmed, cut lengthwise into 1/8-inch slices with a vegetable slicer or mandoline

1 medium fennel bulb, greens trimmed, cut into 1/8-inch wedges

2 pinches cayenne pepper

3 cloves garlic, peeled and finely chopped

6 sprigs basil, leaves only: 5 sprigs finely chopped, 1 sprig leaves whole

6 plum tomatoes, cored, split, seeded, in 1/4-inch dice

1 large Spanish onion, peeled and sliced 1/4 inch thick

8 to 10 medium shiitake or white mushrooms, caps only, sliced 1/4 inch thick

2 sprigs fresh thyme, leaves only, finely chopped

1 pound spinach, leaves only, thoroughly washed and drained

2 pinches freshly grated nutmeg

1/4 cup small black olives (Niçoise)

❧ Preparation

Each vegetable will be cooked separately, set aside to cool, and then assembled in colorful layers in a cake mold.

Preheat broiler. Brush a baking sheet with 1 tablespoon of the olive oil. Sprinkle the sheet with salt, pepper, and 1/2 of the rosemary. Place the zucchini slices one next to the other on the sheet. Brush the top of the zucchini slices with 2 teaspoons of olive oil and sprinkle with salt, pepper, and the rest of the rosemary. Broil for about 5 to 7 minutes or until lightly colored. Turn the slices over and broil for another 5 minutes. Transfer the slices from the broiler as they are done to a plate (some might cook faster than others) and set aside to cool.

Wipe off the baking sheet with a paper towel, brush it with 1 teaspoon of the olive oil, and sprinkle it with salt and pepper. Place the red peppers skin side up and broil until the skin turns black, about 8 to 10 minutes. Transfer the peppers to a plate to cool. When cool, rub off the burnt skin with a paper towel and set the peppers aside.

Wipe off the baking sheet. Brush the sheet with 2 teaspoons of the olive oil and sprinkle it with salt and pepper. Place the slices of eggplant one next to the other on the sheet, brush the top of the eggplant with 1/2 tablespoon of the olive oil, and season with salt and pepper. Broil the eggplant for 8 to 10 minutes or until light brown. Turn them over and broil for another 6 to 8 minutes or until done. (If the eggplant slices are colored but still need some cooking, bake them in the oven for 6 to 8 minutes more at 450 degrees.) When done, remove and set aside on a plate to cool. Turn the broiler off.

Heat 1 tablespoon of the olive oil in a large nonstick pan over medium heat. Add the fennel, salt, pepper, and 1 pinch of cayenne pepper and sweat for 4 to 5 minutes. Add 3/4 cup water, cover for 4 to 5 minutes, remove the cover, and cook until the water has completely evaporated. Remove the fennel from the pan and set aside to cool.

Wipe the pan, place it over medium-low heat, and warm 1/2 tablespoon of the olive oil. Add the garlic and chopped basil and cook for 2 to 3 minutes (do not color the garlic). Add the tomatoes, salt, pepper, and 1 pinch of cayenne pepper and cook for about 12 to 15 minutes, stirring often or until most of the moisture has evaporated. Transfer to a fine-mesh strainer placed over a bowl, drain and cool until needed.

Wipe the pan, place over medium-high heat, and warm 1/2 tablespoon of the olive oil. Add the onion, mushrooms, thyme, salt, and pepper and sweat for 4 to 5 minutes, stirring often. Add 2 tablespoons of water and finish cooking for another 8 to 10 minutes or until all the moisture has evaporated. When done, transfer to a plate to cool.

Wipe the pan, place it over high heat, and warm 1/2 tablespoon of the olive oil. Add the spinach leaves, toss for 2 to 3 minutes, season with salt, pepper, and nutmeg, and cook for 3 to 4 minutes or until all the moisture has evaporated and the spinach has cooked. Transfer to a colander to cool. Press the cooled spinach lightly to extract any remaining water.

To build the vegetable cake, brush a cake mold 8 inches in diameter and 2 inches high with 1 teaspoon of the olive oil and line it carefully with plastic wrap, letting extra wrap hang over the sides.

To line the mold with zucchini slices, place 1 slice of zucchini in the middle of the mold with one end in the center and the other end hanging over the side of the pan. Place the second slice slightly overlapping the first and continue in a circle lining the mold like the petals of a flower.

Spoon a layer of red peppers on the bottom of the mold over the zucchini slices. Press the red peppers down evenly with a spoon.

Spoon a layer of fennel over the pepper and press down evenly.

Spoon a layer of spinach over the fennel and press down evenly.

Spoon a layer of tomatoes over the spinach and press down evenly.

Spread a layer of onion and mushroom mix over the tomatoes and press evenly.

Cover the onion and mushroom mix with an even layer of eggplant and press down.

Fold the ends of the zucchini slices that are hanging over the edge onto the top of the eggplant to seal the cake and wrap the extra plastic wrap over the zucchini.

Place a flat plate the size of the mold over the cake. Put a 4- to 5-pound weight on the plate and flatten the cake for 1/2 hour. Do not refrigerate the cake if you are going to serve it in the next 2 to 3 hours.

Preheat oven to 300 degrees. Remove the plate with the weight and place the mold open end up in a deep pan. Fill the pan with boiling water halfway up the sides of the cake mold. Place the pan with the mold in the oven and warm the cake for about 20 to 30 minutes. Remove the mold from the pan and unwrap the plastic wrap on the top. Place a small round tray over the top of the cake and flip the cake over onto the tray. Remove the mold and plastic wrap and cut the cake into 8 to 10 wedges with an electric knife or a very sharp and long knife. Do not remove the wedges; keep the shape of the cake intact.

❧ Presentation

Present the cake on the round tray. Drizzle the remaining 1/2 tablespoon olive oil over the cake to make it shiny. Decorate the top of the cake with Niçoise olives around the edge and place a few basil leaves in the center.

BROCCOLI PURÉE WITH GINGER

Serves 4

Smooth and flavorful with a sparkle of ginger, this purée complements such delicate white meats as roasted chicken or even grilled fish. You can prepare this recipe up to 3 hours in advance, then reheat it before serving.

Two 1-ounce pieces gingerroot, peeled, a 1/4-inch-thick slice reserved, the rest finely grated

1/2 tablespoon olive oil

1 cup onions, peeled and thinly sliced

1 teaspoon garlic, peeled and chopped

1/2 cup heavy cream

2 pounds very fresh and green broccoli trimmed into florets with 1 inch of stem

Salt, cayenne pepper or freshly ground black pepper

4 cherry tomatoes, washed and thinly sliced

✤ PREPARATION

Wrap the grated ginger in a cotton kitchen towel. Twist the towel tightly over a cup to release the ginger juice. Reserve 1/2 teaspoon of ginger juice and discard any extra juice as well as the grated ginger.

Heat the olive oil in a pan over medium heat. Add the onions, gingerroot slice, and the garlic and sweat for about 5 to 8 minutes or until soft (do not color). Add the heavy cream, bring to a boil, and simmer for 3 to 4 minutes. Discard the ginger slice and keep the cream and onion mixture warm on the side.

Bring 4 quarts water with 1/2 tablespoon salt to a boil in a pot over high heat. Plunge in the broccoli florets and boil for 8 to 10 minutes or until well cooked. Drain in a colander and press against the sides with a wooden spoon to extract any excess water. Transfer the hot broccoli to a blender or food processor and add 1/2 of the cream-and-onion mixture, a pinch of salt and cayenne or black pepper, and purée until smooth. Add the rest of the cream-and-onion mixture and the ginger juice and blend well. Taste for seasoning.

✤ PRESENTATION

Transfer the warm broccoli purée to a warmed serving bowl. Decorate the edges of the bowl with thin slices of cherry tomatoes.

SPRING VEGETABLE CASSEROLE WITH ROSEMARY AND CHIVES

Serves 4 to 6

A celebration of garden-fresh vegetables, woodsy morels, and olive oil, this spring casserole is a perfect vegetarian entrée or a complement to poultry, meat, or fish. Vegetarians can substitute vegetable stock or water for the chicken stock. This recipe can be prepared up to 2 hours in advance and reheated just before serving.

1-1/2 pounds fresh fava beans, shelled; or 1/2 cup sugar peas, ends trimmed

6 baby artichokes

Juice of 1 lemon

3 tablespoons olive oil

1 cup spring onions, peeled, white part only, thickly sliced

1 sprig fresh rosemary, leaves only, chopped

12 baby carrots, peeled, top greens trimmed to 1 inch

12 baby turnips, peeled, top greens trimmed to 1 inch

1 cup chicken stock (see page 370)

Salt, freshly ground black pepper

1/4 pound fresh morels or seasonal mushrooms, caps only

4 ounces haricots verts (very thin green beans), ends trimmed

6 jumbo green asparagus, peeled and cut into 2-inch segments

8 baby zucchinis, rinsed and split lengthwise

1/2 pound fresh peas, shelled

2 cups Boston or Bibb lettuce leaves, cut in 1/4-inch-wide strips

1/4 cup chives, minced

❈ PREPARATION

Plunge the shelled fava beans into 2 cups of boiling water for 1 minute, drain, chill under cold running water, and drain again. Make a slit on the side of each bean and pop the bean out; discard the skins and set the peeled fava beans aside.

Peel off the outer leaves of each artichoke, cut off the stem below the heart, and shape the bottom with a paring knife until round and smooth. Cut off and discard the top leaves 1/2 inch above the heart. Toss the artichokes in the lemon juice and set aside.

Heat 2 tablespoons of the olive oil in a large pan over medium-low heat. Add the sliced spring onions and chopped rosemary and sweat for 5 minutes. Add the artichokes, baby carrots, and baby turnips and sweat for another 5 to 8 minutes. Add 1/2 of the chicken stock and salt and pepper to taste and bring to a boil. Simmer for 10 minutes, add the fresh morels, and cook for another 5 to 7 minutes. The vegetables should be done and the stock evaporated after 15 minutes of cooking. If necessary, add 2 tablespoons chicken stock at a time to keep the vegetables moist while cooking. Set aside until needed.

While the vegetables are cooking, bring 4 quarts water with 1 tablespoon salt to a boil. Add the haricots verts and boil for 2 minutes. Add the asparagus and the zucchini and boil for 3 minutes. Add the fresh peas and the peeled fava beans and cook for 2 minutes more. Drain and cool the vegetables for 2 minutes under cold running water, drain again, and set aside.

When ready to serve, return the artichoke mixture to the pan and heat over high heat. When hot, add the green vegetables and the remaining tablespoon olive oil. Toss well for 3 to 4 minutes, add the lettuce and chives, and toss for another 2 to 3 minutes. Taste for seasoning.

When done, the vegetables should be glazed with the olive oil. If necessary, drain any excess liquid and add a touch more olive oil.

❀ Presentation

Transfer all the vegetables to a warm vegetable bowl or dish. Arrange the most colorful vegetables on top.

SUMMER VEGETABLE CASSEROLE WITH BASIL AND BLACK OLIVES

Serves 4

This celebration of summer vegetables is a refreshing garden salad with a Mediterranean flair.
It can be served either as a vegetarian entrée or as an accompaniment to cold or barbecued seafood, fish, or
meats. The vegetables can be prepared up to 2 hours in advance and refrigerated;
season just before serving.

1/4 cup olive oil

Salt, freshly ground black pepper

*1 sweet red pepper, quartered lengthwise,
stem and seeds discarded*

*1 small zucchini, ends trimmed, cut lengthwise
into thin slices with a mandoline or
vegetable slicer*

*1 small eggplant, ends trimmed, peeled, and cut
widthwise into thin slices*

*16 to 20 yellow wax beans, ends trimmed,
cut in 1/2-inch segments*

3 ears fresh corn, husks and silk removed

1/4 cup small black olives (Niçoise)

*1 celery heart, cut into 1/4-inch slices,
the small yellow leaves reserved for garnish*

*2 medium tomatoes, split, cored, seeded,
in 1/8-inch dice*

3 scallions, white part only, finely sliced

*1 small European hothouse cucumber, peeled,
split lengthwise, seeded, in 1/4-inch dice*

1 bunch watercress, leaves only

3 sprigs basil, leaves only, coarsely chopped

Juice of 2 lemons

6 to 8 drops Tabasco

1 bunch arugula, leaves only

*6 round red radishes, stems and rootlets
trimmed, very thinly sliced,
reserved in ice water*

❦ PREPARATION

Preheat broiler. Brush a baking sheet or shallow roasting pan (large enough to hold each of the vegetables in a single layer) with 1 teaspoon of the olive oil and sprinkle with salt and pepper. Place the red pepper skin side up in the broiler and broil until the skin turns black, about 8 to 10 minutes. Transfer the red pepper to a plate and cool. When cool, rub off the burnt skin with a paper towel and set the pepper slices aside.

Wipe off the baking sheet with a paper towel. Brush it with 1/2 tablespoon of the olive oil and sprinkle with salt and pepper. Place the zucchini and eggplant slices tightly side by side on the sheet. Brush the top of the slices with 1 tablespoon of the olive oil and season with a pinch each of salt and pepper. Broil for 7 to 8 minutes or until lightly brown. Turn the slices over and broil for another 5 to 7 minutes. When done, remove from the pan and set aside to cool.

Bring 3 quarts water with 1/2 tablespoon salt to a boil in a large pot over medium heat. Add the wax beans and boil for 8 to 10 minutes or until very tender. Remove the beans with a slotted spoon to a colander and cool.

Add the corn on the cob to the same boiling water used for the beans and boil for 4 to 5 minutes. Drain and set aside to cool. When cool, remove the kernels from the cob by running a blade under each row of kernels along the length of the cob. Discard the cobs and set the corn kernels aside.

Place the Niçoise olives in a zip-lock plastic bag and seal. Lightly pound with a mallet or rolling pin. Remove the olives and pit them. Cut the pitted olives into small pieces and set aside.

When ready to serve, in a large bowl, combine the wax beans, corn kernels, the sliced celery heart, tomato dice, scallions, cucumber, 1/2 of the Niçoise olives, watercress, basil, juice of 1 lemon, 2 tablespoons of the olive oil, salt, and Tabasco. Toss well and taste for seasoning.

❧ Presentation

Form a ring around the edge of a round casserole by alternating the zucchini and egg-plant slices. Fill the center of the ring with the corn mixture. Place a tight bunch of arugula leaves in the center of the corn mixture. Arrange the red pepper strips around the arugula on top of the corn mixture and place the radish slices over and around the arugula. Sprinkle the whole dish with the remaining chopped Niçoise olives, celery leaves, and a pinch of salt and pepper. Drizzle the remaining lemon juice and olive oil over the top and serve at room temperature.

FALL VEGETABLES ROASTED WITH JUNIPER BERRIES AND WALNUTS

Serves 4 to 6
A festive preparation of fall offerings with the spirit of a bounteous harvest, this dish can be prepared
up to 3 hours in advance and reheated just before serving.

1 tablespoon oil, for cooking

12 to 15 chestnuts, shells slit on the domed face

10 to 12 cloves garlic, separated, skin left on

2 1/2 tablespoons sweet butter

*2 medium leeks, white part only, cut into
1/2-inch-long pieces*

10 brussels sprouts, halved

*1/2 pound small, very firm white turnips,
peeled and cut into 1/2-inch wedges*

*1/2 pound small Yukon Gold potatoes or red
potatoes, peeled and quartered*

*1 teaspoon fresh or dried juniper berries,
ground*

Salt, freshly ground black pepper

*5 ounces porcini mushrooms or seasonal
mushrooms, caps only*

1/2 pound fresh cranberry beans, shelled

2 quarts chicken stock (see page 370)

*1 pound Swiss chard, leaves only,
cut into small pieces*

1/4 cup walnuts, finely chopped

1/2 tablespoon walnut oil

PREPARATION

Preheat oven to 375 degrees. Place 1/2 tablespoon of the cooking oil, the chestnuts, and
the garlic cloves in a small roasting pan and roast in the oven for 30 to 40 minutes.
Remove from heat and set aside to cool. When cool, peel the chestnuts with a knife,
remove the garlic skins, and set aside.

Heat the remaining 1/2 tablespoon oil with 1 tablespoon of the butter in a medium
roasting pan or Dutch oven on top of the stove over medium heat. Add the leeks, brussels sprouts, turnips, potatoes, ground juniper, and salt and pepper to taste and sauté for
4 to 5 minutes over medium heat. Transfer to the oven and roast while tossing often.
After 15 minutes of roasting, add the mushrooms and cook for another 15 to 20 minutes. When done, remove from heat and keep warm.

Place the cranberry beans in the chicken stock, bring to a boil, and simmer for about 10
minutes. Add the Swiss chard and simmer for another 6 to 8 minutes. Drain the beans
and Swiss chard well and add to the roasted vegetables along with the chestnuts, garlic
cloves, and remaining 1-1/2 tablespoons butter. Toss over high heat for 4 to 5 minutes.
Taste for seasoning.

 PRESENTATION

Transfer the warm vegetables to a deep serving dish and sprinkle with the walnuts and walnut oil.

Note: You can substitute dried beans for the fresh cranberry beans. If using dried beans, presoak them in cold water 24 hours prior to cooking. Boil the dried beans for 25 to 30 minutes before adding the Swiss chard.

WINTER VEGETABLE CASSEROLE WITH SPICES AND ORANGE ZEST

Serves 4 to 6

This dish is a tribute to root crops, dried starchy vegetables, spices, and winter-fresh bitter greens.
This casserole will complement roasted game, such as venison, partridge, or pheasant, and can be prepared
up to 2 hours in advance; reheat before serving.

*1/2 cup dried great northern beans,
soaked overnight in cold water, and drained
when ready to cook*

3 quarts chicken stock (see page 370)

*1/4 cup green lentils,
soaked overnight in cold water, and
drained when ready to cook*

*Zest of 1 orange cut into a thin julienne
(matchstick size) and juice of 1 orange*

1-1/2 tablespoons vegetable or olive oil

3 tablespoons sweet butter

*1 medium celeriac, peeled and cut into
2-by-1/4-inch sticks*

*1 fennel bulb, trimmed and cut into small
wedges 1/4 inch thick*

*1 medium parsnip, peeled and sliced
1/8 inch thick*

*3 salsify roots, peeled and cut into
1-inch-long segments*

1 sweet potato, peeled, in 1-inch dice

1 cinnamon stick, 2 inches long

2 cloves

1 bay leaf

1 star anise

Pinch of freshly grated nutmeg

Salt, freshly ground black pepper

*2 radicchio di Treviso or Belgian endives,
ends trimmed,
leaves quartered lengthwise*

*1 bunch broccoli rabe, 3-inch-long florets
with leaves only, stems discarded*

*1/4 pound chanterelles
or seasonal mushrooms*

✤ PREPARATION

Place the drained beans in a pot with 2 quarts of the chicken stock and the lentils in a separate pot with the other quart of chicken stock, both over medium heat. Bring to a boil and simmer the beans for 45 to 60 minutes and the lentils for 30 to 40 minutes. When done, remove from heat and set aside (do not drain).

Bring 2 cups water to a boil in a small pot over medium heat. Add the orange zest, boil for 5 minutes, strain out and set aside.

Preheat oven to 400 degrees. Warm 1/2 tablespoon of the olive oil with 1 tablespoon of the butter in a roasting pan on top of the stove over medium heat. Add the celeriac, fennel, parsnip, salsify, sweet potato, blanched orange zest, cinnamon stick, cloves, bay leaf, star anise, nutmeg, and salt and pepper to taste. Sauté for 2 to 3 minutes, transfer to the oven, and roast, stirring every 5 minutes. After 15 minutes of roasting, add the orange

juice and cook for another 25 to 30 minutes. When done, the vegetables should be glazed, lightly colored, and tender to the fork. Remove from heat, discard the cinnamon, cloves, bay leaf, and star anise, and set the vegetables aside.

Heat 1/2 tablespoon of the olive oil in a large skillet over high heat. Add the radicchio or endives and the broccoli rabe and toss well for 4 to 6 minutes. Season to taste, drain in a colander, and set aside.

Drain the lentils and the beans.

Wipe the skillet clean and heat the remaining 1/2 tablespoon olive oil. Add the chanterelles and toss for 4 to 5 minutes. Season to taste, add the drained beans and lentils, and toss well for 3 to 5 minutes over high heat. Add the remaining 2 tablespoons butter, the radicchio, broccoli rabe, spinach, salt, and pepper and toss for 4 to 5 minutes. Add the root vegetables and toss for 5 to 8 minutes. Taste for seasoning.

✤ PRESENTATION

Transfer the vegetables to a large, warm serving casserole and serve while very hot.

Desserts

Spring Summer Autumn Winter
❀   ❦   🍃   ❄

Sweet Apple Alix 🍃 page 294

Apple, Apple, Apple 🍃 page 295

Baked Apples with Cranberries 🍃 page 298

Caramelized Apple Tart Lyonnaise 🍃 page 299

Roasted Peaches and Blackberries with

    Ginger Caramel Ice Cream ❦ page 300

Blueberry Brioche Bread Pudding ❀ page 303

Oven-Roasted Strawberries with Verbena Ice Cream ❀ page 304

Croustillants of Strawberries ❀ page 305

Crispy Strawberry Purses ❀ page 306

Strawberry Shake with a Red Berry Coulis ❀ page 307

Chocolate and Raspberry Fontaine ❦ page 308

Chocolate Mousse with Honey Popcorn ❄ page 309

Spring Fruits in a Minty Cream ❀ page 310

Summer Fruits with a Watermelon Tequila Granité ❦ page 313

Fall Fruit Fricassée with Caramel Ice Cream 🍃 page 315

Winter's Tropical Fruit in a Spiced Infusion ❄ page 317

Rhubarb and Mango Compote with Strawberry Sorbet ❦ page 319

Fondant au Chocolat ❄ page 320

Chocolate Almond Cake ❄ page 321

Caramelized Walnut Cake 🍃 page 323

Apricot Tarte Tatin with Pistachio Nuts ❦ page 325

SWEET APPLE ALIX

Serves 4 to 6

This dessert is named after my daughter, Alix, who enjoys the family tradition originally created by her grandfather Michael Palmer when he was fixing dessert for his four daughters. Sweet Apple Alix consists of applesauce topped with whipped cream and sprinkled with chocolate chips. The applesauce can be prepared 4 to 5 hours in advance and cooled in the refrigerator until needed. The cream can be whipped and the chocolate grated 1 hour in advance and refrigerated until needed. If you are in a hurry, buy a jar of applesauce, ready-made whipped cream, and chocolate sprinkles. It's an ideal recipe to prepare with your child.

5 McIntosh apples, peeled, quartered, cored, and cut into 1/2-inch chunks

Juice and zest of 1 lemon

1 vanilla bean, split and scraped

1 sprig fresh mint

3 tablespoons granulated sugar

1 cup heavy cream

1 tablespoon confectioners' sugar

4 ounces bittersweet chocolate, at room temperature

4 ounces milk chocolate, at room temperature

PREPARATION

Combine the apple chunks, lemon juice and zest, vanilla, mint, granulated sugar, and 1/4 cup water in a medium-size, heavy-bottomed, nonreactive pot over medium heat. Cover and cook the apples until very soft, about 20 to 30 minutes. Remove from heat, discard the lemon zest, vanilla, and mint, and mash any remaining pieces of apple by hand with a potato masher or fork. Pour the applesauce into a deep glass dessert bowl, smooth the top, and set aside to cool.

Combine the cream and confectioners' sugar in a mixer or food processor and whip until firm. Refrigerate until needed.

Place a grater in the center of a deep plate. Grate the bittersweet and milk chocolate to form small chips. Refrigerate the chocolate chips until ready to serve.

PRESENTATION

Spread the whipped cream evenly over the applesauce and sprinkle with the chocolate chips. Serve cold with a plate of your favorite cookies.

Apple, Apple, Apple

Serves 4

This trilogy of apples combines three distinctive tastes and textures in one dessert: crispy caramelized apple rings, a crunchy apple salad with apple syrup, and a smooth and fragrant apple sorbet. The apple sorbet should be prepared 3 to 5 hours in advance. The caramelized apple rings can be prepared 2 to 3 hours in advance. The apple salad can be prepared 1/2 hour in advance.

For the Apple Sorbet:

7 McIntosh apples, split and cored

Juice of 1/2 lemon

5 tablespoons granulated sugar

For the Apple Salad:

Juice of 1/2 lemon

1/4 cup granulated sugar

2 McIntosh apples, peeled, split, cored, and cut into thin slices

For the Caramelized Apple Rings:

1 McIntosh apple, peeled, cored, and cut into very thin horizontal slices (about 16 rings) with a vegetable slicer or a mandoline

1 tablespoon confectioners' sugar

Preparation

For the Sorbet:

Toss the split apples with the lemon juice in a bowl. Place the apples in a juice extractor and crush. Reserve the apple pulp for the apple salad and stir the granulated sugar into the apple juice. Pour the juice into an ice cream machine and process until the sorbet is firm. Transfer to the freezer until needed.

For the Apple Salad:

Right after making the sorbet, make the apple pulp syrup (so that it has time to cool) by combining in a pot the reserved apple pulp from juicing the apples, above, with 1 cup of water, the lemon juice, and the granulated sugar. Bring to a boil over medium heat and boil for 2 minutes. Strain the syrup through a fine-mesh strainer into a dessert bowl, cool, and refrigerate. Discard the pulp. Add the thin apple slices to the cooled apple syrup and refrigerate until needed.

For the Caramelized Apple Rings:

Preheat oven to 325 degrees. Place the apple rings side by side on a nonstick baking sheet or on a baking sheet lined with parchment paper. Bake the rings until lightly brown, about 5 to 7 minutes.

Turn broiler on. Sprinkle the apple rings with confectioners' sugar and glaze them under the broiler, about 1 to 2 minutes. When glazed, remove from broiler and set aside to cool. Freeze the apple rings until needed to keep crisp.

✒ PRESENTATION

Chill 4 dessert bowls in the freezer for 15 to 30 minutes before serving. Divide the apple salad slices evenly between the 4 frozen dessert bowls. Overlap the slices like the petals of a flower all around the edges of the bowls. Add 2 tablespoons apple syrup per bowl. Place a scoop of apple sorbet in the center of each bowl and decorate each sorbet with 4 caramelized apple rings by sticking one edge of each apple ring into the sorbet.

Clockwise from top:
Caramelized Apple Tart Lyonnaise; Sweet Apple Alix; Baked Apples with Cranberries; Apple, Apple, Apple

Baked Apples with Cranberries

Serves 4

This warm fall dessert is easy to make, colorful, and deliciously fragrant. Use large apples
that will keep their shape, firm texture, and sweet taste when baked (Rome apples, for example).
This recipe can be prepared up to 4 hours in advance.

*Zest of 1 orange: 1/2 finely chopped
and 1/2 whole*

4 Rome or Golden Delicious apples

2 cups fresh cranberries

Juice of 2 oranges

1/4 cup brown sugar, firmly packed

2 tablespoons sweet butter

5 cinnamon sticks

*Sweetened whipped cream or
vanilla ice cream (optional)*

Preparation

Boil the chopped orange zest in 1 quart of water for 10 minutes. Drain and set aside.

Preheat oven to 400 degrees. Slice a 1/4-inch cap off each apple and cut out the stem,
creating a small hole large enough to fit a cinnamon stick through. Set the caps aside.
Core the apples with a melon baller, making a good-size cavity to hold the cranberries.
Discard the apple flesh. Place the cored apples in a small baking pan and evenly divide
half of the cranberries, the chopped zest, the juice of 1 orange, 2 tablespoons of the
sugar, and 1 tablespoon of the butter among the cavities of the cored apples. Stick a cinnamon stick through the hole in each cap and place the apple caps back on top of each
apple, with the cinnamon stick sticking out of the stem hole. Add the remaining cranberries, 2 tablespoons brown sugar, 1 tablespoon butter, whole orange zest, juice of
1 orange, and cinnamon stick to the baking pan around the apples.

Bake the apples for 30 to 40 minutes or until tender when pierced with a knife. Remove
from heat and set aside to cool for 10 minutes.

Presentation

Place the warm apples in the center of a round serving dish. Spoon the sauce around
the apples. You can serve sweetened whipped cream or vanilla ice cream on the side.

CARAMELIZED APPLE TART LYONNAISE

Serves 6 to 8

This tart was the first dessert I had to make as a young apprentice in the pastry department of the Restaurant Nandron in Lyons: an easy, classic, and delicious recipe with a buttery caramelized glaze on top.
The puff pastry dough has to be prepared 24 hours before the tart is fully assembled; you can buy ready-made puff pastry dough as well, or you can find a basic recipe for puff pastry in any classic pastry book.
When done it should be kept chilled until needed.

All-purpose flour, for dusting

1/2 pound puff pastry, rolled into a 6-inch square, 1/2-inch thick, refrigerated until needed

1 egg yolk whisked with 1 tablespoon water

5 Rome or Golden Delicious apples, peeled, split, cored, and sliced into very thin wedges

3 tablespoons sweet butter, softened

1 vanilla bean, split, inside scraped and scrapings mixed with 5 tablespoons sugar

Sweetened whipped cream, crème fraîche, or vanilla ice cream (optional)

PREPARATION

Preheat oven to 400 degrees. Dust a working surface and rolling pin with flour. Place the cold puffed pastry square in the center and evenly roll out the dough, dusting it with flour as needed. Cut into a 14-inch circle. Roll the dough around the rolling pin, then unroll onto a 13-inch round pizza pan or tart pan. Gently press the dough to line the bottom and sides of the pan, leaving a 1-inch edge overhanging. Brush the edge with half of the egg yolk wash, and fold the edge under all around, pinching as you go to make a tightly fluted border. Brush the fluted border with the remaining egg yolk wash.

On top of the dough, make a ring of apple slices around the outer edge of the circle, overlapping the slices every 1/4 inch, forming a rosace (flower shape). Make a second ring of apple slices inside the outer ring. Fill the center of the ring with the remaining apple slices (you may use any broken pieces).

Carefully brush the apples with the butter and evenly sprinkle with the vanilla sugar. Bake the tart for 35 to 40 minutes or until caramelized. Reduce the oven temperature to 325 degrees if necessary to avoid burning. Once the crust is light brown, slide the tart from the pan onto a rack and finish baking on the rack. Cool for 15 minutes before serving.

PRESENTATION

Transfer the caramelized apple tart to a platter and cut into wedges. Optional: Serve sweetened whipped cream, crème fraîche, or vanilla ice cream on the side.

Roasted Peaches and Blackberries with Ginger Caramel Ice Cream

Serves 4

You can make the caramel ice cream and candied ginger 2 to 3 hours in advance. Freeze the ice cream and set aside the candied ginger until ready to serve. You can substitute good-quality commercial caramel-fudge ice cream for the homemade version here, but keep the ginger syrup to drizzle over the ice cream for a fresh ginger taste. You can also roast the peaches 1/2 hour before serving and set aside to cool. Just before serving, reheat the peaches with the blackberries in a pan for 3 to 5 minutes.

For the Ginger Caramel Ice Cream:

1 cup sugar

1 tablespoon fresh gingerroot, peeled and thinly sliced

2 cups heavy cream, chilled

2 cups milk, chilled

7 egg yolks in a bowl, whipped with 1 tablespoon sugar until foamy

For the Candied Ginger:

2 tablespoons fresh gingerroot, peeled,

and cut into a julienne (matchstick size)

1/4 cup sugar

For the Roasted Peaches and Blackberries:

6 medium peaches, ripe but not soft

1 tablespoon sweet butter

1 tablespoon sugar

1 tablespoon fresh gingerroot, peeled and thinly sliced

1 pint blackberries

❧ Preparation

For the Ginger and Caramel Ice Cream:

Combine the sugar, 1 tablespoon water, and the gingerroot in a large copper or heavy-bottom pot over medium heat. Heat the sugar until it starts to turn dark brown. Carefully and rapidly pour in the chilled cream and milk, stirring with a whisk. Bring to a boil and pour over the egg yolks in the bowl while whisking. Transfer the caramel mixture back into the pot over low heat. Stir with a wooden spoon until the mixture reads 175 to 180 degrees on a candy thermometer or until slightly thicker but not yet boiling. Strain the mixture into a bowl and set aside to cool. When cool, transfer to an ice cream machine and freeze until foamy (or according to manufacturer's instructions) and set. Transfer from the ice cream machine to a bowl, cover, and freeze until needed.

For the Candied Ginger:

Combine the gingerroot with the sugar and 3/4 cup water in a small pot over medium heat. Bring to a boil, lower heat, and simmer until the syrup becomes very thick, about 30 minutes, taking care not to let it burn.

Preheat oven to 400 degrees. Drain the candied ginger and spread it on a baking sheet. Dry in the oven for 5 to 8 minutes, remove from heat, and set aside to cool.

For the Roasted Peaches and Blackberries:
Bring 2 quarts water to a boil in a large pot. Plunge in the whole peaches and boil for 1 minute. Remove with a spoon to a colander and cool under cold running water. Delicately peel the peach skins with a small knife, halve the peaches, and remove the pit. Discard the skin and pits and set the halved peaches aside.

Melt the butter in a pan over medium heat. Add the sugar, gingerroot, and the halved peaches hollow side down. Roast in the oven for 5 minutes or until lightly caramelized, turn over, add 1 tablespoon water, and finish cooking for another 5 minutes (add a touch more water if too dry). Remove the roasted peaches from the pan and keep warm.

Add the blackberries to the pan and toss them for 2 to 3 minutes or until slightly soft. Discard the ginger slices and keep the blackberries warm in the pan with the cooking juices.

❧ PRESENTATION

Evenly divide the warm blackberries and a little cooking juice among 4 dessert plates. Arrange 3 warm peach halves, hollow side up, over each serving of blackberries. Place 1 small spoonful of caramel ice cream in each peach hollow and sprinkle with the candied ginger. Serve immediately while still warm.

BLUEBERRY BRIOCHE BREAD PUDDING

Serves 4

This lighter version of bread pudding has a minty flavor and is bursting with
deep-purple baked blueberries. The pudding can be prepared a day in advance.
It is best when refrigerated for at least 6 hours before serving.

1 cup milk

1 cup heavy cream

*1/2 vanilla bean, split and scraped, or a few
drops pure vanilla extract*

*5 sprigs mint, 1 sprig, leaves only,
reserved for garnish*

Zest of 1 lemon, grated

1/2 cup sugar

*4 gelatin sheets or
1 packet unflavored Knox gelatin*

*4 slices brioche or challah bread,
cut 1/3 inch thick*

8 ounces fresh blueberries

❋ PREPARATION

Preheat oven to 325 degrees. Combine the milk, cream, vanilla (bean and scrapings), 4
mint sprigs, and lemon zest in a small saucepan and bring to a boil over medium heat.
Remove from heat, stir in the sugar and gelatin, and let set for 3 minutes. Remove the
mint and vanilla bean.

Place a baking cup 3 inches in diameter and 1-1/2 inches deep top side down on the
center of a slice of bread to cut out a disk the size of the cup. Discard the bread trimmings and set the bread disk aside. Repeat with the remaining 3 bread slices.

Fill 4 baking cups halfway with blueberries. Pour the warm milk mixture over the
blueberries to fill each cup 3/4 full. Place 1 bread disk in each cup over the blueberry
mixture. Transfer to the oven and bake for 20 to 25 minutes (the custard should not be
completely set). Turn on the broiler and broil until the bread is nicely toasted. Remove
from oven and set aside to cool. Refrigerate for several hours before serving.

❋ PRESENTATION

To unmold, run a small blade around the side of each cup and invert the blueberry
bread pudding onto a dessert plate. Garnish with reserved mint leaves.

Oven-Roasted Strawberries with Verbena Ice Cream

Serves 4

Very big, ripe, and juicy strawberries give off a subtle fragrance when roasted and pair well with the lemony flavor of this verbena ice cream. The ice cream can be made up to 5 hours in advance but the strawberries should be roasted just before serving. Butter cookies or almond tuiles go well with this dessert. If you do not have an ice cream maker, serve the verbena sauce chilled instead of processing it in an ice cream machine.

For the Verbena Ice Cream:

3 cups heavy cream

1 cup milk

1 cup plus 3 tablespoons sugar

8 stems fresh verbena or 4 to 5 verbena tea bags

8 egg yolks

For the Roasted Strawberries:

20 large strawberries, hulled

2 tablespoons sweet butter, melted

❋ Preparation

For the Verbena Ice Cream:

Bring the cream, milk, and 1/2 cup of the sugar to a boil in a large saucepan over medium heat. Add the verbena, remove from heat, cover with a lid, and infuse for 5 minutes. Once infused, return to a boil.

In a large bowl, whisk the egg yolks and remaining sugar until smooth and foamy. Pour in the boiling verbena mixture while constantly whisking. Transfer the verbena and egg blend back into the pan over low heat and stir gently with a wooden spatula for 3 minutes or until the blend starts to slightly thicken. Strain the ice cream mixture, discard the verbena, and set aside to cool. When cool, process in an ice cream machine.

For the Roasted Strawberries:

Preheat oven to 400 degrees. Place the strawberries side by side, stem end down, in a baking dish. Add 1 tablespoon water to the dish. Brush the strawberries with the melted butter and sprinkle the 3 tablespoons sugar over the top. Bake for about 6 to 8 minutes or until the strawberries are soft.

❋ Presentation

Place 5 strawberries in a ring in the center of each plate. Scoop the ice cream into the center of the strawberries.

CROUSTILLANTS OF STRAWBERRIES

Serves 4

This beautiful dessert consists of 5 layers of crisp puff pastry disks covered with thinly sliced strawberries topped with whipped cream in a pool of red berry coulis. The puff pastry can be baked up to 1 hour in advance and the berry coulis prepared up to 3 hours in advance. The dessert should be assembled just before serving.

8 ounces puff pastry

2 cups confectioners' sugar

1 pint strawberries, hulled, and thinly sliced

1 cup heavy cream, whipped with 3 tablespoons confectioners' sugar

1/2 cup Red Berry Coulis, strained into a bowl with a fine-mesh strainer and refrigerated until used (see page 307)

❊ PREPARATION

Preheat oven to 400 degrees. Place the puff pastry in the center of a work surface dusted with confectioners' sugar. With a rolling pin, roll the dough out into an 8-by-5-inch rectangle 1/4 inch thick. Tightly roll the dough into a log lengthwise and cut into 1/4-inch slices. With the rolling pin, flatten each slice, pressing it into the confectioners' sugar until it forms a paper-thin round. Cut each piece with a 4-inch round cookie cutter to make even circles. Although only 20 circles are needed for this recipe (5 per *croustillant*), you should end up with approximately 28 circles in case of breakage.

Place circles on a nonstick baking sheet or on a baking sheet lined with parchment paper. Let sit at room temperature for 15 minutes. Bake for 5 to 8 minutes or until golden. Remove from heat and set aside on a wire rack until needed. Use the 20 nicest circles when assembling.

To assemble the dessert, set aside 4 of the nicest circles to top each *croustillant*. Place one circle in the center of each plate. Cover each bottom circle with a layer of sliced strawberries and a dab of whipped cream. Place a second circle over the whipped cream and gently press down. Cover with a second layer of strawberries and a dab of whipped cream. Repeat the same process until you have 4 layers of pastry and strawberries. Top with the reserved circles and a dollop of whipped cream.

❊ PRESENTATION

Drizzle the berry coulis around the *croustillants* and serve immediately.

CRISPY STRAWBERRY PURSES

Serves 4

Baked strawberries in a delicate crisp dough create this wonderful sensation of crunch and warmth coupled with a soft, cold, and refreshing mint sauce.

For the Phyllo Purses:

3 sheets phyllo dough, 12 by 17 inches

1/4 cup sweet butter, melted

3 tablespoons confectioners' sugar

*4 slices pound cake, 2 inches square by
1/2 inch thick*

20 strawberries, hulled

8 mint leaves, 4 finely chopped and

4 reserved for garnish

For the Sauce:

1/2 cup good-quality vanilla ice cream

1/4 cup heavy cream

*1 tablespoon peppermint liqueur or
a few drops peppermint extract*

4 to 6 mint leaves, finely chopped

❀ PREPARATION

For the Phyllo Purses:
Preheat oven to 450 degrees. With a pastry brush, evenly brush 1 sheet of phyllo dough with some of the melted butter. Lightly dust the sheet with some of the confectioners' sugar (using a fine-mesh strainer). Repeat with the second and third sheets of phyllo, and stack all three sheets.

Quarter the phyllo sheets and place 1 slice of pound cake in the center of each phyllo quarter. Arrange 5 strawberries, stem end down, on each cake slice. Brush the strawberries with melted butter and sprinkle with the chopped mint. Gather up the edges of each phyllo quarter to encase the strawberries, leaving a 2-inch opening in the center of the phyllo purse. Brush the outside of the 4 phyllo purses with the remaining melted butter and dust with the remaining sugar.

Bake for 10 to 15 minutes, until the phyllo purses are golden, and remove from heat.

For the Sauce:
While the pastry is baking, combine the ice cream, the heavy cream, mint liqueur, and chopped mint leaves in a bowl and stir until soft and creamy. Keep refrigerated until ready to use.

❀ PRESENTATION

Place each warm phyllo purse on a dessert plate. Spoon the mint sauce around the pastry and garnish with whole mint leaves.

Strawberry Shake with a Red Berry Coulis

Serves 4
This creamy light berry ice cream shake is very easy and quick for a refreshing spring dessert.
It can be served with your favorite cookies or with toasted and sugared brioche.
The red berry coulis can also be served with vanilla or other berry flavored ice cream or to decorate the
Croustillants of Strawberries (see page 305). The coulis can be prepared up to 3 hours in advance
and the shake made just before serving.

For the Strawberry Shake:

8 strawberries: 4 hulled and thinly sliced,
4 whole with the stems on,
slit halfway up from the bottom and
reserved for garnish

1 pint good-quality vanilla ice cream

1 cup Red Berry Coulis

For the Red Berry Coulis:

1/2 pint raspberries

1/2 pint strawberries, hulled and halved

2 tablespoons sugar

Juice of 1/2 lemon

❋ Preparation

For the Strawberry Shake:
Chill the container of a blender or food processor in the freezer for 1/2 hour. Decorate 4
tall glasses or champagne flutes with strawberry slices by pressing one slice at a time
against the insides of the glasses from bottom to top. Chill the decorated glasses in the
freezer until needed.

For the Red Berry Coulis:
Place the berries, sugar, 1/4 cup water, and the lemon juice in a blender or food processor. Purée until very smooth.

Combine the ice cream and the cold berry coulis in the frosted blender or food processor
container and blend until light and smooth. Evenly pour the shake into the decorated
glasses.

❋ Presentation

Slide one slit strawberry onto the rim of each glass and freeze the desserts until ready to
serve, or serve immediately with a tall spoon on the side.

CHOCOLATE AND RASPBERRY FONTAINE

Serves 12

This recipe, created by pastry chef Jacques Torres, is made of crispy phyllo packages stuffed with warm, bitter-sweet chocolate *ganache* topped with raspberries. The fontaines can be prepared 6 to 8 hours in advance, wrapped in plastic wrap and refrigerated, then baked for 8 to 10 minutes just before serving. Once assembled, the fontaines can also be frozen for later use and defrosted for 15 minutes before baking.

7 ounces bittersweet chocolate, chopped

1/2 cup heavy cream

*4 tablespoons raspberry brandy
(eau-de-vie de framboise)*

1/2 cup confectioners' sugar, extra for dusting

8 sheets phyllo dough, 10 by 20 inches

1/2 cup sweet butter, melted

*1 recipe Cocoa Sponge Cake
(see page 321) or commercial pound cake cut
into 12 disks 2-1/2 inches in diameter and
1/2 inch thick with a cookie cutter*

1 pint raspberries

❧ PREPARATION

Place the chopped chocolate in a bowl. Bring the cream to a boil in a small saucepan and pour over the chocolate. Stir until the chocolate has melted, add 2 tablespoons of the raspberry brandy, and combine until smooth. Set the chocolate *ganache* aside to cool.

Bring 1/3 cup water to a boil in a small pot, add the confectioners' sugar, and stir until dissolved. Add the remaining 2 tablespoons raspberry brandy and remove the raspberry syrup from heat.

To assemble, spread 1 sheet of phyllo dough on a work surface, brush with a thin coating of the melted butter, dust with sifted confectioners' sugar, and cover with a second sheet. Brush with the melted butter again and dust with the sugar. Cut the rectangular phyllo dough into 3 equal strips, about 6-1/2 inches wide by 10 inches long. Place a disk of chocolate cake in the center of each strip and moisten each disk with a little of the raspberry syrup. Cover each disk with a generous spoonful of the chocolate *ganache* and place 8 to 10 raspberries on top. First, fold one end of the phyllo dough over the raspberries and then the other, tucking under to form a small closed purse fully encasing the chocolate and raspberries. Repeat this process until you have made 12 packages. Brush each one with butter and refrigerate (or freeze) until ready to bake.

Preheat oven to 400 degrees. Place the packages on a greased baking sheet and sprinkle with more sugar. Bake for 8 to 10 minutes or until lightly browned. Keep warm.

❧ PRESENTATION

Top each fontaine with the remaining raspberries and serve hot.

Chocolate Mousse with Honey Popcorn

Serves 4 to 6

A fun way of making chocolate mousse for children with their favorite snack, this mousse can be made 3 to 5 hours in advance and the popcorn up to 3 hours before serving.

For the Honey Popcorn:

2 tablespoons vegetable oil

1/4 cup popcorn kernels

1/2 cup sugar

2 tablespoons honey

2 tablespoons corn syrup

For the Chocolate Mousse:

8 ounces Swiss milk chocolate, coarsely chopped

2-1/2 tablespoons vegetable oil

1 cup heavy cream, whipped soft and refrigerated

Whipped cream, for serving

✤ Preparation

For the Honey Popcorn:
Place the vegetable oil and the popcorn kernels in a large pot. Cover with a lid, and pop the corn over medium heat, shaking the pan constantly to avoid burning but keeping the lid tightly shut, for about 5 to 6 minutes or until all the corn is popped. Remove from heat, discard any kernels that have not popped, and set aside until needed.

Combine the sugar, honey, corn syrup, and 3 tablespoons water in a heavy-bottom saucepan and cook over medium heat until it registers 350 degrees on a candy thermometer or the sugar has lightly caramelized. Add the popcorn and stir until coated. Transfer the honey popcorn with a spatula onto waxed paper to cool. When cool, break the honey popcorn into small pieces.

For the Chocolate Mousse:
Bring 1 quart water to a simmer in the bottom part of a double boiler, add the chocolate and oil to the top bowl and melt while stirring, or microwave at medium for about 2 minutes. Remove from heat and whisk in 1/4 of the whipped cream while the melted chocolate is still warm. Gently fold in the remaining whipped cream, reserving 2 tablespoons. Fold 3/4 of the honey popcorn into the mousse. Reserve the remaining popcorn for garnish. Spoon the chocolate popcorn mousse into 4 or 6 ramekins 2/3 cup in size. Refrigerate for several hours or overnight.

✤ Presentation

Freeze the ramekins for 10 minutes, run a knife around the edges, dip them in warm water for 10 seconds, and unmold one popcorn mousse onto each serving plate. Garnish with the reserved honey popcorn and serve with a dollop of whipped cream.

SPRING FRUITS IN A MINTY CREAM

Serves 4 to 6

This enchanting dessert captures the joy of the colorful spring bounty with its berries, apricots, cherries, and melon in a refreshing pool of mint cream. The fruits can be prepared up to 1 hour before serving and kept refrigerated, and the mint cream can be made 6 to 8 hours in advance and refrigerated.

For the Minty Cream:

1 cup milk

1 cup heavy cream

1/3 cup sugar

*2 bunches (about 4 ounces) fresh mint:
2 sprigs reserved for garnish,
the rest leaves only, for infusion*

5 egg yolks

1 tablespoon crème de menthe liqueur (optional)

For the Spring Fruits:

*1/2 pint strawberries, hulled,
halved or quartered*

1/2 pint raspberries

1 cup fresh sweet cherries, halved and pitted

2 kiwis, peeled and sliced 1/4 inch thick

*4 ripe apricots, split, pitted, and cut
into 1/4-inch wedges*

*1/4 honeydew melon, peeled, seeded,
and cut into thin slices*

*2 peaches, peeled, pitted, and cut into
1/4-inch wedges*

Juice of 1 lemon

2 tablespoons sugar

*1 sprig fresh mint, leaves only,
finely chopped*

❁ PREPARATION

For the Minty Cream:
Chill a medium-size glass bowl.

Combine the milk, cream, and 1/2 of the sugar in a small pot over medium heat and bring to a boil, stirring constantly. Add 2/3 of the mint leaves for infusion, remove the pot from heat, cover tightly, and let infuse for 5 minutes.

Whisk the egg yolks with the remaining sugar in a medium-size bowl until foamy.

Remove the lid from the mint infusion, return the pot to medium heat, and return to a boil. Carefully pour the hot mint infusion over the egg yolk mixture, whisking constantly until smooth. Strain the cream mixture back into the pot, discard the infused mint leaves, and place over low heat. Continuously stir with a wooden spoon to avoid curdling. Once the cream mixture has slightly thickened and almost reached the boiling point, about 180 degrees, or when steam starts to surface, remove from heat and pour into a bowl. Stir for a few minutes, set aside to cool, then transfer to a blender or food processor.

Bring 1 cup water to a boil in a small pot over medium heat. Add the remaining mint leaves, boil for 1 minute, and strain out the leaves. Add the blanched mint leaves and the crème de menthe, if using, to the blender with the cream mixture. Blend for 2 to 3 minutes until smooth, then strain the mint cream into a container, and refrigerate until needed.

For the Spring Fruits:
Mix all the fruit in a bowl with the lemon juice, sugar, and chopped mint and refrigerate until needed.

❋ PRESENTATION

Spread the mint cream onto the bottom of a large, deep, prechilled dish and arrange the fresh spring fruits over. You can also serve the dessert on individual plates equally dividing the mint cream and fruits. Garnish with the reserved mint sprigs.

Summer Fruits with a Watermelon Tequila Granité

Serves 4 to 5

A frozen watermelon granité flavored with a splash of lime and tequila gives a Southwestern zing to this refreshing summer fruit salad. Other summer fruits can be added to this recipe if you wish. The watermelon granité should be made 6 to 8 hours in advance and the fresh fruits can be prepared up to 1 hour before serving.

For the Watermelon Tequila Granité:

*5 cups watermelon, seeded, rind removed, and cut into 1-inch cubes
(about 3 pounds of watermelon)*

1/2 cup sugar

Juice of 2 limes

1/4 cup tequila (optional)

For the Summer Fruits:

*Zest of 2 limes, cut into a julienne
(matchstick size)*

3 tablespoons sugar

4 fresh figs, trimmed and quartered

1/2 pint blackberries

1 small bunch seedless red grapes, sliced

3 plums, split, pitted, and thinly sliced

1/2 pint blueberries

1/2 small cantaloupe, peeled, seeded, and thinly sliced

Juice of 2 limes

2 tablespoons tequila (optional)

❧ Preparation

For the Watermelon Tequila Granité:
Reserve 1 cup watermelon cubes and blend the rest in a blender or food processor. Add the sugar, lime juice, and the tequila if desired, and blend until smooth. Strain the watermelon juice into a large shallow dish (juice should be 1/2 inch deep). Freeze for 2 hours, making sure the dish is level.

Scrape the iced watermelon juice in the dish with a fork for a light and flaky granite. If not cold enough, freeze for another hour and continue scraping until all the iced juice is made into a snowy granité. Cover with plastic wrap and keep in the freezer until needed.

For the Summer Fruits:
Bring 2 cups water to a boil in a small pot over medium heat. Add the lime zest and boil for 10 minutes. Drain, pat dry with paper towels, and toss the boiled zests in a small bowl with 1 tablespoon of the sugar. Set aside.

In a large bowl, combine the reserved cup of watermelon cubes and all the summer fruits with the lime juice, sugar, and the tequila, if using, and refrigerate until needed.

❧ PRESENTATION

Carefully arrange the summer fruits in small individual serving bowls or on a large, shallow, chilled dish. Sprinkle the watermelon tequila granité and the sugared lime zests over the fruit. Serve immediately.

Fall Fruit Fricassée with Caramel Ice Cream

Serves 4

For this recipe, late harvest fruits and nuts, such as apples, pears, almonds, and chestnuts are tossed with dried fruits, vanilla, and Armagnac and served warm with a rich caramel ice cream. You can prepare it 1 hour in advance and reheat the fruit casserole just before serving. The caramel ice cream should be made less than 3 to 4 hours before serving. You can substitute either a good-quality commercial rum-raisin or butterscotch ice cream if you cannot make the ice cream yourself.

For the Caramel Ice Cream:

7 ounces sugar

1 vanilla bean, split and scraped

2 cups heavy cream, chilled

2 cups milk, chilled

6 egg yolks whisked with 2 tablespoons heavy cream

For the Fruit Casserole:

2 Golden Delicious apples, peeled, split, cored, and sliced into 1/2-inch-thick wedges

2 Anjou pears, firm but ripe, peeled, split, cored, and sliced into 1/2-inch-thick wedges

Juice of 1 lemon

Zest of 1 orange cut into a julienne (matchstick size) and juice of 1 orange

6 tablespoons sugar

1 tablespoon sweet butter

1 tablespoon brown sugar, firmly packed

1 vanilla bean, split and scraped (to enhance the flavor of a split vanilla bean, scrape out the tender paste and add to the dish along with the bean)

1 large ripe red plum, split, pitted, and sliced

1/4 cup fresh or dried cranberries

1 tablespoon raisins

1/4 cup almonds, soaked overnight in 1/2 cup milk

4 prunes, soaked in 2 tablespoons Armagnac (or other brandy) overnight or for a few hours

8 chestnuts in heavy syrup (canned), drained, or 8 candied chestnuts

1 dried fig, sliced

2 tablespoons Armagnac

✒ Preparation

For the Caramel Ice Cream:
Combine the sugar with 1 tablespoon water in a heavy saucepan over medium heat. Add the scraped vanilla bean and let the sugar brown. Very carefully pour the chilled heavy cream and milk over the caramel and stir with a spoon until well mixed. Add the egg yolk mixture and stir with a spoon until almost boiling. Strain the caramel cream, cool, and process in an ice cream machine until done. (Do not overprocess the ice cream or you will ruin the creamy consistency.) Remove when thick and creamy and store in the freezer until ready to serve.

For the Fruit Casserole:
Toss the apple and pear wedges in the lemon juice and set aside.

Boil the orange zest for 20 minutes in 2 cups water with the 6 tablespoons sugar. Drain, discard the sweet water, and set the zest aside.

Melt the butter in a large skillet over high heat. Add the apple and pear wedges and toss for 2 minutes. Add the orange zest, brown sugar, vanilla bean, red plum, cranberries, and raisins, and toss for 2 minutes. Add the almonds, prunes, chestnuts, and fig, and toss for another 2 to 3 minutes. Add the Armagnac and flambé (ignite the alcohol with a match and let it burn out). Add the orange juice. Mix lightly and cook for 1 minute more. Remove the vanilla bean and pour into a deep serving dish.

PRESENTATION

Serve the fall fruit casserole warm with the caramel ice cream scooped on top.

WINTER'S TROPICAL FRUIT IN A SPICED INFUSION

Serves 4 to 6

These fresh tropical fruits are infused with a spiced syrup to create a hot and exotic dessert. This recipe can be prepared up to 6 hours in advance.

For the Tropical Fruits:

1 ripe persimmon, peeled and thinly sliced

1 small, ripe mango, peeled and thinly sliced

3 blood oranges, peeled, seeded, and sectioned

2 clementines, peeled, seeded, and sectioned

1 banana or 3 baby bananas, peeled and sliced

1 small papaya, peeled, seeded, in 1/2-inch dice

2 passionfruit, split in half, the juicy flesh-scooped out and pushed through a strainer with a wooden spoon into a small cup, the seeds discarded

1/2 small pineapple, peeled, cored, and cut into 1/4-inch-thick pieces

1 pink grapefruit, peeled and sectioned

1/4 pomegranate, split, seeds only

3 pieces candied ginger slices, cut into small thin strips and reserved for garnish (optional)

1/2 fresh coconut, meat finely grated

For the Infusion:

1-1/4 cups sugar

3 whole star anise

1 vanilla bean, split and scraped

1 ounce fresh gingerroot, peeled and sliced 1/4 inch thick

2 pieces lemon zest

1 cinnamon stick

5 whole black peppercorns

1/2 teaspoon coriander seeds

✤ PREPARATION

For the Tropical Fruits:
Combine all the fruits, except for the coconut and candied ginger, in a large glass serving bowl.

For the Infusion:
Bring 1 quart water with all the ingredients for the infusion to a boil in a medium saucepan over medium heat. Remove from heat, cover, and set aside to cool for 1/2 hour. Strain the infusion over the fruit, place the vanilla bean, anise star, and cinnamon stick over the fruits for decoration, cover with plastic wrap, and refrigerate overnight or for at least 4 hours.

❧ PRESENTATION

Serve the fruits in chilled bowls, decorated with the candied ginger, if using, and the coconut.

Rhubarb and Mango Compote with Strawberry Sorbet

Serves 4

The earthy and lightly sour taste of rhubarb and the exotic sweet flavor of mango create an original setting for the strawberry sorbet. You can prepare the rhubarb and mango compote up to 4 hours in advance, but the strawberry sorbet is best when prepared 1 hour before serving.

For the Rhubarb and Mango Compote:

1/4 cup sugar

Zest of 1 lemon, finely grated

1 pound rhubarb, ends trimmed, sliced

1 mango (about 1 pound), peeled, thick wedges of mango removed by running the blade of a knife along the pit, the wedges cut into 1/4-inch-thick slices

Juice of 1/2 lemon

For the Strawberry Sorbet:

1 pint strawberries, hulled, 2 strawberries cut in a julienne (matchstick size) and reserved for garnish

2 tablespoons sugar

Juice of 1/2 lemon

❧ Preparation

For the Rhubarb and Mango Compote:

Bring 1/2 cup water with the sugar and lemon zest to a boil in a pot over medium heat. Add the sliced rhubarb and boil for 2 to 3 minutes or until the rhubarb has slightly softened. Remove from heat and add the sliced mango and the lemon juice and set aside to cool. Chill in the refrigerator for 3 to 4 hours or over ice for 30 minutes.

For the Strawberry Sorbet:

Place the strawberries in a food processor or blender with 1/2 cup water, the sugar, and the lemon juice and blend until smooth. Strain and process the puréed strawberries in an ice cream maker or freeze in a bowl, stirring every 15 minutes until frozen.

❧ Presentation

Spoon the rhubarb and mango compote into 4 chilled serving bowls. Place a scoop of sorbet in the center of each bowl and sprinkle with the strawberry julienne.

Fondant au Chocolat

Serves 6 to 8

This easy-to-make chocolate dessert adapted by Jacques Torres combines the richness and taste of a warm chocolate cupcake with the lightness of a soufflé. The chocolate mixture can be prepared up to 5 hours in advance and refrigerated in the cups. Bake just before serving.

7 tablespoons sweet butter

6-1/4 ounces semisweet chocolate,
broken into small pieces

Pinch of salt

5 tablespoons unsweetened cocoa

4 egg whites

2 tablespoons sugar

1/2 cup heavy cream,
whipped until firm with
1 tablespoon confectioners' sugar

✤ Preparation

Preheat oven to 400 degrees. Melt the butter in a small pot over low heat. Remove from heat, add the chocolate, salt, and cocoa, and mix until smooth. Set aside.

Butter 6 to 8 cupcake molds 2 inches in diameter by 1-1/2 inches deep and dust the insides with sugar. Set aside. Whip the egg whites with the sugar until stiff. Slowly pour in the chocolate mixture and gently combine with a rubber spatula. Pour the mixture into the buttered, sugared molds. Bake for 4 to 5 minutes, remove from heat, and unmold immediately by carefully inverting 1 cup on the center of each serving plate.

✤ Presentation

At the table, spoon a dollop of whipped cream on top of each warm cake.

One-Handed Whisking: To help secure a bowl when whisking with one hand and adding something else with the other hand, moisten a kitchen towel, roll it into a coil, and place your bowl in the middle before starting to whisk.

CHOCOLATE ALMOND CAKE

Serves 8

This chocolate cake, layered with a luscious bitter chocolate mousse, a moist and intense
cocoa *génoise,* and crunchy toasted almonds is perfect for special occasions. The cake can be prepared up to
1 day in advance and kept refrigerated.

For the Cocoa Sponge Cake:

1 tablespoon sweet butter

1 tablespoon all-purpose flour

4 egg whites

1/2 cup sugar

4 egg yolks

*1/2 cup all-purpose flour sifted together
with 1/4 cup cocoa powder*

For the Cocoa Syrup:

1/4 cup sugar

1-1/2 tablespoons cocoa powder

For the Chocolate Mousse Filling:

10 ounces bittersweet chocolate

*2 cups heavy cream,
whipped until stiff*

1/2 cup almonds, sliced and toasted

*3-ounce chocolate bar,
scraped into fine curls with a
vegetable peeler or grater*

❖ PREPARATION

For the Cocoa Sponge Cake:
Preheat oven to 350 degrees. Brush an 8-inch springform cake mold with the butter and
dust with the flour.

With an electric mixer, whip the egg whites, slowly adding the sugar, and continue to
whip until stiff. With a spatula, fold in the egg yolks, then gradually incorporate the
sifted cocoa/flour mixture. Pour the batter into the cake mold and bake in the oven for
15 to 18 minutes. Remove from heat when done and unmold on a pastry rack to cool.

For the Cocoa Syrup:
Bring 1/4 cup water, the sugar, and cocoa powder to a boil in a small pot. Remove from
heat and set aside to cool.

For the Chocolate Mousse Filling:
Melt the chocolate in the top of a double boiler until it registers 100 degrees on a candy
thermometer or until hot to the touch. Remove from heat and gently incorporate the
warm chocolate into the whipped cream until smooth. Set aside.

To assemble the cake, place the sponge cake on an 8-inch-round piece of cardboard or on a serving plate. Split the sponge cake horizontally into 2 equal disks with a serrated knife. Slide the top disk to the side. Moisten the bottom disk with 1/2 of the cocoa syrup using a pastry brush. With a spatula, evenly spread 1/2 of the chocolate mousse filling over the moistened disk, then sprinkle 2 tablespoons of the toasted almonds on top. Cover with the top disk, moisten with the rest of the cocoa syrup, and evenly spread the remaining mousse filling on top with a thin coating around the sides.

Decorate the sides of the cake with the remaining sliced almonds, by gently pressing them into the coating. Decorate the top of the cake with the chocolate curls. Refrigerate at least 1 hour before serving.

✤ PRESENTATION

Transfer the cake to a round serving plate and slice it at the table.

Caramelized Walnut Cake

Serves 6 to 8

A deep crunch of caramelized walnuts in a smooth buttery filling is the perfect setting for this fall cake. This cake can be prepared up to 1 day in advance and decorated just before serving.

For the Caramelized Walnuts:

7 ounces shelled walnuts

1 cup sugar

Wedges of 1/4 lemon

2 pieces of orange zest

1/2 vanilla bean, split in half lengthwise

For the Walnut Filling:

6 eggs, separated

1/4 cup sugar

2 sticks sweet butter, very soft

*1 tablespoon hazelnut liqueur
(Eau de Noix or Frangelica)*

For the Cocoa Sponge Cake:

*1 tablespoon hazelnut liqueur
(Eau de Noix or Frangelica)*

1 recipe Cocoa Sponge Cake (see page 321)

Cocoa powder, sifted

For the Walnut Sauce:

Juice of 1 lemon

Juice of 1 orange

1/2 cup heavy cream, chilled

PREPARATION

For the Caramelized Walnuts:
Preheat oven to 400 degrees. Combine the walnuts, sugar, 3/4 cup water, lemon wedges, orange zest, and vanilla bean in a pot over medium heat. Mix well, bring to a boil, and simmer for about 30 to 40 minutes or until the syrup has thickened and very fine bubbles begin to burst at the surface.

Carefully strain the syrup into a bowl and set aside. Discard the lemon wedges, orange zest, and vanilla bean.

Spread the walnuts on a nonstick or greased baking sheet and bake in the oven until well caramelized and dried, about 15 to 20 minutes, tossing every 3 to 5 minutes while baking. When done, remove from heat and set aside to cool. Reserve 8 walnut halves for decoration and coarsely chop the rest.

For the Walnut Filling:
Reduce 1/2 cup of the walnut syrup to 1/4 cup over high heat and keep warm.

Combine the egg yolks and sugar in a bowl. Whisk until white and foamy. Add the butter, mix well, and set aside.

Place the egg whites in the bowl of an electric mixer. Beat at high speed until foamy and firm. Lower speed to medium and slowly and carefully pour in the warm walnut syrup. Switch the mixer back to high speed and beat for 3 to 4 minutes, then reduce speed to low and beat for another 5 minutes. Remove the bowl to the side and with a spatula gently fold in the egg yolk mixture (taking care not to overwork the mixture). Incorporate 4 ounces of chopped walnuts and the hazelnut liqueur and refrigerate until needed.

For the Cocoa Sponge Cake:
In a cup, mix together the hazelnut liqueur, 2 tablespoons of water, and 1/2 tablespoon of walnut syrup. Bake the cocoa sponge cake, remove from the cake mold, and cool. Clean the cake mold as it will be used again. Slice the cake (horizontally) into 3 equal disks. Place the 3 disks side by side on a counter. Brush the top of each disk evenly with the liqueur mixture.

Transfer the bottom disk back into the cleaned cake mold. With a spatula, spread 1/3 of the walnut filling evenly over the disk. Place the middle disk over the layer of filling and spread an equal amount of filling on top of the middle disk. Cover the second layer of filling with the top disk and spread the rest of the filling evenly over the top. Wrap with plastic wrap and refrigerate the cake for 2 to 3 hours.

For the Walnut Sauce:
Reduce the remaining walnut syrup to a brown caramel in a medium pot over high heat, about 8 to 10 minutes. Remove from heat and carefully add the lemon and orange juice all at once. Stir with a whisk, return to medium heat until the caramel melts, and reduce to a thick heavy syrup, about 3 to 5 minutes. Add the heavy cream, bring to a boil, and simmer for 2 to 3 minutes. Transfer the sauce to the container of a blender or food processor, add the caramelized walnuts, and blend until smooth, about 2 to 3 minutes. Strain in a bowl, set aside to cool, and refrigerate until needed.

PRESENTATION

Remove the ring part of the mold around the sides of the cake but leave the cake on the base of the mold. With your fingers, gently press the remaining chopped walnuts all around the sides of the cake. Sprinkle the top of the cake with sifted cocoa powder. Transfer the cake to a round serving dish and decorate the top with the 8 caramelized walnut halves in a circle. Serve the sauce on the side.

Apricot Tarte Tatin with Pistachio Nuts

Serves 4 to 6

A simple adaptation of a classic apple *Tatin,* this upside-down apricot tart has a deep caramel flavor that perfectly balances the acidic apricots and a vanilla ice cream with pistachios on top for a subtle nutty addition. The ice cream can be made 3 to 4 hours in advance and the tart 20 to 30 minutes before serving.

1/2 pound puff pastry (see page 372)

Flour, for dusting

3/4 cup sugar

1 vanilla bean, split and scraped (mix the vanilla scrapings with 1 tablespoon water and discard the pod)

1 pound fresh apricots, halved and pitted

1/4 cup heavy cream

2 tablespoons crushed pistachios

1 pint good-quality vanilla ice cream

❧ Preparation

Preheat oven to 375 degrees. Place the puff pastry in the center of a work surface dusted with flour. With a rolling pin, roll out the dough into a 10-inch circle. Transfer the dough to a greased baking sheet and prick with a fork every 1/2 inch. Place in the oven and bake for 15 to 20 minutes or until golden brown. Remove from heat and set aside to cool.

Sprinkle the sugar in a pan large enough to fit the apricots in a single layer. Add the vanilla water and place the apricot halves side by side (hollow side up) in the pan. Cook over high heat until the apricots are caramelized on the edges. Turn the apricots over, add the cream, and cook until very syrupy. Remove from heat and set aside to cool. Arrange the apricots in an 8-inch tart mold, hollow side up. Place the cooked puff pastry circle on top of the apricots and trim the edges of the dough if necessary. Reheat the tart in the oven for 5 minutes.

❧ Presentation

Invert the tart onto a round platter. Sprinkle with crushed pistachios, slice the tart, and serve with vanilla ice cream on the side.

Seasonal Market Lists

Spring

❋

Mid-March to Mid-June
Vegetables

Artichokes ◆ Asparagus ◆ Avocados ◆ Beets ◆ Carrots ◆ Cucumbers

Dandelion Greens ◆ Fava Beans (Broad Beans) ◆ Garlic Sprouts

Haricots Verts (French String Beans) ◆ Lettuce and Greens

Morels ◆ Peas ◆ Rhubarb ◆ Shallots ◆ Snow Peas

Sweet Peppers ◆ Zucchini

Fruits

Blueberries ◆ Meyers Lemons ◆ Strawberries

ARTICHOKES Grown mainly in California, these edible buds are rich in iron, potassium, fiber, and vitamins. Artichokes have diuretic properties, but the most important fact you should know about them is that they temporarily alter the chemistry of your taste buds and make other foods taste sweeter. There are two types of artichoke: BABY GREEN or PURPLE, and LARGE GREEN. For the large ones, look for heavy artichokes with firm, tightly packed green leaves; avoid black and dry leaves. Size is not a quality factor.

To extract the heart, remove the stem, if any, pull off the leaves from the base, then evenly trim the base and sides with a sharp paring knife until round and smooth. Slice the leaves horizontally just above the heart and rub with half a lemon to prevent discoloring, then boil in water with the juice of a lemon and salt until tender, 20 to 30 minutes. Drain and set aside to cool. Scoop out the chokes and discard them. Use the artichoke hearts, hot or cold, as a garnish for meats and fish or in salads. A wonderful spring soup is *Artichoke and Grilled Eggplant Soup with Lemon and Thyme* (see page 40).

For Baby Artichoke Appetizers: Trim 20 baby artichokes. Cut off the stems and the tips of the leaves. Split the artichokes in half, vertically, and squeeze a lemon over them. In a pan over medium heat, toss them with 3 tablespoons of olive oil, 1 chopped garlic clove, 1 sliced carrot, 1 sliced onion, 1 sprig of fresh thyme, salt, and pepper. Sweat for 5 minutes, and add 1/2 cup of dry white wine and 1 cup of chicken stock. Cook for 20 to 30 minutes. Just before serving, season with 1 chopped clove of garlic, the juice of a lemon, and 2 to 3 tablespoons of olive oil. Toss well with a dozen coarsely chopped basil leaves and 1 tomato, peeled, seeded, and diced. Serve hot or cold.

Try also *Roasted Baby Artichokes with Bacon* (see page 272), a delicious accompaniment for a roast or a fine dish on its own.

ASPARAGUS Reaching peak season from early spring through summer, asparagus is mainly produced in California, Michigan, and Washington. Considered a delicacy, perhaps due to its alleged aphrodisiac properties, asparagus is rich in vitamins A and C. There are 3 main types of asparagus: the large DARK GREEN, PENCIL, and WHITE (less common). Asparagus must be kept refrigerated, otherwise it will lose sugar and flavor and will become tough. Look for firm stalks that have compact tips. Count approximately 7 to 8 large stalks per serving.

For a simple side dish: Clean the stalks, peel them from 2 inches below the tip to the end, and tie them together in a small bunch with kitchen string. Cook in boiling salted water over high heat for about 5 to 7 minutes. Serve them warm right from the water, or plunge in ice water to stop the cooking process, drain, and serve cold with a mustard vinaigrette.

Asparagus can also be steamed or even drizzled with olive oil, chopped rosemary, and seasonings and grilled raw on the barbecue (not too hot) until slightly fork tender. Pencil asparagus do not require peeling but you should keep only 1/3 to 3/4 of the bud ends and discard the stems. They will also cook faster than large ones, about 3 to 4 minutes. White asparagus have a slightly more bitter taste and require careful peeling to prevent stringiness. They are delicious boiled with seafood salad or roasted in butter as a garnish to a sautéed fish fillet or white meat.

For a Warm Appetizer: Roll a very thin slice of prosciutto or cooked ham around each asparagus. Season with pepper and make 4 piles of 3 to 4 asparagus. Spread a sheet of phyllo dough on a flat surface and brush it with melted butter. Place a pile of asparagus on the dough (the tips should stick out by 1 inch), and roll 2 layers of dough around the pile. Cut off the excess dough. Repeat with the other piles. Place the piles in a baking pan, brush with a beaten egg yolk, and sprinkle with Appenzell and Parmesan cheese. Bake at 475 degrees for 5 to 7 minutes. Serve warm.

For other asparagus recipes you can try the refreshing *Asparagus Soup with a Sweet Pepper Coulis* (see page 34) or the *Black Sea Bass in a Lemon Broth with Asparagus* (see page 183).

AVOCADOS Grown mainly in Southern California, this tropical pear-shaped fruit is one of the most nutritious of foods. With a perfectly balanced pH, avocados are rich in vitamins from A to K, iron, potassium, and usable carbohydrates.

The two main varieties are the HAAS, considered the best, with a thick black leathery skin, and the FUERTE, with a thin, smooth green skin. Choose firm avocados that yield to gentle pressure (rock-hard avocados have been picked before they were mature and will rot before they ripen). Avocados should be bought a few days in advance and ripened at home wrapped in a newspaper. Prepare them just before serving. Once cut, they brown rapidly, so sprinkle them with lemon juice.

For a Chicken and Avocado Salad with Black Olives: In a pan, sauté 2 boneless and skinless chicken breasts with 2 tablespoons of olive oil, salt, and pepper until done, 15 to 20 minutes. Cool and slice into 1/2-inch cubes. Skin, pit, and dice 2 avocados. Pit and chop 2 ounces of cured American black olives. Add 1 minced shallot, 2 raw sliced white mushrooms, and a sprig of chopped tarragon. Mix all the ingredients in a bowl and season with a dressing of olive oil, balsamic vinegar, 1 teaspoon of dry mustard, a few drops of Tabasco, and salt and pepper.

For cocktail parties, an ideal hors d'oeuvre is the *Avocado Dip with Sesame Seeds* (see page 17).

BEETS California, New Jersey, Ohio, and Texas are the largest producers of beets. Sweet in taste but low in calories, beet roots are rich in phosphorus, potassium, calcium, and magnesium. The early crops are the best: Look for small and tender roots with fresh, crisp leaves. Avoid large, woody, and bruised ones. Do not cut the stems too short (leave about 1 inch) and do not peel before cooking or they will lose flavor and nutritional value.

To cook beets the size of a golf ball: Boil for at least 1 hour, until tender. Wear disposable gloves and use a sheet of parchment paper on your work surface to avoid stains. (Table salt removes beet root stains.)

For a Salad of Roasted Beets: Preheat the oven to 400 degrees. Add 1 pound of small beets to a pan along with 1 tablespoon of cooking oil, a few cloves, and 3 sprigs of thyme. Cover the pan with foil, and roast until fork tender, about 1 hour. When done, cool, peel, and slice the beets. Add 1 chopped shallot, two teaspoons of chopped parsley, 1 teaspoon of tarragon, 2 tablespoons of red wine vinegar, and 3 tablespoons of peanut or walnut oil, 1/4 cup of minced toasted walnuts, salt, and pepper. Toss well and serve with a few slivers of Parmesan cheese on top.

CARROTS Grown mainly in California and Texas, carrots are rich in potassium, pectin, fiber, and vitamin A. Carrot juice is an easy-to-digest, high-energy drink. Look for crisp, fresh, smooth, and well-shaped carrots. Avoid wilted, soft, and shriveled ones. The best are the young, bright-orange, medium-size California carrots. Chop off the top greens, as they take moisture from the root.

For Braised Pork and Carrots: Brown a 3-pound blade end of pork loin in 1/4 cup of oil in a heavy pan over high heat. Add a few peeled cloves of garlic, 1 sliced onion, 4 carrots thickly sliced, one bouquet garni (made of 4 sprigs of parsley, 1 sprig of fresh thyme, 1 bay leaf, and 1 small leek cleaned and folded in half, tied up with kitchen string), a pinch of sugar, 2 cloves, salt, and pepper. Add a bottle of dry white wine, cover, and braise in the oven for 2-1/2 hours at 300 degrees. Add water if too dry. Sprinkle with freshly chopped Italian parsley before serving.

Try the delicious *Carrot, Artichoke, and Broccoli Terrine* (see page 100), the perfect appetizer for a large party.

CUCUMBERS Cucumbers grow mainly in Florida and Mexico. Rich in water and vitamins A and C, low in calories and sodium, cucumbers are refreshing and have diuretic properties. Look for the European hothouse variety; they are 12 to 15 inches long with dark green skin. Select the firm ones and avoid the puffy or shriveled ones. To make cucumbers more digestible and less bitter, peel, halve lengthwise, scoop out the seeds with a spoon, slice, place in a colander, sprinkle with salt, and drain for 30 minutes before serving.

Try making *Cucumber Cones with Mint and Lime* (see page 19), a light vegetarian snack.

DANDELION GREENS Grown mainly in California, dandelion is a wild springtime plant picked before it flowers. Rich in vitamins A, B, and C, calcium, and iron, and low in calories, dandelion is a diuretic and helps liver function. Look for fresh, bright green leaves

with the stems and root intact (they will stay fresher). Avoid wilted, yellowing leaves.

To prepare a Dandelion Salad: Allow about 1/2 pound per serving. Cut off the roots, wash thoroughly, and drain well. This bittersweet green is delicious prepared with crispy bacon, warm poached quail eggs (break and cook them for 1 minute in simmering water with 1 tablespoon vinegar), garlic toasts, and chopped shallots with a mustard vinaigrette.

FAVA BEANS (BROAD BEANS) Grown mainly in California, this member of the pea family, a staple food during the Middle Ages, can cause an inherited allergy called favism. Rich in protein, iron, fiber, potassium, and vitamins A and C, fava beans come in large pods. Look for fresh, green pods and avoid wilted and damaged ones. One pound of fava beans in the pod yields about 1 cup shelled. Once shelled, fava beans need to have their tough outer skin removed. To do so, plunge the beans into boiling water for 1 minute. Drain and cool under cold running water. Make a small incision with your finger at one end of each bean and pop the bean out of its skin (discard the skins). The beans are now ready to be used.

The sweet and delicate taste of fava beans can enrich many other ingredients, such as fish, crustaceans, poultry, or lamb. You will find a recipe for *Lobster with a Fava Purée and Black Trumpets* (see page 149), or try the *Chicken Casserole with Morels, Fava Beans, and Spring Potatoes* (see page 204).

GARLIC SPROUTS Garlic sprouts are young bulbs with a mild garlic flavor that are often used in Chinese and other Asian cooking. They are well paired with tiny roasted spring potatoes, available locally toward later spring. (Try to find very small potatoes, the size of a marble, for they are the best in the world.) Just rub the potatoes under cold water to clean them and roast whole with a few scraps of fresh duck foie gras, the garlic bulbs, and seasonings; serve over slices of seared fresh foie gras and sprinkle with coarse sea salt. *For 4 servings, use about 1 bunch of garlic bulbs, cleaned and cut 2 inches long (green discarded), 1 pound of tiny spring potatoes, and 8 ounces of fresh duck liver (foie gras).*

HARICOTS VERTS (FRENCH STRING BEANS) Imported mainly from Europe, Africa, Central America, and the Caribbean, haricots verts are delicate and tasty. The long thin pods are hand picked while they are still young. Haricots verts are rich in vitamins A and C and low in calories. Look for tiny crisp beans. Snap one in two to test crispness and to make sure it has no strings.

To cook haricots verts for a simple side dish: Trim the ends of each bean, then wash and drain. Plunge into plenty of boiling salted water and cook for 5 to 6 minutes for a crunchy (al dente) consistency. Drain and plunge immediately into ice-cold water to stop the cooking process and preserve the bright green color. Drain and wrap in a cotton kitchen towel to preserve moisture until ready to use.

For Haricots Verts with a Creamy Lemon Dressing: Mix 1 teaspoon of dry mustard with 3 tablespoons crème fraîche or sour cream, add the juice of a lemon, and salt and pepper to taste. Toss 1 pound of cooked haricots verts with the dressing. Place on a bed of Bibb lettuce and sprinkle with toasted sliced almonds and chopped roasted sweet red pepper.

A salad with haricots verts and other spring vegetables is perfect for a light lunch; try the *Chicken Salad Tepee with Walnuts and Chives* (see page 69).

LETTUCE AND GREENS Most lettuce and salad greens are grown in California, Arizona, and Florida, but when the spring season approaches, local growers all over the country offer a wonderful assortment of very fresh and delicate salad greens. Salad greens are rich in vitamins A, C, and E, as well as iron and calcium. The popular BUTTERHEAD lettuce has a round head with a yellow heart and a tender, buttery texture. BOSTON lettuce is slightly larger in size with a lighter and crisper heart; it is excellent in *Lobster Salad Le Régence* (see page 84). BIBB lettuce has a small head of crunchy green leaves and a small yellow heart; it is very good when cut into wedges, washed thoroughly, and dipped in or drizzled with *Basil and Anchovy Dip with Radishes* (see page 9). Other spring and summer greens of varying tastes and colors include LOLLO ROSSA, a small head with reddish-brown and curly leaves, delicate in taste and texture; OAKLEAF, the same color as Lollo Rossa but with leaves in the shape of oak leaves (it's also available with green leaves); and the most interesting and widely popular today, MESCLUN, a mix of many different baby greens. These include spicy greens such as mustard or mizuna, tender greens such as oakleaf or Lollo Rossa, and crunchy baby tatsoi, baby spinach, or wild watercress, plus many more depending on the grower's imagination. Mesclun may also include edible flowers such as chrysanthemums, daylilies, geraniums, nasturtiums, pansies, roses, and violets.

MORELS From Oregon, the fresh Morel mushroom is abundant during spring. Its conical cap is deeply furrowed in a honeycomb pattern and ranges in color from

light brown to blond, varying in size as well. Morels are better cooked than raw. *To prepare a simple side dish: Remove the stems, split them in half if large, rinse and pat dry, then sauté in a very hot pan with a touch of cooking oil until all moisture has evaporated. Add seasonings, a touch of fresh butter, freshly minced chives, and 1 bunch of watercress leaves.*

Morels are also excellent with scrambled eggs for brunch *or with breaded bay scallops: Season and toss the scallops in flour, dip in melted butter, and roll in fresh bread crumbs, then broil until golden and serve on top of sautéed morels. Allow about 1/4 pound of morels and about 2 ounces of scallops per serving.*

A delicious side dish using morels is my *Morel Custard with a Shallot Jus* (see page 266).

PEAS Grown mainly in California, Texas, and Florida, green peas are also called ENGLISH PEAS. High in protein, rich in vitamins A, B, and C, potassium, phosphorus, and iron, peas are a highly nutritious food. Look for firm green pods, velvety to the touch, neither too small nor too dry. To test for freshness, snap open a pod and taste a pea. Peas should be eaten as soon as possible after being purchased, as their sugars start converting to starch once picked.

To cook, plunge them in boiling salted water for 3 minutes, drain, and chill in ice water to set their bright green color. Drain again and keep refrigerated until ready to use (cold in salads or warm in butter or olive oil as a side dish).

For a Pea Casserole or Soup: Sweat 1 cup of either minced leeks or pearl, spring, or white onions for 2 minutes at low heat in 1 tablespoon of butter. Add 1 sprig of rosemary, a piece of bacon or smoked ham, and 1 pound of freshly shelled raw peas. Sweat for 5 minutes. Add 1/2 cup of boiling chicken stock (1 quart for a soup), a pinch of sugar, salt, and pepper. Simmer for 8 to 10 minutes. For the pea casserole, discard the rosemary and bacon, add 1 tablespoon of butter and 1/2 teaspoon of chopped rosemary; for the soup, pour into a blender or food processor, add 1/2 cup of hot heavy cream, blend until smooth, and serve sprinkled with small pieces of crisp bacon and chives.

Peas are also delicious with shellfish, and may be substituted for the fava beans in the *Lobster with a Fava Purée and Black Trumpets* (see page 149).

RHUBARB Washington and Michigan are the largest producers of this vegetable. Often thought of as a fruit, rhubarb is also known as "pie plant." Rich in vitamins

A, B, and C, potassium, and calcium, rhubarb helps digestion with a gentle laxative effect. There are 2 types of rhubarb: FIELD GROWN, tart and tangy with dark red stalks, and the HOT-HOUSE variety, ranging from light pink to light red. These have a milder flavor and fewer strings. Look for firm, crisp, brightly colored, fairly thick stalks. Avoid wilted or flabby ones with spots or brown areas.

To cook, remove and discard the leaves (they are toxic), trim the stem ends, wash, and cut on the bias into 1/4-inch-thick slices. Cook with very little liquid (seasoned water or sweet wine for fish or meat, or in a heavy syrup for dessert) for about 3 to 5 minutes.

Rhubarb can be served as an interesting and unexpected accompaniment to steamed fish or shellfish (plain or flavored with dill), or with roasted duck or squab: Cut into long thick slices and sauté in butter with sugar until caramelized. Serve at dessert as marmalade or sorbet. Warm or cold, it is very delicious, but be careful to sweeten it enough; rhubarb has no natural sugar.

For a Rhubarb Mousse: Cut the stalks of 1/2 pound of rhubarb into 1-inch pieces. Cook with 1 tablespoon of water, a slice of lemon, 2 sprigs of mint, and 1 tablespoon of sugar. Bring to a boil and stir for 3 to 4 minutes. Stir with a spoon and remove from the heat when softened. Let cool, refrigerate, drain if there is too much liquid (the mixture should be on the thick side), and discard the lemon and the mint. Mix with an equal amount of whipped cream, and add sugar to taste. Serve with sliced strawberries or raspberries and a warm pound cake.

A compote of rhubarb is a refreshing dessert in *Rhubarb and Mango Compote with Strawberry Sorbet* (see page 319).

SHALLOTS Grown mainly in California, Oregon, and Washington, shallots are small, onionlike bulbs with brown skin. Their flavor is less harsh than that of garlic and more subtle than that of onions. Shallots stimulate the appetite and are more easily digestible than onions. They grow in multiple bulbs and range in size from 1 to 2 inches long, depending on the variety. Look for plump and firm ones; avoid those that are soft or sprouting. Traditional in Bordeaux cooking, shallots are mainly used to flavor sauces. They are delicious with steamed mussels or tossed in butter with a splash of red wine vinegar and chopped parsley, and served over steaks. Shallots can also be eaten raw and minced in a warm potato salad with chives and parsley.

For a Custard of Caramelized Shallots with Thyme: Sweat

1/2 pound of minced shallots over low heat with 1 table-spoon of butter, 1 teaspoon of chopped fresh thyme, 1 tea-spoon of sugar, and salt and pepper to taste. Add 2 to 3 tablespoons of water while cooking. Once they have turned a light caramel color, set aside to cool. Blend them with 3 eggs, 1-1/2 cups of cream, 1 pinch of nutmeg, salt, and freshly ground pepper, until smooth. Strain and pour into 6 small buttered 4-ounce cups. Bake in the oven in a water bath at 250 degrees for 45 minutes or until set. Serve along-side roast beef or sirloin steak.

For a shallot-flavored broth of clams, try the *Marinière of Littleneck Clams and Salmon with Champagne and Caviar* (see page 156).

SNOW PEAS Also called sugar peas, pea pods, or "mange tout" (which means "eat all" in French), snow peas are grown mainly in California. Rich in protein, potassium,

phosphorus, iron, and vitamins A, B, and C, they are a highly nutritious food. The pod is tender—and the peas inside are tiny—so they are eaten whole. Always trim the ends. Look for small, crisp, shiny green pods that feel velvety to the touch. Avoid dull and yellowish ones. To set their bright-green color once cooked, blanch the peas in boiling salted water for 3 minutes, then chill them in cold water.

To prepare a Snow Pea Garnish: Sweat 1 minced leek with 1 sprig of rosemary in 2 tablespoons of butter for 4 minutes. Add 1/2 pound of snow peas, a pinch of sugar, salt, pepper, and 2 tablespoons of water and simmer until done, about 10 minutes. Discard the rosemary and serve with roasted squabs or baby chickens that have also been flavored with rosemary while roasting.

Sugar snaps, a shorter and fatter pod with a thicker skin and tiny peas inside, are also available in the spring.

They are just as sweet as snow peas and should be prepared the same way.

Rosemary might be the best fragrant herb to pair with sweet pea pods, as in the recipe *Gulf Shrimp and Sugar Pea Risotto with Rosemary* (see page 112).

SWEET PEPPERS California, Florida, Mexico, and Holland are the largest producers of sweet peppers. Low in calories, rich in vitamins A, B, C, and E, potassium, and fiber, peppers can be difficult to digest when eaten raw. They come in many colors: green, red, yellow, orange, purple, etc. Look for peppers that are firm, smooth, and shiny with bright, fresh stems.

Always remove the seeds and the inner white veins before preparing. To skin peppers: Split them lengthwise, remove the seeds and stems, lay them skin side up on a pan, and broil until the skin blackens. Remove, cool, and peel by rubbing the skin off under cold running water.

For Chicken Drumsticks and Rice with Red Peppers: Roast 8 seasoned chicken drumsticks in a casserole over high heat. When brown, add 1 minced onion, 2 minced peppers, and 1 chopped clove of garlic. Sweat for 5 to 8 minutes. Add 1 tablespoon of Madras curry powder, and 1 cup of converted rice, stir well, and add 3 cups of chicken stock. Cook in the oven at 350 degrees for about 20 to 30 minutes. Serve in the casserole.

Cold or hot, broiled sweet peppers bring a distinctive taste to dishes such as *Broiled Mackerel with Radicchio di Treviso and Sweet Peppers* (see page 173).

ZUCCHINI Grown mainly in Florida, Texas, and California, zucchini is a young summer squash. Low in calories and sodium, it is rich in vitamins A and C, potassium, and iron. Look for dark-green, firm and unblemished zucchini under 7 inches (the smaller, the sweeter). Avoid soft or large ones. Used primarily in Mediterranean cuisine, zucchini are edible in their entirety; even their orange blossoms, stuffed or fried, are a delicacy.

For a Zucchini and Shrimp Appetizer: Sauté 1 cup of sliced zucchini and 1 pound of peeled and deveined shrimp over high heat with 1 tablespoon olive oil for 3 to 4 minutes. Add 3 pieces of orange peel, 10 basil leaves, salt, and pepper. Once cooked, discard the orange peels and serve topped with orange segments and drizzled with olive oil.

A healthful and easy-to-prepare recipe, *Baby Chicken and Squash Casserole with Rosemary* (see page 203), captures the spirit of spring.

BLUEBERRIES Grown mainly in Michigan and New Jersey, cultivated blueberries are bigger and sweeter than wild ones. Rich in vitamins A and C and potassium, blueberries are very nutritious. Look for plump, dark-blue, even-shaped berries. They should be clean, dry, and have no leaves. Avoid soft ones as well as those that come in cartons stained with juice (a sign of over-ripeness).

Try a Warm Blueberry Pie: In a bowl, whip 2 eggs with 5 tablespoons of sugar until white and foamy. Add 1/2 cup of heavy cream, 1/3 cup of all-purpose flour, 1-1/2 tablespoons of melted butter, and the grated zest of 1/2 an orange. Butter a tart mold, pour in the mixture, and add 1 pint of blueberries on top. Bake in the oven at 350 degrees for about 20 to 25 minutes. Serve warm.

In the style of old-fashioned bread pudding, I have created a lighter version with blueberries and lemon zest. See the recipe for *Blueberry Brioche Bread Pudding* (see page 303).

MEYERS LEMONS In speciality stores during the spring and early summer you will find the sweet-tasting Meyers lemon, a tree-ripened lemon with a sweet taste and a tender edible rind. It is excellent sliced thin into seafood salad or cut into thick slices, seasoned with a pinch of salt and sugar, then sautéed in olive oil until tender with chicken breasts or veal scaloppine.

STRAWBERRIES Grown mainly in California and Florida, low in calories, rich in protein, potassium, iron, vitamins B and C, strawberries are easy to digest. Look for fragrant, red, unblemished ones with fresh green stems. Avoid cartons stained with the juice, which means some of the berries are bruised or rotten. DRISCOLL strawberries are very large berries with long green stems. Although more expensive, their delicate fragrance and sweet taste makes them worth every penny.

For a Strawberry Cocktail: In a blender, mix 1 cup of orange juice with 1 pint of strawberries, 1 cup diced pineapple, the juice of a lemon, 2 tablespoons of sugar (optional) and 10 ice cubes. Blend well and serve in tall glasses with a large straw. Place a strawberry on the rim of the glass for decoration.

Strawberries can also be roasted, as in the recipe for *Oven-Roasted Strawberries with Verbena Ice Cream* (see page 304).

SUMMER

❖

MID-JUNE TO MID-SEPTEMBER

VEGETABLES

Arugula ❖ Basil ❖ Celery ❖ Eggplant ❖ Pea Shoots ❖ Pink Radishes

Porcini Mushrooms ❖ Scallions (Green Onions)

Sweet Corn ❖ Swiss Chard ❖ Tomatoes ❖ Yellow Squash

Yellow Wax Beans (Butter Beans) ❖ Watercress

FRUITS

Apricots ❖ Blackberries ❖ Cantaloupe ❖ Grapes ❖ Litchi Nuts

Mangoes ❖ Nectarines ❖ Peaches ❖ Plums

Raspberries ❖ Red Currants ❖ Sweet Cherries ❖ Watermelon

ARUGULA California is the main producer of this Mediterranean salad green. Rich in vitamins A and C, arugula is a member of the mustard family, easy to grow in a sunny corner of the garden. Look for small dark-green leaves; avoid yellowing and wilted ones. This pungent green has a peppery taste that nicely complements such bland greens as Boston or Bibb lettuce. Arugula is also delicious with walnuts or pine nuts. Like spinach, it can be cooked but requires more cooking time.

For a side dish of Warm Creamy Arugula (for 4 servings): Clean and blanch the leaves of 4 bunches (or 2 pounds) of arugula in boiling salted water for 5 minutes. Drain, cool under cold running water, and drain again. Finely chop the arugula. Melt 1/2 tablespoon of butter in a pot over medium heat. Sweat 1/4 cup of chopped onions for 5 minutes. Add 3 teaspoons of chopped garlic, the arugula, 1 pinch of nutmeg, 1/3 cup heavy cream, and 1 tablespoon of grated Parmesan cheese. Stir well and cook at low heat for 10 to 15 minutes. Serve with roasted chicken or veal chops.

For an Arugula Salad: Use 2 bunches of cleaned arugula leaves, 1/2 cup finely diced celery hearts, 1/2 cup diced Black Forest ham, and 1/2 cup diced English Cheddar. Mix with 3 tablespoons of chopped walnuts, 2 tablespoons of chopped shallots, and serve with a dressing made of 1 tablespoon of honey mustard, 1 tablespoon of balsamic vinegar, and 2 tablespoons of sunflower oil. Season and toss well.

Other spicy greens available during the summer, such as mustard and mizuna greens, can be prepared in similar ways. Try also the *Squid and Arugula Salad with Sesame Seeds* (see page 78).

BASIL California and Florida are the largest producers of basil, but it is also grown locally. Rich in vitamin C, basil stimulates the appetite and aids digestion. Look for firm, fragrant, medium-size bright-green leaves. Avoid

wilted, yellowing leaves and flower buds (an indication of bitterness). To store, wrap in a wet paper towel, place in a zip-lock bag, and refrigerate (wash the leaves just before using). Widely used in Mediterranean cooking, basil is the tomato's best companion.

You can also find PURPLE basil on the market. Its very pungent, dark purple leaves are wonderful with seafood. There is also PICCOLO basil, a tasty decorative variety bred like a bonsai to have small leaves.

For a Cold Swordfish Salad with Basil: Cut 1 pound of swordfish steak into 1/2-inch cubes. Season with salt and pepper and sauté in a pan with 2 teaspoons of oil for 3 minutes. Drain swordfish cubes on paper towels, cool, and mix with 1 cup of peeled, seeded, and cubed tomatoes (in 1/2-inch dice), 2 tablespoons of minced chives or scallions, 1 yellow and 1 red sweet pepper (broiled, peeled, and cubed), and 1 bunch of basil leaves, cleaned and coarsely chopped. Serve with a dressing made with the juice of 1/2 orange and

1/2 lemon, 1 tablespoon Spanish sherry vinegar, 3 tablespoons peanut oil, 1 teaspoon peanut butter, and 1 teaspoon dry mustard. Toss well and serve over a bed of arugula.

For a Basil and Anchovy Dip: In a blender or food processor, combine 10 to 12 anchovies drained of their oil with the cleaned leaves of 1 bunch of basil, 1 teaspoon freshly ground black pepper, 1 peeled clove of garlic, and 1/3 cup of olive oil. Serve with cleaned and cut-up raw vegetables on ice, sprinkled with drops of lemon juice.

Another basil-scented dish is the *Skate and Tomatoes in a Pistou Broth* (see page 188).

CELERY California and Florida are the biggest producers of celery. Traditionally a remedy for hangovers, celery is low in calories and rich in fiber, calcium, iron, and vitamin C. There are 2 main types: the GREEN variety, strongly flavored and best for cooking, and the GOLDEN variety, also called "celery heart," which is white-colored and best for eating raw. Look for fresh leaves with crisp and solid stalks.

For a Gratin of Heart of Celery: Cut off and discard the top 4 inches of 1 bunch of celery. Remove the first layer of stalks. You should be left with the most tender part, the heart, which will be about 6 inches long. Quarter the celery heart lengthwise. Place the pieces in a roasting pan with salt, pepper, butter, and chicken stock to the level of the celery. Cover with foil and braise in the oven at 400 degrees for 60 to 80 minutes. When cooked, drain. Brush the pieces with 1 tablespoon Dijon mustard, sprinkle them with 1 tablespoon bread crumbs, and place under the broiler for 3 minutes, or until golden.

A cold and vibrant soup for a hot summer day is the *Green Celery Soup with Pink Radishes* (see page 37)

EGGPLANT Florida, New Jersey, and California are the largest producers of eggplant. Low in calories, eggplants are rich in vitamin C, potassium, and calcium. They come in different shapes and colors but the main variety has a dark purple color and oblong shape. Look for the ones that are firm, heavy (in relation to size), free of bruises, dark and shiny, with a green and fresh-looking cap. An oval mark at the blossom end indicates fewer seeds and firmer flesh, a round mark indicates the opposite. Small eggplants are firmer with fewer seeds. Avoid dull, shriveled skin with bruises or brown spots. Eggplant is used in numerous Eastern and Mediterranean dishes along with tomatoes, zucchini, garlic, and olives.

Other varieties include the long, thin, and light purple JAPANESE eggplant with few seeds, the short, deep-purple, and firm ITALIAN eggplant, as well as the WHITE eggplant with many seeds.

For Stuffed Eggplant with Cumin: Split 2 eggplants lengthwise. Brush each half with olive oil and add seasoning to taste. Place on a baking sheet skin side down and bake at 350 degrees for 40 to 60 minutes, or until very soft. Cool and scoop out the flesh without breaking the skin. Set the shells aside. Chop the flesh finely and set aside. Heat 1 tablespoon of the olive oil in a pan over medium heat. Sweat 1/3 cup chopped white onions, 1 tablespoon chopped garlic, and 1 teaspoon cumin for 3 minutes. Add and sweat 1 cup of finely chopped white mushrooms for 5 minutes. Add the chopped eggplant, salt, and pepper, and cook for 20 minutes (or until most of the moisture has evaporated). Cool, then fill the eggplant shells. Cover with slices of tomato, sprinkle with cumin, olive oil, salt, and pepper, and bake at 350 degrees for 10 to 15 minutes. Serve with roasted lamb or poultry flavored with cumin while cooking.

A great dip for a cocktail party is the *Eggplant Dip with Country Bread* (see page 8). Try also one of my trademark soups, *Eggplant and Crab Garbure with Cumin and a Tomato Confit* (see page 48).

PEA SHOOTS In Chinese markets you will find fresh pea shoots (the very tender leaves of snow peas), which can be cleaned, tossed in a hot pan with olive oil, a touch of chopped garlic, and seasonings to taste for 1 to 2 minutes and served over grilled or broiled seafood.

PINK RADISHES Grown mainly in California, pink radishes help clean your teeth and are low in calories and rich in potassium, fiber, and vitamin C. The RED GLOBE is the most common. Look for bunches of small radishes with bright cherry-red skin. They should be smooth, firm, and well rounded; the top leaves should be fresh and green. Avoid cracks, soft spots, and sprouting.

To prepare, remove greens leaving 1 inch of the stem for convenient handling. Cut off the root tips and with a paring knife scrape off any dirt around the greens. Wash in cold water and dry. Serve as an appetizer along with celery heart sticks and an avocado dip (see recipe in hors d'oeuvres section on page 17).

Pink Radishes are also featured in the refreshing *Curried Tuna Tartare with Pink Radishes and a Green Celery Sauce* on page 92.

PORCINI MUSHROOMS Also called BOLETUS or CEPE, this mushroom has a smooth, rounded, thick brown cap and a bulbous stalk. There are many varieties available both imported from Italy and France and harvested in the Midwest and Oregon. From midsummer through mid-fall this is a pure delicacy for mushroom enthusiasts, with its meaty texture and flavorful taste. Look for firm mushrooms, not too wet, and with a little choke under the cap. To clean them, wipe them gently with a damp towel and remove the sandy base of the stalk if necessary. You may also remove the choke if too thick, greenish, and slimy, a sign that the porcini were picked in very humid weather.

You can roast, grill, or barbecue porcini whole with olive oil, unpeeled garlic cloves, fresh thyme, and seasonings. You can cut them in thick slices and toss them in a very hot pan with cooking oil until soft and tender, then add chopped shallots and fresh herbs (chives, parsley, tarragon, chervil) and serve alongside a roasted chicken. Small porcini are excellent sliced raw in a salad with a light seasoning and splashes of red wine vinegar and walnut oil.

SCALLIONS (GREEN ONIONS) California, Arizona, and Texas are the largest producers of scallions. Low in calories, scallions are rich in potassium, niacin, and vitamins A and C. Scallions are white onions harvested when they are very young. Sold by the bunch, look for straight bright-green scallions with white bulbs. Avoid curved ones (old and tough) and those larger than 1/2 inch in diameter (not as sweet). Store them in a plastic bag in the refrigerator.

To prepare, cut off the roots and 1/3 of the green stem. Peel off one layer of white skin. Rinse and dry. Their mild flavor makes them perfect to eat raw, thinly sliced in salads. They can also be braised whole with fresh rosemary and small cubes of bacon.

For Baby Chickens with Scallions: Discard the roots and the green part of 1 bunch of scallions. Cut the white bulbs into 1-inch slices. Place the scallions around 2 baby chickens seasoned to taste and seared in a roasting pan with 1 tablespoon of oil until golden. Add 1 tablespoon minced bacon, 1 cup of sliced small new potatoes, a peeled and sliced garlic clove, and a sprig of fresh thyme. Roast for 30 to 40 minutes at 400 degrees, tossing often.

SWEET CORN Grown mainly on the East Coast and in Florida, sweet corn is one of the world's most popular crops. Low in calories, it is rich in carbohydrates, proteins, and vitamins A and B. Since corn converts its sugar into starch as soon as it's picked, choose sweet corn from your local market and cook it the same day. Look for small, thin, bright-green ears with full husks, soft silks, and plump kernels. Avoid dry or yellowed husks and shriveled kernels.

For Corn Pancakes: Remove the kernels from 6 cobs with a knife (you should have about 2 cups of corn). Melt 1 tablespoon of butter in a pot over medium heat. Sweat 2 tablespoons of white onions for 3 minutes. Put the corn in a blender or food processor and add the sweated onions, 3 eggs, 3 tablespoons of flour, 3/4 cup of milk, 2 tablespoons of chopped parsley, 1 pinch of sugar, salt, and pepper. Blend for 1 minute, keeping a slightly coarse texture. In a nonstick pan brushed with oil, put tablespoons of the mix at 3-inch intervals around the pan over medium heat. Color, turn over and color the other side.

Another delicious recipe using sweet corn is *Corn Risotto with Bacon and Chanterelles* (see page 109).

SWISS CHARD A member of the beet family, Swiss chard is grown mostly in the Southern states. Low in calories, it is rich in calcium, iron, phosphorus, and vitamins A and C. Look for long white or reddish-purple ribs with bright green and crisp leaves. Swiss chard has a less pronounced flavor than spinach but can be prepared in the same ways. One pound raw serves 2. During winter months, you can substitute other greens such as kale or turnip and collard greens for Swiss chard. Always blanch it first before using it in a recipe.

To blanch, separate the leaves from the stems. Peel and julienne the stems (matchstick size). Soak and wash the leaves and stems 4 times. Plunge the Swiss chard in boiling salted water for 6 to 8 minutes. Cool under cold water, press to drain well, and coarsely chop.

For Swiss Chard Gratin: Blanch 2 pounds of cleaned Swiss chard leaves. Sweat 1 cup of onions with 2 tablespoons of butter for 3 minutes in a large pan over medium heat. Add 1/2 tablespoon of garlic and 1/2 teaspoon of chopped rosemary and cook for 2 more minutes. Add 1/2 pound cleaned white mushrooms minced in a blender or food processor. Add the blanched Swiss chard, mix well, and cook for about 20 minutes, until all moisture has evaporated. When done, cool and then add 2 beaten eggs with 1/2 cup of heavy cream. Mix well, pour into a shallow baking dish, and sprinkle with 1/2 cup of grated Swiss cheese. Bake in the oven at 325 degrees for 30 to 45 minutes. If needed, finish

cooking under the broiler to color the cheese.

Another great recipe is *Veal Chops with Ginger and Swiss Chard Strudel* (see page 227). The strudel can be served alone as the centerpiece for a vegetarian meal.

TOMATOES Florida and California are the largest producers of tomatoes in the country. Low in calories, tomatoes are rich in potassium, fiber, and vitamins A and C. They are available in different sizes, shapes, and varieties (field-grown, vine-ripe, plum, cherry, and now a very popular yellow tomato). Look for locally grown summer tomatoes, picked red-ripe on the vine, such as the BEEFSTEAK variety. Choose them ripe, heavy, unblemished, well shaped, and plump. Avoid overripe, soft, or bruised tomatoes, as well as the cheaper commercial varieties; they are hard, thick-skinned, tasteless, and have never seen the sun. Do not refrigerate tomatoes, except to chill them just before serving in a refreshing salad. The best liked of summer vegetables, the *Pomme d'Amour,* or "Apple of Love," as the French used to call it, can be used in a variety of dishes. In general, use small tomatoes for salads, medium ones for stuffing, and large ones for sauces.

Summer is the time to prepare and freeze a Tomato Sauce

for winter months: Warm 1/4 cup olive oil in a cast-iron pot over medium heat. Sauté 2 tablespoons of chopped garlic, 2 sprigs of fresh thyme, 2 tablespoons of chopped shallots, and the leaves of 2 basil sprigs for 5 minutes. Add 5 pounds of very ripe beefsteak or plum tomatoes, peeled, seeded, and cubed. Toss well and add 1 teaspoon of sugar, 1 teaspoon of salt, and pepper to taste. Bring to a boil, lower heat, and simmer very gently for 2 hours while stirring often, or bake the sauce in a 325-degree oven for a few hours. Crush the tomatoes to a coarse consistency and season to taste. To store for winter months, let cool, then place in small plastic containers for 2 or 4 portions, seal well, and freeze. Serve with a bowl of cooked fresh pasta tossed with olive oil, chopped garlic, and minced basil, and sprinkle with Parmesan cheese.

You will find *Chilled Tomato Soup with a Basil Guacamole,* a most refreshing soup full of summer vegetables, on page 38.

YELLOW SQUASH Florida is the main producer of this summer squash. Low in calories, yellow squash is rich in potassium, iron, vitamins A and C, and it is easily digested. Its shape and size are similar to zucchini. Harvested when half grown, yellow squash are best when under 7 inches long, having tender and edible rinds and seeds. Look for shiny, firm skin free of bruises. Yellow squash also come in baby size and in a round shape called PATTYPAN.

For Barbecued Yellow Squash: Cut 1 pound of squash 1/4 inch thick lengthwise and marinate for 1 hour with 2 tablespoons oil, 1 clove of garlic, 1/2 chopped jalapeño pepper, 1/2 tablespoon chopped rosemary, and salt. Barbecue or broil for 2 to 4 minutes on each side. Serve alongside barbecued lamb chops, baby chicken, or red snapper marinated the same way.

YELLOW WAX BEANS (BUTTER BEANS) Florida and California are the leading producers of this variety of string beans. Low in calories, yellow wax beans are rich in potassium and vitamins A, B, and C. Look for firm, crisp, and regularly shaped beans with a pale yellow color. Break one in half to make sure they snap crisply and have no strings. The smaller ones are usually more tender. Avoid shriveled, soft, or overgrown beans. One pound serves 4 to 6.

To prepare, trim and cut them at an angle into 2-inch-long pieces. Wash and drain. Plunge them in boiling salted water for 7 to 10 minutes, or until tender. Drain, cool under cold water, and drain again.

For a Yellow Wax Bean Garnish: Toss 1 pound of blanched

beans in a pan with 2 tablespoons of butter or olive oil, 1 clove of chopped garlic, 6 sprigs of chopped Italian parsley, salt, and pepper. Serve with barbecued chicken or flank steak, topped with 2 cups of sautéed minced shiitake mushrooms tossed with 2 tablespoons of minced shallots.

Tuna Steak with Watercress and Yellow Wax Beans (on page 166) is a delicious way to use this bean.

WATERCRESS California and Florida are the largest producers of this member of the mustard family. Rich in calcium, iron, and vitamins A and C, this leafy green with a peppery taste is low in calories. Look for bunches with small, tender stems with fresh and crisp deep-green leaves. Sort out the bad sprigs, rinse, and drain before cutting the leaves off the stems. If used in a salad, keep only the leaves and 1/2 inch of the stems.

Watercress can also be cooked, as in the Beet and Watercress Risotto with Pancetta (see page 106).

To prepare a Watercress and Egg Salad: Clean 4 bunches of watercress, discard the stems, and toss with 1 tablespoon of red wine vinegar, 2-1/2 tablespoons olive or walnut oil, salt, pepper, 1/4 cup of chopped cheddar cheese, 4 slices of crisp bacon cut into pieces, and 2 tablespoons of chopped walnuts. Top with 4 warm soft-boiled eggs (boiled for 7 minutes), shelled and split, and drizzle 1 tablespoon Dijon mustard diluted with 1/2 tablespoon of vinegar and 1/2 tablespoon water. Sprinkle with 1 tablespoon of chopped chives.

APRICOTS The season for apricots begins mid-spring and lasts through the end of August. California produces 20 percent of the world's apricot harvest. Low in calories, apricots are rich in potassium, iron, fiber, and vitamins A and C. Look for strong-scented fruit with a soft, velvety skin. (The flavor depends on ripeness.) Choose them plump and rather soft but not mushy. Avoid pale, bruised, or rock-hard fruit. Firm apricots will ripen in a few days at room temperature.

For an Apricot Fruit Soup: Cut 1 pound of pitted apricots into thin wedges. Add 1 pint of raspberries and set aside. Boil 1 cup of water with 2 tablespoons of sugar, a split vanilla bean, a lemon peel, an orange peel, and a large sprig of mint. Cover, remove from heat, and infuse for 30 minutes. Strain over the fruits and refrigerate until cold. Serve chilled.

Try the Apricot Tarte Tatin with Pistachio Nuts (see page 325), which is another delicious way to prepare apricots.

BLACKBERRIES Oregon, Texas, and Washington are the main producers of blackberries. Rich in vitamins C and B, low in calories, and easily digestible, blackberries are usually sold by the pint or half pint. The fruit of a prickly shrub, blackberries are ripe when every red drupelet turns black. Look for plump, bright berries free of dirt and moisture. Sort out and discard any bruised fruit to prevent decay from spreading.

Blackberries can be served cold or warm, as in Roasted Peaches and Blackberries with Ginger Caramel Ice Cream (see page 300).

CANTALOUPE California, Arizona, and Texas are the largest growers of this popular melon. Rich in potassium, and vitamins A and C, cantaloupe is low in calories and contains 90 percent water. Look for heavy, fragrant, and firm melons (5 inches in diameter) with a smooth end at the stem. (When ripe, cantaloupes separate from the vine, leaving a smooth scar). Avoid those with soft or watery spots, cracks, or rot. Keep at room temperature for a few days to ripen.

For an appetizer: Grind pepper over slices of seeded cantaloupe. The pepper spices and enhances the taste of the melon without modifying it.

For a Melon Granité: Blend 1/2 pound of puréed melon with 1/3 cup of port wine, the juice of 1 lemon, and 2 to 3 tablespoons of sugar (depending on the sweetness of the melon). Pour into a shallow pan. Place in the freezer. When frozen, grate the melon with the prongs of a fork to obtain a flaky texture. Keep frozen until ready to use. Serve in frosted glasses topped with red currants or blackberries.

GRAPES In late summer, grapes become available from many regions, including the unique CONCORD grape from upstate New York, and the tiny and very sweet CHAMPAGNE grape from California.

LITCHI NUTS This true Asian delicacy is found in Chinese markets and will complement any summer fruit salad. The round fruit (1 to 2 inches in diameter) has a pink to brownish skin. Once peeled, the flesh is white, sweet, and juicy. Discard the pip.

MANGOES Grown in Florida and imported from Mexico and the Caribbean in spring to midsummer, and from South America during the winter, mango is the most common fruit in tropical areas. Rich in potassium and vitamins A and C, mangoes come in many different sizes, colors, and shapes. The quality of a mango is determined by the amount of fiber in its meat and the pungency of its skin. The most widely available

mangoes in the United States are the HAYDEN and TOMMY ATKINS varieties. Weighing 1 to 2 pounds they both have green skin with yellowish blossom ends and reddish stem ends. Haydens have bright orange meat and Tommy Atkins bright yellow meat; both are sweet, juicy, and with little fiber. Look for smooth-skinned mangoes that yield to gentle pressure and have a fruity aroma emanating from the stem end. Avoid very soft or bruised fruit, those with large black spots, as well as very green or rock-hard ones (picked prematurely). Mangoes will continue to ripen at room temperature.

To prepare, peel the mango, lay it lengthwise, and cut the meat off each side of the large, flat, center pit.

A refreshing recipe for early summer is the *Rhubarb and Mango Compote with Strawberry Sorbet* (see page 319).

NECTARINES California is the largest producer of this fruit. Low in calories, rich in fiber, vitamins A and C, and phosphorus, nectarines are almost twice as nutritious as peaches. Closely related to the peach, nectarines come in different sizes and colors. Look for plump and unblemished fruit with a rich color fading slightly along the seam. Once picked they don't gain in sweetness; therefore they should be harvested as close to maturity as possible. Sweet nectarines should be fragrant and the skin should be yellow-orange with a bright red blush.

For Warm Nectarines and Blackberries with Star Anise: Split and remove the pits of 4 nectarines. Place the halves on a buttered baking pan, skin side down. Add to each half 1 star anise and 1 teaspoon each butter and sugar. Bake at 375 degrees until soft, 15 to 20 minutes. Discard the star anise and set the nectarines aside. Pour 1 tablespoon of Pernod or anisette into the baking pan, add the juice of 2 oranges, and reduce by half on top of the stove over medium heat. Add 1 tablespoon of sugar and 1/2 pint of blackberries, mix well over medium heat for 1 minute, and pour over the warm nectarines.

PEACHES Peaches are available from mid-spring through the summer. The United States grows 25 percent of the world's crop of fresh peaches. Georgia, California, New Jersey, Pennsylvania, and the Southern states are the largest producers. A good source of carbo-

hydrates and potassium, as well as vitamins A, B, and C, peaches (called "Venus's bosom" by Louis XIV) are highly digestible. Most vitamins are in the skin, so you may consider not peeling but just washing them before eating. The blush on the skin is not a quality factor, but depends on the variety of the fruit. Look for fragrant, firm, and unblemished peaches with a deep color. Avoid green skin, bruised, or rock-hard peaches. If they are slightly firm, ripen them at room temperature for a few days, stored in a brown bag with a few holes. Use them as soon as they become ripe.

For Warm Peaches with Red Currants and Vanilla Ice Cream: Peel 4 peaches by plunging them in boiling water for 1 to 2 minutes and cooling them under cold running water. Quarter them and discard the stones. In a pot over medium heat, prepare a caramel by boiling 2 tablespoons of sugar with 1/2 tablespoons of water until light brown. Add the peaches and 1 tablespoon of whiskey and toss well. Cover and cook for 2 minutes. Add 1 cup of red currants and cook for 1 minute more. Serve warm over a scoop of vanilla ice cream.

More difficult to find and absolutely delicious for its juicy flesh and delicate perfume is the WHITE peach. Look for them at roadside stands and farmer's markets. This variety has a pink and white skin. Toward late summer and early fall, you may also find the blush burgundy peach called *Pêche de Vignes,* or WINE peach, named because of its similar color to grapes. These peaches are excellent for poaching in sweet red wine flavored with spices.

PLUMS California, Washington, and Oregon are the largest producers of this fruit. Low in calories, plums are rich in vitamins A, B, and C. There are more than 140 varieties of plums in the United States and all vary in shape and color. They are easily found in local markets during the summer months. The FRIAR is a large plum with deep black skin, amber flesh, and a small stone. Look for plump, well-colored fruit, firm or slightly soft. Avoid overripe or bruised fruit.

For Poached Plums and Figs in Cabernet: Mix 1/2 bottle of Cabernet wine with 7 ounces of sugar, 2 sticks of cinnamon,

2 slices of orange, and 1 clove and boil for 10 minutes over high heat. Split and pit 1 pound of Friar or purple plums and split 1 pound of fresh figs. Strain the wine over the plums and figs and boil for 2 minutes. Remove from heat, set aside to cool, and refrigerate overnight. Serve cold with a scoop of cinnamon ice cream.

Raspberries California, Washington, and Oregon are the largest raspberry producers. Low in calories, raspberries are rich in calcium, iron, phosphorus, fiber, and vitamins A, B, and C. Look for fully colored, plump, and dry berries, free of bruises and mold. Avoid stained cartons; it usually means there are overripe berries at the bottom. Rich in pectin, raspberries are the best fruit for jams and jelly.

For a Frozen Raspberry Soufflé: Blend 2 cups of raspberries with 1/4 cup of water and the juice of 1 lemon in a blender. Strain, mix with a spoon into a pint of firmly whipped heavy cream, and refrigerate. Boil 7 ounces of sugar with 2 tablespoons water until syrupy, about 5 minutes. With an electric beater, whip 4 egg whites until stiff. Gently pour the cooked sugar over the whites, while beating at medium speed for 3 minutes. With a spoon, slowly add the beaten egg whites to the raspberry-cream mixture. Wrap aluminum foil around a soufflé mold (2/3 of the foil should be standing over the rim) and secure with tape. Pour the mixture into the mold up to the rim of the foil. Freeze overnight. When ready to serve, remove the foil and cover the top of the soufflé with a layer of fresh raspberries.

Enjoy pastry chef Jacques Torres's incredibly delicious dessert of crispy phyllo dough with melting chocolate and raspberries, called Chocolate and Raspberry Fontaine (see page 308).

Red Currants California is the main producer of this red berry. Rich in pectin and vitamin C, red currants are mainly used to make jams and jellies. Look for well-colored, plump, and unblemished fruit. Avoid shriveled or bruised ones. To eat them fresh, wash and drain 1 pint of red currants, toss them in 2 tablespoons of sugar to mellow their sour flavor, and eat them with your fingers. Acidic enough for a pickling effect, they can be used in salads or with a seafood or roasted poultry preparation.

For a Squid and Red Currant Salad: Cut 1/2 pound of squid into 1/4-inch slices. Clean, and cook for 3 to 4 minutes with a drop of vinegar, 1 sliced onion, and a bay leaf in 1 quart of boiling water. Drain and set aside to cool. Blanch 1/4 pound of yellow wax beans in salted water for 7 to 10 minutes. Drain and set aside. Blanch 1/4 pound green beans for 4 to 5 minutes in the same water. Drain and set aside. Combine 1 to 2 large heads of chopped radicchio with the squid and the beans. Prepare the dressing with 2 tablespoons of mayonnaise, 1 tablespoon of Dijon mustard, 2 tablespoons of heavy or sour cream, the juice of 1 orange and 2 lemons, 1 sprig of chopped tarragon, 1 tablespoon minced chives, salt, and pepper. Place in a dome shape and decorate with avocado wedges. Sprinkle 1/4 pint of cleaned red currants on top.

Red currants are also delicious when simply served over vanilla ice cream.

Sweet Cherries Although sweet cherries are grown in most Northern states, Washington is the leading supplier. Low in calories, cherries are rich in potassium and vitamin A, B, and C. The color of the fruit depends on the variety. The most popular varieties are the Bing (extra large and black), the Royal Anne (large and yellow-red), and the Lamberts (smaller and red). Look for cherries with the stems still attached. Choose firm, well-matured, and well-colored fruit. Avoid hard or sticky cherries and ones with dark-colored stems (too old). Refrigerate and wash just before serving.

For a Cherry Tart: Split and pit 1 pound of cherries. Whip 2 whole eggs with 1 egg yolk and 2 ounces of sugar until foamy and white. Whip in 1/4 cup of flour, 1 cup of milk, and 2 tablespoons of melted butter. Pour the tart mix into a buttered tart mold. Spread the cherries nicely on top and bake at 350 degrees for 30 to 40 minutes. Cool, refrigerate for 2 hours, and unmold. Serve with whipped cream on the side.

You can substitute pitted cherries for blueberries in the Blueberry Brioche Bread Pudding (see page 303).

Watermelon This easy-to-love summer fruit is available in both red and yellow varieties, with seeds or seedless. A great way to prepare watermelon, along with other summer fruits, is in my Summer Fruits with a Watermelon Tequila Granité (see page 313).

AUTUMN

MID-SEPTEMBER TO MID-DECEMBER

VEGETABLES

Cabbage ◆ Cauliflower

Garlic ◆ Leeks ◆ Lima Beans ◆ Mushrooms

Pumpkins ◆ Squash ◆ White Truffles

FRUITS AND NUTS

Apples ◆ Chestnuts ◆ Cranberries ◆ Dates ◆ Figs

Grapes ◆ Italian Plums ◆ Papaya ◆ Pears

Persimmons ◆ Pomegranates ◆ Quinces ◆ Walnuts

CABBAGE Grown all over the United States and an excellent cleanser for both teeth and the digestive system, cabbage is low in calories and rich in vitamin C, potassium, and fiber. SAVOY is a round yellow-green cabbage and is excellent *in soups or as a side dish: Remove the core and take the leaves apart. Boil for 2 minutes then drain. In a pot with 1 tablespoon of butter, sweat 1 small chopped onion, 1 clove of garlic, and 1 sliced carrot for 5 minutes. Add the cabbage and cook slowly for 1 hour or until very tender. In general, the longer you cook cabbage, the sweeter it tastes.*

RED CABBAGE has a dark purple tint and is delicious in salads or *as a side dish for duck, turkey, or roast pork: Slice the cabbage leaves into 1/2-inch strips. Poach them for 5 minutes in boiling water, then drain and cook slowly in an ovenproof pot on top of the stove with butter, pieces of apple, pearl onions, 1/2 cup of vinegar, 1 teaspoon of sugar, and 1 cup of chicken stock. Cover with a lid and braise in the oven for 1-1/2 hours at 375 degrees.*

WHITE CABBAGE has very tight leaves and is used for coleslaw and sauerkraut. Although inexpensive and high in yield, white cabbage is not as tasty or delicate for cooking as red and savoy.

Several recipes in this book feature cabbage, such as *Cabbage and Lobster Soup with Chives* (see page 42), *Salmon in a Polenta Crust with Red Cabbage* (see page 186), and *Cabbage Stuffed with Apples and Cranberries* (see page 273).

CAULIFLOWER Cauliflower season begins midsummer and peaks in the fall. Grown mainly in California and New York, cauliflower is low in calories and rich in vitamin C. Always make sure that the leaves are of a blue-green color and look crisp, with very white florets— good signs of freshness. Cauliflower is a perfect vegetable for soups.

To make Cauliflower Soup: Break a head into small pieces and discard the leaves and the hard stem. Sweat a minced leek in a pot. Add 1 quart of hot chicken stock and the cauliflower and boil for 30 minutes. Pour the soup into a blender and, if you are not on a diet, add 1/2 cup of heavy cream. Blend until smooth and serve hot with chopped crisp bacon. You can also serve this soup cold with a small spoon of whipped cream mixed with Madras curry powder on top.

Another delicious soup is *Curried Cream of Cauliflower and Apple Soup* (see page 54).

GARLIC California produces 90 percent of the fresh garlic sold in the United States. Garlic, known for its antibacterial powers, is rich in potassium, calcium, fiber, iron, and vitamin C. Its color ranges from white to pink. Bulb size varies from small to very large. Look for large, plump, and firm garlic heads with tight and unbroken sheaths. Avoid bulbs that are stained, soft, or shriveled, as well as heads with small green sprouts.

Store in a cool, dry place. The flavor of garlic, compatible with all foods except sweets, varies with the way it is prepared. To avoid a bitter and unpleasant aftertaste, garlic should never be cooked to a dark-brown color. If cooked whole and unpeeled (around a roast), the taste is mild. If mashed to a paste its taste is more pungent.

If you are a garlic fanatic, try a Garlic Sauce (this recipe can be prepared in advance): Boil 1/2 cup of diced potatoes until tender, drain and mash them in a bowl. Add 2 table-spoons of finely chopped garlic, 2 tablespoons mayonnaise, and while whisking, add 3/4 cup of olive oil. Boil 2 pinches of saffron in 2 tablespoons of water for 1 minute. Continue whisking the garlic sauce and add the saffron water, salt and pepper, and 3 to 4 drops of Tabasco. Serve alongside seafood or crudités.

On page 110 you will find a recipe using succulent, sweet roasted garlic—*Green Risotto with Roasted Squab and Garlic Cloves.*

LEEKS This vegetable grows best in cool climates and is available year round with two main harvests: spring and then fall for very sweet and tender leeks. California, New Jersey, Michigan, and Virginia are the largest producers of this vegetable rich in calcium, potassium, and vitamin C. Always look for crisp light green leeks. One of the basic ingredients in French cuisine, leeks are always consumed cooked. The best part is the white bulb, which is used *as a base for soups: 1 sweated leek with 1 quart of chicken stock and 1 baking potato are the basic proportions for 2 servings. You can add as many vegetables as you want to this base: pumpkin, mushrooms, carrots, broccoli, etc. Boil for 20 to 30 minutes. Purée in your food processor or blender if you prefer a smooth texture (creamy soups), or cut the vegetables in small dice for a chunky, country taste.*

One of my specialities is the *Crisp Paupiette of Sea Bass in a Barolo Sauce* served on a bed of sweet leeks (see page 164).

LIMA BEANS The Southern states are the largest producers of lima beans. These pale green beans are rich in carbohydrates, vitamins A and B, potassium, phosphorus, and calcium. Look for plump, small, velvety beans with an even color. These beans come in a small variety called BABY LIMA and a large one called FORDHOOK. Both have a delicate texture and mild aroma. Figure on approximately 1 pound of unshelled beans for 2 servings.

For a simple side dish: In a pot over medium heat, warm 1/2 tablespoon of olive oil. Add 2 tablespoons of chopped white onion, 1 teaspoon of finely chopped garlic, and 1 sprig of fresh sage and sweat for 3 minutes. Add 2 cups of lima beans, 1 cup of chicken stock, and pepper to taste. Simmer for 20 to 30 minutes or until tender, adding salt when they are 3/4 of the way cooked to prevent hardening. Before serving, drain and toss with 1 tablespoon of butter or olive oil. Season to taste and serve with crispy bacon on top.

MUSHROOMS California and Pennsylvania provide the best cultivated mushrooms. They are low in calories and rich in protein. When you choose mushrooms, always look for the firm and unbroken ones; make sure that they are not damp, and that they have kept their fragrance. Except for wild PORCINIS and CHANTERELLES, generally you should discard the stems. Never soak mushrooms; if you want to clean them, just wipe off the dirt with a damp cloth or rinse them under running water with the help of a brush, and dry with a towel.

For most recipes, cut the mushrooms into pieces and sauté them in a pan with oil over very high heat. Fry them quickly before they lose too much of their water. They will always shrink by 1/3 when cooked. Serve them with chopped shallots, garlic, and fresh herbs as a side dish to roasted poultry or sautéed fillet of fish, over creamy pasta, or in scrambled eggs. Mushrooms are a versatile vegetable with lots of character.

Besides the traditional white button mushrooms, many other varieties are cultivated today and often originate in other countries, like the pungent and earthy brown CREMINI and PORTOBELLO from Italy. Some other well-known varieties include:

ASIAN MUSHROOMS Some exotic Asian mushrooms, a little spicier and with varying flavors and textures, have been widely available in the United States for the past ten years. The most popular is the SHIITAKE mushroom, with a brown, flat cap, which adapts to many preparations; the NAMEKO or HONEY mushroom, a tiny brown and webbed mushroom excellent in soups and sauces; ENOKI, a small cluster of white caps with long stems used in salads, soups, or stir-fry; and HON-SHIMEGI, a small, beige, closed-cap mushroom with very tender flesh.

CHANTERELLES California, Washington, and Oregon grow these low-calorie, fiber-rich mushrooms available from midsummer through the fall season. Chanterelles are golden orange and look like curving trumpets with small ribs under their caps. They grow in cool and damp pine forests. This mushroom is much sought after for its pleasant and delicate taste. Look for firm and dry chanterelles; avoid discolored or dehydrated ones.

To clean them, cut off the tip of the stem and scrape off the dirt around it. Rinse under cold running water and drain. Figure on approximately 3 ounces of raw chanterelles per serving.

On page 154 there is a recipe for *Sweet-Water Prawn and Chanterelle Casserole with Garlic.*

OYSTER MUSHROOMS Also known as PLEUROTUS, this is a very large grey, yellow, or white mushroom cultivated primarily in the fall. Oyster mushrooms grow in clusters at the base of trees.

To prepare an Oyster Mushroom Garnish: Rinse the mushrooms briefly if needed, cut off and discard the stems. To reduce their slight bitterness, boil the oyster mushrooms for 3 to 5 minutes in a covered pot with a small amount of water (1/4 cup per pound) and the juice of 1/2 lemon. Drain and sauté in a hot pan with butter, seasoning, and herbs (sage or savory). Serve as a garnish to meat, poultry, or fish.

PUMPKINS Colorado and California grow the most pumpkins, which are actually winter squash. Rich in vitamin A and potassium, pumpkins were the staple food for the American Indians and early settlers. When using a pumpkin for carving, choose a CONNECTICUT FIELD, JACK O' LANTERN, or HOWDEN variety, free of bruises and spots. The eating varieties should be mature with a rich orange color. Look for hard and heavy pumpkins, but not too large for cooking. Avoid bruises and cracks. Pumpkin is very good in soups and gratin dishes as well as in pie.

SQUASH Many varieties of delicious squash are available in the fall, such as the SWEET DUMPLING TURBAN, KABOCHA, GOLDEN NUGGET, or BUTTERCUP. For a delicious squash soup try the *Cinnamon Squash Soup with Chicken Liver Toasts* (see page 46).

Other squash include:

ACORN SQUASH Acorn squash is a small, round, green or yellow/white squash with thick ribs. A sweet and light variety that is very nutritious, acorn squash can be prepared like spaghetti squash.

BUTTERNUT SQUASH This squash is grown in most states—just look for your local varieties. Loaded with minerals and vitamins A, B, and C, butternuts are easy to digest. They are one of the cheapest vegetables during harvest season. Use the butternut in soups with a touch of cinnamon powder.

SPAGHETTI SQUASH Florida and California are the largest producers of spaghetti squash. Rich in potassium and vitamins A and C, this type of squash is a cross between the summer and winter varieties. Look for a bright yellow shell, firm and free of bruises. Avoid lightweight ones. One large squash serves 3 to 4. As this squash is slightly bland, it needs either herbs or spices to enhance its flavor. *To prepare as a side dish: Brush a baking pan with olive oil, cover it with aromatic herbs (thyme, rosemary, or sage) or with dry seeds (coriander, fennel, cumin, cloves, juniper berries) and cinnamon sticks. Split the squash lengthwise, scrape out the seeds, season with salt and pepper, and place it in the pan skin side up. Bake in the oven at 350 degrees for 45 to 60 minutes or until tender. Remove and discard the spices, pull out the inside with a fork, and transfer to a bowl (the flesh will separate like spaghetti). Add 2 tablespoons of butter or cream and season to taste. Toss well and return the spaghetti to the shells.*

WHITE TRUFFLES Very expensive subterranean fungi imported from Italy, white truffles are found only in specialty food shops. Flavorful over risotto, pasta, eggs, and salads, they have a uniquely strong and penetrating odor when thinly sliced raw over food. They should never be peeled or washed but rubbed lightly with a wet towel or brush. Truffles can be stored for a few days in a jar with Italian arborio rice: The smell of the truffles will penetrate the rice and you can then use it for a risotto served with grated Parmesan cheese and white truffles on top.

I created a recipe that combines an inexpensive baked potato with the most expensive food on earth: white truffles (see page 277). This ensemble elevates the potato to a rich and unique indulgence.

To create a beautiful garnish of fall bounty, try the recipe for *Fall Vegetables Roasted with Juniper Berries and Walnuts* (see page 288).

APPLES Grown in most states (Washington and Michigan are the biggest producers), apples come in many varieties. They are rich in dietary fiber and vitamin C, and low in fat. Look for apples with smooth, clean skin free of bruises. One of the most popular varieties is RED DELICIOUS, representing almost half of the production in this country. It has a rich red skin with shades of light red and is best used fresh. Good apples for both cooking and eating fresh are GOLDEN DELICIOUS, with light green to yellow skin, lightly juicy and sweet with a tender texture very good in desserts such as the *Caramelized Apple Tart Lyonnaise* (see page 299); McINTOSH, which has two-toned red and green skin and is fragrant with a crisp texture, excellent when in season for sorbet, as in the recipe for *Apple, Apple, Apple* (see page 295); JONATHAN, with light red stripes over yellow or deep red areas, small to medium in size, tart and rich in flavor when in season, with a crunchy skin; the green GRANNY SMITH, which has a firm and white flesh and a tart taste; and the ROME, with a large round shape and often brilliant red color, the best apple for baking because it will retain its shape, firm texture, and sweet taste once baked. Try it in the *Baked Apples with Cranberries* (see page 298).

Other apples that can be eaten fresh or used in dessert recipes include the EMPIRE from New York State, which is a cross between McIntosh and Red Delicious with a dark red skin and a mildly tart, juicy white flesh. An early apple or summer apple is the GALA, very sweet and aromatic under an orange-yellow skin with stripes of red.

If using apples in marmalades, sauces, compotes, chutneys, etc., it is better to mix a few varieties to diversify the taste and texture of the dish. A great apple dessert for children is the *Sweet Apple Alix* (see page 294).

CHESTNUTS Of Mediterranean origin, chestnuts were considered a staple food in Europe. Rich in starches and sugar, they are used as a vegetable as well as in desserts. They are wonderful when cooked in ashes or roasted. Look for clean, whole shells and avoid cracked shells, insect blight, and decay. Refrigerate and use while fresh. Always make an incision on each side of the chestnut so it peels easily. *For a garnish with roasted duck, turkey, or goose, peel off the chestnuts' outer skin and fry the chestnuts in hot oil until crisp, about 3 to 4 minutes, then remove the inner second skin. Spread the peeled chestnuts all around your roasted bird in the last 30 minutes of cooking along with a whole garlic clove, pearl onions, pieces of apple, whole mushrooms, and fresh thyme sprigs.*

A purée of chestnuts is a delicious garnish for venison: Once they are peeled, cover 1 pound of chestnuts with chicken stock and boil with 1/2 cup chopped celeriac. When tender (about 25 to 35 minutes) drain, and crush the chestnuts and celeriac with a fork. Add 3 to 4 tablespoons butter, seasoning, and 1/4 cup of hot heavy cream. The purée should be chunky and lightly creamy.

CRANBERRIES Grown in Wisconsin, Massachusetts, New Jersey, Oregon, and Washington, cranberries were used by the Northeastern American Indians to garnish game. Low in calories and sodium, cranberries are high in fiber and pectin. Cranberry juice is an excellent kidney flush: It dissolves minerals and excessive acids. Fresh berries can be frozen for months and used throughout the year *as a relish for duck, turkey, pork, and sausages: Boil the cranberries for 4 to 5 minutes in just enough maple syrup to soak them. Add the juice of 1 lemon, 1 orange peel, and a stick of cinnamon. Drain the excess syrup before serving.*

DATES During the fall season dates are a rich and satisfying snack or addition to desserts. Less sweet than dried dates, fresh dates should be plump and glossy. For desserts they can be made into *a creamy filling for puff pastry: Pit the dates, purée the pulp in a blender or food processor with the same quantity of pastry cream (use a classic pastry cream recipe) until smooth, then transfer to a bowl. With a spatula, add in the same quantity of sweetened whipped heavy cream, flavor the date cream with a few drops of rum, and spoon the mixture in between 3 layers of baked puff pastry.*

FIGS The season for figs begins in midsummer and continues through mid-fall. California is the largest producer of figs. Toward the second half of summer fresh California PURPLE figs, WHITE figs, and MISSION figs will be at their peak. The mission fig is a small, intense, and richly flavored fig similar to the wild Mediterranean fig. Known for their laxative and digestive properties, figs are rich in potassium, calcium, and vitamins A, B, and C. There are hundreds of different varieties and their color ranges from white, green, or purple to black. The skin is edible in all varieties. They also come in different shapes and sizes, from round to oblong. Sweetness and taste depend on ripeness. Look for soft, plump fruit with a rich color. Check the navel at the blossom end: The skin will show a few cracks when the fruit is ripe. Avoid hard, underripe fruit, as well as bruised or blemished ones with a fermenting odor. Figs are highly perishable. Washed gently just before serving, they can be served fresh in fruit salads, or with prosciutto, or cooked in tarts.

Try a Fig Delight: Discard any stems and cut a cross halfway down the stem end of 8 figs. Open each quarter halfway down. Sprinkle with confectioners' sugar and cinnamon. Bake in a preheated 400-degree oven for 5 to 8 minutes. Serve hot with vanilla ice cream or whipped cream.

GRAPES Many varieties of grapes are at their peak during fall, including the imported MUSCAT grape from Italy, a very large and delectable variety with a yellowish berry when ripe and a sweet musky flavor (the most yellow are the muskiest in flavor). Choose grapes that are unblemished, plump, and ripe. An excellent garnish for roasted game, poultry, or sautéed foie gras, grapes are wonderful as a snack or dessert, plain and simple.

ITALIAN PLUMS The season for these plums begins in midsummer and lasts through the fall. California, Washington, and Oregon are the main producers of the elongated "freestone" plums, which are usually dried to become prunes because the pit separates easily from the flesh. Rich in vitamin A, calcium, and potassium, prunes are famous for their laxative properties. When buying fresh ones look for slightly soft, deep purple plums and avoid hard, poorly colored, underripe fruit as well as overripe ones. Allow them to mature at room temperature.

Try a Crispy Scone Plum Pie: Split 1 pound of Italian plums (for an 8-inch tart) and discard the pits. Fill the tart mold with the halved plums skin side down. Sprinkle the plums with brandy and sugar. Cover with the crumbs of a scone. Sprinkle again with melted butter and brown sugar and bake for 20 minutes at 400 degrees. Serve warm with whipped cream or vanilla ice cream.

PAPAYA Spring and late fall are the best seasons for papaya. Imported from Hawaii, Mexico, and the Dominican Republic, papayas are picked firm with a green skin that turns yellow when ripe. The healing powers of papaya are legendary. It is one of the most nutritious of fruits. Rich in vitamin A, B, and C, calcium, magnesium, and potassium, papaya contains papain, similar to the pepsin in digestive juices, and is recommended to sooth stomach irritation and indigestion. Papayas can be used in salads, sorbets, shakes, or even plain with just a touch of lime and sugar.

PEARS You will have the pick of pears from fall through the winter. Mainly grown in California, Oregon, and Washington, pears are high in fiber, vitamins A, B, and C, mineral salts, and iodine. Look for firm (but not rock-hard) ones without bruises or cuts. Pears ripen from the inside out, then rot very quickly once they have reached maturity. To hasten the ripen-ing process, place in a brown bag with a few holes. Once ripe, they should yield when gently pressed. You will find four primary varieties: the BARTLETT (yellow or red), good for canning and desserts; the ANJOU, which has a yellow-green skin and keeps its shape during cooking or baking; the Bosc, a very fragile variety, and the COMICE, with thin yellow-green skin. Considered the best pear in the world for its creamy, smooth, and tasty flesh, the Comice can be used as an accompaniment for game, in chutney, and for desserts.

Try a Pear Chutney: Peel, split, and core 1 pound of pears and cut into 1-inch chunks. In a pot over medium heat, add 1 tablespoon olive oil and sweat 1/2 cup of onions for 5 minutes. Add 1/2 tablespoon of sugar, 1/4 cup of dry white wine, 1 clove, 1/2 tablespoon cumin, 1 pinch of anise powder (or 2 star anise), and 1 pinch of Madras curry powder, then cover and let simmer for 35 to 45 minutes. Serve with roasted game bird, duck, or squab.

A favorite French winter dessert is the Poires Belle Hélène: Peel, split 4 pears in half and core. Cook them for 15 to 20 minutes in 1 quart of boiling water with the juice of 1 lemon, 1 cup of sugar, and 1 vanilla bean. Drain and set the pears aside to cool. In a double-boiler, melt 8 ounces of bittersweet chocolate with 1/2 cup of heavy cream. Roast 2/3 cup of slivered almonds in the oven at 350 degrees for 8 to 10 minutes. In individual serving bowls, place 2 pear halves and a generous scoop of vanilla ice cream. Cover with the melted chocolate and the roasted almonds.

PERSIMMONS   The Japanese national fruit is the PERSIMMON, grown widely in California. Its peak season is from fall through midwinter. When choosing persimmons, look for glossy, very ripe fruit that is soft to the touch with bright orange skin. Persimmons have a very high nutritional value and a musky sweet taste similar to apricot-papaya. When very ripe, they have a custardy texture. To eat, either split in half and scoop out the pulp with a spoon, or peel and slice into fruit salad. If the persimmon is not ripe enough it will have an awful mouth-puckering astringent taste, but once ripe it is pure sensuality.

POMEGRANATES (CHINESE APPLES) California produces most of this fruit. The pomegranate is low in calories and rich in phosphorus, iron, calcium, and vitamin C. Look for large, heavy fruit with red and smooth skin free of cracks and bruises. Keep in a plastic bag and store in the refrigerator. Split the fruit to eat the ruby kernels (do not eat the white membranes). Or spoon out the juicy kernels and use them to decorate salads and desserts. You can also use a juice extractor to squeeze out the juice and then sweeten it to make grenadine drinks, ices, or fruit soup. Beware of pomegranate stains for they are extremely difficult to remove.

One of my recipes featuring pomegranate is *Winter's Tropical Fruit in a Spiced Infusion* (see page 317).

QUINCES   The best fruit for a marmalade is the quince. A fall fruit with a tart taste, once sweetened and cooked its agreeable fruity flavor is released, one that is distinctive but similar to an apple or pear. The quince can also be used in fruit chutney. It looks similar to a yellow apple, but it is very bitter in taste when raw so it must always be cooked.

For 1/2 pound of Quince Marmalade: Peel, quarter, and seed 4 fruits, cut each quarter into 2 or 3 pieces. Boil 3 quarts of water and plunge the quinces in for 5 minutes.

Drain and transfer to another pot, add 2 cups of water, 1-1/2 cups of sugar, 1 split vanilla bean and 1 piece of lemon peel. Cook over medium heat until very soft, about 30 to 45 minutes, discard the vanilla bean and lemon peel, mash the marmalade with a potato masher, and set aside to cool. Serve warm with a scoop of vanilla ice cream or as a spread over lemon pound cake slices.

WALNUTS California is the biggest producer of this nut. High in protein, phosphorus, and vitamins B and D, walnuts have a high level of natural oils. Look for slightly rough and hard golden-brown shells with cream-white kernels. Walnuts can be eaten fresh from the tree or dried. (Kernels regain most of their fresh flavor if soaked in milk overnight.) They are used in soups, salads, desserts, oils, etc.

Try Walnuts in Red Wine: Gently boil 1 cup of walnuts with 1 cup of Rhône or Spanish wine, 1 teaspoon of sugar, 1 clove, an orange peel, a few black peppercorns, and 1 bay leaf for 30 minutes. Cool, discard the wine, and slice the walnuts into a mushroom soup or serve them on top of a red wine stew, or with a terrine of game.

WINTER

✤

MID-DECEMBER TO MID-MARCH

VEGETABLES

Black Truffles ✦ Broccoli ✦ Brussels Sprouts ✦ Cardoon ✦ Celeriac (Celery Root)

Chicory, Endive, and Escarole ✦ Collard Greens

Dried White Beans ✦ Fennel ✦ Jerusalem Artichokes

Kohlrabi ✦ Mâche ✦ Parsnips ✦ Potatoes

Radicchio ✦ Radishes ✦ Salsify (Scorzonera) ✦ Spinach

Sweet Potatoes ✦ Turnips

FRUITS

Bananas ✦ Dried FruitsGrapefruit ✦ Kiwi

Oranges ✦ Pineapple ✦ Tropical Fruits

BLACK TRUFFLES Winter is the season for BLACK TRUFFLES, subterranean fungi that grow in the soil around the roots of particular oak trees located primarily in Périgord (southwest France) but are now also widely available from the Vaucluse region in Provence, from Spain, and from Italy. Very expensive but worth every bite when very fresh, firm, and strongly aromatic. Look for well-rounded and unbroken truffles. Brush them lightly with a wet brush to remove any dirt; you will recognize a good truffle by its firmness, woodsy smell, and marbleized flesh with white veins when sliced. A favorite way to prepare them is to toss thinly sliced truffles in a salad of mâche and season with a few drops of lemon juice, a good extra-virgin olive oil, salt, and pepper. Their aroma will delicately perfume seafood, poultry, or game when cooked with it.

The black truffle is highlighted in one of my signature dishes, *Maine Sea Scallops in Black Tie* (see page 151), a striking creation in contrasting colors, textures, and tastes that exemplifies the influence of black truffles in French cooking. On page 277 is an inspired version of the classic American baked potato, twice baked and stuffed with black truffles and butter—a simple way to enjoy the true taste of this delicacy.

BROCCOLI Grown mainly in California, broccoli comes from the cabbage family (in Italian, broccoli means "cabbage sprout"). Low in calories, rich in vitamins A and C and in minerals, this is one of the most frequently used vegetables in Italian and Asian cooking. Look for crisp, firm, compact heads and avoid yellow florets. Depending on the variety, broccoli can be dark green or purple. BROCCOLI RABE is a small leafy variety with a more bitter taste than regular broccoli. You can steam

1/2 pound of broccoli florets in 5 minutes.

For a delicious and easy winter treat try *Broccoli Purée with Ginger* (see page 282).

For a Shrimp and Broccoli Rabe Casserole: Trim off half of each stem of 1 bunch of broccoli rabe, discarding the bottom. In a large and very hot pan, stir-fry 1 pound of large peeled and deveined shrimp for 1 minute with 2 tablespoons of olive oil, add the broccoli rabe, add seasoning and a pinch of cayenne pepper. After 3 to 4 minutes, when the broccoli rabe starts to wilt and the shrimp is cooked, add 1 tablespoon of chopped garlic, 1/4 cup of sliced toasted almonds, and 1 teaspoon of finely chopped rosemary. Toss well and serve.

BRUSSELS SPROUTS Grown mainly in California, this cold-weather crop is a member of the cabbage family. Rich in vitamins C and A, potassium, thiamine, and iron, brussels sprouts stimulate the digestive system. Look for small, bright-green sprouts that are firm and compact; avoid yellow or soft ones. Brussels sprouts are usually sold by the pint (1 pint serves 4). Trim the stem and cut a deep X into the bottom of the sprout to allow even and rapid cooking.

To prepare as a side dish: Boil in plenty of salted water for 4 to 5 minutes. Cool under cold running water and drain. Sauté in 2 tablespoons of butter with a minced shallot and 1 teaspoon of chopped rosemary. Toss until lightly colored.

CARDOON This is a rare but delectable vegetable that I am very attached to; see page 267 for *Gratin of Cardoon Francine*, the recipe my grandmother prepares for us regularly in Lyons. Popular among Italian communities in America, cardoons look like large celery stalks and taste similar to artichokes.

CELERIAC (CELERY ROOT) This winter member of the celery family grown mainly in Northern California is rich in phosphorus and easy to digest. Look for medium-size, plump and heavy roots (12 to 16 ounces) and avoid very large roots, which are often hollow. Discard the greens; only the root of this vegetable is edible, raw or cooked. Its taste is a cross between celery and walnuts. Always rub the peeled celeriac with lemon to keep it white. Celeriac is a wonderful garnish for game, or even cut very thin and added to salads—see the *Celeriac and Escarole Salad with Apple Chips* on page 86.

For a Celeriac Purée: Peel the root, cut into 1-inch pieces, and cook until very tender in salted water with lemon juice. Drain the celeriac and blend in a blender or food processor until smooth, then pass through a food mill or sieve. Heat in a saucepan over a low flame to remove excess moisture. Add a little butter and heavy cream for a smoother texture. (For a thicker purée, use 1 part potato to 3 parts celeriac. Cook both together and process as above.)

CHICORY, ENDIVE, AND ESCAROLE These salad greens are often confused: All chicory and endive come from the same family, but their names vary regionally. Mainly grown in Florida and New Jersey but also imported from France and Italy (the more yellow and tender varieties), these greens are a good diuretic and a good source of fiber, potassium, and vitamin A. CURLY CHICORY grows in bunched heads with narrow, ragged edged leaves that curl at the end. The center is yellow-white and sweet. The outer greens are bitter and tough. A delicious winter recipe is the warm *Salad of Crispy Sweetbreads with Curly Chicory and Condiments* (see page 62). ESCAROLE has deep green leaves that form a slightly crumpled compact head. When choosing these greens, always select a head with a heart of fresh pale yellow leaves. BELGIAN ENDIVE should have firm creamy-white leaves blending to pale yellow at the tip. Judge any salad green by looking at the base of the stem. It is especially important with Belgian endive that the stem end be firm and white, not brown or bruised.

Prepare a seasonal salad with any of those greens and pecans or walnuts, a minced apple, chives, and crisp bacon. *For the dressing, blend 1 part walnut oil, 2 parts corn oil, 1 part red wine vinegar, salt, and pepper.*

Belgian endive can be prepared raw in salads or cooked—*an excellent accompaniment for many roasts, such as veal, chicken, or guinea fowl: Split the endives in half lengthwise (2 per person) and sauté in an ovenproof casserole with a finely chopped carrot, a few tablespoons of chopped fresh fennel, and 1/4 cup butter. Braise the endive and vegetables in 1 cup of chicken stock with the juice of 1 lemon and 1 pinch of sugar. Cover the casserole with foil and bake at 400 degrees until the endive is tender, about 30 to 40 minutes. Once cooked, remove the endive and the chopped vegetables. Sauté 1 cup of sliced mushrooms in 1 tablespoon of hot oil, add 1 tablespoon chopped fresh tarragon, and combine the mushrooms with the endive, carrots, and fennel. Serve this garnish along with your roast.*

You will find another recipe for endive on page 278: *Roasted Endives Wrapped in Bacon with Juniper and Orange.*

COLLARD GREENS From the cabbage family, collards have thick green leaves with a slight bitterness and are excellent in spicy preparations, soups, or cooked plain with olive oil and garlic.

DRIED WHITE BEANS Grown mainly in the Midwest, NAVY and GREAT NORTHERN beans are similar to their Italian and French counterparts, the cannellino and the coco, respectively. They are very rich in protein as well as mineral salts and vitamins. Try to choose beans from this year's harvest. Before cooking, soak them in water and store in the refrigerator overnight, or just soak them for 3 to 4 hours in warm water (to return moisture to the flesh). Never soak them for more than 5 hours in warm water, or they might ferment. To reduce the flatulence associated with beans, change their soaking water every few hours and cook them in fresh water.

A typical winter dish is a Shoulder of Lamb with a White Bean Garnish: The lamb should be boneless and weigh about 3 pounds. Have your butcher tie the roast for you. Season and brown the roast in a heavy skillet in 1/4 cup of hot oil for about 5 minutes and set aside. Boil 3 cups of presoaked white beans for 10 minutes, then set aside. Finely dice 1 onion, 1 carrot, 1/2 stalk of celery, and 1 clove of garlic. Sweat these vegetables in 3 tablespoons of butter in an ovenproof casserole, then add 1 tablespoon of tomato paste. Add a bouquet garni (2 sprigs of parsley, 1 sprig of thyme, 1 bay leaf, a stalk of celery, and the greens of 1 leek, tied together with kitchen string), toss for 2 to 3 minutes, add 1 cup of white wine and 1 cup of tomatoes (peeled, seeded, and diced), the drained white beans, and the lamb and cover with chicken stock (or cold water) to a level of 2 inches above the beans. Add salt and pepper to taste. Cook covered in a preheated 300-degree oven for 2 hours, or until the lamb is tender. (Add water if the dish gets too dry.) To serve, remove the bouquet garni, cut off the string around the lamb, and slice the meat. Serve the beans in a deep dish with the meat on top, and sprinkle with fresh chopped parsley and olive oil.

FENNEL Of Mediterranean origin, fennel is now grown in California and New Jersey. Low in calories, fennel is a digestive stimulant, and is known for its sweet, mild, aniseed flavor. Look for crisp, white bulbs with very fresh light-green leaves. Trim greens and outer leaves and keep the layers of outer skin for flavoring soups, stews, or stocks.

For appetizers, crunchy fresh fennel is delicious with a dip made of chopped sun-dried tomatoes and pine nuts, mixed with olive oil, freshly ground black pepper, salt, and a touch of garlic. Fennel is also a wonderful garnish for fish and shellfish: Cut the fennel in wedges, cook in light chicken stock until tender. Drain, then toss in butter, salt, pepper, and basil leaves. Serve hot.

A wonderful, simple recipe using fennel is the *Salmon Salad with Fennel, Walnuts, and Chives* (see page 61).

JERUSALEM ARTICHOKES This vegetable is the tuberous root of the sunflower plant and has a crisp texture and lightly sweet taste. Once peeled it can be used boiled and puréed with butter or cut matchstick size and added to salads.

KOHLRABI Another member of the cabbage family, kohlrabi is available during the winter months. This is a green or purple vegetable with a swollen stem topped with green leaves whose taste is a combination of turnip and cabbage. *For a simple and delicious side dish: Peel, dice, and sweat 1 pound of Kohlrabi with 1/4 cup chopped onions, 1 apple, 1 tablespoon Madras curry powder, and seasonings, then add 1/2 cup heavy cream and simmer until tender. Purée in a blender or food processor. Serve with sautéed pork chops seasoned with curry.*

MÂCHE Also called CORN SALAD or LAMB'S LETTUCE, mâche has spoon-shaped, dark-green leaves and is one of the most delicate and pleasant salad greens. Imported from France and Holland, but also grown locally, it has a sweet hazelnut flavor. Rich in vitamins A and C, mâche is a diuretic and stimulates the intestines. Choose crispy fresh dark-green leaves, and count about 2 handfuls per person. Try to keep the leaves in a cluster but remove the root and any yellow leaves, wash thoroughly, then dry in your salad spinner.

To prepare a vinaigrette for a mâche salad: Crush a clove of garlic in a bowl until you have a paste, add a pinch of salt, freshly ground black pepper, 1 teaspoon of mustard, 1 tablespoon of red wine vinegar, and 3 tablespoons of walnut or peanut oil. Toss with the mâche and serve with a roasted baby chicken and homemade potato chips.

PARSNIPS Grown in Massachusetts, Illinois, Washington, and Northern California, these root vegetables need cold weather to convert their starch into sugar. Rich in potassium and vitamin C, parsnips look like an off-white carrot. Their flavor is an interesting mixture of sweet potatoes, nuts, and parsley. Look for small to medium-size roots. They should be plump and crisp. Avoid soft, cracked, and shriveled parsnips, or those with dry skin. Always peel them before using. This richly flavored vegetable adds sweetness to stews and soups.

Try a Parsnip and Walnut Soup: Peel 1 pound of parsnips and cut into 1-inch dice. Wash and mince 1 leek (white part only—discard the greens). Sweat the leek in 1 tablespoon of butter for a few minutes in a 2-quart casserole over medium heat. Add the parsnips, 1-1/2 quarts of chicken stock, 1 tablespoon of chopped walnuts, and a pinch of salt. Boil gently for 30 minutes. Pour into a blender and add 1/2 cup heavy cream. Blend, then strain. Toast 1/2 cup of chopped walnuts in the oven for 5 minutes at 400 degrees and sprinkle them over the hot soup.

POTATOES A staple in the diet of every country in the Western world, the potato is high in vitamin C and rich in protein, potassium, calcium, phosphorus, and starch. Large quantities are produced in the northern states from east to west, with a peak in supplies from early fall through winter. Potatoes should be stored in a cool place to prevent sprouting. Major varieties include the RUSSET or IDAHO, a white-fleshed potato with a long, cylindrical or slightly flattened shape, an all-purpose potato useful for baking, frying, and mashing because of its starchy and dry flesh; the KENNEBEC or MAINE potato, a white-fleshed variety with large, round tubers and smooth skin often used for boiling in soups, mashing, and frying. The small RED potato has a thin skin that does not require peeling, therefore is it used for boiling and in salad preparations. It is also excellent split and roasted in the oven around a roasting chicken with garlic cloves, thyme, and wedges of onions; the NEW potato is also a very firm and fresh potato that can be prepared the same way as the RED; the YUKON GOLD is a relatively new potato on the market and could be the tastiest of all, with its rich yellow flesh excellent for mashed potatoes and also for roasting and panfrying. This potato comes in large or small sizes and the skin is thin enough to retain when cooking.

Other local potatoes are available from summer through winter, and the best is certainly the FINGERLING potato, a small oblong potato with a moist fresh flesh and a sweet taste. This potato is delicious roasted whole, boiled, or sliced and panfried. Just rub the skin under water to clean it. Other interesting varieties are the PERUVIAN PURPLE potato, a deep purple and starchy potato with a delicate taste and strange color similar to that of the small PINK potato. Both are very good for boiling and using in salads with a sharp vinegar dressing and a sprinkle of crisp bacon. Try them in the salad called *Smoked Fish with Potatoes and Quail Eggs* on page 76.

RADICCHIO This variety of red chicory, originally from the Veneto province of Italy, is now grown in California. Rich in vitamin C, it has important diuretic properties. The more common and less seasonal RADICCHIO DI VERONA has a round head and short red leaves with white stalks and veins. It is used raw, mainly for salads, for its delicate slightly bitter taste and crisp texture that combine well with other greens such as arugula, escarole, or endive. The RADICCHIO DI TREVISO, available only during winter and imported from Italy, has long, thin, red leaves with a long, thick root. It can be served sautéed or grilled, more rarely raw in salads.

When cooked, its delicate, very bitter and peppery taste makes radicchio a perfect counter to seafood such as shrimp, crab, lobster, or scallops.

A typical example is the *Crab and Radicchio Risotto with Basil* (see page 113).

As an appetizer, try a Radicchio Salad with a Vinegar Cream Dressing and Garlic Toast: Cut 6 ounces of radicchio di Verona into large strips. Trim the crust from 4 slices of white bread and cut the bread into small cubes. Chop a clove of garlic and mix with a teaspoon of olive oil. Toss the bread crumbs in the oil, and toast them in the oven until crisp. Chop 1 ounce of chives. Mix 1/3 cup heavy cream with 1-1/2 tablespoons of sherry vinegar. Salt and pepper to taste. Toss the radicchio with the chives and dressing. Garnish with the garlic croutons and crushed hazelnuts.

RADISHES Winter radishes are available, either BLACK or WHITE (ICICLE, DAIKON). Black ones are very pungent in flavor and should be used sparingly in salads or cooked with other winter vegetables. Icicle and daikon, which are Oriental varieties, are milder in flavor but slightly hotter than regular radishes. They are excellent when finely shredded and seasoned with rice vinegar to create an Oriental salad for seafood.

SALSIFY (SCORZONERA) With a taste similar to that of artichoke hearts, salsify (or OYSTER PLANT) is a root vegetable imported mainly from Belgium. These rather thin, long, black roots are rich in calcium and iron. Look for firm black salsify, avoid sprouting roots or those with mold. To prevent the juice from coloring your hands, countertop, or cutting board, be sure to wear disposable gloves and place parchment paper on the work surface. With its delicate and nutty taste, salsify complements meats such as pork, roasts, and lamb but also can be the garnish on a fish dish like *Black Sea Bass with an Herb Crust and Salsify* (see page 192).

To prepare as a side dish: Peel the salsify and cut into 2-inch pieces. Boil them in water with a pinch of salt and the juice of 1 lemon for 10 to 15 minutes, or until tender. Drain, then serve with butter, seasoning, and chives alongside a roast or fish.

SPINACH Although it is available year-round, spinach season reaches its peak in winter. This mineral-rich vegetable is grown primarily in California, Texas, and New Jersey. Unlike many other winter vegetables, spinach is extremely rich in vitamins A, B-complex, C, E, and K, as well as potassium, iron, and fiber. Spinach must be cooked very quickly to retain its vitamins.

Although very digestible, spinach is not recommended for people with liver problems or kidney stones. There are two varieties of spinach: CURLY and FLAT LEAF. The crinkled leaves of curly spinach are tougher and less sweet than the delicate flat leaf spinach, which is best for salads. Choose small, crisp, deep-green leaves. Cut off the stems and wash several times in plenty of water. (Because it is grown in sandy soil, spinach must be cleaned thoroughly.) Be aware that cooked spinach will loose 4/5 of its raw volume.

To serve spinach as a simple side dish, sauté it in slightly browned butter with a dash of chopped garlic, a pinch of grated nutmeg, salt, and pepper.

To prepare as a side dish with roasted chicken: Blanch the leaves of 3 bunches for 2 minutes in salted water. Drain, cool under cold running water, transfer to a colander, and press to remove excess moisture. Butter your chicken and roast it in a 425-degree oven with thyme, salt, and pepper. After 15 to 20 minutes of cooking add 15 peeled garlic

cloves. Cook for another 20 to 30 minutes for a 3-pound chicken. In the last 10 minutes of cooking, remove the excess fat from the pan, add the blanched spinach, and mix with the cloves of garlic around the chicken. Season to taste. Carve and serve the chicken over the spinach.

SWEET POTATOES Grown mainly in North Carolina, Louisiana, and California, sweet potatoes are low in sodium, high in starch, and rich in potassium and vitamins A and C. Look for red-skinned sweet potatoes. They are larger, firmer, and more moist than white varieties. They should be unblemished, with firm ends and no soft spots. Avoid potatoes that are dull, dry, and shriveled. A favorite Southern vegetable, the sweet potato can be baked, candied, mashed, puréed, or made into biscuits, breads, or fritters.

They are delicious as a side dish for game: Peel and slice the potatoes into 1/4-inch dice. Simmer in chicken stock until done but firm, about 15 to 20 minutes. Drain and toss in a

hot pan with a touch of maple syrup. Sprinkle grated nutmeg on top before serving.

The best-tasting baked sweet potatoes with bacon and spices are in the recipe for *Quail Salad with Sweet Potatoes, Red Cabbage, and Celeriac Chips* (see page 64).

TURNIPS Mainly grown in California, Colorado, and Indiana, turnips, a staple food in Northern and Central Europe before the introduction of the potato, come in many varieties. Usually rounded and white in color with a purple top, turnips are low in calories, rich in potassium and vitamin C. Choose small, firm, heavy turnips with smooth skin and avoid overgrown, bruised, or withered ones. To prepare, remove a 1/4-inch-thick layer of skin by peeling with a small paring knife. Mainly used to flavor soups and stews, turnips are also very delicate when braised and caramelized, as in the recipe for *Caramelized Turnips with Rosemary and Honey* (see page 275).

BANANAS The United States is the leading importer of bananas, the most widely consumed fruit in this country. The cheapest of exotic fruits, bananas are mainly imported from Central America. Rich in vitamins A and B, niacin, iron, phosphorus, potassium, and calcium, the banana helps digestion. Nutritionally loaded and with a high energy value, raw bananas are an ideal food for growing children. The CAVENDISH is the leading commercial variety. Since bananas ripen off the tree, they are the perfect fruit for export. Always choose yellow bananas with a touch of green at either end. Never refrigerate unripe bananas. They should be eaten when they become speckled—an indication that the fruit is at its lowest starch and highest sugar content. Bananas also come with a red skin—RED BANANA—slightly shorter and fatter than the yellow one, with a thick texture and a rich, aromatic, and sweet taste. They are excellent in desserts and blended in drinks, but are less available than the yellow ones. The most fun member of the banana family is the CHICADITA, or LADYFINGER, a tiny yellow banana that is very sweet, fragrant, and a popular item in Spanish markets.

For a Chocolate Banana Terrine: Line a loaf pan with plastic wrap. Place 5 whole peeled bananas in the pan. Melt 1 pound of bittersweet chocolate in 1 cup of boiling heavy cream. Pour over the bananas and refrigerate overnight. Unmold, remove the wrap and serve in 1/2-inch-thick slices with walnut halves and a dollop of vanilla ice cream.

DRIED FRUITS Raisins, prunes, and dried figs, apples, pears, apricots, dates, cherries, cranberries, and exotic fruits are very tasty and nutritious. Try to make sure they are from this year's harvest. They can be used in puddings and other desserts, wild rice, or as a garnish for game. They can be eaten plain or moistened for desserts. *For moistened dried fruits (such as a mix of prunes, cherries, cranberries, and raisins): Prepare a marinade made with 1 quart of water, 4 tablespoons of sugar, 1 orange peel, a cinnamon stick, and a clove. Boil for 5 minutes. Remove from heat and pour over the dried fruits. Let cool and keep in the refrigerator overnight. Drain and serve the fruits with a slice of freshly baked sponge cake and whipped cream, or for breakfast as an energy supplement.*

GRAPEFRUIT Grown mainly in Florida and California, American grapefruits make up 95 percent of the world's production. Low in calories, rich in vitamins A, B, and C, and potassium, grapefruits help reduce cholesterol and detoxify the body. They are usually seedless and should be tree ripened. Depending on the variety, the skin will be pale yellow for white flesh or orange-red for pink flesh. The pinker the flesh, the sweeter the grapefruit. Look for thin-skinned, firm, and heavy fruits.

For a Pink Grapefruit and Honey Dessert: Peel and section 2 pink grapefruits. Place them in a bowl with 1 tablespoon of honey and let macerate overnight in the refrigerator. Serve with a scoop of honey ice cream.

KIWI Mainly grown in California or imported from New Zealand, this fruit was named after the national symbol of New Zealand, the Kiwi bird. Mostly a year-round fruit, kiwi is rich in protein, iron, calcium, phosphorus, potassium, and vitamin C, and one kiwi has more crude fiber than a bowl of bran flakes. The HAYWARD is the best variety. The fruit is ripe when soft to the touch. A kiwi will ripen at room temperature in a couple of days.

For a Lemon and Kiwi Mousse with Strawberries: Mix 6 peeled kiwis with the juice of 3 lemons, 1/3 cup of water, and 6 tablespoons of sugar in a blender or food processor and strain. Whisk in 2 packets of unflavored Knox gelatin diluted in 1 tablespoon of boiling water and fold in 3 cups of stiffly whipped heavy cream. Add 6 diced strawberries. Pour in a bowl and refrigerate overnight. Unmold and decorate with sliced strawberries and kiwis.

ORANGES California, Arizona, Florida, and Texas are the main producers of the sweet orange varieties. Rich in vitamin C and free of sodium, oranges vary in size, shape, color, and degree of sweetness. Look for plump, firm, and heavy fruit and avoid those with a thick-textured or bruised skin. The main varieties are:

BLOOD ORANGE Less acidic than common oranges, this small- to medium-size fruit with red-speckled flesh and a berry taste is suitable for eating fresh and juicing.

NAVEL Easy to peel and usually seedless, this orange is best for eating fresh or in recipes requiring orange segments.

VALENCIA This variety accounts for half of the total orange production and is best used for juice.

MANDARIN Smaller than the common orange, this easy-to-peel citrus fruit comes in different categories:

TANGELOS The largest of the mandarin family, this juicy and sweet fruit is a cross between a tangerine and a grapefruit.

TANGERINES This deep-orange mandarin is also sweet and juicy and highly aromatic.

CLEMENTINES Imported from Spain and North Africa, this small, generally seedless, sweet, and juicy citrus fruit is the ultimate snack for children and grown-ups alike.

For your Sunday brunch try using tangerine juice in your Mimosa cocktail—it enhances the flavor.

Chocolate Tangerines are a great treat for the holidays: Peel, and remove the membrane from each segment. Dry the tangerine segments on a plate for a few hours, then dip each segment halfway in melted bittersweet chocolate. Place on a sheet of waxed or parchment paper and place the chocolate-dipped wedges in the refrigerator to harden. Serve with coffee or as an after-school snack for the kids.

PINEAPPLE This tropical fruit is imported mainly from Hawaii, Mexico, and Central American countries. Pineapple has the highest mineral content of any fruit, and is also rich in vitamin C and fiber. The best variety is the CAYENNE from Hawaii. It has a greenish-orange skin and is deep yellow inside. Pineapples must be picked when mature or they will never ripen, for they have no starch reserve to convert into sugar after they are picked. Look for pineapples that carry a string label reading "Jet-fresh from Hawaii." To know if they are ripe, look for a golden-orange skin and fragrance (scratch the bottom to see how fragrant they are). The leaves on top should be fresh and deep green. Avoid pineapples with bruises, or with dull brown leaves. If the pineapple needs a little more maturing, don't refrigerate it but stand it upside down in a warm place;

this will allow the sugar to flow toward the top instead of fermenting at the bottom.

Make your own pineapple jam for breakfast or tea: Finely chop 1 pound of fresh, peeled pineapple. Cook in a deep copper or other nonreactive pan with 1/2 cup of water and 1/2 cup of sugar for about 45 minutes over medium-low heat. Stir occasionally. To test if the jam has the right consistency, pour a drop on a plate and make sure it's not too runny. Set aside to cool and store in the refrigerator in a clean jar with a lid.

You will find a use for pineapples, bananas, and grapefruit in *Winter's Tropical Fruit in a Spiced Infusion* (see page 317).

TROPICAL FRUITS Tropical fruits add a refreshing note to winter desserts. For example, COCONUTS are an excellent snack for kids but require some work to break and peel. The STARFRUIT or CARAMBOLA, often from New Zealand, has a golden color and refreshing tartness, but is quite bland in taste. It is wonderful mixed with other tropical fruits in chutney or jams. CHERIMOYAS, also known as CUSTARD APPLES, look strange, with a brown speckled skin, but contain a luscious sweet and juicy pulp with a taste that combines that of litchi nuts, pineapples, and bananas. PEPINO MELON, also called MELON PEAR, is usually imported from New Zealand. This fruit has an oval shape, a pale lemon skin with purple stripes, and a cantaloupe-cucumber taste; it should be ripe and have the sweet aroma of honeysuckle when purchased. PRICKLEY PEAR, the fruit of the cactus plant, has a fresh fruity taste and refreshing quality. Lightly soft and reddish when ripe, once peeled it can be used in exotic winter fruit salads, with a squeeze of lime, a sprinkle of sugar, and a splash of tequila.

BASIC RECIPES

BASIC CHICKEN OR VEGETARIAN STOCK

Yields 4 to 5 quarts

This basic chicken stock requires 2 hours of simmering to extract the rich flavors of the chicken bones and vegetables and is used in various recipes. For a vegetarian stock, eliminate the chicken bones and triple the quantity of vegetables and tomato or V-8 juice.

This stock can be made in advance and kept frozen.

6 to 8 pounds chicken bones, wings, legs, and necks included, skinned and trimmed of fat

1 tablespoon coarse sea salt or 1/2 tablespoon table salt

3 medium carrots, peeled and split lengthwise

2 medium whole leeks, split lengthwise

3 stalks celery, cut into 4- to 5-inch segments

1 medium onion, peeled and split

1 medium turnip, peeled and split

2 large white mushrooms, halved

4 sprigs fresh parsley

1 teaspoon black peppercorns

1 small bay leaf

2 cloves garlic, peeled

1 clove

1 sprig fresh thyme

1/2 cup tomato juice or V-8 juice

PREPARATION

Place the chicken bones in a large bowl under cold running water until clean. Drain, transfer the bones to a large stockpot, and cover with cold water to about 3 to 4 inches above the bones (approximately 6 to 7 quarts of water). Add the salt and bring to a boil, uncovered, over high heat. Once boiling, lower heat to simmer and skim the surface for 10 minutes or until clear of foam and fat. Add all the vegetables, spices, and the tomato or V-8 juice, stir, and return to a boil. Once boiling, reduce heat and simmer, uncovered, for 2 hours. Remove the stockpot from heat and let cool for 30 to 45 minutes. Carefully transfer the broth with a ladle to a fine-mesh strainer set over a large bowl. Discard the bones and vegetables and let the stock cool to room temperature for a few hours, or cool rapidly by placing bowl in a bath of ice water. Divide the stock into pint or quart plastic containers with lids and freeze until needed.

BASIC CHICKEN JUS

Yields 4 to 6 cups

This basic chicken jus, a concentrate of roasted chicken bones and vegetables, is used in various meat, poultry, and fish recipes. It can be prepared in advance and kept in the freezer in individual 1-cup plastic containers until needed. Other jus can be made by substituting various poultry, meat, fish, or game bones as well as lean scraps of meat.

2 tablespoons oil, for cooking

1 tablespoon sweet butter

4 to 5 pounds chicken bones, wings and necks included, carcass broken into pieces, skinned, and trimmed of fat, or 3 to 4 pounds chicken wings

1/2 cup shallots, peeled and sliced 1/2 inch thick

1 cup carrots, peeled and sliced 1/2 inch thick

1/2 cup celery, sliced 1/2 inch thick

12 to 15 cloves garlic, with skin, lightly crushed

1/2 cup plum tomatoes, split, seeded, and chopped

1/2 cup white mushrooms, halved

4 sprigs fresh parsley, tied with a string

1 sprig fresh thyme

1 bay leaf

1 teaspoon black peppercorns

2 teaspoons salt

1 teaspoon coriander seeds

PREPARATION

Preheat oven to 425 degrees. Heat a very large Dutch oven or roasting pan in the oven for 10 minutes. Add the cooking oil, butter, and bones to the pan, toss well, and roast in the oven for 20 to 30 minutes, tossing every 5 minutes. Spoon off half of the fat released while cooking. Add all the remaining ingredients, toss well, and roast for another 20 to 30 minutes, tossing every 5 minutes until the bones and vegetables have caramelized (if using a large roasting pan, the ingredients may cook faster). Transfer the pan to the stove top and reduce oven temperature to 375 degrees. Add 3 quarts boiling water, stir well over high heat while scraping the sides and bottom of the pan, and bring to a boil. Transfer the casserole back to the oven and braise for 1-1/2 to 2 hours while stirring every 20 to 30 minutes or until liquid is reduced by a third. Remove the pan and let cool for 30 to 40 minutes. Strain the jus through a fine-mesh strainer into a bowl and discard the bones and vegetables. Let the jus cool for 1 to 2 hours, or cool rapidly by placing the bowl in a bath of ice water. Pour into 1-cup plastic containers with lids and freeze until needed.

FRANÇOIS PAYARD'S QUICK PUFF PASTRY

Yields 1-3/4 quarts
Our talented pastry chef at Restaurant Daniel, François Payard, uses this basic puff pastry recipe
in many of his spectacular and delicious desserts.

*1 pound all-purpose flour
11 ounces sweet butter in 1/2-inch cubes
1 teaspoon salt*

PREPARATION

Coarsely mix all the ingredients in a bowl for 5 minutes with a hand blender (with a pastry attachment) or in a food processor with the hook attachment at low speed. Remove from the bowl and form a ball. Cut a 1/2-inch-deep cross on the dough, cover with plastic wrap, and refrigerate for 20 minutes.

Dust a work space and rolling pin with flour. Unwrap the dough and dust with flour. Roll the dough out into a rectangle, about 1/2 inch thick. Fold the dough in thirds, wrap with plastic, and refrigerate for 20 minutes. Repeat this process two more times, letting the dough rest in between. The dough is now ready to be rolled out to the required dimensions.

Freeze unused dough in plastic wrap.

ERRATUM

The recipe for "FRANCOIS PAYARD'S QUICK PUFF PASTRY" on page 372 omitted the following ingredient:

1-1/4 CUPS WATER

SUPPLIERS

Here is a list of suppliers I personally use for my restaurant:

AUX DELICES DES BOIS
4 LEONARD STREET
NEW YORK, NY 10013
TEL: (212) 334-1230
FAX: (212) 334-1231
Seasonal fresh wild mushrooms and specialty produce imported from France

D'ARTAGNAN
399-419 ST. PAUL STREET
JERSEY CITY, NJ 07306
TEL: (800) 327-8246
FAX: (201) 792-6113
Fresh foie gras, game, poultry, and homemade pâtés

BERRY BEST FARMS
P.O. BOX 189
LAMBERTVILLE, NJ 08530
TEL.: (609) 397-0748
FAX: (609) 397-2437
Fresh preserves and jam, seasonal produce and flowers

GRACE'S MARKETPLACE
1237 THIRD AVENUE
NEW YORK, NY 10021
TEL: (212) 737-0600
Gourmet specialty foods

ALL-CLAD COOKWARE
ALL-CLAD METALCRAFTERS, INC.
RD #2
CANONSBURG, PA 15317
TEL: (412) 745-8300
For fine cookware (also available in major department stores and specialty shops)

M. SLAVIN AND SONS FISH, LTD.
122 THATFORD AVENUE
BROOKLYN, NY 11212
TEL: (718) 346-6734
FAX: (718) 485-6569
All kinds of fresh fish and seafood

ROD MITCHELL
BROWNE TRADING CORP.
260 COMMERCIAL STREET
PORTLAND, ME 04101
TEL: (207) 766-2402
FAX: (207) 766-2404
Maine fish, seafood, and exceptional Russian caviar

SALUMERIA BIELLESE
376 EIGHTH AVENUE
NEW YORK, NY 10001
TEL: (212) 736-7376
Italian and French charcuterie

SWEET WATER AQUA
P.O. BOX 298
EDGEWATER, NJ 07020
TEL: (800) 477-2967
FAX: (201) 224-5688
Freshwater blue prawns

PAPRIKAS WEISS IMPORTER
1572 SECOND AVENUE
NEW YORK, NY 10028
TEL: (212) 288-6117
Spices and condiments

GOURMAND
66 SOUTH PICKETT STREET
ALEXANDRIA, VA 22304
TEL: (703) 461-0600
FAX: (703) 461-0198
Gourmet specialty foods

URBANI TRUFFLES USA
262 MOTT STREET
SUITE 206-207
NEW YORK, NY 10012
TEL: (212) 941-4710
FAX: (212) 941-4715
Fresh black and white truffles, canned black truffles, truffle juice, truffle oil

BERNARDAUD NORTH AMERICA
41 MADISON AVENUE
NEW YORK, NY 10010
TEL: (212) 696-2433
Fine porcelain Limoges

VALRHONA CHOCOLAT
1901 AVENUE OF THE STARS
SUITE 1774
LOS ANGELES, CA 90067
TEL: (310) 277-0401
FAX: (310) 277-4092
Fine French chocolate for desserts

PROP CREDITS

All china thanks to:

BERNARDAUD LIMOGES
777 MADISON AVENUE
NEW YORK, NY 10021

KEESAL & MATHEWS
1244 MADISON AVENUE
NEW YORK, NY 10128

L.S. COLLECTION
765 MADISON AVENUE
NEW YORK, NY 10021

SARA
952 LEXINGTON AVENUE
NEW YORK, NY 10021

VILLEROY & BOCH
974 MADISON AVENUE
NEW YORK, NY 10021

INDEX

Acorn Squash Risotto with Spices, 107–8

anchovy(ies)
Basil and Anchovy Dip with
Summer Radishes, 9
Pappardelle Meridionale, 128–29

apple(s), 353
Apple, Apple, Apple, 295–96
Baked, with Cranberries, 298
Cabbage Stuffed with Cranberries
and, 273–74
Caramelized Apple Tart Lyonnaise,
299
Celeriac and Escarole Salad with
Apple Chips, 86–87
Curried Cream of Cauliflower and
Apple Soup, 54–55
Fall Fruit Fricassée with Caramel Ice
Cream, 315–16
Roast Loin of Pork with Purée of
Curried Cauliflower and,
246–47
Sweet Apple Alix, 294
Sweet Potato Purée with Fruits and
Spices, 276
Wild Partridge with a Red Cabbage
Confit and Fall Fruit
Chutney, 256–57

apricot(s), 343
Crispy Duck with Spices, Spinach
Purée, and Roasted, 208–9
Dried, Braised Veal Shank with
Lemon, Thyme, and, 234–35
Spring Fruits in a Minty Cream,
310–12
Tarte Tatin with Pistachio Nuts, 325

artichoke(s), 328
Baby, Appetizer, 328
Baby, Crab Salad with a Lemon
Confit and, 74–75
Baby, Roasted with Bacon, 272
Baby, Stuffed with Almonds and
Chives, 18
Gratin of Squab with Spring
Vegetables, 212–13
Jerusalem, 361
Leg of Baby Lamb with Lemon,
Tomatoes, Olives, and,
239–40
Pheasant Salad with Walnuts, Crisp
Celery, and, 254–55
Soup with Grilled Eggplant, Lemon
and Thyme, 40–41
Terrine of Carrot, Broccoli, and,
100–101

arugula, 338
Beef Sticks with Pickle Dip and, 14
Fresh Sardine Fillets with, 23–24
Salad, 338
Salad with Squid and Sesame Seeds, 78
Warm Creamy, 338

asparagus, 329–30
appetizer, 329–30
Black Sea Bass in a Lemon Broth
with, 183–84
Gratin of Squab with Spring
Vegetables, 212–13
Salad with Spinach and Prawns in a
Pesto Sauce, 68
Soup with a Sweet Pepper Coulis,
34–35
Spaghetti Sirio Maccioni (Spaghetti
Primavera), 126–27
Spring Vegetable Casserole with
Rosemary and Chives,
283–84

avocado(s), 330
Cherry Tomatoes Stuffed with Crab
Guacamole, 4
Chicken Salad Tepee with Walnuts
and Chives, 69–70
Chilled Tomato Soup with a Basil
Guacamole, 38–39
Dip with Sesame Seeds, 17
Lobster Salad Le Régence, 84–85
Salad with Chicken and Black Olives,
330

Baby Chicken and Squash Casserole
with Rosemary, 203

bacon
Corn Crêpes with Lobster and,
144–46
Corn Risotto with Chanterelles and,
109
Roasted Baby Artichokes with,
272
Roasted Endives Wrapped in, with
Juniper and Orange, 278
Baked Apples with Cranberries, 298
Baked Potatoes on a Bed of Sea Salt
with Fresh Truffles, 277

banana(s), 365
Chocolate Banana Terrine, 365
Sweet Potato Purée with Fruits and
Spices, 276
Winter's Tropical Fruit in a Spiced
Infusion, 317–18

Barbecued Yellow Squash, 342

Barolo Sauce, 164–65

Basic Chicken Jus, 371

Basic Chicken or Vegetarian Stock, 371

basil, 338–39
and Anchovy Dip with Summer
Radishes, 9
Guacamole, Chilled Tomato Soup
with, 38–39
Mussels and Baby Vegetable Stew
with, 142–43
Oil, 130, 132
Risotto of Crab and Radicchio with,
113
Salad with Cold Swordfish and, 339
Skate and Tomatoes in a Pistou
Broth, 188
Spinach and White Asparagus Salad
with Prawns in a Pesto Sauce,
68
Summer Vegetable Casserole with
Black Olives and, 285–87
Tapenade and Quail Eggs on Toast, 5

bean(s)
Cranberry, Tuna Salad with Black
Olives and, 67
dried white, 360–61
Fall Vegetables Roasted with Juniper
Berries and Walnuts, 288–89
Shoulder of Lamb with a White
Bean Garnish, 360–61
Soup with Swiss Chard and Ricotta
Toasts, 51
Summer Vegetable Casserole with
Basil and Black Olives,
285–87
Tuna Steak with Watercress and
Yellow Wax, 166
Winter Vegetable Casserole with
Spices and Orange Zest,
290–91
see also fava beans

beef
Hanger Steak with Scallions and
Shredded Corn Crêpes, 224
Rib-Eye Steak with Stuffed Marrow
Bones and Turnips, 220–21
Short Ribs Miroton, 222
Sirloin Napoleon with Black Olives
and Zucchini, 223
Sticks with Arugula and a Pickle
Dip, 14
Tenderloin with Glazed Onions in
Balsamic Vinegar, 225–26

Terrine of Leek and, 102–3

beet(s), 330
Risotto with Watercress and
Pancetta, 106
Roasted Baby, with Szechuan
Pepper, 268
Salad of Roasted, 330
Steamed Cod on a Salad with Mâche
and, 179–80

The Best Chilled Tomato Salad, 73

beverages
Strawberry Cocktail, 336
Strawberry Shake with a
Red Berry Coulis, 307

blackberry(ies), 343
Roasted Peaches and, with Ginger
Caramel Ice Cream, 300–301
Summer Fruits with a Watermelon
Tequila Granité, 313–14
Warm Nectarines and, with Star
Anise, 344

Black Sea Bass in a Lemon Broth with
Asparagus, 183–84

Black Sea Bass with an Herb Crust and
Salsify, 192–93

blueberry(ies), 336
Brioche Bread Pudding, 303
Pie, 336

bouillon
Chicken, with Lime, Coriander, and
Mint, 52–53

Braised Leg of Lamb Cleopatra, 237–38

Braised Pork and Carrots, 330

Braised Rabbit with Pappardelle Pasta
and Sage, 262–63

Braised Veal Shank with Lemon,
Dried Apricots, and Thyme,
234–35

Bread Pudding, Blueberry Brioche, 303

broccoli, 358–59
Purée with Ginger, 282
Spaghetti Sirio Maccioni (Spaghetti
Primavera), 126–27
Terrine of Carrot, Artichoke, and,
100–101

broccoli rabe, 358–59
Casserole of Shrimp and, 359
Gulf Shrimp and Butterfly
Dynamite, 119–20

Winter Vegetable Casserole with
Spices and Orange Zest,
290–91

Broiled Blue Prawns with Ginger,
138–39

Broiled Mackerel with Radicchio di
Treviso and Sweet Peppers,
173–74

Broiled Pompano with Condiments and
Olive Oil, 185

Broiled Squab and Endives with Cumin
and Pine Nuts, 210–11

brook trout, see trout

brussels sprouts, 359

cabbage, 348
Quail Salad with Sweet Potatoes,
Celeriac Chips, and, 64–65
Red, Salmon in a Polenta Crust with,
186–87
Soup with Lobster and Chives, 42–43
Steamed Halibut with Rosemary
and, 171
Stuffed, with Apples and
Cranberries, 273–74
Wild Partridge with a Red Cabbage
Confit and Fall Fruit
Chutney, 256–57

cake(s)
Caramelized Walnut, 323–24
Chocolate Almond, 321–22
Eggplant and Lamb, with a Garlic
Jus, 241–42
Vegetable Cake Provençal, 279–81

Calf's Liver with Fresh Pea Croquettes,
230–31

cantaloupe, 343
Appetizer, 343
Melon Granité, 343
Summer Fruits with a Watermelon
Tequila Granité, 313–14

Caramel Ice Cream, 315–16

Caramelized Apple Tart Lyonnaise, 299

Caramelized Turnips with Rosemary
and Honey, 275

Caramelized Walnut Cake, 323–24

cardoon, 359
Gratin of, Francine, 267

carpaccio
Salmon, with Minted Couscous,
96–97
Tuna, with Celeriac and Tarragon,
98–99

carrot(s), 330
Braised Pork and, 330
Creamy Rabbit Casserole with Nine
Spring Herbs, 260–61
Curried Grouper with Summer
Vegetables, 175–76
Gratin of Squab with Spring
Vegetables, 212–13
Maryland Crab and Carrot Gratin
with Coriander, 161
Mussels and Baby Vegetable Stew
with Basil, 142–43
Spring Vegetable Casserole with
Rosemary and Chives,
283–84
Terrine of Artichokes, Broccoli, and,
100–101

casserole(s)
Baby Chicken and Squash, with
Rosemary, 203
Chicken, with Morels, Fava Beans,
and Spring Potatoes,
204–5
Creamy Rabbit, with Nine Spring
Herbs, 260–61
Pea, 334
Shrimp and Broccoli Rabe, 359
Spring Vegetable, with Rosemary
and Chives, 283–84
Summer Vegetable, with Basil and
Black Olives, 285–87
Sweet-Water Prawn and Chanterelle,
with Garlic, 154
Winter Vegetable, with Spices and
Orange Zest, 290–91

cauliflower, 348–49
Curried Cream of Cauliflower and
Apple Soup, 54–55
Roast Loin of Pork with Purée
of Curried Apple and,
246–47
Soft-Shell Crab and Cauliflower
Grenobloise, 140–41
Soup, 349

caviar
Marinière of Littleneck Clams and,
with Champagne and, 156
Potato and Salted Cod Galettes with
Chives and, 169–70
Spring Potatoes with Chives and, 20

celeriac (celery root), 360
  Carpaccio of Tuna with Tarragon
    and, 98–99
  Crispy Golden Squid and, 25–26
  Purée, 360
  Quail Salad with Sweet Potatoes,
    Red Cabbage and, 64–65
  Salad with Escarole, Apple Chips
    and, 86–87
  Winter Vegetable Casserole with
    Spices and Orange Zest,
    290–91

celery, 339–40
  Cabbage and Lobster Soup with
    Chives, 42–43
  Curried Grouper with Summer
    Vegetables, 175–76
  Curried Tuna Tartare with a Green
    Celery Sauce and Pink
    Radishes, 92–93
  Gratin of, 269, 340
  Gratin of Squab with Spring
    Vegetables, 212–13
  Pheasant Salad with Walnuts,
    Artichokes, and, 254–55
  "Rillettes" with Salmon and, 16
  Soup with Pink Radishes, 37
  Summer Vegetable Casserole with
    Basil and Black Olives,
    285–87

chanterelles, 351
  Casserole with Sweet-Water Prawns
    and Garlic, 154
  Corn Risotto with Bacon and, 109
  Tomatoes Stuffed with a Ragout of
    Rabbit, Rosemary and, 258–59

chard, see Swiss chard

cheese(s)
  Gratin of Cardoon Francine, 267
  Parmesan, Crispy Rolls of Salsify
    with Prosciutto and, 10
  Ricotta Toasts, Swiss Chard and
    Bean Soup with, 51
  Tartlets with a Sweet Pepper Confit,
    27–28

cherry(ies), sweet, 346
  Spring Fruits in a Minty Cream,
    310–12
  Tart, 346

Cherry Tomatoes Stuffed with Crab
  Guacamole, 4

chestnut(s), 354
  Fall Fruit Fricassée with Caramel Ice
    Cream, 315–16

Fall Vegetables Roasted with
    Juniper Berries and Walnuts,
    288–89
  Garnish, 354
  Purée, 354

chicken
  and Avocado Salad with Black
    Olives, 330
  Baby, and Squash Casserole with
    Rosemary, 203
  Baby, with Scallions, 341
  Casserole with Morels, Fava Beans,
    and Spring Potatoes, 204–5
  Crispy, Cooked Under a Brick with
    Garlic, Lemon, and Herbs,
    202
  Curry Salad Le Cirque, 80–81
  Drumsticks and Rice with Red
    Peppers, 336
  Herb, Walnut, and Lemon Dip with,
    13
  Hot and Crusty, My Way, 214–15
  Jus, Basic, 371
  Salad, in a Spring Vegetable Broth,
    82–83
  Salad Tepee with Walnuts and
    Chives, 69–70
  Salad with Avocado and Black
    Olives, 330
  Stock, 370

Chicken Bouillon with Lime, Coriander,
  and Mint, 52–53

chicken liver
  Toasts, with Cinnamon Squash
    Soup, 46–47

chicory, 360
  Salad of Crispy Sweetbreads with
    Condiments and Curly,
    62–63

Chilled Tomato Soup with a Basil
  Guacamole, 38–39

chive(s)
  Chicken Salad Tepee with Walnuts
    and, 69–70
  Potato and Salted Cod Galettes with
    Caviar and, 169–70
  Salmon Salad with Fennel, Walnuts,
    and, 61
  Soup with Cabbage, Lobster and,
    42–43
  Spring Potatoes with Caviar and, 20
  Spring Vegetable Casserole with
    Rosemary and, 283–84
  Stuffed Baby Artichokes with
    Almonds and, 18

chocolate
  Cake with Almond and, 321–22
  Fondant au Chocolat, 320
  Mousse with Honey Popcorn, 309
  and Raspberry Fontaine, 308
  Sweet Apple Alix, 294
  Tangerines, 366
  Terrine with Banana and, 365

chutney(s)
  Fall Fruit, 256–57
  Pear, 355

clam(s)
  Marinière of Littleneck Clams and
    Salmon with Champagne
    and Caviar, 156

clementine(s), 366
  Winter's Tropical Fruit in a Spiced
    Infusion, 317–18

coconut
  Winter's Tropical Fruit in a Spiced
    Infusion, 317–18

cod
  Potato and Salted Galettes, with
    Caviar and Chives, 169–70
  Steamed, on a Beet and Mâche Salad,
    179–80

Cold Brook Trout with Mint and
  Lemon, 167–68

collard greens, 360

confit
  Lemon, 74–75
  Red Cabbage, 256–57
  Red Onion, 155
  Sweet Pepper, 27–28
  Tomato, 48–49

corn, 341
  Crêpes, Hanger Steak with Scallions
    and, 224
  Crêpes, with Lobster and Bacon,
    144–46
  Pancakes, 341
  Risotto with Bacon and Chanterelles,
    109
  Soup with Nutmeg, 33
  Summer Vegetable Casserole with
    Basil and Black Olives,
    285–87

coulis
  Fennel, 157
  Red Berry, 307
  Sweet Pepper, 34–35
  Tomato, 130, 132

couscous
  Carpaccio of Salmon with Minted, 96–97
  Cold Brook Trout with Mint and Lemon, 167–68
  Cucumber Cones with Mint and Lime, 19

crabmeat
  Cherry Tomatoes Stuffed with Crab Guacamole, 4
  Eggplant and Crab Garbure with Cumin and a Tomato Confit, 48–49
  Maryland Crab and Carrot Gratin with Coriander, 161
  Risotto of Radicchio, Basil and, 113
  Salad with Baby Artichokes and a Lemon Confit, 74–75
  Soft-Shell Crab and Cauliflower Grenobloise, 140–41
  Stuffed Tomatoes with Fennel Coulis and, 157–58
  Trenette with Lemongrass and, 125

cranberry(ies), 354
  Baked Apples with, 298
  Cabbage Stuffed with Apples and, 273–74
  Fall Fruit Fricassée with Caramel Ice Cream, 315–16

Creamy Rabbit Casserole with Nine Spring Herbs, 260–61

crêpe(s)
  Corn, Hanger Steak with Scallions and, 224
  Corn, with Lobster and Bacon, 144–46

Crisp Paupiette of Sea Bass in Barolo Sauce, 164–65

Crispy Chicken Cooked Under a Brick with Garlic, Lemon, and Herbs, 202

Crispy Duck with Spices, Spinach Purée, and Roasted Apricots, 208–9

Crispy Golden Squid and Celeriac, 25–26

Crispy Rolls of Salsify with Prosciutto and Parmesan, 10

Crispy Strawberry Purses, 306

Crispy Tomato Toast Michel Guérard, 12

Croquettes, Fresh Pea and Calf's Liver, 230–31

Croustillants of Strawberries, 305

Crusty Sweetbreads with Hot Mustard, Bacon, and a Shallot Jus, 232–33

cucumber(s), 330
  Cones with Mint and Lime, 19
  Smoked Salmon Sticks with a Sherry Dip, 15
  Soup with Coriander and Smoked Trout, 32
  Summer Vegetable Casserole with Basil and Black Olives, 285–87

Cured Duck Pot-au-Feu with an Herb Oil, 200–201

currant(s), 346
  Salad of Squid and Red, 346
  Warm Peaches with Vanilla Ice Cream and, 345

Curried Cream of Cauliflower and Apple Soup, 54–55

Curried Grouper with Summer Vegetables, 175–76

Curried Tuna Tartare with Pink Radishes and a Green Celery Sauce, 92–93

custard(s)
  Caramelized Shallots with Thyme, 334–35
  Morel, with a Shallot Jus, 266
  Zucchini, Gulf Shrimps with Sweet Red Peppers and, 147–48

dandelion greens, 330–32

date(s), 354

dip(s)
  Avocado, with Sesame Seeds, 17
  Basil and Anchovy, with Summer Radishes, 9
  Crispy Golden Squid and Celeriac, 25–26
  Eggplant, with Country Bread, 8
  Herb, Walnut, and Lemon, with Chicken Chunks, 13
  Pickle, Beef Sticks with Arugula and, 14
  Sherry, Smoked Salmon Sticks with, 15

dried fruits, 365

duck
  Crispy, with Spices, Spinach Purée, and Roasted Apricots, 208–9

Cured Duck Pot-au-Feu with an Herb Oil, 200–201

eel
  Smoked Fish with Potatoes and Quail Eggs, 76–77

egg(s)
  The Best Chilled Tomato Salad, 73
  Salad with Watercress and, 343
  Tapenade and Quail, on Toast, 5

eggplant, 340
  and Crab Garbure with Cumin and a Tomato Confit, 48–49
  Dip with Country Bread, 8
  and Lamb Cake with a Garlic Jus, 241–42
  Mussels and Baby Vegetable Stew with Basil, 142–43
  Pappardelle Meridionale, 128–29
  Rosace with Zucchini and Thyme, 270
  Soup with Artichoke, Lemon, and Thyme, 40–41
  Stuffed, with Cumin, 340
  Summer Vegetable Casserole with Basil and Black Olives, 285–87
  Vegetable Cake Provençal, 279–81
  Vegetarian Penne, 123–24

endive, 360
  Broiled Squab with Cumin, Pine Nuts, and, 210–11
  Pig Knuckles with Lentils, Oregano, and, 243–45
  Roasted, Wrapped in Bacon with Juniper and Orange, 278

escarole, 360

Fall Fruit Fricassée with Caramel Ice Cream, 315–16

Fall Vegetables Roasted with Juniper Berries and Walnuts, 288–89

fava beans, 332
  Chicken Casserole with Morels, Spring Potatoes, and, 204–5
  Lobster with a Fava Purée and Black Trumpets, 149–50
  Mussels and Baby Vegetable Stew with Basil, 142–43
  Skate and Tomatoes in a Pistou Broth, 188

fava beans (cont.)
Spring Vegetable Casserole with
Rosemary and Chives, 283–84

fennel, 361
appetizers, 361
Coulis, Stuffed Tomatoes with Crab
and, 157–58
Curried Grouper with Summer
Vegetables, 175–76
Herb, Walnut, and Lemon Dip with
Chicken Chunks, 13
Salmon Salad with Walnuts, Chives,
and, 61
Sea Scallops with Cumin and Fresh,
159–60
Vegetable Cake Provençal, 279–81
Winter Vegetable Casserole with Spices
and Orange Zest, 290–91

Fettuccine with Mushrooms, Sweet
Garlic, and Thyme, 121–22

fig(s), 354
Delight, 354
Poached Plums and, in Cabernet,
345–46
Stuffed Quail with Swiss Chard
Leaves and Fresh, 206–7
Summer Fruits with a Watermelon
Tequila Granité, 313–14

fish, see specific types of fish

Flounder Diable with Spinach and Salsify,
196–97

Fondant au Chocolat, 320

François Payard's Quick Puff Pastry, 372

Fresh Sardine Fillets with Arugula,
23–24

Frozen Raspberry Soufflé, 346

fruits
dried, 365
tropical, 366
see also specific fruits

garlic, 349
Crispy Chicken Cooked Under a Brick
with Lemon, Herbs, and, 202
Eggplant and Lamb Cake with Jus
of, 241–42
Fettuccine with Mushrooms, Thyme,
and, 121–22
Green Risotto with Roasted Squab
and, 110–11

Sauce, 349
Sweet-Water Prawn and Chanterelle
Casserole with, 154

garlic sprouts, 332

ginger
Broccoli Purée with, 282
Broiled Blue Prawns with, 138–39
Caramel Ice Cream, 300–301
Flavored Oil, 118

granité
Melon, 343
Watermelon Tequila, 313–14

grape(s), 343, 354
Summer Fruits with a Watermelon
Tequila Granité, 313–14

grapefruit, 365
Pink Grapefruit and Honey Dessert,
365
Winter's Tropical Fruit in a Spiced
Infusion, 317–18

gratin
of Cardoon Francine, 267
of Celery Heart, 269, 340
Maryland Crab and Carrot, with
Coriander, 161
of Squab with Spring Vegetables, 212–13
Swiss chard, 341

Green Celery Soup with Pink Radishes, 37

Green Risotto with Roasted Squab and
Garlic Cloves, 110–11

grouper
Curried, with Summer Vegetables,
175–76
with Fingerling Potatoes and Morels,
194–95

guacamole
Basil, Chilled Tomato Soup with a,
38–39
Crab, Cherry Tomatoes Stuffed
with, 4

guinea fowl
Roasted, in a Salt Crust Roger Vergé,
216–17

Gulf Shrimp and Butterfly Dynamite,
119–20

Gulf Shrimp and Sugar Pea Risotto with
Rosemary, 112

Gulf Shrimp with Sweet Red Pepper and
Zucchini Custard, 147–48

halibut
Steamed, with Cabbage and
Rosemary, 171

Hanger Steak with Scallions and
Shredded Corn Crêpes, 224

haricots verts (French string beans), 332
Chicken Salad Tepee with Walnuts
and Chives, 69–70
with a Creamy Lemon Dressing, 332

Herb, Walnut, and Lemon Dip with
Chicken Chunks, 13

Herb Oil, 200–201

Herb Ravioli with Basil Oil and a Tomato
Coulis, 130–32

honeydew melon
Spring Fruits in a Minty Cream,
310–12

Honey Popcorn, with Chocolate Mousse,
309

hors d'oeuvres
Avocado Dip with Sesame Seeds,
17
Baby Artichoke, 328
Basil and Anchovy Dip with
Summer Radishes, 9
Beef Sticks with Arugula and a
Pickle Dip, 14
Cheese Tartlets with a Sweet Pepper
Confit, 27–28
Cherry Tomatoes Stuffed with Crab
Guacamole, 4
Crispy Golden Squid and Celeriac,
25–26
Crispy Rolls of Salsify with
Prosciutto and Parmesan,
10
Crispy Tomato Toast Michel
Guérard, 12
Cucumber Cones with Mint and
Lime, 19
Eggplant Dip with Country Bread,
8
Fennel, 361
Fresh Sardine Fillets with Arugula,
23–24
Herb, Walnut, and Lemon Dip with
Chicken Chunks, 13
Red Snapper and Sun-Dried Tomato
Roulade with Lime, 6
Salmon and Celery "Rillettes," 16
Smoked Salmon Sticks with a Sherry
Dip, 15

Spring Potatoes with Caviar and
Chives, 20
Stuffed Baby Artichokes with
Almonds and Chives, 18
Tapenade and Quail Eggs on Toast, 5
Warm Asparagus, 329–30
Zucchini and Shrimp, 336

Hot and Crusty Chicken My Way,
214–15

ice cream
Caramel, Fall Fruit Fricassée with,
315–16
Ginger Caramel, Roasted Peaches
and Blackberries with,
300–301
Verbena, Oven-Roasted Strawberries
with, 304

Jerusalem artichokes, 361

kiwi(s), 365
Mousse with Lemon and, 365
Spring Fruits in a Minty Cream,
310–12

kohlrabi, 361

lamb
Braised Leg of, Cleopatra, 237–38
Chops Champvallon, 236
Eggplant and Lamb Cake with
Garlic Jus, 241–42
Leg of Baby, with Lemon,
Tomatoes, Artichokes, and
Olives, 239–40
Shoulder, with a White Bean
Garnish, 360–61

leek(s), 351
Crisp Paupiette of Sea Bass in a
Barolo Sauce, 164–65
Terrine of Beef Shank and,
102–3

Leg of Baby Lamb with Lemon,
Tomatoes, Artichokes, and
Olives, 239–40

Leg of Venison with Stuffed Mini-
Pumpkins, 251–53

lemon(s)
Artichoke and Grilled Eggplant

Soup with Thyme and,
40–41
Black Sea Bass in Broth of, with
Asparagus, 183–84
Cold Brook Trout with Mint and,
167–68
Confit, Crab Salad with Baby
Artichokes and, 74–75
Herb, Walnut, and Lemon Dip with
Chicken Chunks, 13
Meyers, 336
Mousse with Kiwi and, 365

Lemongrass, Trenette with Crabmeat
and, 125

Lentils, Pig Knuckles with Endives,
Oregano, and, 243–45

lettuce and salad greens, 330–32

lima beans, 351

lime(s)
Chicken Bouillon with Coriander,
Mint, and, 52–53
Cucumber Cones with Mint and, 20
Red Snapper and Sun-Dried Tomato
Roulade with, 6

litchi nuts, 343

liver
Calf's, with Fresh Pea Croquettes,
230–31
chicken, see chicken liver

lobster
Corn Crêpes with Bacon and, 144–46
with a Fava Purée and Black
Trumpets, 149–50
and Pompano Sottha Khunn, 190–91
Ravioli on Spinach Leaves in a
Ginger Broth, 117–18
Salad Le Régence, 84–85
Soup with Cabbage and Chives,
42–43

mâche, 361
Steamed Cod on a Salad of Beets
and, 179–80
vinaigrette for, 361

mackerel
Broiled, with Radicchio di Treviso
and Sweet Peppers, 173–74

Maine Sea Scallops in Black Tie, 151–52

mango(es), 343–44
Rhubarb and Mango Compote with
Strawberry Sorbet, 319

Winter's Tropical Fruit in a Spiced
Infusion, 317–18

Marinière of Littleneck Clams and
Salmon with Champagne
and Caviar, 156

Marmalade Quince, 356

Maryland Crab and Carrot Gratin with
Coriander, 161

Melon Granité, 343

Meyers lemons, 336

Minty Cream, Spring Fruits in a, 310–12

monkfish
Roasted, Biriatou, 189

morels, 332–34
Chicken Casserole with Fava Beans,
Spring Potatoes, and, 204–5
Custard, with a Shallot Jus, 266
Grouper with Fingerling Potatoes
and, 194–95

mousse
Chocolate, with Honey Popcorn, 309
Lemon and Kiwi, 365
Rhubarb, 334

mushroom(s), 332–34, 341, 351
Chicken Casserole with Morels, Fava
Beans, and Spring Potatoes,
204–5
Corn Risotto with Bacon and
Chanterelles, 109
Curried Grouper with Summer
Vegetables, 175–76
Eggplant and Lamb Cake with
Garlic Jus, 241–42
Fall Vegetables Roasted with Juniper
Berries and Walnuts,
288–89
Fettuccine with Sweet Garlic,
Thyme, and, 121–22
Grouper with Fingerling Potatoes
and Morels, 194–95
Lobster with a Fava Purée and Black
Trumpets, 149–50
Morel Custard with a Shallot Jus,
266
Oyster Mushroom Soup with
Walnuts in Red Wine, 57
Sweet-Water Prawn and Chanterelle
Casserole with Garlic, 154
Tomatoes Stuffed with a Ragout of
Rabbit, Chanterelles, and
Rosemary, 258–59
Vegetarian Penne, 123–24

Mussels and Baby Vegetable Stew with
Basil, 142–43

Napoleon of Tuna with a Mosaic Salad,
94–95

nectarine(s), 344
Warm Blackberries and, with Star
Anise, 344

nut(s)
Almonds, Stuffed Baby Artichokes
with Chives and, 18
Chocolate Almond Cake, 321–22
litchi, 343
Pine Nuts, Broiled Squab and
Endives with Cumin and,
210–11
Pistachio, Apricot Tarte Tatin with,
325
Walnut, Herb, and Lemon Dip with
Chicken Chunks, 13
walnuts, 356
Walnuts, Caramelized Cake with,
323–24
Walnuts, Chicken Salad Tepee with
Chives and, 69–70
Walnuts, Fall Vegetables Roasted
with Juniper Berries and,
288–89
Walnuts, Pheasant Salad with Crisp
Celery, Artichokes, and,
254–55
Walnuts, Salmon Salad with Fennel,
Chives and, 61
Walnuts, Soup with Parsnips and,
361
Walnuts in Red Wine, 356
Walnuts in Red Wine, Oyster
Mushroom Soup with, 57

oil(s)
Basil, 130, 132
Ginger-Flavored, 118
Herb, 200–201

olive(s)
Chicken and Avocado Salad with
Black, 330
Leg of Baby Lamb with Lemon,
Tomatoes, Artichokes, and,
239–40
Salad with Chicken and Avocado,
330
Sirloin Napoleon with Zucchini and
Black, 223

Summer Vegetable Casserole with
Basil and, 285–87
Tapenade and Quail Eggs on Toast, 5
Tuna Salad with Cranberry Beans
and Black, 67

onion(s)
Beef Tenderloin with Glazed, in
Balsamic Vinegar, 225–26
Creamy Rabbit Casserole with Nine
Spring Herbs, 260–61
Eggplant and Lamb Cake with
Garlic Jus, 241–42
Roasted Monkfish Biriatou, 189
Sea Scallops with Mashed Potatoes
and a Red Onion Confit, 155

orange(s), 365–66
Roasted Endives Wrapped in Bacon
with Juniper and, 278
Sweet Potato Purée with Fruits and
Spices, 276
Winter's Tropical Fruit in a Spiced
Infusion, 317–18
Zucchini with Orange Zest and
Rosemary, 271

Oven-Roasted Strawberries with
Verbena Ice Cream, 304

oyster mushroom(s), 351
Garnish, 351
Soup with Walnuts in Red Wine, 57

Pancakes, Corn, 341

Pancetta, Risotto of Beet, Watercress,
and, 106

papaya(s), 355
Winter's Tropical Fruit in a Spiced
Infusion, 317–18

Pappardelle Meridionale, 128–29

parsnip(s), 361
Soup with Walnuts and, 361
Winter Vegetable Casserole with
Spices and Orange Zest,
290–91

Partridge, Wild, with a Red Cabbage
Confit and Fall Fruit
Chutney, 256–57

passionfruit
Winter's Tropical Fruit in a Spiced
Infusion, 317–18

pasta
Braised Rabbit with Pappardelle and
Sage, 262–63

Fettuccine with Mushrooms, Sweet
Garlic, and Thyme, 121–22
Gulf Shrimp and Butterfly
Dynamite, 119–20
Herb Ravioli with Basil Oil and a
Tomato Coulis, 130–32
Lobster Ravioli on Spinach Leaves in
a Ginger Broth, 117–18
Pappardelle Meridionale, 128–29
Route with Scallops, Peas, and Black
Truffles, 134–35
Spaghetti Sirio Maccioni (Spaghetti
Primavera), 126–27
Trenette with Crabmeat and
Lemongrass, 125
Vegetarian Penne, 123–24

pea(s), 334
Calf's Liver with Fresh Pea
Croquettes, 230–31
Casserole or Soup, 334
Curried Grouper with Summer
Vegetables, 175–76
Gratin of Squab with Spring
Vegetables, 212–13
Lobster and Pompano Sottha
Khunn, 190–91
Route with Scallops, Black Truffles,
and, 134–35
snow, 335
Spaghetti Sirio Maccioni (Spaghetti
Primavera), 126–27
Spring Vegetable Casserole with
Rosemary and Chives,
283–84
Suckling Pig with Snow Peas,
Radishes, and Rosemary,
248–50
Sugar, Risotto of Gulf Shrimp,
Rosemary, and, 112
sugar snaps, 335–36

peach(es), 344–45
Roasted Blackberries and, with
Ginger Caramel Ice Cream,
300–301
Spring Fruits in a Minty Cream,
310–12
Warm, with Red Currants and
Vanilla Ice Cream, 345

pear(s), 355–56
Chutney, 355
Fall Fruit Fricassée with Caramel Ice
Cream, 315–16
Poires Belle Hélène, 356
Wild Partridge with a Red Cabbage
Confit and Fall Fruit
Chutney, 256–57

pea shoots, 340

pepper(s), sweet, 336
    Asparagus Soup with a Coulis of,
        34–35
    Broiled Mackerel with Radicchio di
        Treviso and, 173–74
    Cheese Tartlets with a Confit of,
        27–28
    Chicken Drumsticks and Rice with
        Red, 336
    Gulf Shrimp with Sweet Red Pepper
        and Zucchini Custard,
        147–48
    Lobster and Pompano Sottha
        Khunn, 190–91
    Roasted Monkfish Biriatou, 189
    Vegetable Cake Provençal, 279–81

Peppered Tuna and Shoestring Potatoes
    with a Shallot Jus, 177–78

persimmon(s), 356
    Winter's Tropical Fruit in a Spiced
        Infusion, 317–18

Pheasant Salad with Walnuts, Crisp
    Celery, and Artichokes,
    254–55

pie(s)
    Crispy Scone Plum, 354
    Warm Blueberry, 336

Pig Knuckles with Endives, Lentils, and
    Oregano, 243–45

pineapple(s), 366
    jam, 366
    Winter's Tropical Fruit in a Spiced
        Infusion, 317–18

pink radishes, see radish(es)

plum(s), 345–46, 354
    Crispy Scone Plum Pie, 354
    Poached Figs and, in Cabernet, 345–
        46
    Summer Fruits with a Watermelon
        Tequila Granité, 313–14
    Wild Partridge with a Red Cabbage
        Confit and Fall Fruit
        Chutney, 256–57

Poires Belle Hélène, 356

polenta
    Salmon in a Polenta Crust with Red
        Cabbage, 186–87

pomegranate(s), 356
    Winter's Tropical Fruit in a Spiced
        Infusion, 317–18

pomelo
    Salad with Smoked Trout,
        Radicchio, and, 89

pompano
    Broiled, with Condiments and
        Olive Oil, 185
    Lobster and, Sottha Khunn,
        190–91

popcorn
    Honey, Chocolate Mousse with, 309

porcini mushrooms, 341

pork
    Braised, with Carrots, 330
    Pig Knuckles with Endives, Lentils,
        and Oregano, 243–45
    Roast Loin of, with Curried
        Cauliflower and Apple
        Purée, 246–47
    Suckling Pig with Snow Peas,
        Radishes, and Rosemary,
        248–50

potato(es), 362
    Baked, on a Bed of Sea Salt with
        Fresh Truffles, 277
    Chicken Casserole with Morels, Fava
        Beans, and Spring, 204–5
    Fall Vegetables Roasted with Juniper
        Berries and Walnuts, 288–89
    Grouper with Fingerling, and
        Morels, 194–95
    Lamb Chops Champvallon, 236
    Peppered Tuna and Shoestring, with
        a Shallot Jus, 177–78
    and Salted Cod Galettes with Caviar
        and Chives, 169–70
    Sea Scallops with Mashed, and a Red
        Onion Confit, 155
    Smoked Fish with Quail Eggs and,
        76–77
    Spring, with Caviar and Chives, 20
    sweet, see sweet potato(es)

Pot-au-Feu, Cured Duck, with an Herb
    Oil, 200–201

poultry, see chicken; duck; guinea fowl;
    quail; squab

prawns, see shrimp

prosciutto
    Crispy Rolls of Salsify with
        Parmesan and, 10

prune(s)
    Fall Fruit Fricassée with Caramel Ice
        Cream, 315–16

puff pastry
    Croustillants of Strawberries, 305
    date filling for, 354
    François Payard's Quick, 372
    Maine Sea Scallops in Black Tie,
        151–52

pumpkin(s), 353
    Leg of Venison with Stuffed Mini-,
        251–53

purée
    Apple and Cauliflower, 246–47
    Broccoli, with Ginger, 282
    Celeriac, 360
    Chestnut, 354
    Fava Bean, 149, 150
    Spinach, 208–9
    Sweet Potato, with Fruits and Spices,
        276

quail
    Salad with Sweet Potatoes, Red
        Cabbage, Celeriac Chips and,
        64–65
    Stuffed, with Fresh Figs and
        Swiss Chard Leaves,
        206–7

quail eggs
    The Best Chilled Tomato Salad, 73
    Smoked Fish with Potatoes and,
        76–77
    Tapenade and, on Toast, 5

quince(s), 356
    Marmalade, 356

rabbit
    Braised, with Pappardelle Pasta and
        Sage, 262–63
    Creamy Casserole with Nine Spring
        Herbs, 260–61
    Tomatoes Stuffed with a Ragout of
        Chanterelles, Rosemary, and,
        258–59

radicchio, 362
    Broiled Mackerel with Sweet
        Peppers and, 173–74
    Risotto of Crab, Basil and, 113
    Salad, 362
    Salad with Smoked Trout, Pomelo
        and, 89
    Winter Vegetable Casserole with
        Spices and Orange Zest,
        290–91

radish(es), 340–41, 362
  Basil and Anchovy Dip with
    Summer, 9
  Curried Tuna Tartare with a Green
    Celery Sauce and Pink, 92–93
  Green Celery Soup with Pink, 37
  Suckling Pig with Snow Peas,
    Rosemary, and, 248–50
  Summer Vegetable Casserole with
    Basil and Black Olives,
    285–87

raspberry(ies), 346
  Chocolate and Raspberry Fontaine,
    308
  Frozen Soufflé, 346
  Red Berry Coulis, 307
  Spring Fruits in a Minty Cream,
    310–12

Red Berry Coulis, 307

red snapper
  and Sun-Dried Tomato Roulade
    with Lime, 6
  Whole, Baked with Dill and
    Cracked Peppercorns,
    181–82

rhubarb, 334
  and Mango Compote with
    Strawberry Sorbet, 319
  Mousse, 334

Rib-Eye Steak with Stuffed Marrow
  Bones and Turnips, 220–21

risotto
  Acorn Squash, with Spices, 107–8
  Beet and Watercress, with Pancetta,
    106
  Corn, with Bacon and Chanterelles,
    109
  Crab and Radicchio, with Basil, 113
  Green, with Roasted Squab and
    Garlic Cloves, 110–11
  Gulf Shrimp and Sugar Pea, with
    Rosemary, 112

Roasted Baby Artichokes with Bacon, 272

Roasted Baby Beets with Szechuan
  Pepper, 268

Roasted Endives Wrapped in Bacon
  with Juniper and Orange,
  278

Roasted Guinea Fowl in a Salt Crust
  Roger Vergé, 216–17

Roasted Monkfish Biriatou, 189

Roasted Peaches and Blackberries with
  Ginger Caramel Ice Cream,
  300–301

Roast Loin of Pork with Curried
  Cauliflower and Apple
  Purée, 246–47

Rosace, Zucchini and Eggplant, with
  Thyme, 270

Route with Scallops, Peas, and Black
  Truffles, 134–35

salad(s)
  Apple, Apple, Apple, 295–96
  Arugula, 338
  The Best Chilled Tomato, 73
  Celeriac and Escarole, with Apple
    Chips, 86–87
  Chicken, in a Spring Vegetable
    Broth, 82–83
  Chicken and Avocado, with Black
    Olives, 330
  Chicken Curry, Le Cirque, 80–81
  Chicken Tepee, with Walnuts and
    Chives, 69–70
  Cold Swordfish and Basil, 339
  Crab, with Baby Artichokes and a
    Lemon Confit, 74–75
  of Crispy Sweetbreads with Curly
    Chicory and Condiments,
    62–63
  Dandelion, 332
  greens, 330–32, 360
  Hot and Crusty Chicken My Way,
    214–15
  Lobster, Le Régence, 84–85
  Mosaic, Napoleon of Tuna with,
    94–95
  Pheasant, with Walnuts, Crisp Celery,
    and Artichokes, 254–55
  Quail, with Sweet Potatoes, Red
    Cabbage, and Celeriac Chips,
    64–65
  Radicchio, 362
  Roasted Beet, 330
  Salmon, with Fennel, Walnuts, and
    Chives, 61
  Smoked Fish with Potatoes and
    Quail Eggs, 76–77
  Smoked Trout and Radicchio, with
    Pomelo, 89
  Spinach and White Asparagus, with
    Prawns in a Pesto Sauce, 68
  Spring Fruits in a Minty Cream,
    310–12

Squid and Arugula, with Sesame
    Seeds, 78
  Squid and Red Currant, 346
  Steamed Cod, with Beet and Mâche,
    179–80
  Summer Fruits with a Watermelon
    Tequila Granité, 313–14
  Tuna, with Cranberry Beans and
    Black Olives, 67
  vinaigrette, 361
  Watercress and Egg, 343

salmon
  Carpaccio of, with Minted Couscous,
    96–97
  Marinière of Littleneck Clams and,
    with Champagne and Caviar,
    156
  in a Polenta Crust with Red
    Cabbage, 186–87
  "Rillettes" with Celery and, 16
  Salad with Fennel, Walnuts, and
    Chives, 61
  Smoked Fish with Potatoes and
    Quail Eggs, 76–77
  Smoked Salmon Sticks with a Sherry
    Dip, 15

salsify, 362
  Black Sea Bass with an Herb Crust
    and, 192–93
  Crispy Rolls of, with Prosciutto and
    Parmesan, 10
  Flounder Diable with Spinach and,
    196–97
  Soup with Bay Scallops and Sorrel, 45
  Winter Vegetable Casserole with
    Spices and Orange Zest,
    290–91

sardine(s)
  Fresh, Fillets with Arugula, 23–24
  Pappardelle Meridionale, 128–29

sauce(s)
  Barolo, 164–65
  Garlic, 349
  Tomato, 342

scallions (green onions), 341
  Baby Chickens with, 341

scallop(s)
  Bay, Salsify Soup with Sorrel and, 45
  Maine Sea Scallops in Black Tie,
    151–52
  Route with Peas, Black Truffles,
    and, 134–35
  Sea, with Fresh Fennel and Cumin,
    159–60

Sea, with Mashed Potatoes and a Red
  Onion Confit, 155

sea bass
  Black, in a Lemon Broth with
    Asparagus, 183–84
  Black, with an Herb Crust and
    Salsify, 192–93
  Crisp Paupiette of, in Barolo Sauce,
    164–65

Sea Scallops with Fresh Fennel and
  Cumin, 159–60

Sea Scallops with Mashed Potatoes and a
  Red Onion Confit, 155

shallot(s), 334–35
  Crusty Sweetbreads with Hot Mustard,
    Bacon and Jus of, 232–33
  Custard of Caramelized with
    Thyme, 334–35
  Morel Custard with Jus of, 266
  Peppered Tuna and Shoestring
    Potatoes with Jus of, 177–78

shellfish, see clam(s); crabmeat; lobster;
    mussels; scallop(s); shrimp

Short Ribs Miroton, 222

shrimp
  Broiled Blue Prawns with Ginger,
    138–39
  Casserole of Broccoli Rabe and, 359
  Gulf, and Butterfly Dynamite,
    119–20
  Gulf, with Sweet Red Pepper and
    Zucchini Custard, 147–48
  Risotto of Sugar Peas, Rosemary, and
    Gulf, 112
  Salad with Spinach and White
    Asparagus in a Pesto Sauce, 68
  Sweet-Water Prawn and Chanterelle
    Casserole with Garlic, 154
  Zucchini and Shrimp Appetizer, 336

Sirloin Napoleon with Black Olives and
  Zucchini, 223

Skate and Tomatoes in a Pistou Broth,
  188

Smoked Fish with Potatoes and Quail
  Eggs, 76–77

Smoked Salmon Sticks with a Sherry
  Dip, 15

Smoked Trout and Radicchio Salad with
  Pomelo, 89

snow peas, 335
  Garnish, 335

Soft-Shell Crab and Cauliflower
  Grenobloise, 140–41

sorbet
  Apple, Apple, Apple, 295–96
  Strawberry, Rhubarb and Mango
    Compote with, 319

sorrel
  Salsify Soup with Bay Scallops and,
    45

soufflé
  Frozen Raspberry, 346

soup(s)
  Apricot Fruit, 343
  Artichoke and Grilled Eggplant,
    with Lemon and Thyme,
    40–41
  Asparagus, with a Sweet Pepper
    Coulis, 34–35
  Cabbage and Lobster, with Chives,
    42–43
  Cauliflower, 349
  Chicken Bouillon with Lime,
    Coriander, and Mint, 52–53
  Chilled Tomato, with a Basil
    Guacamole, 38–39
  Cinnamon Squash with Chicken
    Liver Toasts, 46–47
  Corn, with Nutmeg, 33
  Cucumber and Coriander, with
    Smoked Trout, 32
  Curried Cream of Cauliflower and
    Apple, 54–55
  Eggplant and Crab Garbure with
    Cumin and a Tomato Confit,
    48–49
  Green Celery, with Pink Radishes,
    37
  Oyster Mushroom, with Walnuts in
    Red Wine, 57
  Parsnip and Walnut, 361
  Pea, 334
  Salsify, with Bay Scallops and Sorrel,
    45
  Swiss Chard and Bean, with Ricotta
    Toasts, 51

Spaghetti Sirio Maccioni (Spaghetti
  Primavera), 126–27

spinach, 362–63
  Eggplant and Lamb Cake with
    Garlic Jus, 241–42
  Flounder Diable with Salsify and,
    196–97
  Lobster Ravioli on, in a Ginger
    Broth, 117–18

Maine Sea Scallops in Black Tie,
  151–52
Purée of, Crispy Duck with Spices
  and Roasted Apricots, 208–9
Salad with White Asparagus and
  Prawns in a Pesto Sauce, 68

side dish, 363

spread(s)
  Salmon and Celery "Rillettes," 16

Spring Fruits in a Minty Cream, 310–12

Spring Potatoes with Caviar and Chives,
  20

Spring Vegetable Casserole with
  Rosemary and Chives,
  283–84

squab
  Broiled, with Endives, Cumin and
    Pine Nuts, 210–11
  Gratin of, with Spring Vegetables,
    212–13
  Green Risotto with Garlic Cloves
    and Roasted, 110–11

squash, 353
  Acorn, Risotto with Spices and,
    107–8
  Barbecued Yellow, 342
  Casserole with Baby Chicken and
    Rosemary, 203
  Soup with Chicken Liver Toasts and
    Cinnamon, 46–47
  yellow, 342
  see also zucchini

squid
  Crispy Golden, and Celeriac, 25–26
  Salad of Red Currants and, 346
  Salad with Arugula and Sesame
    Seeds, 78

Steamed Cod on a Beet and Mâche
  Salad, 179–80

Steamed Halibut with Cabbage and
  Rosemary, 171

stew(s)
  Cured Duck Pot-au-Feu with an
    Herb Oil, 200–201
  Mussels and Baby Vegetable, with
    Basil, 142–43

stock(s)
  Chicken, 370
  Vegetarian, 370

strawberry(ies), 336
  Cocktail, 336

strawberry(ies) (cont.)
    Crispy, Purses, 306
    Croustillants, 305
    Oven-Roasted, with Verbena Ice
        Cream, 304
    Red Berry Coulis, 307
    Shake with a Red Berry Coulis,
        307
    Sorbet, Rhubarb and Mango
        Compote with, 319
    Spring Fruits in a Minty Cream,
        310–12
strudel
    Swiss Chard, Veal Chops with
        Ginger and, 227–29
Stuffed Baby Artichokes with Almonds
    and Chives, 18
Stuffed Eggplant with Cumin, 340
Stuffed Quail with Fresh Figs and Swiss
    Chard Leaves, 206–7
Stuffed Tomatoes with Crab and Fennel
    Coulis, 157–58
sturgeon
    Smoked Fish with Potatoes and
        Quail Eggs, 76–77
Suckling Pig with Snow Peas, Radishes,
    and Rosemary, 248–50
sugar snaps, 335–36
Summer Fruits with a Watermelon
    Tequila Granité, 313–14
Summer Vegetable Casserole with
    Basil and Black Olives,
    285–87
Sweet Apple Alix, 294
sweetbreads
    Crispy, with Hot Mustard, Bacon,
        and a Shallot Jus, 232–33
    Salad of Crispy, with Curly Chicory
        and Condiments, 62–63
sweet potato(es), 363–65
    Purée, with Fruits and Spices, 276
    Quail Salad with Red Cabbage,
        Celeriac Chips, and, 64–65
    side dish, 363–65
    Winter Vegetable Casserole with
        Spices and Orange Zest,
        290–91
Sweet-Water Prawn and Chanterelle
    Casserole with Garlic, 154

Swiss chard, 341–42
    Bean Soup with Ricotta Toasts and, 51
    Fall Vegetables Roasted
        with Juniper Berries and
        Walnuts, 288–89
    Gratin, 341
    Stuffed Quail with Fresh Figs and,
        206–7
    Veal Chops with Ginger and Strudel
        of, 227–29
swordfish
    Cold Salad with Basil, 339

tangerine(s), 366
    Chocolate, 366
Tapenade and Quail Eggs on Toast, 5
tart(s)
    Apricot Tarte Tatin with Pistachio
        Nuts, 325
    Caramelized Apple Tart Lyonnaise,
        299
    Cheese Tartlets with a Sweet Pepper
        Confit, 27–28
    Cherry, 346
terrine(s)
    Beef Shank and Leek, 102–3
    Carrot, Artichoke, and Broccoli,
        100–101
    Chocolate Banana, 365
toast(s)
    Chicken Liver, Cinnamon Squash
        Soup with, 46–47
    Crispy Tomato Toast Michel
        Guérard, 12
    Eggplant Dip with Country Bread, 8
    Fresh Sardine Fillets with Arugula,
        23–24
    Red Snapper and Sun-Dried Tomato
        Roulade with Lime, 6
    Ricotta, Swiss Chard and Bean Soup
        with, 51
    Smoked Salmon Sticks with a Sherry
        Dip, 15
    Tapenade and Quail Eggs on, 5
tomato(es), 342
    The Best Chilled Tomato Salad, 73
    Cherry, Stuffed with Crab
        Guacamole, 4
    Chilled Soup, with a Basil
        Guacamole, 38–39
    Confit, Eggplant and Crab Garbure
        with Cumin and, 48–49

Coulis, Herb Ravioli with Basil Oil
        and, 130–32
    Crispy Golden Squid and Celeriac,
        25–26
    Crispy Tomato Toast Michel
        Guérard, 12
    Eggplant and Lamb Cake with
        Garlic Jus, 241–42
    Leg of Baby Lamb with Lemon,
        Artichokes, Olives, and,
        239–40
    Mussels and Baby Vegetable Stew
        with Basil, 142–43
    Pappardelle Meridionale, 128–29
    Red Snapper and Sun-Dried Tomato
        Roulade with Lime, 6
    Roasted Monkfish Biriatou, 189
    Sauce, 342
    Skate and, in a Pistou Broth, 188
    Stuffed, with Crab and Fennel
        Coulis, 157–58
    Stuffed with a Ragout of Rabbit,
        Chanterelles, and Rosemary,
        258–59
    Summer Vegetable Casserole with
        Basil and Black Olives,
        285–87
    Vegetable Cake Provençal, 279–81
Trenette with Crabmeat and
    Lemongrass, 125
tropical fruits, 366
trout
    Cold Brook, with Mint and Lemon,
        167–68
    Smoked, Cucumber and Coriander
        Soup with, 32
    Smoked, Salad with Radicchio,
        Pomelo, and, 89
truffle(s)
    Baked Potatoes on a Bed of Sea Salt
        with Fresh, 277
    black, 358
    Lobster Salad Le Régence, 84–85
    Maine Sea Scallops in Black Tie,
        151–52
    Route with Scallops, Peas, and,
        134–35
    white, 353
tuna
    Carpaccio of, with Celeriac and
        Tarragon, 98–99
    Curried Tuna Tartare with Pink
        Radishes and a Green Celery
        Sauce, 92–93

Napoleon of, with a Mosaic Salad,
94–95
Peppered, and Shoestring Potatoes
with a Shallot Jus, 177–78
Salad with Cranberry Beans and
Black Olives, 67
Steak with Watercress and Yellow
Wax Beans, 166

turnip(s), 365
Caramelized, with Rosemary and
Honey, 275
Fall Vegetables Roasted with Juniper
Berries and Walnuts, 288–89
Gratin of Squab with Spring
Vegetables, 212–13
Mussels and Baby Vegetable Stew
with Basil, 142–43
Rib-Eye Steak with Stuffed Marrow
Bones and, 220–21
Spring Vegetable Casserole with
Rosemary and Chives,
283–84

veal
Braised Shank, with Lemon, Dried
Apricots, and Thyme, 234–35
Chops, with Ginger and Swiss Chard
Strudel, 227–29
Vegetable Cake Provençal, 279–81
Vegetarian Penne, 123–24

venison
Leg of, with Stuffed Mini-Pump-
kins, 251–53
Verbena Ice Cream, 304

Walnuts in Red Wine, 356
Warm Creamy Arugula, 338
Warm Peaches with Red Currants and
Vanilla Ice Cream, 345
watercress, 343
and Egg Salad, 343
Risotto with Beet and Pancetta, 106
Tuna Steak with Yellow Wax Beans
and, 166
watermelon, 346
Tequila Granité, 313
Whole Red Snapper Baked with Dill
and Cracked Peppercorns,
181–82
Wild Partridge with a Red Cabbage
Confit and Fall Fruit
Chutney, 256–57
Winter's Tropical Fruit in a Spiced
Infusion, 317–18
Winter Vegetable Casserole with
Spices and Orange Zest,
290–91

yellow wax beans, 342–43
Garnish, 342–43
Tuna Steak with Watercress and,
166

zucchini, 336
Baby Chicken and Squash Casserole
with Rosemary, 203
Curried Grouper with Summer
Vegetables, 175–76
Custard, Gulf Shrimp with Sweet
Red Pepper and, 147–48
Mussels and Baby Vegetable Stew
with Basil, 142–43
with Orange Zest and Rosemary,
271
Rosace with Eggplant and Thyme,
270
and Shrimp Appetizer, 336
Sirloin Napoleon with Black Olives
and, 223
Spaghetti Sirio Maccioni (Spaghetti
Primavera), 126–27
Spring Vegetable Casserole with
Rosemary and Chives,
283–84
Summer Vegetable Casserole with
Basil and Black Olives,
285–87
Vegetable Cake Provençal, 279–81

ABOUT THE AUTHOR

DANIEL BOULUD was raised in Lyons, France, on his family's farm. After working in some of the most prestigious restaurants in both Europe and America, he was elected executive chef at New York City's Le Cirque restaurant in 1986. He was voted one of America's ten best chefs by *Food and Wine* magazine and designated Best Chef of the Year by Chef in America Association. Under his command, Le Cirque was chosen by Gault Millau as the best restaurant in the United States and was awarded four stars by *The New York Times*. He has appeared on *Late Night with David Letterman, Live with Regis & Kathie Lee,* and PBS's *Cuisine Rapide* with Pierre Franey. His new restaurant, Daniel, opened in the spring of 1993.